Criminal
Procedure

Third Edition

*No class
Wed. 12th 12012*

Judy Hails, J.D., LL.M.
California State University–Long Beach

*Adj. 85
Case briefs
For
extra credit
Do 3 of
these
1 page each*

WADSWORTH
CENGAGE Learning™

Australia • Brazil • Japan • Korea • Mexico • Singapore • Spain • United Kingdom • United States

**Criminal Procedure,
Third Edition**
Judy Hails

For product information and technology assistance, contact us at **Cengage Learning Customer & Sales Support, 1-800-354-9706**

For permission to use material from this text or product, submit all requests online at **www.cengage.com/permissions**
Further permissions questions can be emailed to **permissionrequest@cengage.com**

Library of Congress Control Number: 2002108901

ISBN-13: 978-1-928916-23-9

ISBN-10: 1-928916-23-6

Wadsworth
10 Davis Drive
Belmont, CA 94002
USA

Cengage Learning is a leading provider of customized learning solutions with office locations around the globe, including Singapore, the United Kingdom, Australia, Mexico, Brazil, and Japan. Locate your local office at **www.cengage.com/global**

Cengage Learning products are represented in Canada by Nelson Education, Ltd.

To learn more about Wadsworth, visit
www.cengage.com/wadsworth

Purchase any of our products at your local college store or at our preferred online store **www.ichapters.com**

Printed in the United States of America
6 7 8 9 10   15 14 13 12 11

ED020

Contents

Chapter 3

The Warrant Process   43

Chapter 4

Other Search and Seizure Issues   67

Chapter 5

Interrogation and Identification Procedures   91

Chapter 6

Authority of Other Investigative Agencies   111

Chapter 7

The Criminal Complaint and Arraignment 133

Chapter 8

Indictments and Preliminary Hearings 153

Chapter 9

Pretrial Court Proceedings 175

Chapter 10

Preparation of a Case for Trial   205

Chapter 11

The Trial   231

Chapter 12

Special Trials   265

Chapter 13

The Sentencing Hearing   285

Chapter 14

Chapter 15

Chapter 16

Dedication

To Miriam and Kahina
My Twin Inspirations

Preface

Criminal Procedure, 3rd edition is designed to help students and officers understand how activities in both law enforcement and corrections interface with court proceedings. This text will demystify the judicial process and help the reader understand the importance of collecting evidence and documenting facts that may not appear relevant to the crime being investigated. A knowledge of the lengthy court process that follows the arrest makes it easier for officers to prepare to testify and, thus, assist the prosecutor. Obtaining convictions will be easier because officers can efficiently focus on what needs to be done. Study questions at the end of each chapter are designed to develop a better understanding of the process in your local area.

Ideally, a student should complete an introductory course in criminal justice prior to taking this class. There is sufficient material in this book, however, to provide necessary background information for those who have not and to refresh the memories of those who have not reviewed the topic recently. A course in evidence is recommended for all students planning careers in law enforcement, but it is not required in order to comprehend this text. Chapters 2 through 5 cover Fourth and Fifth Amendment issues. Some colleges have a separate course on these topics, others include them in the evidence course, while a third approach is to teach these important issues as part of criminal procedure. They are included in this book for the convenience of all; the individual instructor can decide how much coverage to give them in order to dovetail with other parts of the curriculum.

Chapter 1 places the police in the larger context of American government. Two crucial encounters that police have with the public are addressed in Chapter 2—detention for questioning and arrest. Both the powers of arrest and Fourth Amendment constraints are covered. Chapter 3, which focuses primarily on the Fourth Amendment warrant clause, discusses arrest and search warrants. It provides detailed instruction on preparing affidavits, obtaining warrants and executing them. Chapter 4 covers many other search and seizure issues frequently encountered by patrol officers. Chapter 5's main emphasis is confessions and *Miranda,* although it also addresses identification procedures and the right to counsel. Many of the county, state, and federal agencies who interact with local law enforcement are discussed in Chapter 6.

The remaining chapters of this book follow the chronological order of court proceedings. Chapter 7 covers the first steps in the journey—interaction with the prosecutor when obtaining a criminal complaint. Detailed information is given on what facts must be included in this legal document. The arraignment that follows formally launches the criminal case. Felonies are screened by a judge at the preliminary hearing or by grand jurors when an indictment is sought. Chapter 8 discusses these two processes in detail.

Many of the behind-the-scene activities that precede the start of a criminal trial are discussed in Chapters 9 and 10. Utilization of suppression motions to activate the Exclusionary Rule and the Fruit of the Poison Tree Doctrine is explained. While the prosecutor is in charge of the case at this stage, it is important for law enforcement officers to be familiar with the issues involved so they will be prepared when called to testify at pretrial hearings. Investigators must understand what they are expected to do to prepare the case for trial and the types of information the prosecutor will need to effectively question each witness. All officers involved should review the case focusing on what questions are likely to be asked when they testify during trial.

No two trials are alike but there are many similarities. Chapter 11 follows the presentation of evidence at a typical trial. Officers need to understand the rules on direct and cross examination and what can be done on rebuttal. Several special mini-trials are discussed in Chapter 12: evaluation of the defendant's mental competency; adjudication of the defendant's plea of not guilty by reason of insanity; and the penalty phase of capital murder trials. Juvenile court hearings are also considered in this chapter.

The sentencing hearing, discussed in Chapter 13, follows a conviction. In nearly all cases, the judge at this proceeding may consider facts that were not introduced to establish the defendant's guilt. Presenting appropriate evidence at the sentencing hearing frequently has a major impact on the length of the defendant's sentence.

The case is not final until the appeal is over. Chapter 14 reviews the appellate process and discusses direct appeals as well as avenues used to reach the state's highest court and the United States Supreme Court. *Habeas corpus* proceedings are also outlined.

Most decisions related to the defendant's punishment and/or rehabilitation are not made in the courtroom. Chapter 15 looks at the due process requirements for each of the hearings involved in the correctional system. Both institutional hearings, such as those which impose discipline or set parole dates, and proceedings related to community based corrections, such as probation revocation hearings, are discussed. The newly developed procedures to commit sexually violent predators to secure mental health facilities at the end of their prison terms are summarized.

Civil suits play an increasingly large role in our lives. Chapter 16 discusses various forms of litigation that result from on-duty activities of law enforcement and correctional officers. Suits typically filed in state courts and under the federal Civil Rights Act are covered. Forfeiture proceedings used to seize a defendant's property are also outlined.

Judy Hails

About the Author

Judy Hails has taught criminal law and procedure for over 25 years. She is currently a Professor in the Department of Criminal Justice at California State University, Long Beach and has also been a Visiting Assistant Professor at Illinois State University (1981–83) and an adjunct professor at John Jay College in New York City (1978–80).

Dr. Hails is a former sergeant with the Los Angeles County Sheriff's Department. Her education includes: B.S. in mathematics from Loma Linda University; M.S. in criminology from CSU Long Beach; J.D. from Southwestern University School of Law and an LL.M. in criminal justice from New York University School of Law.

She has published four well-received books, *Criminal Evidence, Criminal Procedure, Criminal Procedure: A Case Approach,* and *Criminal Law* all published by Copperhouse along with numerous articles in professional journals on criminal procedure, prisoner's rights, and domestic violence.

Dr. Hails is a past president of both the California Association of Administration of Justice Educators and the Western and Pacific Association of Criminal Justice Educators; she also served a three-year term as trustee for Region V of the Academy of Criminal Justice Sciences. She is an inactive member of the California State Bar.

Criminal Justice as Part of the American Legal System

Outline

Key Terms

bench trial	freedom of speech	U.S. Code
bills of attainder	geographical jurisdiction	U.S. Congress
common law	jurisdiction	U.S. Constitution
cruel and unusual	jury nullification	U.S. Courts of Appeal
punishment	precedent	U.S. District Court
defendant	self-incrimination	U.S. Supreme Court
double jeopardy	state constitution	venue
due process	subject matter jurisdiction	writ of certiorari
equal protection	sunset laws	writ of habeus corpus
ex post facto	unreasonable searches	
Exclusionary Rule	and seizures	

Learning Objectives
Learning Objectives

After reading this chapter, the student will be able to

- Explain six sources of criminal law.
- Explain how a bill becomes a law.
- Describe the structure of the judicial system.
- Explain the authority of federal and state courts.
- Describe the roles of the following participants in the criminal justice system: law enforcement, prosecutor, defendant, defense attorney, judge, and jury.

The criminal justice system must exist within the structure of the American legal system. This chapter will discuss the sources of federal and state law as well as the structure of the legislature, the judicial system, and the authority of the state and federal courts. It will close with a look at the roles of law enforcement, prosecution, and defense in criminal trials as well as the roles of the judge and jury.

1-1 Sources of Law

No single code book contains all the laws. Due to the federal system of government used in the United States, there are at least two layers of laws: state and federal. Cities and other municipal agencies also enact laws.

1-1a Federal Laws

There are two distinct types of federal law: the United States Constitution and the United States Code. The Constitution is binding on all levels of government in the United States. The U.S. Code has provisions that apply to the entire nation and others that are only used in federal territories such as Washington, D.C., and the national parks.

U.S. Constitution

A few provisions of the **U.S. Constitution** apply to criminal laws. *Ex post facto* laws are prohibited. Laws that make conduct criminal that was legal at the time it was done are ex post facto. So are laws that make the penalty more severe than was authorized at the time the crime was committed. A law which changes the rules of evidence to make it easier for the prosecution to obtain a conviction than it was at the time the crime was committed is also ex post facto.

No **bills of attainder** may be passed by the legislature. A bill of attainder was used by the British Parliament to impose the death penalty and required that the person's property be forfeited to the government. The constitutional prohibition also includes bills of pains and penalties, which were used to impose criminal penalties without trials for non-capital crimes. These bills were passed by the legislature and there was no trial. The key is that individuals are either named, easily identified members of a group or described in terms of conduct.

The *writ of habeus corpus* is used by a person to challenge illegal confinement. The Constitution prohibits suspension of the *writ of habeus corpus* except when required due to rebellion or invasion.

The majority of what we call "constitutional rights" come from the Bill of Rights and the Fourteenth Amendment. While the Bill of Rights was originally enacted to prevent oppressive conduct by the federal government, the U.S. Supreme Court has used the due process clause of the Fourteenth Amendment as a vehicle for applying many, but not all, of the provisions of the Bill of Rights to state actions.

The following is a brief summary of the constitutional amendments that apply to local law enforcement. Chapters 2 through 5 deal with many of these issues. An in-depth study of these principles is required to function effectively as a police officer. It is recommended that anyone planning a career in law enforcement take a separate course devoted to them.

First Amendment

The First Amendment provides for **freedom of speech,** freedom of assembly, freedom of the press, freedom of religion, and the right to petition the government for redress of grievances.

Nearly all speech is protected by the First Amendment. A few categories, such as obscenity (pornography, not profanity) and "fighting words," are not protected. The key to freedom of speech is that the minimum restraint necessary must be used and that the law must be "content neutral." A law is unconstitutional if it forbids both legally protected speech and speech that is not protected. It is also impermissible to base decisions on the content of the speech. For example, a law prohibiting speeches in the park would be "overbroad" because it would cover both protected and unprotected speech. Refusing to give a parade permit to a racist group because the town does not approve of the opinions expressed would violate the "content neutral" requirement.

Freedom of the press is a difficult issue in criminal cases because the defendant has the right to trial by an impartial jury. Inflammatory media coverage may make it impossible to find jurors who are not already prejudiced against the defendant. The press has access to any court hearing that is open to the public and may publish any information it discovers on its own. The court may be closed to the press only if there is a specific, compelling reason for closure, such as emotional trauma to a young child who is testifying regarding being molested. The judge may issue gag orders, which forbid disclosure of information to the press by prosecutors and defense attorneys. When used, such gag orders must be very limited in scope.

Criminal laws may not be designed to interfere with a person's exercise of religion. Laws, such as bigamy and a prohibition on possession of peyote, that have a purpose other than deterring religious activities are allowed. The government cannot establish religion. Conditions of probation that include attending church are forbidden.

Fourth Amendment

The Fourth Amendment prohibits **unreasonable searches and seizures.** A "reasonable expectation of privacy" test has been used instead of restricting the amendment to "persons, houses, papers, and effects" (the words used in the amendment). The Fourth Amendment is violated if a person's reasonable expectation of privacy is invaded by government agents. A person who does not take reasonable steps to protect his/her privacy cannot complain that the Fourth Amendment has been violated.

Probable cause is defined as a group of facts that would convince a reasonable person that an event occurred. The Fourth Amendment sets probable cause as the minimum standard for issuing warrants. Probable cause must be established under oath or affirmation. This is usually done by a written affidavit signed under penalty of perjury. Specific facts must be given which, under the totality of the circumstances, establish probable cause to arrest an individual for a specified crime (arrest warrant) or to search a specific location for items of evidence listed in the warrant (search warrant). A neutral magistrate or judge must review the facts and determine that probable cause exists to issue the warrant.

Probable cause is mentioned in the "warrant clause" of the Fourth Amendment, but the Supreme Court has also used this standard for making warrantless arrests. A full search of the person and area under his/her immediate control is permitted whenever there is a legal custodial arrest. Some other searches may also be done on probable cause even though no warrant has been obtained.

Only unreasonable searches or seizures are prohibited. The Court has attempted to set standards that fit the circumstances. Items left where they can be seen by an officer who is legally at the location are considered in "plain view" and no unreasonable search has occurred. Cars on a public roadway are subject to many vehicle code regulations and, due to their windows, have a lesser expectation of privacy than houses or other enclosed areas. Therefore, the Court has relaxed the warrant requirement in many instances where vehicles are involved.

The Court also recognized law enforcement's need to investigate suspicious conduct when there is no right to make an arrest. The "reasonable suspicion" standard, which requires less certainty of criminal activity than probable cause, can be used for this purpose.

Fifth Amendment

The Fifth Amendment applies to **self-incrimination:** any testimonial communication that can be used to incriminate a person. It is personal: a person can only claim its protection if he/she would face criminal charges

based on what he/she said. The *Miranda* warnings have made this amendment famous. *Miranda* warnings must be given prior to custodial interrogation. A suspect may waive these rights if the waiver is knowing,
intelligent, and voluntary.

The Fifth Amendment also prohibits **double jeopardy.** This applies
whenever a person is tried for the same crime after being acquitted or convicted except when the defendant successfully appealed and the conviction
was reversed. It also prohibits conviction (either at one trial or sequential
trials) on a crime and any lesser included offense included in that crime.

Sixth Amendment

Numerous rights related to criminal trials are listed in the Sixth
Amendment: speedy trial, public trial, impartial jury, being informed of
the charges prior to trial, right to cross-examine witnesses who testify for
the prosecution, right to subpoena witnesses for the defense, and assistance of counsel. These rights will be covered in considerable detail in
Chapter 11.

Eighth Amendment

This amendment prohibits excessive bail and fines. It also forbids **cruel
and unusual punishment.** In 1976 the Supreme Court held that the death
penalty is not cruel and unusual punishment if appropriate procedural
safeguards are used to prevent arbitrary jury decisions.

Due Process

While **due process** consists of both substantive due process and procedural due process, the majority of the cases applying to criminal law are
procedural. Laws that are vague violate due process. So do laws that give
police too much discretion.

Equal Protection

Equal protection is used to prohibit racial discrimination. It also applies
to gender discrimination. Discrimination on the basis of ability to pay also
violates equal protection in some circumstances. The poor must be provided with attorneys at government expense during court proceedings
from arraignment through sentencing and the first appeal. Jail sentences,
either directly or due to revocation of probation, cannot be imposed for
failure to pay fines if the defendant has made bona fide efforts but is
unable to pay.

United States Code

The **U.S. Code** contains laws enacted by the United States Congress. There must be some power delegated to the federal government in the Constitution or its amendments as a basis for each law. Some federal powers, such as regulation of interstate commerce, have been interpreted broadly enough to allow federal laws on interstate car theft, kidnapping, and other crimes. The Civil Rights Act is an example of laws passed to enforce an amendment to the Constitution.

Congress serves as the legislature for federal territories (such as Washington, D.C.), national parks, military bases, and post offices. This results in sections of the U.S. Code which cover criminal offenses ranging from petty theft to murder. Laws passed for this purpose are not binding on the states.

1-1b State Laws

State Constitutions

Each state has its own constitution. Some are extremely long, others quite brief. The **state constitution** establishes the framework for the state's government. Terms of office for the governor and other officials are usually set in the constitution. How the legislature is elected and the length of members' terms are specified. Judicial selection procedures and the length of the terms for judges are usually included in state constitutions.

Many other items may be included in a state's constitution. Most include a "Bill of Rights," which guarantees certain rights for people living in the state. States that allow constitutional amendment by the initiative process frequently have amendments on subjects normally handled by the legislature.

The state constitution and its Bill of Rights must give residents all the rights afforded by the U.S. Constitution and Bill of Rights. This is the minimum acceptable standard. Each state can give its residents more rights than are mandated by the federal constitution. For example, a state can require police to obtain arrest warrants under circumstances where warrants were not required under the Fourth Amendment. This does not violate the U.S. Constitution because it gives residents more rights.

State Statutes

The process for enacting new laws and amending old ones is set out in the state constitution. This usually involves a simple majority vote of both houses of the state legislature, but each state is free to establish different procedures. For example, a two-thirds majority may be required to raise taxes.

Each state is free to decide what acts are criminal, provided the laws do not violate the U.S. Constitution or Bill of Rights. There is no requirement that state criminal laws be the same. This results in a wide variety of crimes and punishments. Two states may use the same name, such as burglary, for crimes that do not have similar elements. Actions that are criminal in one state, such as gambling, may be legal in another. A criminal act may be a felony in one state but a misdemeanor in another.

Local Law

Each state delegates authority to local entities, such as counties, cities, and townships. This is usually specified in the state constitution. The local entities have the right to enact laws, frequently called ordinances. It is not uncommon to find enforcement of city ordinances restricted to law enforcement officers employed by the city which enacted the ordinances.

Statewide laws, such as those in the penal code, usually preempt local ordinances. This means that, if there is a conflict between the state law and the local law, the state law is considered the only valid law on the subject. Sometimes a state law is written specifically authorizing municipalities to enact ordinances for more complete coverage of special problems. When this happens, the state laws will not preempt local ordinances on the same subject.

Common Law

Common law has a variety of meanings depending on the context in which it is used. The common law system is the legal system of England. Most of the American colonies derived their legal systems from English common law. Some of its characteristics in criminal cases include the presumption that a person is innocent until proven guilty, the requirement that a case be heard before a neutral magistrate, and the stipulation that a jury is composed of laypeople rather than professional jurists.

"Common law" is also used to refer to the body of law that was brought to this country from England in the seventeenth century. "Common law burglary" refers to the definition of burglary that was used in England at that time. Many states now have statutes which say that the common law no longer applies. The intent of these code sections is to emphasize that the laws enacted by the legislature rather than the traditional definitions are to be used. Even so, if a statute uses common law terms and the legislature did not define them, the courts will look to the common law when applying the statute.

Another feature of common law is heavy reliance on **precedent.** When judges apply the law, they are supposed to follow the decisions already issued by higher courts. A court has the authority to reverse itself, and thus change the rule, but it does not have the authority to make a rule inconsistent with prior opinions of higher courts. When a new issue arises, the judge should review the precedents that exist for similar issues and try to apply law in a manner consistent with existing precedent.

1-2 Structure of the Legislative System

1-2a Federal

The **U.S. Congress** is divided into the Senate and the House of Representatives. Each state, regardless of population, has two senators, each of whom is elected by the entire state. Senators serve six-year terms, with one third of the seats up for election every two years.

There are 435 seats in the House of Representatives. Seats are allocated based on population. Boundaries are redrawn every 10 years after the national census in an attempt to keep the population in each district approximately equal. Each state has a minimum of one seat in the House, but there is no upper limit on how many representatives a state may have. Members of the House of Representatives serve two-year terms; all seats are up for election every other year.

Any legislator may introduce a bill into the house in which he/she is a member. Many more bills are introduced than are passed into law. Special interest groups, including law enforcement, labor unions, business and professional organizations, and private individuals, ask their representatives to "carry" bills. They frequently draft the bill and try to find other legislators who will coauthor the bill. Once the bill is introduced, these groups lobby other legislators to support the bill; opposing interest groups lobby for negative votes. Lobbying efforts range from contacting the legislators (in person or by mail, telephone, e-mail, and FAX) to providing volunteer staff to help with a campaign. After passage of the bill, there may be lobbying to have the president sign or veto it.

A bill must be passed by both houses of Congress. If amendments change the bill after it has been approved by one branch of Congress, a conference committee is formed to try to reconcile the differences, and then both the House and Senate must vote to approve the resulting bill. Bills that are not passed by the end of the two-year congressional session die. If they are reintroduced in the next session, the process starts over.

The final step is approval by the president. The president can either sign the bill, veto it, or leave it unsigned. If the president vetoes a bill while Congress is in session, the bill can still become law if two thirds of both houses vote to override the veto.

1-2b State

There are no restrictions in the U.S. Constitution on how the individual states operate their legislatures. Nearly all have established bicameral (divided into two houses) legislatures similar to the House and Senate. One house may have more members than the other. For example, the state senate may have 40 members while the assembly has 80. To do this, a senate district would have twice the population of an assembly district.

The Supreme Court has ruled that districts for each house of the state legislature must be divided so that each elected representative is from a district of approximately the same population. This applies to both houses in a bicameral system even though the U.S. Senate is allowed to operate under a different system.

The process of enacting a law in the state legislature is similar to that used in Congress. A bill is introduced into one of the legislative bodies and, if passed there, goes to the other. Only after passage by both does it go to the governor. The governor has the power to veto legislation. Some states give the state legislature the power to override a veto. A bill that does not become law can be introduced in the next legislative session.

The process of asking a legislator to introduce a bill and lobbying is similar at the state and federal levels. There is a greater opportunity for individuals and civic groups to try to influence the process at the state level, due to the fact that each legislator represents fewer people. The wider range of activities the state controls also results in more interaction with local groups. Mothers Against Drunk Drivers (MADD) is a good example of a group which has been very successful in lobbying state legislatures.

Most criminal laws become effective on January 1 of the year following passage rather than the date the governor signed the bill. Sometimes the effective date is sooner; most states provide for this if special procedures are followed. Occasionally a law will not become operative for two or more years. This is usually done so that necessary equipment purchases and training can be completed before the law goes into effect. If the bill does not follow the normal rule, the bill must state the date it will take effect.

Legislation usually remains in effect until repealed or amended. A recent trend has been to make **sunset laws.** These laws are enacted with an end date stated in the bill. State laws may mandate that all laws on certain topics take effect for only a limited period of time. For example, the California law authorizing electronic surveillance warrants expired after five years. This gave the legislature the chance to review the use of wiretaps and decide whether it should make the law permanent, change it, or discontinue authorization for wiretaps.

1-3 Structure of the Judicial System

The structures of the federal and state judicial systems for handling criminal cases are similar. Two exceptions are noted: state courts typically have more layers in order to facilitate handling of misdemeanors and other minor crimes; the federal system has separate courts for special purposes, such as bankruptcy courts. Each level of court must follow precedent. The courts are organized geographically, with appeals going up the organization chart in a predetermined order.

1-3a Federal

Criminal charges for violations of federal law are filed and trials are held at the **U.S. District Court.** There is at least one U.S. District Court in each state. States generating large caseloads will have more than one district, each using the state's name—for example, the Southern District of New York. Where the district covers a large land mass, there may be courthouses at several cities; each is called an office.

Appeals are heard by the **U.S. Courts of Appeal** (circuit courts). These are organized geographically in circuits. There are currently 11 circuits, which handle the 50 states plus one for cases regarding the federal government and another for the District of Columbia. For example, the proper designation for the federal appellate court for Pennsylvania, New Jersey, and Delaware is the United States Third Circuit Court of Appeal (see Figure 1-1).

Appeals are usually heard by a panel of three appellate judges. A majority vote is required. The number of panels of judges in each circuit is usually determined by the workload. In special circumstances a rehearing can be requested *en banc*. This means that a larger panel, sometimes all the justices of the circuit, will hear the case.

Each circuit has equal standing. Circuit courts must follow precedent established by the United States Supreme Court. They are not bound by decisions of other circuits, but they may use them as a basis for decisions if they agree with the legal reasoning used.

Figure 1-1

Geographical Organization of United States Circuit Courts of Appeal

First Circuit	Maine, Massachusetts, New Hampshire, Puerto Rico, Rhode Island
Second Circuit	Connecticut, New York, Vermont
Third Circuit	Delaware, New Jersey, Pennsylvania
Fourth Circuit	Maryland, North Carolina, South Carolina, Virginia, West Virginia
Fifth Circuit	Louisiana, Mississippi, Texas, Virgin Islands
Sixth Circuit	Kentucky, Michigan, Ohio, Tennessee
Seventh Circuit	Illinois, Indiana, Wisconsin
Eighth Circuit	Arkansas, Iowa, Minnesota, Missouri, Nebraska, North Dakota, South Dakota
Ninth Circuit	Alaska, Arizona, California, Guam, Hawaii, Idaho, Montana, Nevada, Northern Mariana Islands, Oregon, Washington
Tenth Circuit	Colorado, Kansas, New Mexico, Oklahoma, Utah, Wyoming
Eleventh Circuit	Alabama, Florida, Georgia
Federal Circuit	Matters related to federal government
District of Columbia Circuit	Acts similar to a state court for crimes and civil matters arising in the District of Columbia

The **U.S. Supreme Court** is at the top of the federal judicial system. Cases are heard by a panel of nine justices. Federal law requires that the Supreme Court hear some cases, such as border disputes between states. Most cases come by petition for writ of *certiorari* (frequently called *cert*). This petition asks the court to accept the case. Four of the nine justices must vote to grant a ***writ of certiorari*** before a case will be scheduled for a hearing. Granting the writ does not indicate the Supreme Court will reverse the lower court's decision: some of the justices may have voted to grant *cert* because they favor reversing the lower court's decision while the remaining justices may want to affirm it. Oral arguments are held a few months after *cert* is granted, and an opinion is usually issued within the next six to nine months.

1-3b State

While the basic structure of the state courts closely resembles the federal system, the names used may be different. Most states call the highest court the Supreme Court, but some do not. New York designates it the Court of Appeals; the Supreme Court in New York conducts felony trials. A few states, such as Texas, have specially designated courts, which hear only criminal appeals.

Most state courts separate felony and misdemeanor trials. Typically all cases start in the same courts. These courts are frequently called municipal courts or justice courts, although numerous other titles are used. Many states transfer felonies to a higher court for trial. The case stays in the trial court through sentencing.

The use of two separate courts results in different appellate procedures for misdemeanors and felonies. The basic rule is that an appeal goes to the next higher court on the organization chart. A state may have misdemeanor appeals heard by judges who normally preside over felony trials. Felony appeals are more likely to be heard in the intermediary-level court equivalent to the federal court of appeal (names vary from state to state).

The highest court in each state functions much like the United States Supreme Court: cases are usually heard only if the justices grant a hearing. The most frequent exception is for cases in which the death penalty has been imposed: the state Supreme Court, instead of the lower-level appellate courts, may be required to hear these cases (see Figure 1-2).

1-4 Authority of the Courts

Courts can make binding decisions only if they have authority over the case. This is called **jurisdiction.** An individual court must also have authority to hear the case. This is called **venue.** Even with appropriate jurisdiction and venue, the Exclusionary Rule restricts the courts' right to enter convictions based on unconstitutionally seized evidence.

1-4a Jurisdiction

The jurisdiction of a court is based on two things: whether there is authority over the place where the crime occurred and whether there is authority over the subject matter involved.

Geographical Jurisdiction

A state has **geographical jurisdiction** over all crimes committed within its geographical boundaries. Sometimes there is also jurisdiction for acts that occur out of state. A simple example is a person who stands 10 feet from the state line and shoots someone in another state. The state where the injury occurred would have jurisdiction even though the defendant never set foot in the state. Crimes occurring through the mail, telephone, FAX, and so on would also result in jurisdiction if there were harm within the state.

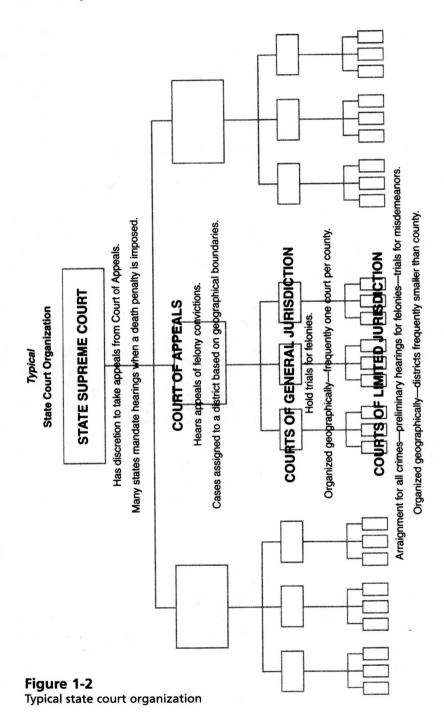

Figure 1-2
Typical state court organization

Federal jurisdiction is somewhat similar. It covers acts done inside the United States or its territories (including overseas military bases and embassies). In some situations it also covers injuries to United States citizens that occur while they are overseas.

Subject Matter Jurisdiction

Subject matter jurisdiction means that the court has the authority to hear cases on this subject. State courts cannot try cases based on another state's criminal laws.

A court of general jurisdiction usually can hear any felony under that state's laws. It can also hear cases in which the charges include both felonies and misdemeanors. If a state has a separate level of courts that conduct arraignments and misdemeanor trials, they are said to be of limited jurisdiction because they cannot hear felony trials. Cases involving only misdemeanors must be tried in these courts.

In criminal cases, federal courts have subject matter jurisdiction only over crimes in the United States Code. An indictment cannot contain both federal and state charges.

Venue

Venue divides cases between courts within the state or federal system. The legislature draws geographical boundaries for each court. If a case is filed in the wrong court, it may be dismissed for lack of venue. The prosecution usually has the right to refile the case in the correct court district. For example, a robbery that occurs in Cook County must be filed in that county's courts. The prosecutor may need to check the map to determine which court to use if the crime occurred near the boundary line.

Either side may request a change of venue after the case has been correctly filed. One reason for a change of venue is to find an impartial jury when there has been inflammatory media coverage before the trial. When a change of venue is granted, the case will be moved to a different county and heard by a jury from the new location. The prosecutor will be from the original locale.

1-4b Exclusionary Rule

In 1961 the United States Supreme Court expanded the **Exclusionary Rule** to cover state courts. The Exclusionary Rule mandates that both state and federal judges have been required to exclude evidence obtained in violation of the Fourth and Fifth Amendments. Over the years exceptions have been made, so that some unconstitutionally seized evidence can be used at trial.

The basic rule remains that unconstitutionally seized evidence, as well as evidence obtained as the result of the original action (Fruit of the Poison Tree), cannot be used by the prosecution in state or federal trials.

States have the authority to make their own Exclusionary Rules as long as the constitutionally required rule is followed. State policy may dictate that there is a greater expectation of privacy in certain situations, such as booking people arrested for the most trivial offenses, which mandate more protections for the person than found in the United States Constitution. Our federal system of government allows states to do this. The reverse is not true: states may not give the police authority to act in violation of the Fourth Amendment as interpreted by the United States Supreme Court.

1-5 Roles of the Participants in the Justice System

The American legal system assigns distinct roles to the participants in the criminal justice system. Some, such as the roles of the prosecutors and defense attorneys, are in conflict with each other.

1-5a Law Enforcement

Law enforcement functions include preventing crime, apprehending criminals, and engaging in other activities which protect and serve the community they police. The philosophy of each law enforcement agency is a reflection of the community it serves.

Investigating criminal activity and making arrests are clearly police functions. Patrol officers must carefully observe human behavior and be suspicious when it appears criminal activity is occurring. Officers have the right to make an arrest whenever there is probable cause that the person has committed a crime. In addition to probable cause, the officer may consider other factors when deciding to make an arrest: Is there a need to arrest the suspect in order to prevent further violence? Will the victim prosecute? How serious is the crime? Will warning the suspect, rather than making an arrest, sufficiently deter future violations? Are there other, more serious calls that need to be handled immediately?

The Supreme Court has characterized law enforcement as being involved in the "often competitive job of ferreting out crime." Pressures to make arrests, due either to a public outcry or to the officer's desire to further his/her own career, may influence the actions taken. The Court has been reluctant to view police officers as acting objectively. Requiring judicial review of warrant applications is a buffer in the process designed to insert an impartial observer between the police and the suspected criminal.

Investigations done after an arrest may show that the suspect is not the person who committed the crime. The police have a duty to release the person under these circumstances unless there is probable cause that the suspect committed some other crime. The police function is to find the truth, not merely to obtain convictions. All information discovered by the police, whether it shows guilt or innocence, must be made available to the prosecutor.

1-5b Prosecutor

The prosecutor, like the police, is part of the executive branch of government. The prosecutor serves as a gatekeeper of the judicial process. Cases are reviewed and decisions made on what charges, if any, will be filed. The prosecutor does not have to file the same charges the police used when making the arrest.

While probable cause is sufficient to file the case, the prosecutor always keeps in mind that it takes proof beyond a reasonable doubt to obtain the conviction. A more legalistic approach is taken when reviewing the case: Is there admissible evidence which will result in a conviction? Are the eyewitnesses credible? Have the defendant's Fourth and Fifth Amendment rights been violated?

Other factors also influence the prosecutor's decision. One is workload. Minor charges may be rejected if there are already more cases awaiting trial than the prosecutor can handle. Cases may be rejected if there is doubt that they can be "won," even though the prosecutor personally believes the suspect is guilty.

Another consideration is public attitudes. These attitudes will likely be reflected in the minds of the jurors who will be selected for the trial. Judicial attitudes also influence the prosecutor. If the local judge has a reputation for giving extremely light sentences for some cases, such as minor batteries, the prosecutor may decide it is not worthwhile even to file the charges.

Plea bargaining also reflects these considerations. Plea bargaining is one device used to reduce the workload. The prosecutor is in charge of making a "deal" which is just—the defendant should receive a sentence that appropriately reflects the seriousness of the offense(s). Prosecutors may tip the scales by overcharging in order to be able to offer the defendant a good "bargain." Overcrowded court calendars and sentencing practices of local judges also influence the final decision.

The prosecutor is charged with seeking justice. Any evidence indicating the defendant's innocence must be disclosed to the defense attorney. The prosecutor also has a duty not to introduce perjured testimony and not to seek inflammatory pretrial publicity that could bias potential jurors. The prosecutor has the power to ask the court to dismiss charges "in the interest of justice," even though the defendant may be believed to be guilty. This power can be used to drop charges when a defendant has agreed to cooperate with the prosecution or to become a police informant. Sometimes it is used because the defendant is suffering from a terminal illness.

1-5c Defendant

A criminal suspect is considered a **defendant** once the charges have been filed in court. The defendant is presumed innocent until proven guilty. This gives the defendant the right to refuse to cooperate with the police. The Fifth Amendment protects the defendant from being forced to make incriminating statements. It also prohibits the inference that the defendant's silence is an admission of guilt.

1-5d Defense Attorney

The role of the defense attorney is to protect the defendant. Constitutionally this is based on a combination of the Fifth Amendment right not to incriminate oneself, Sixth Amendment right to counsel, and the due process right to be convicted by proof beyond a reasonable doubt. Added to this is the traditional attorney-client privilege covering confidential communications. Confessions by the defendant to his/her attorney or the defense attorney's personal belief that the client is guilty does not change the duties of the defense attorney.

The defense attorney is charged with doing everything in his/her legal power to defend the accused. The defense attorney should seek an acquittal or a dismissal. When plea bargains are possible, the attorney has the responsibility to use his/her best legal judgment in advising the client on the available options. Motions should be filed to suppress any evidence that the police obtained in violation of the defendant's Fourth and Fifth Amendment rights. At trial, the defense attorney should make appropriate objections to evidence the prosecution tries to admit and aggressively cross-examine witnesses and attempt to impeach them. The Sixth Amendment right to counsel includes all of these tactics, which force the prosecution to meet its burden of proof.

The attorney must not resort to illegal tactics, such as introducing testimony known to be false or tampering with the evidence, in order to gain the client's freedom. Conduct in court should not be designed to threaten and intimidate witnesses beyond the scope of legitimate cross-examination.

During opening statements, cross-examination, and closing arguments, the defense attorney should not allude to evidence that is inadmissible or use unfounded innuendos to imply that witnesses have been untruthful or have withheld facts.

1-5e Judge

The judge serves as a neutral referee in the American criminal justice system. A judge who has a personal stake in a case is required to recuse (remove) him-/herself from the case. This would occur if the judge or a member of the judge's immediate family were a defendant, victim, or witness in the case. It also applies if the judge previously was a member of the law firm which is representing one side in the case. Sometimes judges are removed from cases because they have made statements indicating personal biases about the cases or similar cases.

Judges in nearly all states are now required to have experience as members of the state bar. The legal training and experience gained prior to taking the bench give them background in both the rules of law and the practical application of law to courtroom situations.

In a jury trial the judge acts as a referee. The judge listens to objections and makes rulings on the admissibility of evidence. He/she controls the tenor of the courtroom by cautioning the attorneys and witnesses about their emotional outbursts and flamboyant conduct. The judge can control the line of questioning to avoid harassment of the witness. Rulings the judge makes on the jury instructions control the law of the case. Jury instructions related to particular defenses have decisive impacts on many cases.

There is no jury in a **bench trial.** The judge decides both the law and the facts. In addition to the normal judicial function of ruling on the admissibility of evidence and objections to questions, the judge personally evaluates the evidence and decides the guilt or innocence of the defendant. This unique combination of roles is used only if both the prosecution and the defense agree to waive a jury trial.

1-5f Jury

The jury listens to the evidence that is admitted at trial and applies the law given in the jury instructions. The collective opinions of the jury should equate to the judgment of a "reasonable person." The jury's function is also to serve as a jury of the defendant's peers. This implies that jury members are the conscience of the community. While they are given instructions on what the law is, they also have the authority to temper their decision as they believe justice requires.

The jury may totally reject the jury instructions and acquit a person. This is called **jury nullification.** The opposite is not true: the conviction will be reversed if the jury convicts the defendant of a crime not included in the jury instructions. Jury nullification occurs most often when community standards do not parallel the letter of the law. Double jeopardy prevents the prosecution from refiling a case under these circumstances. An example is acquitting an elderly person who had killed a terminally ill spouse who was in excruciating pain and was begging to die.

Chapter Summary

The criminal justice system is governed by a combination of federal and state laws. Small portions of the U.S. Constitution apply to criminal justice, but the First, Fourth, Fifth, Sixth, and Eighth Amendments plus the due process and equal protection clauses of the Fourteenth Amendment have major impacts. A few sections of the U.S. Code apply to criminal conduct in the states.

Most laws directly affecting local law enforcement either are in the state constitution or enacted by the state legislature. The U.S. Constitution gives the states a great deal of leeway in making criminal laws. There is no requirement that states have the same crimes, that punishment for the same crimes be equal, or that crimes with the same names have similar definitions. States usually give local municipalities authority to enact laws on some issues.

The American legal system is largely based on the British common law model. Many of our crimes started with the definition in use at the time settlers came to America from England. Statutes enacted by state legislatures have largely replaced common law crimes. The old definitions are still used if new laws use the old terms but fail to define them.

Federal laws are enacted by the U.S. Congress. A bill can be introduced into either house of Congress but must be passed by both houses. It then goes to the president, who may either sign it or veto it. State laws follow similar paths through the state legislature and then to the governor.

The state and federal legal systems consist of three or more tiers. Criminal arraignments are held at the lowest tier, and the case works its way up the organization chart. The courts are organized geographically: which court the case goes to depends on where the crime occurred.

A court can act only if it has jurisdiction. Federal courts have jurisdiction over crimes described in the U.S. Code. State courts have jurisdiction over crimes committed in the state. A court must also have venue over a case; this means the crime occurred within the geographical boundaries of the judicial district.

The role of law enforcement is to enforce laws by making arrests. Officers have discretion not to arrest, even though there is probable cause. The prosecutor screens cases prior to filing them. In addition to deciding if there is probable cause, the prosecutor considers a variety of other factors, including the admissibility of evidence, workload, and community attitudes.

Our legal system presumes the defendant innocent until proven guilty. The Fifth Amendment gives the defendant a privilege against self-incrimination. The defense lawyer's duty is to protect the defendant's rights. He/she is to be considered innocent unless the prosecution has established guilt beyond a reasonable doubt at trial. The defense attorney has the duty to represent the defendant, whether or not the defense attorney personally believes the defendant is guilty. There is no right to use illegal tactics, such as introducing perjured testimony, to accomplish this goal.

The judge presides over the trial and makes rulings on the admissibility of evidence. He/she also controls the demeanor of the courtroom and rules on jury instructions. In a bench trial, the judge also weighs the evidence to determine guilt.

The jury hears the evidence at trial and decides whether the prosecution has established guilt beyond a reasonable doubt. The jury is sworn to follow the jury instructions but has the authority to ignore the instructions and vote for acquittal. In this way, the jury acts as the conscience of the community.

Study Questions

Study Questions

1. Explain which provisions of the U.S. Constitution apply to a state's authority to enact criminal laws.
2. Explain how the following amendments to the U.S. Constitution apply to a state's criminal justice system:
   a. First Amendment
   b. Fourth Amendment
   c. Fifth Amendment
   d. Sixth Amendment
   e. Eighth Amendment
   f. Fourteenth Amendment (due process and equal protection clauses)
3. Explain how laws in the United States Code apply to criminal acts in a state.
4. Describe the interaction between the U.S. Constitution and state constitutions.
5. Describe the ways state laws may provide rights different from those in the U.S. Constitution and Bill of Rights.
6. How does English common law affect the American criminal justice system?
7. Describe the structure of the federal legislative system and of the legislative system in the state and city where you live.
8. Diagram the process used to enact a law in the U.S. Congress and in your state legislature.
9. Describe the structure of the federal judicial system and of your state's judicial system.
10. How are jurisdiction and venue determined in federal courts? in the courts in your state?
11. Explain the role of precedent in judicial opinions.
12. Explain the exclusionary rule.
13. Describe the role of law enforcement in making arrests and obtaining convictions in the criminal justice system.
14. Describe the roles of the prosecutor and the defense attorney in the criminal justice system.
15. Describe the roles of the judge and the jury in the criminal justice system.

True or False Questions

T **1.** The *writ of habeas corpus* is guaranteed by the U.S. Constitution and can be suspended only if there is a rebellion or invasion in the United States.

T **2.** New state laws must be approved by the state legislature and then sent to the state governor.

F **3.** The Sixth Amendment gives the defendant in a criminal case the right to demand a jury trial in all felony cases.

T **4.** The Fourth Amendment prohibits unreasonable searches and seizures conducted by city police officers.

F **5.** The U.S. Constitution requires that the court systems of all states follow the same organizational structure as the federal courts.

F **6.** The Equal Protection Clause of the Fourteenth Amendment applies only to legislation passed by the U.S. Congress.

F **7.** Each state's constitution must be approved by the U.S. Congress.

T **8.** A criminal trial for a suspect accused of violating federal law will be held in the U.S. District Court for the state where the crime was committed.

T **9.** State courts have geographical jurisdiction over crimes committed within their boundaries.

F **10.** The Exclusionary Rule, which prohibits the use of evidence seized in violation of the Fourth Amendment, applies only in federal courts.

Chapter

2

Authority of Police to Detain and Arrest

Outline

Key Terms

arrest warrant required
booking search
Chimel v. California
deadly force
felony arrest
Interstate Agreement
  on Detainers
jurisdiction

misdemeanor arrest
nondeadly force
out-of-state warrants
patdown (frisk)
peace officer
probable cause
protective sweep
reasonable suspicion

search incident
  to the arrest
Terry v. Ohio
Uniform Criminal
  Extradition Act
Uniform Act
  on Fresh Pursuit

Learning Objectives

After reading this chapter, the student will be able to

- Explain who has the legal status of a peace officer.
- Explain the jurisdiction of a peace officer.
- Explain the authority of a peace officer to stop a person for questioning.
- Explain the authority of a peace officer to search a person who has been detained.
- Describe the arrest powers of a peace officer.
- Identify circumstances where an officer must have a warrant in order to make an arrest.
- Explain the scope of the search that is allowed incident to an arrest.
- Describe the extent of the search that is allowed when a person is booked into a jail facility.

Police have the authority to detain people if there is a reasonable suspicion that criminal activity is occurring. Traditionally, police have been given more authority than other members of the community to make arrests. The officer's power of arrest is controlled by both the Fourth Amendment and the laws of the state where the arrest is made.

2-1 Peace Officers

Everyone has the right to make arrests for crimes that occur in their presence. They are allowed to use appropriate levels of force in defense of themselves, other people, and their homes and property. Peace officers have these powers plus authority that is granted by the laws of the state in which they are employed. The Fourth Amendment places some limitations on the powers that a state can grant its peace officers.

2-1a Peace Officer Defined

State law defines who is a peace officer and what authority he/she can exercise. The test of who is a **peace officer** is based on two criteria: who the employer is and in what capacity the person is employed. Many states mandate specific training courses and background checks be completed within the first year of employment in order to maintain peace officer status.

Police departments, highway patrol, and sheriffs' departments are the best known local law enforcement agencies. A wide variety of others exist: transit authorities, airports, regulatory agencies, park rangers, fire wardens, probation and parole officers, and correctional officers. There are also peace officer positions within agencies not thought of as law enforcement, such as consumer affairs, children's protective services, and agencies that license doctors, lawyers, and other professions. States may designate some law enforcement positions as peace officers for all purposes while restricting others to on-duty activities within the jurisdiction that employs them.

More limited authority is given to some peace officers, particularly reserve officers and those who work as investigators for agencies which are not primarily enforcement agencies. For example, California designates investigators of the Department of Toxic Substance Control as peace officers only for enforcement of laws related to their primary duty; for other crimes, they have the same powers as a private citizen.

Not everyone who works for a law enforcement agency is a peace officer. Clerical personnel are not peace officers; neither are people in a variety of other service positions, such as field evidence technicians and community service officers. State law may designate some jobs as non-peace officer positions. Local agencies may also decide that some jobs do not require the powers of a peace officer. Converting peace officer positions to civilian positions generally adds specialized personnel to the department and reduces salary expenses.

Authorization to carry a firearm typically is part of peace officer status. A state may restrict this right to on-duty hours for some positions, such as consumer fraud investigators. It may even designate some positions as not authorized to carry weapons at all. Local agencies may have more restrictive policies than the state law.

2-1b Jurisdiction of Peace Officers

Peace officers are charged with enforcing the laws of the state in which they are employed. The **jurisdiction** of peace officers is usually based on geographical boundaries. A peace officer acts under the same authority as does a non-peace officer when out of the jurisdiction. Three exceptions apply: travel into another part of the state while investigating a crime which occurred locally; fresh pursuit which goes out of the state; and arrests and detainers for crimes committed in another state.

Within the State

Officers employed by a city police department usually are authorized to act as peace officers within their city both on- and off-duty. They can act as peace officers in other jurisdictions within the state if this is necessary in the performance of their primary duties (for example, a detective going to another city to make an arrest). They may also make arrests anywhere in the state for crimes occurring in their presence or if there is an immediate danger to life or property.

Mutual aid agreements between cities, or a city and another level of government, also give officers the authority to exercise peace officer powers outside the jurisdiction where they are employed. Formal contracts are usually developed by the agencies involved. Officers may be allowed to respond with only an informal request, such as an "officer needs help" call; more structured procedures usually apply when officers are sent on longer-term assignments to help with riots, natural disasters, or special events.

Uniform Fresh Pursuit Act

Each state's laws, and the authority of its peace officers, extend only to its geographical boundaries. Criminals fleeing the police do not respect state lines. The **Uniform Act on Fresh Pursuit** was enacted by all 50 states, so that officers could go into an adjoining state to make an arrest. Note that it applies only to felony arrests; an arrest warrant is not required. The key provision is

> Any peace officer of another State, who enters this State in fresh pursuit, and continues within this State in fresh pursuit, of a person in order to arrest him on the ground that he has committed a felony in the other State, has the same authority to arrest and hold the person in custody, as peace officers of this State have to arrest and hold a person in custody on the ground that he has committed a felony in this State (California Penal Code Section 852.2).

Officers must be in pursuit at the time they cross the state line. The pursuit does not, however, have to start at the time of the crime. There is no restriction on how far the officers may go. What is mandatory is that the pursuit started in the state where the crime occurred and continued until the arrest was made.

Once a fleeing felon has been arrested, he/she must be taken without unnecessary delay to the local magistrate in the state where the arrest was made. A hearing is held to determine the lawfulness of the arrest. If the magistrate rules the arrest was legal, the suspect remains in custody, so that an extradition warrant can be prepared by the state where the crime occurred. The person is released if it is determined that the arrest was not lawfully made.

2-1c Out-of-State Warrants and Detainers

The mobility of criminals necessitates procedures to arrest criminals who leave the state under circumstances that do not amount to hot pursuit. Similar legislation enacted by nearly all the states covers two possibilities: authorizing local officers to make arrests on out-of-state warrants and placing a "hold" on a person who is serving a sentence in another state.

Out-of-State Warrants

Authority to make arrests based on out-of-state warrants is found in the **Uniform Criminal Extradition Act.** The key provision reads

> . . . it is the duty of the Governor of this State to have arrested and delivered up to the executive authority of any other State any person charged in that State with treason, felony, or other crime, who has fled from justice and is found in this State.

The extradition process requires that the state in which the crime occurred send a copy of an indictment, information, or arrest warrant with accompanying affidavits to justify the return of the person arrested.

A court hearing is held in the state where the arrest was made. Its purpose is to inform the person arrested of the extradition request and to verify that the documents establish **probable cause.** The authorities requesting extradition must show that the suspect was in their state when the crime occurred. If the person who was arrested objects to the extradition, he/she can file a petition for *writ of habeas corpus.*

Detainers

A detainer is used to prevent the release of an inmate because there are other criminal charges pending. The agency that filed the detainer takes custody of the inmate at the time he/she is due to be released. Most states have procedures that enable a law enforcement agency to place a detainer on inmates being held in another jail or prison in their state.

The **Interstate Agreement on Detainers** is used when a detainer has been filed against an inmate by an out-of-state agency. It can be used if any of the following court documents have been filed in a case—indictment, information, or complaint. The Uniform Act allows the inmate to have pending charges tried while he/she is serving the current sentence.

An inmate must be notified if a detainer has been filed. The inmate may then demand a trial on the charges. Once the demand has been made, the state filing the detainer has 180 days, plus necessary continuances, to bring the case to trial. The inmate is transported to the location where the trial will be held but remains in custody throughout the proceedings. Failure to bring the case to trial within the time limits specified results in dismissal of the charges without the right to refile them.

At the end of the trial (or when charges are dismissed), the inmate is returned to the state where he/she was serving a sentence. Sometimes the two sentences can be served concurrently, even though the convictions occurred in two different states. The inmate will be returned to the state that filed the detainer, if necessary, after the original sentence is completed in order to serve any time remaining on that state's conviction.

2-2 Use of Force

Anytime an officer has the right to detain someone, there is a corresponding right to use force to prevent that person from leaving. This applies to both temporary detentions and arrests. The Fourth Amendment requires that the force used must always be reasonable under the circumstances

(*Graham v. Connor*, 490 U.S. 386, 104 L.Ed. 2d 443, 109 S.Ct. 1865 [1989]). **Deadly force** is justified *only if* a life is in danger (*Tennessee v. Garner*, 471 U.S. 1, 85 L.Ed. 2d 1, 105 S.Ct. 1694 [1985]).

Nondeadly force must also be used in a reasonable manner. The rationale for using force is to detain and subdue the suspect. Only tactics reasonably necessary to achieve these objectives are allowed. The amount of force allowed correlates with the suspect's actions: more force is permitted if the suspect becomes combative; less force is authorized as the suspect's resistance diminishes. No force is authorized once the suspect is passive.

2-3 Detaining of a Suspect for Questioning

Police frequently observe something that indicates that further investigation is needed. Many times the initial observation does not give the officer enough information to make an arrest, but there is definitely something going on that needs to be checked out. The Supreme Court agreed that the police should have the power to stop a suspect for brief questioning in these situations.

2-3a Stop for Questioning

In **Terry v. Ohio** (392 U.S. 1, 20 L.Ed. 2d 889, 88 S.Ct. 1868 [1968]), the leading case, the Court authorized temporary detention for questioning if there are specific articulable facts which lead a reasonable police officer to believe that criminal activity is occurring. A police officer may consider the fact that the suspect acted nervous and took evasive actions (including fleeing the scene) when the officer approached. Information from victims, witnesses, and informants may be considered by the officer. Mere hunches are not enough. The officer may not stop a person based solely on the fact that the person is associating with "known criminals" or is at a location where criminal activity, such as drug sales, frequently occurs. The officer may consider reliable hearsay. The Supreme Court, however, invalidated a stop based on an anonymous call stating that there was a man on the corner with a gun in his pocket. It stated that accepting such uncorroborated information made it too easy for someone to call the police and cause problems for an innocent person.

The standard for detention is frequently called **reasonable suspicion.** It differs from probable cause to arrest in several ways. Reasonable suspicion does not require as many facts as are needed to make an arrest. The officer must be able to cite specific facts that led to the belief that criminal

---

Terry v. Ohio
392 U.S. 1, 20 L.Ed. 2d 889, 88 S. Ct. 1868 (1968)

Issue: Search of Person Who Has Been Detained but Not Arrested

"We merely hold today that, where a police officer observes unusual conduct which leads him reasonably to conclude in light of his experience that criminal activity may be afoot and that the persons with whom he is dealing may be armed and presently dangerous, where, in the course of investigating this behavior, he identifies himself as a policeman and makes reasonable inquiries, and where nothing in the initial stages of the encounter serves to dispel his reasonable fear for his own or others' safety, he is entitled for the protection of himself and others in the area to conduct a carefully limited search of the outer clothing of such persons in an attempt to discover weapons which might be used to assault him. Such a search is a reasonable search under the Fourth Amendment, and any weapons seized may properly be introduced in evidence against the person from whom they were taken."

---

activity was present, but it is not necessary to identify a specific crime believed to be in progress. To make an arrest, the officer must believe that it is more probable than not that the suspect committed a specific crime. Reasonable suspicion requires that a "reasonable officer," based on experiences patrolling the area, would believe that some criminal activity were occurring. The decision to arrest is based on an objective test: what a "reasonable person" would conclude.

2-3b Request Identification

The Supreme Court recognized a legitimate need for police to stop individuals and demand identification if there is reasonable suspicion of criminal activity. State laws authorizing such stops must set specific standards establishing what type of identification is acceptable (*Kolender v. Lawson,* 461 U.S. 352, 75 L.Ed. 2d 903, 103 S.Ct. 1855 [1983]).

2-3c Patdown for Weapons

The Supreme Court, recognizing that it is frequently necessary to search a suspect for the safety of the officer, authorized protective searches during a temporary detention if the officer has a reasonable suspicion that the suspect is armed or dangerous. The limited search permitted in *Terry* is designed solely for the protection of the officer. There is no automatic right to search every person stopped. Officers must have a reasonable suspicion that the search is needed for their protection. If a person is stopped, for example, because there is reasonable suspicion that a violent crime is in progress, the right to search logically follows. If the situation involves a non-aggressive person believed to be preparing to commit a theft, there may be no right to search.

The officer may **patdown (frisk)** the suspect's outer clothing for weapons. This logically includes checking purses, back packs, or items that the person is carrying. If the officer feels something believed to be a weapon, he/she may retrieve the suspicious object. If, in fact, the object seized is not a weapon, whatever was seized will still be admissible. On the other hand, if the officer feels something in the suspect's pocket that does not resemble a weapon, there is no right to retrieve it.

One exception to this rule applies when contraband is "plainly detected through the sense of touch" during a patdown for weapons (*Minnesota v. Dickerson*, 508 U.S. 366, 124 L.Ed. 2d 334, 113 S.Ct. 2130 [1993]). This is a very limited exception: the officer must be able to determine that an item is contraband while conducting a normal patdown. The Court pointed out that examination of a suspicious but unidentified object, in order to identify it as contraband, is not allowed. The Court rejected a seizure made after an officer discovered a small lump in a suspect's pocket during a legal patdown and persisted in "squeezing, sliding, and otherwise manipulating the contents of the defendant's pocket" prior to concluding that the object was rock cocaine.

2-3d Search of Vehicles

There is no special rule that allows police officers to stop a car or other vehicle. Police do not have the authority to randomly stop cars, merely to check their registration or to see if the driver has a valid license (*Delaware v. Prouse*, 440 U.S. 648, 59 L.Ed. 2d 660, 99 S.Ct. 1391 [1979]). A car can be stopped, however, if there is reasonable suspicion that the driver has violated the vehicle code. These stops can be based on reasonable suspicion. The Supreme Court recognized the right of the police officer to order the driver and passengers to get out of a vehicle that was stopped under these circumstances (*Pennsylvania v. Mimms*, 434 U.S. 106, 54 L.Ed. 2d 331, 98 S.Ct. 330 [1977]); *Maryland v. Wilson*, 519 U.S. 408, 137 L.Ed. 2d 41, 117 S.Ct. 883 [1997]). They can be searched only if some other test is triggered, such as having a bulge in a pocket that looks like a gun.

Even though no vehicle code violation has occurred, the facts may provide reasonable suspicion that the occupants of the car are involved in criminal activity. These cars can be stopped under *Terry's* authority to detain suspects temporarily. Officers have the authority to conduct a search of the passenger compartment for weapons if there is an objectively reasonable belief that the suspect is potentially dangerous; searching for weapons is permitted even if the officers have decided to release the suspects (*Michigan v. Long*, 463 U.S. 1032, 77 L.Ed. 2d 1201, 103 S.Ct. 3469 [1983]). The rationale is that a suspect who has been released may return to the car, retrieve the weapon, and assault the officers.

2-3e Fingerprinting

The Supreme Court has held that a suspect may not be detained and taken to the police station for fingerprinting unless there is probable cause to arrest or the suspect consents. It is legal, however, to fingerprint a person at the scene.

2-3f Interrogation

Questioning during temporary detention does not require *Miranda* warnings. The right to interrogate during a *Terry* stop does not include taking the suspect to the police station for questioning. Transportation to the station can be done only if the suspect consents or has been arrested (*Dunaway v. New York*, 442 U.S. 200, 60 L.Ed. 2d 824, 99 S.Ct. 2248 [1979]).

2-4 Arrest

Traditionally, the authority of a peace officer to make a felony arrest was different from what was allowed for misdemeanors. In addition to these distinctions, the Supreme Court has mandated arrest warrants under some circumstances.

2-4a Probable Cause to Arrest

All arrests made by police officers must be based on probable cause. *Black's Law Dictionary* gives a good definition of probable cause to arrest:

> Probable cause exists where the facts and circumstances would warrant a
> person of reasonable caution to believe that an offense was or is being com-
> mitted. The existence of circumstances which would lead a reasonably pru-
> dent man to believe in guilt of arrested party; mere suspicion or belief,
> unsupported by facts or circumstances, is insufficient. . . . Probable cause
> justifying officer's arrest without warrant has been defined as situation
> where officer has more evidence favoring suspicion that person is guilty of
> crime than evidence against such suspicion, but there is some room for
> doubt.

If an arrest warrant has already been issued, the existence of the warrant establishes probable cause, even though the officer executing it has no knowledge of the facts of the case. The defense will have the opportunity to challenge the validity of the warrant after the suspect has been arraigned.

An officer may use facts obtained from informants in order to establish probable cause. The "totality of the circumstances" test is used to determine if probable cause exists. Both the facts and the credibility of the person providing the information must be considered. While the fact that a person has previously provided information that proved to be true is important, it is not mandatory that there be an established track record. Other factors considered include whether significant details were provided; motive to lie; inherent probability that the scenario could have occurred in the manner reported; and the reputation of the individual providing the information.

2-4b Felony Arrest

A peace officer is authorized to make a **felony arrest** whenever he/she has probable cause to believe that a felony has been committed. The arrest is legal, even though no felony actually occurred, as long as there were sufficient facts to establish probable cause. A peace officer also needs probable cause that the person to be arrested committed the crime; absolute certainty is not required.

2-4c Misdemeanor Arrest

The traditional rule is that a peace officer may make a **misdemeanor arrest** *only if* the offense occurred in his/her presence. As with felonies, there must be probable cause that the crime occurred and that the suspect is the person who committed it. Some state statutes modify this rule and allow officers to arrest for certain misdemeanors, even though the officers did not observe the crime occurring. Typically this expanded rule authorizes the arrest of juveniles, anyone suspected of drunk driving, a person who commits battery on his/her spouse, and a few other misdemeanors. The popularity of this rule has resulted in the legislature's frequently adding to the list of exceptions. Each officer must be familiar with the law that currently applies.

Officers lack authority to arrest for misdemeanors that occurred when they were not at the scene unless the state law has expanded their authority. In situations where the officer cannot make a misdemeanor arrest for this reason, there are three alternatives:

- Have someone who witnessed the misdemeanor make a "citizen's arrest."
- Obtain an arrest warrant based on affidavits containing statements of people who witnessed the offense.
- Make no arrest.

2-4d When Arrest Warrants Are Required by the Fourth Amendment

While officers frequently enter buildings to rescue people, there is no general right to enter private property to conduct a criminal investigation (*Mincey v. Arizona*, 437 U.S. 385, 57 L.Ed. 2d 290, 98 S.Ct. 2408 [1978]). The United States Supreme Court interpreted the Fourth Amendment as requiring a warrant to make an arrest in a residence unless there is an emergency, such as hot pursuit or someone screaming for help, or if someone with authority over the residence consents. This rule applies to both felonies and misdemeanors. An arrest warrant is sufficient if officers want to enter the suspect's dwelling (*Payton v. New York*, 445 U.S. 573, 63 L.Ed. 2d 639, 100 S.Ct. 1371 [1980]), but a search warrant is needed to enter the home of another person to arrest the suspect (*Stegald v. United States*, 451 U.S. 204, 68 L.Ed. 2d 38, 101 S.Ct. 1642 [1981]).

Knock notice procedures must be followed at dwellings. Prior to entering, the officer must (1) knock or otherwise draw attention to his/her presence; (2) announce the purpose of the visit; and (3) wait long enough for a cooperative person to comply. After this three-step procedure has been followed, the officer may use force to enter if admittance has been denied or there was no reply. See section 3-4a, "Knock Notice," for details about knock notice.

2-4e Search Incident to Arrest

Officers are allowed to search the suspect at the time of arrest, but what is found during this search cannot be used to establish probable cause for the original arrest. The prerequisite for this search is that the officer made a legal arrest and is taking the suspect into custody. It applies to all situations where the legislature has given the officer the authority to make an arrest; it does not matter whether the offense is serious or not. The basic rule is that the **search incident to the arrest** may include a thorough search of the person arrested and the area under his/her immediate control. Only searches done at the scene *immediately after* the arrest qualify for this exception to the warrant requirement; searches done later must be justified on some other grounds.

Chimel v. California
395 U.S. 752, 23 L.Ed. 2d 685, 89 S.Ct. 2034 (1969)

Issue: Search Incident to an Arrest

"Application of sound Fourth Amendment principles to the facts of this case produces a clear result. The search here went far beyond the petitioner's person and the area from within which he might have obtained either a weapon or something that could have been used as evidence against him. There was no constitutional justification, in the absence of a search warrant, for extending the search beyond that area."

Everything found on the person or under his/her immediate control is admissible. There are no restrictions on the thoroughness of the search conducted when the suspect is arrested and taken into custody. Only the area searched is restricted. Anywhere the arrested person could reach to obtain weapons or destroy evidence can be searched. This "arms reach" rule (sometimes called the "wingspan rule") is applied without considering the fact that the suspect is handcuffed at the time the search is conducted. Anywhere he/she could reach if not restrained is included. Officers may open cupboards, look under beds, and inspect things that are within reach. Items seized do not have to be specifically related to the crime for which the person was arrested.

Arrests frequently involve either the driver or passenger of a car. The Supreme Court has allowed a search of the entire passenger compartment, including the glove box and console, incident to the custodial arrest of an occupant of the car (*New York v. Belton*, 453 U.S. 454, 69 L.Ed. 2d 768, 101 S.Ct. 2860 [1981]). An extensive search of anything in the passenger compartment, including luggage and parcels, is allowed. It must be done at the time of the arrest, but the suspect may be removed from the car before the search. Searches of other parts of the vehicle, such as the trunk, are not permitted unless another exception to the warrant requirement applies. See section 4-5, "Vehicle Searches," for more details on car searches.

When an arrest is made in a home or another building, officers may be concerned about attacks by people who may be hiding there. A **protective sweep** is a quick visual check of the area for people who may harm the officers. At the time of an arrest, and without any additional facts indicating danger, officers may look in the area immediately adjoining the place where they are making an arrest (*Maryland v. Buie*, 494 U.S. 325, 108 L.Ed. 2d 276, 110 S.Ct. 1093 [1990]). This would justify looking in walk-in closets but not opening drawers in a dresser. For the officer to go farther, such as into another room, the Supreme Court requires that the officer

---

Maryland v. Buie

494 U.S. 325, 108 L.Ed. 2d 276, 110 S.Ct. 1093 (1990)

Issue: Protective Sweep of Building

"We also hold that as an incident to the arrest the officers could, as a precautionary matter and without probable cause or reasonable suspicion, look in closets and other spaces immediately adjoining the place of arrest from which an attack could be immediately launched. Beyond that, however, we hold that there must be articulable facts which, taken together with the rational inferences from those facts, would warrant a reasonably prudent officer in believing that the area to be swept harbors an individual posing a danger to those on the arrest scene."

---

conducting the search have a reasonable suspicion that someone is present who might attack the officers.

Searches during non-custodial arrests are handled under different rules. Traffic stops are a typical example of non-custodial arrests. This is a less serious crime (or possibly only an infraction); therefore, it justifies a less intrusive invasion of the suspect's privacy. If the suspect will be released at the scene, officers may not conduct a thorough search. With a non-custodial arrest, the right to search is the same as the one allowed under *Terry*—a protective patdown may be done if there is reasonable suspicion that the suspect is armed.

2-5 Booking

Booking occurs when the person who has been arrested enters jail or a holding facility. It also happens if a person reports directly to the jail to serve all or part of his/her sentence. Inmates who serve weekends or leave the facility on work furlough are subject to booking searches each time they reenter the jail. The reason for allowing booking searches is to prevent weapons and contraband from entering the jail. Whether the person has been searched recently or not, the permissible **booking search** is the same: it includes a thorough search of the person and any items in his/her possession at that time (*United States v. Edwards*, 415 U.S. 800, 39 L.Ed. 2d 771, 94 S.Ct. 1234 [1974]). Closed containers may be opened and searched (*Illinois v. Lafayette*, 462 U.S. 640, 77 L.Ed. 2d 65, 103 S.Ct. 2605 [1983]).

The booking search is usually the most extensive search of the person that occurs. Due to the fact that weapons and drugs can easily be hidden, strip searches and inspections of body cavities are permitted. Reasonable attempts to preserve privacy, such as shielding the strip search area from public view and having searches conducted by officers of the same gender as the suspect, are required. Combative inmates who defy control by booking personnel, or those who attempt to flee the booking area during a strip search, waive protection of their privacy. Several states have restricted the right to conduct strip searches and body cavity searches if a person was arrested for a misdemeanor.

The courts recognize a minor exception to *Miranda* for the booking process. Questions related to name, address, person to notify in case of an emergency, date of birth, and a few other biographical facts are permitted. *Miranda* applies if questioning at booking is extended in order to obtain information to be used in a criminal investigation.

Chapter Summary

Peace officers are given more authority than the average citizen to make arrests. Who has peace officer status is determined by the type of agency that employs the person and the job performed. Most, but not all, peace officers are permitted to carry weapons.

Peace officers have authority within the jurisdiction (city, county, etc.) that employs them and while performing their official duties in other parts of the state. In hot pursuit, they may follow a fleeing felony suspect into another state. Officers may also make arrests based on out-of-state warrants. A person serving a sentence in one state may be detained when his/her sentence has expired and transported to another state for trial on pending charges.

The right to detain a suspect implies the authority to use force to do so. The Fourth Amendment authorizes the use of reasonable force. This is judged on the totality of the circumstances. Deadly force may be used *only* if someone's life is endangered. Nondeadly force may be used in other situations, but excessive force is never allowed.

The traditional rule is that peace officers have the authority to make arrests based on probable cause that a felony has occurred. Officers usually may arrest for misdemeanors only if the crime occurred in their presence; if it did not, an arrest warrant may be needed. Warrants are also required to make arrests (felony or misdemeanor) inside a home except when there is an emergency. An arrest warrant is sufficient if the suspect is in his/her own home; a search warrant is required to enter another person's home to arrest the suspect.

The police may detain someone for questioning if there is reasonable suspicion that criminal activity is occurring. A patdown for weapons may be done if there is reasonable suspicion that the suspect is armed. A person may be asked for identification while stopped, but the state must set specific standards for the types of identification the officer may request.

Officers may search the suspect incident to a custodial arrest. The scope of this search includes the person and anything within his/her immediate control. This search must be done at the time and place of the arrest. If the person is in a car when arrested, the entire passenger compartment may be thoroughly searched.

A comprehensive search is allowed at the time of booking. This includes a strip search and body cavity search, as well as a check of the contents of everything in his/her possession. Some states have restricted strip searches of suspects booked on misdemeanor charges.

Study Questions

1. Explain who has peace officer status in your state.
2. What is the authority of a peace officer to act within the city employing the officer? to act within the state where employed? to go into another state to make an arrest?
3. Explain the authority of a peace officer to make an arrest under a warrant issued in another state.
4. Explain the process for detaining a person for prosecution on a crime committed in your state if that person is currently serving a prison sentence in another state.
5. When may a peace officer detain a person for questioning if there is no authority to make an arrest? How extensive a search may be done under these circumstances?
6. When may a peace officer stop a person and demand identification? What types of identification may be required in your state?
7. Explain the right of a peace officer to use deadly force and to use non-deadly force.
8. When is a police officer in your state allowed to make a felony arrest? a misdemeanor arrest?
9. If a police officer makes a custodial arrest, how extensive a search is allowed at the time the arrest is made?
10. How extensive a search is permitted when a person is booked into jail? If laws in your state are more restrictive than the rule given by the U.S. Supreme Court, explain the restrictions that are placed on the booking search.

True or False Questions

T **1.** A city police officer can make an arrest using an arrest warrant for a crime committed in another state.

T **2.** A city police officer who is in hot pursuit of a fleeing felony suspect has the authority to follow the suspect into another state to make an arrest.

T **3.** A police officer may detain a suspect for brief questioning if there is reasonable suspicion that the person is involved in criminal activity at the time.

4. A person may be searched for weapons during a detention based on *Terry v. Ohio* only if an officer has probable cause to believe that the person has a concealed weapon.

T **5.** A police officer who has probable cause to believe a person has committed a crime never needs an arrest warrant.

F **6.** A search warrant is needed to search the car that a person was driving at the time of his/her arrest.

7. At the time of a valid custodial arrest, the officer may conduct a thorough search of the person being arrested and the area under the arrested person's immediate control.

8. Under traditional rules, a police officer may make an arrest for a misdemeanor without an arrest warrant only if the misdemeanor is committed in the officer's presence.

9. The purpose of the protective sweep that is allowed at the time of an arrest is to prevent the destruction of evidence at the scene.

F **10.** Based on U.S. Supreme Court decisions, a person who is being booked into a jail may be thoroughly searched only if he/she is being booked for a felony.

Chapter 3

The Warrant Process

Outline

Key Terms

abstract of the warrant	executing a warrant	probable cause
affidavit	(serving a warrant)	recalled warrant
affirmation	*Illinois v. Gates*	return on a search warrant
anonymous informant	"John Doe" warrant	stale information
bench warrant	knock notice	telephonic search warrants
confidential informants	neutral magistrate	totality of the
electronic surveillance	oath	circumstances test
warrants	Plain View Doctrine	

Learning Objectives

Learning Objectives

After reading this chapter, the student will be able to

- Explain the basic requirements for issuing an arrest warrant and a search warrant.
- Explain what should be in an affidavit used to obtain a warrant.
- Describe the process for obtaining a warrant.
- Describe how a search warrant should be executed.
- Illustrate how an arrest should be made with a warrant.
- Demonstrate the appropriate procedure for entering a residence to serve a warrant.
- Explain what should be listed on the return on a search warrant.

The processes for issuing arrest warrants and search warrants are similar. Both require probable cause. This chapter discusses the process for obtaining warrants.

3-1 Meeting the Basic Requirements

The second half of the Fourth Amendment is referred to as the warrant clause:

> . . . no Warrant shall issue, but upon probable cause, supported by Oath or affirmation, and particularly describing the place to be searched, and the person or things to be seized.

This mandates several things: probable cause; facts supported by oath or affirmation; the particular description of location to be searched; and the particular description of what is to be seized.

Sometimes it appears that someone may destroy evidence while the warrant is being obtained. The U.S. Supreme Court allows officers to keep the area under surveillance and, if necessary, detain individuals during the period that the warrant is sought. Officers should reconcile their need to preserve evidence with the privacy interests of the individual. The search may not be conducted until after the warrant has been issued.

3-1a Warrant Requirements in the Fourth Amendment

Probable Cause

Probable cause is defined as the group of facts which would cause a reasonable person to conclude that it is more likely than not that a given fact exists. The Supreme Court has made it clear that the judge must independently determine that there is probable cause to issue the warrant. This can be done only if the judge is given the facts of the case. Section 3-2, "Drafting Affidavits," addresses this issue in detail.

Oath or Affirmation

This requirement has been interpreted to mean that the person making the statement formally promises to tell the truth. An **oath** is a solemn declaration to God that a statement is true. An **affirmation** is a solemn declaration to tell the truth when no oath is taken. An affirmation is used when the person objects to taking an oath for religious or other conscientious reasons. Most states allow a person to sign a statement under penalty of perjury that the facts contained in the document are true. This statement is called an **affidavit.** Some states require affidavits to be notarized. An affidavit meets the Fourth Amendment requirements for an oath or affirmation.

One or more affidavits accompany the application for the warrant. Sometimes the judge will have the officer or another person who is present take an oath and answer additional questions. When the judge does this, the dialogue will be transcribed and a copy attached to the warrant application.

Particular Description of the Location to Be Searched

A warrant authorizes intrusion into another person's privacy. For this reason, the warrant must contain a description of the area where the officers have the right to go. The information contained in the affidavits, plus any sworn oral testimony the judge hears, must establish probable cause that there is evidence at a specific location. The warrant itself must state exactly where the officers will be authorized to search.

Particular Description of What Is to Be Seized

In addition to stating where the officers may go, the warrant must specify what they are looking for. Officers may look only in places where the items to be seized might be located. If the warrant is for the seizure of large objects—for example, 25-inch TV sets—the officers may look only where items this large can be concealed. On the other hand, if the warrant is for stolen coins, the officer may look almost anywhere because the coins can be hidden in very small places. The Plain View Doctrine goes with the officer as long as he/she is searching in a place permitted by the warrant. This means that items not listed on the warrant may be seized *provided that* the officers can identify the items as either evidence or contraband without moving them to look for identifying characteristics, such as serial numbers.

3-1b Arrest Warrant

The Fourth Amendment covers an arrest: it is a seizure of the person. To obtain an arrest warrant, the affidavits need to establish two things: probable cause that a specific crime was committed; and probable cause that the person named committed this crime. The warrant is frequently worded in the same manner as the complaint which the prosecutor files to start a criminal prosecution. In many states, the warrant substitutes for the complaint, thus avoiding duplicate paperwork.

An arrest warrant needs to specify the person to be arrested in sufficient detail so that the officer serving the warrant can verify that the correct person is being arrested. This is particularly important because many warrants are entered into the National Crime Information Center (NCIC) network and the arrest made by an officer totally unfamiliar with the case. A detailed description, including as many of the following as possible, should be included: name, aliases, age and/or date of birth, height, weight, ethnicity, and social security number. Approximations, such as "age 20 to 25," may be used when necessary. An arrest warrant may be issued even though the legal name of the suspect is unknown. This is called a **"John Doe" warrant.** It refers to a specific person whose name is unknown although an alias may be known. A "John Doe" warrant should have particularly detailed descriptions of the suspect, along with as many aliases as possible, in order to avoid arresting innocent people. Some prosecutors have obtained arrest warrants based on the results of DNA tests performed on evidence found at the scene. In these cases, the technical description of the DNA is included in the warrant, plus any physical identification that the victim and/or eye witnesses provided (see Figure 3-1).

An arrest under a warrant is valid if the officer uses reasonable care to verify that the person arrested is the same person named in the warrant. The wrong person may be arrested if the suspect has a popular name or is using a false ID, but the arrest and subsequent search will be valid as long as sufficient care was taken. Officers are protected from civil liability for false arrest when they exercise due care.

Arrest warrants are usually valid for at least a year. Many states make the warrant valid for a period equal to the statute of limitations on the crime. Some crimes, such as murder, have no statute of limitations; arrest warrants for these crimes remain valid indefinitely. Officers need to be familiar with the rule in their jurisdiction, so they can determine if an arrest warrant is still valid. Automated warrant systems need to be programmed to purge warrants that have expired.

Figure 3-1
Typical affidavit to accompany application for an arrest warrant

State of California

County of Los Angeles

AFFIDAVIT IN SUPPORT OF PROBABLE CAUSE ARREST WARRANT

Your affiant, Officer Mary Black, is employed as a peace officer for the Metropolitan Police Department and has attached hereto and incorporates by reference official reports and records of a law enforcement agency. These reports were prepared by law enforcement officers and contain factual information and statements obtained from victims, witnesses, and others which establish the commission of the following criminal offense(s): PC 459 - Residential Burglary, by the following person: John DeHaviland Smith.

WHEREFORE, your affiant prays that a warrant of arrest be issued for said person. (signed) Officer Mary Black.

Just as the powers to arrest are more limited for misdemeanors than for felonies, the service of misdemeanor warrants may be more restricted than that of felony warrants. Felony warrants can usually be served 24 hours a day. The officer may make the arrest in public or enter private buildings, including houses, at any time. Many states allow the service of misdemeanor warrants 24 hours a day in public places, but residences may be entered to serve the arrest warrant only during "daytime." The hours that are "daytime" are specified in the code and usually are not tied to sunrise and sunset. For example, "daytime" may be 6:00 A.M. to 10:00 P.M. An accurate watch is essential if the arrest is to be made near these time limits: an arrest made under a misdemeanor warrant at 10:05 P.M. would be invalid.

The term **bench warrant** is used to refer to an arrest warrant issued by a judge after a conviction. A common reason for issuing a bench warrant is failure to appear in court in response to a citation. State laws govern issuing bench warrants. Usually they can be served by peace officers in the same manner as misdemeanor warrants.

An arrest warrant can be recalled. This means that the court which issued the warrant withdraws the warrant. One reason for a **recalled warrant** is that the person has surrendered voluntarily. Another is that facts discovered after the warrant was issued show that there is no longer probable cause to support a warrant. It is important to establish procedures to identify recalled warrants and to remove them from computerized databases. An arrest based on a recalled warrant is not valid.

3-1c Search Warrant

A search warrant must identify the place to be searched and the items to be seized. This information is necessary, so that officers executing the search warrant will know what they are allowed to do. The affidavits containing the facts used to establish probable cause become part of the court record, but these facts do not need to be stated on the search warrant (see Figure 3-2).

In most urban areas, the address is used to describe the place to be searched. Even so, it is useful to include other descriptive information, such as "the white house on the northeast corner of Third and Spring." The courts have permitted the search of a house even though the street number in the warrant was wrong when the description made it obvious what location was to be searched. In most cases the description needs to be more specific than just the address: the portion of the building to be searched needs to be stated. For example, if the informant told the police

Figure 3-2
A typical search warrant

Search Warrant No. 8-24

1	STATE OF CALIFORNIA	1 1" scar on left thumb,
2	COUNTY OF ORANGE	2 ///
3	SEARCH WARRANT	3 for the following property: a 16" gold
4	PEOPLE OF THE STATE OF	4 chain with attached gold coin ring in
5	CALIFORNIA to any sheriff, police	5 which is mounted a 1095 US $20 gold
6	officer or other peace officer in the	6 coin; the letters "TRU" in the motto
7	County of Orange; PROOF by affidavit	7 "In God We Trust" are noticeably worn
8	having been made before me by Investi-	8 down as compared with the other letters;
9	gator James Green, No. 274, Orange	9 and articles of personal property tending
10	County Sheriff's Office, that there is	10 to establish the identity of the current
11	probable cause to believe that the	11 resident of the premises, including utility
12	property described herein may be found	12 company receipts, rent receipts, canceled
13	at the locations set forth herein and that	13 mail envelopes, and printed return-ad-
14	it ___was stolen or embezzled___	14 dress stickers,
15	you are therefore commanded to search	15 ///
16	(1) the premises at 118 N. Main Street,	16 ///
17	Cara Linda, California, a one-story	17 and to seize it if found and bring it
18	brown frame house, being the first house	18 forthwith before me, or this court, at the
19	on the northeast corner of Main and 2nd	19 courthouse of this court.
20	Streets, enclosed by a chain-link fence	20 This warrant may be served only be-
21	and identified with the numerals "118"	21 tween the hours of 7:00 o' clock a.m.
22	painted on the curb directly in front of	22 and 10:00 o' clock p.m.
23	the house, including all rooms, attics,	23 ///
24	basements, garages, outbuildings and	24 Given under my hand and dated this
25	trash containers at these premises, and	25 12th day of August, 2001.
26	(2) the person of Julie Smith, a female	26 ——————————————
27	African American, approximately 22 years,	27 Judge of the Superior Court
28	5'4", 120 lbs., short/curly black hair,	28 of the County of Orange.

that the suspect keeps a supply of drugs in the kitchen cupboards, the warrant should be issued for the search of the kitchen cupboards, not the entire house. Items found while walking to the kitchen will be covered by the plain view doctrine. This is true even though the warrant was originally sought for the items left in plain view but the judge granted a more restrictive warrant.

A search warrant is valid only if the information used to obtain it was obtained recently. Information that was not obtained recently is called stale. **Stale information** cannot be used if the time lapse is such that the item to be seized may have been moved to another location before the warrant was issued. This will depend on the facts of the case and the type of evidence sought. Drugs are highly mobile, and dealers are notorious for their evasive conduct. Information on where a dealer is keeping drugs is stale if it is more than a few days old. Some items, such as built-in appliances which have been installed in the kitchen, are rarely moved. Information on the location of these items would not become stale for a long time.

Search warrants are valid for a limited period of time. This is an extension of the staleness concept used to issue a warrant: waiting a lengthy period before conducting the search makes it more likely that the items sought will have been removed from the location. State law sets the maximum time period, frequently 10 days or less. A warrant that is executed after it has expired is not valid, and any evidence found while trying to execute it will be inadmissible.

Search warrants may be executed only once. This ordinarily means that, once officers enter the location in order to conduct the search, some members of the investigative team must stay until the job is complete. The fact that the warrant would have been valid for a few more days does not give officers the right to return and search the premises again.

State laws vary on when search warrants may be executed. A common practice is to make search warrants valid only in the daytime unless the judge has indicated otherwise when issuing the warrant. To obtain this consent the judge must be given specific facts indicating there is a need to conduct the search at night. State law should be consulted to determine what hours qualify as "daytime." It cannot be automatically assumed that "daytime" is defined the same for misdemeanor arrest warrants and search warrants.

3-1d Electronic Surveillance Warrants

The Supreme Court approved **electronic surveillance warrants** but required a more particularized showing of necessity than is needed for other warrants. Congress reacted by passing the Omnibus Crime Control and Safe Streets Act of 1968. Title III of this act applies to electronic surveillance. Many states have passed laws adopting this federal legislation; others have passed their own laws for this type of warrant. Federal law allows judges to issue warrants for wiretaps and other forms of electronic surveillance. Some state laws are more restrictive.

Electronic surveillance warrants may be issued only for crimes specified in Title III or the equivalent state law. This usually covers only major felonies. To obtain this type of warrant there must be probable cause that specific types of conversations will occur during the surveillance. In addition to the normal showing of probable cause, the affidavits must establish that normal investigative techniques have been tried and do not work or that there is a special reason to believe that they will not work. The warrant application must name all suspects whose conversations are likely to be seized during the surveillance. Unlike normal warrants, the electronic surveillance application must be approved by the head of the prosecutorial agency (attorney general, district attorney, etc.) or a specific designee before submission to a judge. The warrant is valid for a maximum of 30 days. The Supreme Court interpreted Title III as implicitly authorizing whatever actions are necessary to install, maintain, and retrieve the necessary electronic equipment. Some state statutes specifically prohibit covert entries.

Officers must take reasonable steps to minimize intrusion into the privacy of non-suspects while conducting the surveillance: once it is determined that a conversation is not related to the crimes under investigation, the conversation should not be monitored. The warrant can be extended only with a showing that probable cause still exists for the wiretap. A transcript of what was seized is submitted to the court after the surveillance is complete; this is much like the return on a search warrant.

The Foreign Intelligence Surveillance Act (FISA) of 1978 established procedures, in many ways similar to Title III, for obtaining wiretaps on agents working for foreign countries who are suspected of spying on the United States. The USA PATRIOTS Act of 2001 (HR 3162), passed in the aftermath of the September 11 terrorist attack, expanded FISA to cover terrorist activities. It is now possible for federal agents to obtain electronic surveillance warrants to monitor people suspected of plotting terrorist acts. The USA PATRIOTS Act also added provisions to Title III to allow government agencies to more freely share information obtained by wiretaps. A new provision allows federal judges to issues orders for the interception of e-mail.

3-2 Drafting Affidavits

At one time, warrant applications read "The undersigned officer has information from a reliable informant that establishes probable cause to believe that . . . ." The Supreme Court has made it clear that this is not acceptable because the judge is the one who must determine whether probable cause exists to issue a warrant. The judge may rely on facts submitted by the officers but must independently conclude that probable cause exists. For the judge to do this, the affidavit must contain detailed facts.

The judge must consider two issues when determining whether probable cause exists: Are the facts in the warrant application sufficient to establish probable cause? Is the source of the facts sufficiently reliable? At one time the Supreme Court required judges to determine these two things independent of each other. In 1983, *Illinois v. Gates* (462 U.S. 213) changed that rule: judges now consider the issues together, using a **totality of the circumstances test.**

Information comes to the police from several avenues: firsthand observation by a police officer; statements by victims and eye witnesses; and informants. An affidavit or oral statement under oath made on firsthand observations are considered the most reliable: they are stated under penalty of perjury. Statements by victims and witnesses are generally considered reliable unless there is a motive to provide false information. A more common problem, particularly with the victim, is that there is insufficient detail. Robbery victims, for example, may be adamant that the robber had a large gun but may be unable to give more than sketchy details on what the robber and getaway car looked like. Unfortunately, this lack of detail makes it impossible to establish probable cause unless the police have additional information.

Police informants pose a different problem. Many informants have ulterior motives: gaining their release; negotiating a plea bargain; being paid for information; or seeking revenge on a former partner in crime. An **anonymous informant** is a person whose identity is unknown. When an informant calls the police department, the officers may have no idea who provided the information and no way to ask for more details. Other times there may be a person who calls periodically and whose voice the officer recognizes but whose true identity remains unknown. Police also have **confidential informants:** people who give information after obtaining a promise that their identity will not be revealed. Since the police actually know who these people are, they may be able to vouch for their reliability.

Under the totality of the circumstances test, a judge may consider information from previously untested informants and anonymous informants. The affidavit should identify the source of the information. The quantity and quality of information provided is crucial for this purpose. Rather than looking for proof that an informant has previously given reliable information, the judge may look at the facts given in the present case. Extensive details that only a person with firsthand knowledge of the facts could provide can be used to validate the information, even though the source is unknown to the police. Police verification of some of the details given by the informant is required as well. It is not necessary to verify enough facts to establish probable cause. Neither is it mandatory that any single fact that was verified show criminal activity. The cumulative impact of numerous facts, each apparently innocent when viewed in isolation, can be used to corroborate an informant.

· The facts from *Illinois v. Gates* demonstrate the Supreme Court's reasoning. On May 3, 1978, the Bloomingdale Police Department received an anonymous handwritten letter in the mail which read

> This letter is to inform you that you have a couple in your town who strictly make their living on selling drugs. They are Sue and Lance Gates, they live on Greenway, off Bloomingdale Rd. in the condominiums. Most of their buys are done in Florida. Sue his wife drives their car to Florida, where she leaves it to be loaded up with drugs, then Lance flies down and drives it back. Sue flies back after she drops the car off in Florida. May 3 she is driving down there again and Lance will be flying down in a few days to drive it back. At the time Lance drives the car back he has the trunk loaded with over $100,000.00 in drugs. Presently they have over $100,000.00 worth of drugs in their basement.
>
> They brag about the fact they never have to work, and make their entire living on pushers.
>
> I guarantee if you watch them carefully you will make a big catch. They are friends with some big drug dealers, who visit their house often.
>
> Lance & Susan Gates
> Greenway
> in Condominiums

The United States Supreme Court stated that it was inclined to agree with the Illinois Supreme Court that this anonymous letter, standing alone, did not establish probable cause. The application for the warrant to search the Gates' home included the anonymous letter plus the following facts learned during a police investigation of the case:

> An Illinois driver's license had been issued to Lance Gates, residing at a stated address in Bloomingdale; a confidential informant examined financial records and provided a more recent address; L. Gates had a reservation on Eastern Airlines flight 245 from Chicago to West Palm Beach on May 5 at 4:15 P.M.; surveillance of flight 245 revealed that Gates boarded the flight; surveillance in Florida observed Gates arrive in West Palm Beach and take a taxi to a nearby Holiday Inn; Gates went to a room registered to Susan Gates; 7:00 A.M. the next morning Gates and an unidentified woman left the

motel in a Mercury bearing Illinois license plates and drove northbound on an interstate frequently used by travelers going to Chicago; the license plate on the Mercury was registered to a Hornet station wagon owned by Gates; driving time from West Palm Beach to Bloomingdale was approximately 22 to 24 hours.

The U.S. Supreme Court, using the totality of the circumstances test, held that the search warrant was valid. Note the amount of detail given in the affidavit.

The judge cannot determine if probable cause exists unless he/she receives detailed information. Drafting a good affidavit is a time-consuming process. Rushing through it may result in the application's being rejected or the warrant's being declared invalid by an appellate court. The judge's action will be reviewed solely on the facts available to the judge prior to signing the warrant: additional facts known to the officers, but not conveyed to the judge under oath or in an affidavit, may not be considered.

In *Massachusetts v. Upton*, 466 U.S. 727 (1984), the Supreme Court stated that the totality of the circumstances test completely replaced *Aguilar*'s two-pronged test, which required proof of the reliability of the informant. The case involved the following facts:

At noon on September 11, 1980, Lt. Beland of the Yarmouth Police Department assisted in the execution of a search warrant for a motel room reserved by one Richard Kelleher at the Snug Harbor Motel in West Yarmouth. The search produced several items of identification, including credit cards, belonging to two persons whose homes had recently been burglarized. Other items taken in the burglaries, such as jewelry, silver and gold, were not found at the motel.

At 3:20 P.M. on the same day, Lt. Beland received a call from an unidentified female who told him that there was "a motor home full of stolen stuff" parked behind #5 Jefferson Ave., the home of respondent George Upton and his mother. She stated that the stolen items included jewelry, silver, and gold. As set out in Lt. Beland's affidavit in support of a search warrant:

"She further stated that George Upton was going to move the motor home any time now because of the fact that Ricky Kelleher's motel room was raided and that George Upton had purchased these stolen items from Ricky Kelleher. This unidentified female stated that she had seen the stolen items, but refused to identify herself because 'he'll kill me,' referring to George Upton. I then told this unidentified female that I knew who she was, giving her the name of Lynn Alberico, who I had met on May 16, 1980, at George Upton's repair shop off Summer St., in Yarmouthport. She was identified to me by George Upton as being his girlfriend, Lynn Alberico. The unidentified female admitted that she was the girl that I had named, stating that she was surprised that I knew who she was. She then told me that she'd broken up with George Upton and wanted to burn him. She also told me that she wouldn't give me her address or phone number but that she would contact me in the future, if need be."

Following the phone call, Lt. Beland went to Upton's house to verify that a motor home was parked on the property. Then, while other officers watched the premises, Lt. Beland prepared the application for a search warrant, setting out all the information noted above, in an accompanying affidavit. He also attached the police reports on the two prior burglaries, along with the lists of the stolen property.

The United States Supreme Court explained its holding that the affidavit was sufficient to justify issuing the search warrant:

Examined in light of *Gates,* Lt. Beland's affidavit provides a substantial basis for the issuance of the warrant. No single piece of evidence in it is conclusive. But the pieces fit neatly together and, so viewed, support the magistrate's determination that there was "a fair probability that contraband or evidence of crime" would be found in Upton's motor home. The informant claimed to have seen the stolen goods and gave a description of them which tallied with the items taken in recent burglaries. She knew of the raid on the motel room—which produced evidence connected to those burglaries—and that the room had been reserved by Kelleher. She explained the connection between Kelleher's motel room and the stolen goods in Upton's motor home. And she provided a motive both for her attempt at anonymity—fear of Upton's retaliation—and for furnishing the information—her recent breakup with Upton and her desire "to burn him."

* * *

In concluding that there was probable cause for the issuance of this warrant, the magistrate can hardly be accused of approving a mere "hunch" or a bare recital of legal conclusions. The informant's story and the surrounding facts possessed an internal coherence that gave weight to the whole. Accordingly, we conclude that the information contained in Lt. Beland's affidavit provided a sufficient basis for the "practical, common-sense decision" of the magistrate. . . .

In *United States v. Leon,* 468 U.S. 897 (1984), the lower court found that the affidavits contained insufficient evidence to establish probable cause. The United States Supreme Court accepted this finding. The affidavit was based on the following facts:

In August 1981, a confidential informant of unproved reliability informed
an officer of the Burbank Police Department that two persons known to
him as "Armando" and "Patsy" were selling large quantities of cocaine and
methaqualone from their residence at 620 Price Drive in Burbank, Cal. The
informant also indicated that he had witnessed a sale of methaqualone by
"Patsy" at the residence approximately five months earlier and had observed
at the time a shoebox containing a large amount of cash that belonged to
"Patsy." He further declared that "Armando" and "Patsy" generally kept only
small quantities of drugs at their residence and stored the remainder at
another location in Burbank.

On the basis of this information, the Burbank police initiated an extensive investigation focusing first on the Price Drive residence and later on
two other residences as well. Cars parked at the Price Drive residence were
determined to belong to respondents Armando Sanchez, who had previously been arrested for possession of marijuana, and Patsy Stewart, who had
no criminal record. During the course of the investigation, officers observed
an automobile belonging to respondent Ricardo Del Castillo, who had previously been arrested for possession of 50 pounds of marijuana, arrive at
the Price Drive residence. The driver of the car entered the house, exited
shortly thereafter carrying a small paper sack, and drove away. A check of
Del Castillo's probation records led the officers to respondent Alberto Leon,
whose telephone number Del Castillo had listed as his employer's. Leon had
been arrested in 1980 on drug charges, and a companion had informed the
police at that time that Leon was heavily involved in the importation of
drugs into this country. Before the current investigation began, the Burbank
officers had learned that an informant had told a Glendale police officer
that Leon stored a large quantity of methaqualone at his residence in
Glendale. During the course of this investigation, Burbank officers learned
that Leon was living at 716 South Sunset Canyon in Burbank.

Subsequently, the officers observed several persons, at least one of
whom had prior drug involvement, arriving at the Price Drive residence and
leaving with small packages; observed a variety of other material activity at
the two residences as well as at a condominium at 7901 Via Magdelena; and
witnessed a variety of relevant activity involving respondents' automobiles.
The officers also observed respondents Sanchez and Stewart board separate
flights for Miami. The pair later returned to Los Angeles together, consented
to a search of their luggage that revealed only a small amount of marijuana,
and left the airport.

An experienced narcotics investigator drafted the affidavit and sought
a warrant to search 620 Price Drive, 716 South Sunset Canyon, 7901 Via

Magdelena, and automobiles registered to each of the respondents for an extensive list of items believed to be related to the respondents' drug-trafficking activities.

The lower-court judge did not question the reliability and credibility of the informant, but stated

> Some details given tended to corroborate, maybe, the reliability of [the informant's] information about the previous transaction, but if it is not a stale transaction, it comes awfully close to it; and all the other material I think is as consistent with innocence as it is with guilt.

Note that the one drug sale the informant claimed to have witnessed occurred five months prior to the information being given to the police; the search warrant was issued after an additional month of police investigation. Although numerous people were seen leaving the locations with small packages, there was no verification that any of these packages contained illegal drugs.

The facts in *Massachusetts v. Sheppard*, 468 U.S. 981 (1984), show the type of detailed information the Supreme Court considers adequate in describing the location to be searched. The investigation showed

> The badly burned body of Sandra Boulware was discovered in a vacant lot in the Roxbury section of Boston at approximately 5 A.M., Saturday, May 5, 1979. An autopsy revealed that Boulware had died of multiple compound skull fractures caused by blows to the head. After a brief investigation, the police decided to question one of the victim's boyfriends, Osborne Sheppard. Sheppard told the police that he had last seen the victim on Tuesday night and that he had been at a local gaming house (where cards games were played) from 9 P.M. Friday until 5 A.M. Saturday. He identified several people who would be willing to substantiate the latter claim.
>
> By interviewing the people Sheppard had said were at the gaming house on Friday night, the police learned that although Sheppard was at the gaming house that night, he had borrowed an automobile at about 3 A.M. Saturday morning in order to give two men a ride home. Even though the trip normally took only fifteen minutes, Sheppard did not return with the car until nearly 5 A.M.
>
> On Sunday morning, police officers visited the owner of the car Sheppard had borrowed. He consented to an inspection of the vehicle. Bloodstains and pieces of hair were found on the rear bumper and within the trunk compartment. In addition, the officers noticed strands of wire in the trunk similar to wire strands found on and near the body of the victim. The owner of the car told the officers that when he last used the car on

Friday night, shortly before Sheppard borrowed it, he had placed articles in the trunk and had not noticed any stains on the bumper or in the trunk.

An affidavit was drafted containing these facts. It requested a warrant to search Sheppard's residence for the following items:

[a] fifth bottle of amaretto liquor, 2 nickel bags of marijuana, a woman's jacket that has been described as black-grey (charcoal), any possessions of Sandra D. Boulware, similar type wire and rope that match those on the body of Sandra D. Boulware, or in the above Thunderbird. A blunt instrument that might have been used on the victim, men's or women's clothing that may have blood, gasoline burns on them. Items that may have fingerprints of the victim.

The following items seized during the search were admissible: a pair of bloodstained boots, bloodstains on the concrete floor, a woman's earring with bloodstains on it, a bloodstained envelope, a pair of men's jockey shorts and women's leotards with blood on them, three types of wire, and a woman's hairpiece, subsequently identified as the victim's.

3-3 Obtaining a Warrant from a Judge

In addition to preparing necessary affidavits, there are usually preprinted forms that must be completed requesting a warrant. In many jurisdictions, the prosecutor's office reviews and screens warrant applications before they are submitted to a judge. The prosecutor's office may also assist with the clerical work involved. Sometimes the local judges will only review applications that the prosecutor has already approved. It is not uncommon for the person seeking the warrant also to prepare the warrant in advance, so that it is ready for the judge's signature.

Sometimes there are several different preprinted forms available, each designed for a specific type of case. When this is true, it is important to use the appropriate form or to make corrections that delete all references to facts not established in the affidavits. For example, a form designed for a drug case may have a preprinted paragraph describing drug paraphernalia that can be seized. If used for a non-drug case, this paragraph and any other references to seizing drugs must be removed. Leaving them in the warrant would make the warrant invalid because it authorized a search for things for which probable cause had not been established.

Once the paperwork has been completed, the application can be presented to a judge or magistrate. Both local laws and customs should be consulted to determine which judge reviews warrant applications. In most states, an arrest warrant must be obtained in the jurisdiction where the crime occurred. Search warrants are normally issued by judges in the jurisdiction where the search will be conducted. If there is reason to believe that the suspect fled and hid evidence in a different county, it may be necessary to go to two different courts in order to obtain the necessary warrants.

Most states give trial court judges the authority to grant warrants. Where the court system is large, some judges may be assigned to criminal cases, while others are in the civil division. Professional courtesy calls for presenting applications to the judges who hear criminal cases. The presiding judge may designate one judge to hear all warrant applications. It is very common to have one judge "on call" for reviewing warrant applications at night and on weekends. Ask the prosecutor's office which judge to see and what local rules apply.

The application may be submitted only once. If the judge refuses to issue a warrant, the officers may not take the same application to a different judge. The officers have the option of continuing their investigation, drafting new affidavits, and seeking the warrant again. Sometimes the officers know of facts that were left out of the original affidavits that can be added for this purpose.

The judge who issues a warrant must be a **neutral magistrate.** "Magistrate," as used here, means a judge or another person to whom state law gives the power to issue warrants. "Neutral" means that the person has no personal interest in the case. If a judge's salary is in any way based on the number of warrants issued, as opposed to the number of applications reviewed or a flat salary, the judge is not neutral. The warrant is not valid, even though probable cause was clearly established and any reasonable judge would have granted the warrant. If a state authorizes ranking members of a law enforcement agency to act as magistrates, those persons cannot issue warrants. Again, the potential conflict of interest, not the facts of the individual case, invalidates the warrant. Judges who are personally involved in the case are not considered neutral. This occurs when the judge, or a member of his/her immediate family, is the victim of the crime in the case for which the warrant is being sought.

Once the judge has reviewed the warrant, it is important that the warrant be completed correctly and signed by the judge. If a warrant was prepared before presenting the paperwork to the judge, it is important to review it to make sure that the judge has agreed to everything that is listed. Lines may be drawn through items that the judge has refused to grant.

Some states allow search warrants to be issued over the telephone or at night and on weekends. These warrants are sometimes called **telephonic search warrants.** Normally a conference call is set up with the officer, the prosecutor, and the judge. The officer is placed under oath and tells the judge the facts that should be in the affidavit. The judge can ask questions. If the judge grants the warrant, the officer or prosecutor fills out the warrant and signs the judge's name. The entire conference call is recorded and a transcript made. The transcript will take the place of the affidavit in the court file. A few states also authorize judges to issue warrants based on e-mail documents that are made under oath and that establish probable cause.

3-4 Executing Warrants

The process of acting under a warrant to make an arrest or a search is called **executing a warrant,** or **serving a warrant.** What is done will vary somewhat, depending on whether a search or an arrest is being conducted.

3-4a Copy of the Warrant

The person who is named in the warrant or whose property is to be searched is normally entitled to see a copy of the search warrant at the time it is served. The person who receives the warrant is not allowed to stop the execution of the warrant: legal challenges to the warrant can be made in court at a later time. Presenting a copy of the warrant merely notifies the person that the officers have the legal authority to enter and search. Once this authority has been established, people on the premises do not have a legal right to resist the search.

Officers executing a search warrant take copies with them when they go to the location where the search will be conducted. Search warrants are either printed in duplicate or photocopied for this purpose. A copy is given to an adult with apparent authority over the premises that are being searched. If no one is present, a copy is left in a conspicuous location.

Arrest warrants are handled differently when the warrant is entered into a computerized data bank. The arrest is frequently made by officers who were not involved in the investigation. An officer has probable cause to make the arrest if the person detained matches the description of the person named in a warrant listed in the computer. A brief statement of the warrant, called an **abstract of the warrant,** will be requested. This is immediately sent by teletype, FAX, or other teleprocessing equipment to the location where the suspect will be booked. A complete copy of the arrest warrant must be filed with the court before arraignment. The suspect will be arraigned in the same manner as other persons arrested by the local police department. If the warrant is not from the local jurisdiction, the case will then be transferred to the court that issued the warrant. For out-of-state warrants, this will require extradition proceedings unless the suspect waives them.

3-4b Knock Notice

Entering a residential unit (home, apartment, motel room, etc.) involves the invasion of someone's privacy. Another reason for requiring warnings is to avoid harm to the officers by residents who believe burglars or other criminals are breaking into their homes. The process is frequently called "**knock notice**" or "knock and announce." In *Wilson v. Arkansas,* 514 U.S. 927 (1995), the Supreme Court held that the Fourth Amendment mandates these procedures, except in emergencies. Four requirements must be considered.

Knock

Officers must knock, ring the doorbell, or use some other appropriate method to inform people in the residence that they are there.

Announcement of Identity and Purpose

Officers must in some way announce their official capacity and why they are demanding entry—for example, "Police officers! We have a search warrant." This must be done with appropriate wording and loud enough so anyone inside who wishes to cooperate will be aware of what is going on.

Waiting Period

After making the necessary announcement, officers must wait long enough so a cooperative person could open the door. The length of time required depends on the circumstances. For example, it is very brief if officers at the front door can see into the living room and know that people are only a few feet from the door; a longer wait is required if officers arrive in the middle of the night and a person who is likely to be asleep in a distant bedroom must respond.

Entry

Officers may enter after knocking, announcing, and waiting. Force may be used to gain entry to serve a warrant if no one answers the door or someone refuses to open the door.

The fact that no one appears to be home does not excuse compliance with knock notice. Knock notice may be excused for any one of the following reasons: serious danger to the officers; high probability of destruction of evidence; or strong possibility that the suspect will escape. Officers should learn local standards for completely avoiding knock notice and when partial compliance is sufficient.

3-4c Plain View

The **Plain View Doctrine** applies to observations made while executing both search and arrest warrants. Observations officers make from a vantage point where they are authorized to be do not require separate justification. This applies to observations, but not to actions such as examining objects or turning them over to search for serial numbers in order to run a computer check to determine if the items are stolen.

When serving an arrest warrant, the Plain View Doctrine primarily applies to items discovered while trying to locate the person named in the warrant. Officers may look anywhere a person might be hiding, but not in cupboards or other containers too small to conceal a person. With search warrants, the scope of the search is justified based on the size of the items sought. Anything known to be contraband or stolen property or to have other evidentiary value found while looking in areas large enough to hide items listed in the warrant is admissible. Searching areas too small to conceal the smallest item listed on the warrant is not permitted. Anything found while doing so is inadmissible.

The Supreme Court has recognized the safety needs of the officers while executing warrants. Officers may quickly do a protective sweep through adjacent areas and look for anyone who might attack them. Any place large enough for a person to hide may be checked. Anything found in plain view while doing this cursory search is admissible.

3-5 Filing a Return on a Search Warrant

The **return on a search warrant** is basically an inventory which is filed with the court and becomes a permanent part of the case file. It is frequently printed on the back of the warrant. The officers executing the warrant must fill in the information requested by the court: date and time when the warrant was executed; the officer(s) who executed the warrant; and an itemized inventory of everything seized while executing the warrant. Items found in plain view should also be included in the inventory. A copy of this itemized list usually must be left at the location when the items are seized. If officers were unable to serve the warrant, this fact will be noted on the return.

Chapter Summary

The Fourth Amendment requires probable cause for the issuance of a warrant. Facts must be stated under oath or affirmation or in an affidavit. The place to be searched must be precisely described in the warrant. Any items the warrant authorizes the police to seize must also be described in detail. An arrest warrant needs a sufficient description of the person to be arrested, so that the officers can verify that the correct person is being detained.

The totality of the circumstances test is currently used to determine if probable cause has been established. It is no longer necessary to establish that the informant has previously given reliable information. The judge may consider all the facts presented in the affidavits. Sufficient details must be given, so that the judge will be convinced that there is enough credible information to establish probable cause. This can be based on a combination of information from informants and facts discovered during police investigations. Stale information may not be used to obtain search warrants. It is important that the facts show the items sought are still at the location the police wish to search.

The affidavits and any forms required by the local court are submitted to a judge. In large courts, there is usually one judge designated to review the warrant applications. Local court rules may require the prosecutor to review the application before it is presented to the judge. A warrant application can be presented only once. If denied, additional facts must be included before another attempt can be made to have the warrant issued.

Officers must comply with knock notice prior to entering residences to serve either an arrest or search warrant, unless there is an emergency creating a danger of harm to the officer, destruction of the evidence, or escape of the suspect. When a search warrant is executed a copy of the warrant must be given to a responsible adult at the location or a copy left in a conspicuous place if no one is present. Plain view accompanies the officers.

An officer in the field needs to confirm that the suspect matches the description of a person who is listed in the computer as having an outstanding arrest warrant. An abstract of the arrest warrant should be obtained immediately. A copy of the actual warrant will be needed in order to arraign the suspect. Arraignment will occur in the court for the district where the arrest was made. The suspect will then be transferred to the court that issued the warrant.

A return on the warrant is filed with the court. It will indicate when the warrant was executed and list anything that was seized. This form is also used to record the fact that the warrant was not served.

Study Questions

1. List four things specifically required by the Fourth Amendment before a search warrant can be issued.
2. Define probable cause. When seeking a warrant, who determines if probable cause exists?
3. Explain probable cause for a search warrant.
4. Explain probable cause for an arrest warrant.
5. Describe the current test judges are required to use to determine if probable cause has been established to issue a warrant.
6. Define the following:
   a. oath
   b. affirmation
   c. affidavit
7. According to the law in your state, how long is a misdemeanor arrest warrant valid? a felony warrant? Are there crimes for which arrest warrants do not expire?
8. According to the law in your state, what restrictions are placed on the service of
   a. misdemeanor arrest warrants?
   b. felony arrest warrants?
   c. search warrants?
9. Define the following:
   a. bench warrant
   b. recall of a warrant
   c. execution (service) of a warrant
10. Clip newspaper articles on a current criminal investigation. Draft an affidavit for
    a. a search warrant.
    b. an arrest warrant.
11. Explain how the Plain View Doctrine applies to the execution of
    a. an arrest warrant.
    b. a search warrant.

12. Explain the process used in your local court for obtaining search warrants and arrest warrants. Include
    a. the role the prosecutor plays in the process.
    b. the necessary paperwork.
    c. which judge should be contacted.
    d. the location and times the judge will review warrant applications.
13. Explain knock notice. Under the law of your state, when are officers excused from compliance with knock notice?
14. Explain the process for arresting a person based on information in the police computer network that there is an arrest warrant for that person if a warrant was issued
    a. in your city.
    b. in another part of your state.
    c. in another state.
15. What is the return on a search warrant? Explain the function of the return.

True or False Questions

T **1.** An arrest warrant may be issued based on a person's alias if his/her full legal name is not known.

T **2.** A judge should use the totality of the circumstances test to determine if probable cause has been established in an application for an arrest warrant.

T **3.** Facts obtained from informants cannot be used in the affidavit for a search warrant.

T **4.** A judge may not rely on stale information when evaluating probable cause to issue a search warrant.

T **5.** A search warrant must be signed by a judge who has authority over the location to be searched.

F **6.** Officers are not required to announce their presence prior to entering a home to conduct a search if they have a valid search warrant.

F **7.** Items not listed in a search warrant, that are found while properly executing a search warrant, may not be introduced into evidence at trial.

F **8.** The return on a search warrant is filed with the court only if the search warrant was never executed.

9. A police officer who is making an arrest based on an arrest warrant does not need to have a copy of the original arrest warrant in his/her possession at the time of the arrest.

10. Once an arrest warrant has been issued it cannot be recalled.

Other Search
and Seizure
Issues

O u t l i n e

Key Terms

abandoned property
aerial searches
apparent authority
Chambers v. Maroney
Closed Container Rule
closed containers
controlled delivery

inventory
Misplaced Reliance
  Doctrine
New York v. Belton
probable cause
reasonable suspicion
roadblocks

Schneckloth v. Bustamonte
search incident to the arrest
South Dakota v. Opperman
vehicle searches
voluntary consent

Learning Objectives

Learning Objectives

After reading this chapter, the student will be able to

- Explain when investigators need a search warrant to enter a crime scene.
- Describe the operation of the Plain View Doctrine.
- Identify situations where abandoned property can be seized by police without a warrant.
- Explain the appropriate procedures for obtaining consent to search.
- Explain the boundaries of searches that are allowed when a vehicle has been stopped based on reasonable suspicion that a person in the vehicle is involved in criminal activity.
- Explain the limits on searches conducted when a person in a vehicle has been arrested.
- Demonstrate the type of search that is allowed when officers have probable cause that a vehicle contains evidence of a crime.
- Describe the officer's right to inventory an impounded car.
- Explain the rules that govern an officer's right to obtain blood, breath, or urine samples from a suspect.
- Describe how the Misplaced Reliance Doctrine applies to statements that a suspect makes to friends and accomplices.
- Explain special rules that apply when officers seize closed containers.

Patrol officers must constantly be alert for situations that require search warrants. The basic rule is that a warrant is required *unless* there is an exception to the Fourth Amendment that applies. Making warrantless arrests and detaining suspects based on reasonable suspicion were covered in Chapter 2. This chapter will discuss other common exceptions to the warrant requirement frequently encountered by officers on patrol. Officers working the field need to take a complete course on search and seizure and frequent refresher classes because the Supreme Court decides new cases on these topics every year.

4-1 Entry to Investigate

There is no special right to enter or remain at a location merely because it is a crime scene. Emergencies, such as looking for people who need immediate medical attention, temporarily excuse compliance with the warrant requirement. An arrest warrant is required to enter the suspect's residence in order to make an arrest; a search warrant is needed to enter the home of a third party in order to arrest the suspect (*Payton v. New York*, 445 U.S.

573, 63 L.Ed. 2d 639, 100 S.Ct. 1371 [1980]); *Stegald v. United States,* 451 U.S. 204, 68 L.Ed. 2d 38, 101 S.Ct. 1642 (1981). See section 2-4, "Arrest." Officers do not have more leeway during the investigation of a crime. The Supreme Court specifically rejected the contention that there is a "murder scene" exception to the Fourth Amendment (*Mincey v. Arizona*).

Entering private property after medical aid has been rendered requires a search warrant unless someone consents to the intrusion.

Mincey v. Arizona
437 U.S. 385, 57 L.Ed. 2d 290, 98 S.Ct. 2408 (1978)

Issue: Warrantless Entry of House to Investigate a Crime

"Moreover, the mere fact that law enforcement may be made more efficient can never, by itself, justify disregard of the Fourth Amendment. The investigation of crime would always be simplified if warrants were unnecessary. But the Fourth Amendment reflects the view of those who wrote the Bill of Rights that the privacy of a person's home and property may not be totally sacrificed in the name of maximum simplicity in enforcement of the criminal law. For this reason, warrants are generally required to search a person's home or his person unless 'the exigencies of the situation' make the needs of law enforcement so compelling that the warrantless search is objectively reasonable under the Fourth Amendment. See, e.g., *Chimel v. California* (search of arrested suspect and area within his control for weapons or evidence); *Warden v. Hayden* ('hot pursuit' of fleeing suspect); *Schmerber v. California* (imminent destruction of evidence).

"Except for the fact that the offense under investigation was a homicide, there were no exigent circumstances in this case, as, indeed, the Arizona Supreme Court recognized. There was no indication that evidence would be lost, destroyed, or removed during the time required to obtain a search warrant. Indeed, the police guard at the apartment minimized that possibility. And there is no suggestion that a search warrant could not easily and conveniently have been obtained. We decline to hold that the seriousness of the offense under investigation itself creates exigent circumstances of the kind that under the Fourth Amendment justify a warrantless search."

The same knock notice rules that apply when serving search warrants and making arrests must be complied with when investigating criminal activity. These rules apply when entering a residence but do not need to be followed when commercial property or public buildings are involved. Briefly stated, the officers must (1) knock; (2) announce their identity and purpose; and (3) wait long enough for a cooperative person to admit them to the house. A more complete discussion of knock notice and its exceptions is found in section 3-4a, "Knock Notice."

4-2 Plain View Doctrine

The Plain View Doctrine is one of the most useful exceptions to the warrant requirement. It has three key elements:

- Objects must be where officers can observe them.
- Officers must be legally at the location where the observation was made.
- Probable cause is required to seize what was observed.

4-2a The Observation

Finding an object in plain view is not considered a search because no one looked for something that was hidden. The items must have been left where the officers could see them without disturbing things they had no right to touch. Officers are not allowed to conduct a search by moving things or otherwise examining them for identifying marks; neither may they squeeze soft-sided luggage to determine what is inside. This does not prevent the officer from moving to a better vantage point to observe objects already in plain view. For example, an investigator may walk around the room and stretch or bend in order to see items more clearly. Most courts also allow the use of flashlights and binoculars.

The Supreme Court made it clear that items do not have to be discovered inadvertently to qualify for the plain view doctrine (*Horton v. California*). In the leading case, officers had requested a warrant to search for stolen property and weapons, but the judge issued one that authorized only a search for stolen property. While executing the search warrant, officers could not locate any stolen property, but they did find weapons. The court held that these weapons were in plain view and legally seized, even though the officers suspected that the weapons were in the house before going to the location.

The Supreme Court recently addressed the issue of thermal imaging. A police department had used a heat detection device to scan houses. The fact that excessive heat was detected in the attic of a house was used, along with utility records and other facts, to obtain a search warrant for marijuana plants being grown under heat lamps in the attic. The Court found that the thermal imaging device violated the resident's reasonable expectation of privacy because it was not in common use. The bounds of the reasonable expectation of privacy will change as technology advances.

Horton v. California

496 U.S. 128, 110 L.Ed. 2d 112, 110 S.Ct. 2301 (1990)

Issue: Plain View Doctrine

"It is, of course, an essential predicate to any valid warrantless seizure of incriminating evidence that the officer did not violate the Fourth Amendment in arriving at the place from which the evidence could be plainly viewed. There are, moreover, two additional conditions that must be satisfied to justify the warrantless seizure. First, not only must the item be in plain view, its incriminating character must also be 'immediately apparent.' . . . Second, not only must the officer be lawfully located in a place from which the object can be plainly seen, but he or she must also have a lawful right of access to the object itself."

4-2b Legally on Premises

For the Plain View Doctrine to operate, the officers must be legally at the location where the observation was made. The most common situations involve making arrests, field interviews, and car stops and executing search warrants. Arriving at the point where the observation was made as the result of a Fourth Amendment violation makes the Plain View Doctrine inapplicable. For example, if the officer entered the house without complying with knock notice, nothing observed inside qualifies for the Plain View Doctrine.

Aerial searches are an extension of the Plain View Doctrine. As long as the aircraft is complying with FAA regulations and any other rules that apply, the observer is legally at the location. Building a fence around a backyard shows a subjective expectation of privacy, but objectively this does not matter if the area is seen from an aircraft overhead. Observations made from a plane qualify whether made during routine patrol, from commercial flight paths, or as a result of chartering a plane exclusively to view an otherwise inaccessible area (*California v. Ciraolo*, 476 U.S. 207, 90 L.Ed. 2d 210, 106 S.Ct. 1809 [1987]).

4-2c Probable Cause to Seize

The fact that the item was in plain view and the officers were legally present indicates that there has been no unreasonable search. The final issue deals with the right to seize the item. To do this, there must be probable cause: the facts must indicate it is more likely than not that the item seized is evidence of a crime or is contraband (*Arizona v. Hicks*, 480 U.S. 321, 94 L.Ed. 2d 347, 107 S.Ct. 1149 [1987]).

The determination that probable cause exists must be made *without* moving the item to look for clues, such as serial numbers. Once probable cause has been established, the item can be seized on the spot without a warrant.

Observations too limited to constitute probable cause may provide useful leads in the investigation. The observation can also be included, along with other facts, in an affidavit when applying for a warrant to conduct a search of the location.

4-3 Abandoned Property

One of the key points in the Supreme Court's analysis of search and seizure issues is the expectation of privacy. The Fourth Amendment applies only if *both* an objective and a subjective expectation of privacy exist. The subjective part of the analysis focuses on a person's efforts to protect his/her privacy. The objective aspect means that society is willing to protect the privacy interest.

Seizing **abandoned property** is not an unreasonable search because there is neither an objective nor a subjective expectation of privacy. In most cases, the fact that the property has been abandoned clearly indicates that the previous owner no longer has any interest in it. This is clear when the property has been discarded in a public place. A more difficult question arises when trash has been sealed in opaque plastic bags and left at a location designated for garbage pickup. The Supreme Court ruled that there is no objective expectation of privacy in these circumstances (*California v. Greenwood*, 486 U.S. 35, 100 L.Ed. 2d 30, 108 S.Ct. 1625 [1988]). Strangers, animals, snoops, or the garbage collector could rummage through the trash or even give it to the police.

Determining when something has been abandoned may be problematic. Dumping it in a public trash can and littering the highway are pretty obvious examples of abandonment. A person who merely puts an item in a trash can inside his/her own home still has the right to retrieve it. Hiding something in a public place—for example, under a rock in the forest—could be considered either way. Items that a person attempts to throw away while being pursued by police, but prior to being apprehended, are considered abandoned (*California v. Hodari D.*, 499 U.S. 621, 113 L.Ed. 2d 690, 111 S.Ct. 1547 [1991]). The rules regarding searches incident to an arrest or a *Terry* stop apply only *after* the person has been detained.

4-4 Consent

Officers do not need a warrant if they have consent to search. On the other hand, probable cause to search cannot be based solely on the fact that a person refused to give consent. Three key points must be considered to determine if valid consent has been obtained for a search:

- The standard for obtaining consent
- Who can give consent
- What can be searched based on the consent

4-4a Standard for Consent

Schneckloth v. Bustamonte (1973) established that **voluntary consent** for a search waives Fourth Amendment rights. The Supreme Court has, however, specifically refused to require officers to warn suspects that there is a constitutional right to refuse to consent to a search. Each case must be analyzed on the totality of the circumstances that were present when the officer asked for permission to search.

Some factors clearly indicate that the consent is coerced. For example, consent is not voluntary if the police inform someone that a search warrant is being executed. Allowing the police to enter under these circumstances is considered to be merely acquiescing to authority (*Bumper v. North Carolina,* 391 U.S. 543, 20 L.Ed. 2d 797, 88 S.Ct. 1788 [1968]). By stating they have a warrant, the police, in effect, inform people that they do not have the right to refuse.

Courts look at all of the facts surrounding the request for consent. Officers do not need reasonable suspicion to stop a person and ask for consent to search. The fact that officers drew their guns weighs very heavily against the consent being voluntary. Other applicable factors include the education and intelligence of the suspect, intentional intimidation by the police, and the fact that the suspect already knew his/her rights. For example, uniformed officers approached people on a bus and asked for permission to search luggage. The officers testified that the people on the bus were informed that they had the right to refuse to consent, and none

---

Schneckloth v. Bustamonte
412 U.S. 218, 36 L.Ed. 2d 854, 93 S.Ct. 2041 (1973)

Issue: Voluntary Consent to Search

"Similar considerations lead us to agree with the courts of California that the question whether a consent to a search was, in fact, 'voluntary' or was the product of duress or coercion, express or implied, is a question of fact to be determined from the totality of all the circumstances. While knowledge of the right to refuse consent is one factor to be taken into account, the government need not establish such knowledge as the sine qua non of an effective consent."

---

of the officers drew their guns or threatened the passengers in any manner. A passenger, who was subsequently arrested for possession of drugs, testified that he did not feel free to leave the bus. The Court held that consent was valid and saw no distinction between a stop in the close confines of a bus and one on the street (*Florida v. Bostick,* 501 U.S. 429, 115 L.Ed. 2d 389, 111 S.Ct. 2382 [1991]).

4-4b Who Can Consent?

Consent must be given by someone with **apparent authority** over the area to be searched (*United States v. Matlock,* 415 U.S. 164, 39 L.Ed. 2d 242, 94 S.Ct. 988 [1974]); *Illinois v. Rodriguez,* 497 U.S. 177, 111 L.Ed. 2d 148, 110 S.Ct. 2793 [1990]). Officers may rely on reasonable appearances that a person lives in a house or owns a business. Ownership, however, is not essential. Police cannot rely on consent from people whose personal privacy is not at stake. The key again is reasonable expectation of privacy. Landlords cannot consent to searches of a tenant's apartment; nor can hotel personnel grant permission to search a guest's room.

If two people have equal rights to a location, either one may consent to a search. This commonly applies to husband-wife and roommate situations. For example, either roommate can consent to a search of the kitchen, but one cannot consent to a search of the other's room if they have separate bedrooms.

The parent-child relationship is more complicated. If a young child is living at home, the parent can consent to a search of the child's room and possessions. Very young children do not have the authority to consent to police entering the house. Neither do children have the right to consent to searches of their parents' room or other private areas of the house.

Older children may have their own privacy interests. Paying rent, or the fact that the parents recognize the child's right to exclude them from

---

Illinois v. Rodriguez

497 U.S. 177, 111 L.Ed. 2d 148, 110 S. Ct. 2793 (1990)

Issue: Consent to Enter a House

"As with other factual determinations bearing upon search and seizure, determination of consent to enter must 'be judged against an objective standard: would the facts available to the officer at the moment . . . "warrant a man of reasonable caution in the belief"' that the consenting party had authority over the premises? If not, then warrantless entry without further inquiry is unlawful unless authority actually exists. But if so, the search is valid."

the room, may indicate a parent cannot give consent. On the other hand, if a parent frequently enters the room to clean or put away the laundry, the child may have limited privacy. Even if the parent can consent to police entering the room, teenagers may still have an expectation of privacy regarding locked containers kept in their rooms.

Probationers and parolees pose a different question. Many states permit searches of these people on less than probable cause; consent to searches may be a condition of probation or parole. The Supreme Court approved this practice. In the case before the Court, searches based on "reasonable grounds," but less than probable cause, were authorized under the supervision of the probation officer (*Griffin v. Wisconsin*, 483 U.S. 868, 97 L.Ed. 2d 709, 107 S.Ct. 3164 [1987]).

4-4c Scope of the Search

The area to be searched and how long officers can search are governed by the conditions that accompanied the consent. Once consent has been given, officers can search anything in that area (including closed containers), unless the person giving the consent placed restrictions on what may be searched. For this reason, officers usually make a very general request, such as "Do you mind if I look around?" Consent can be withdrawn at any time without explaining why it is terminated (*Florida v. Jimeno*, 500 U.S. 248, 114 L.Ed. 2d 297, 111 S.Ct. 1801 [1991]).

Plain view accompanies a consent search; anything seen during the search can be seized if there is probable cause to tie it to a crime. The facts may also indicate that some other exception to the warrant requirement applies. Evidence discovered during the search may create probable cause for an additional search. If so, these facts should be included in an affidavit to be considered by the judge when the officers apply for a search warrant.

4-5 Vehicle Searches

Cars and other vehicles have become very important parts of our daily lives; they are highly visible and heavily regulated. Their extensive exposure to public view, coupled with detailed licensing requirements and safety inspections, support the conclusion that there is a lesser expectation of privacy in vehicles than in homes. The mobility of vehicles is viewed as creating an urgency not present when evidence is found in buildings. For all of these reasons, the rules for searching vehicles are different than those for other locations.

Motor homes are usually treated like vehicles (*California v. Carney,* 471 U.S. 386, 85 L.Ed. 2d 406, 105 S.Ct. 2066 [1985]). Even though they possess many of the characteristics of houses, they still have the ability to leave the scene. This creates exigent circumstances not present with more traditional dwellings. If, on the other hand, the motor home is immobilized—for example, if the wheels have been removed and it is placed on blocks—it is treated as a dwelling.

4-5a   Search of Car When the Suspect is Detained Based on Reasonable Suspicion

There are two prerequisites for the search of a car for weapons during a field interview:

- Specific articulable facts that caused the officers to believe that at least one of the occupants of the vehicle is involved in criminal activity.

AND

- At least a **reasonable suspicion** that the vehicle contains weapons the suspect might use against the officers.

While this type of vehicle search allows police to search the entire passenger compartment, it is more limited than the search incident to a custodial arrest. Weapons are the only things officers may legitimately attempt to find. This means that only areas large enough to conceal a weapon can be searched. Anything found while the officers are properly conducting this type of search is admissible under the Plain View Doctrine.

Michigan v. Long
463 U.S. 1032, 77 L.Ed. 2d 1201, 103 S.Ct. 3469 (1983)

Issue: Search of Car Stopped Based on Reasonable Suspicion

"In *Terry v. Ohio*, we upheld the validity of a protective search for weapons in the absence of probable cause to arrest because it is unreasonable to deny a police officer the right 'to neutralize the threat of physical harm,' when he possesses an articulable suspicion that an individual is armed and dangerous. . . . In the present case, respondent David Long was convicted for possession of marijuana found by police in the passenger compartment and trunk of the automobile that he was driving. The police searched the passenger compartment because they had reason to believe that the vehicle contained weapons potentially dangerous to the officers. We hold that the protective search of the passenger compartment was reasonable under the principles articulated in *Terry* and other decisions of this Court."

The search for weapons can be done while the suspects are out of the car. The right to search applies *even if* the officers know that the suspect will be allowed to drive away. When establishing this rule, the Court recognized that, as soon as the suspect is released, he/she may retrieve weapons from the car and assault the officer.

Non-custodial arrests, such as traffic tickets, also fall under this rule. It is important to note that the second prerequisite, reasonable suspicion that the vehicle contains weapons, does not automatically follow from the decision to make a non-custodial arrest. Officers must be able to state specific facts that create reasonable suspicion that weapons are present.

4-5b Search of a Vehicle as Incident to Arrest

The **search incident to the arrest** normally covers the person and area under his/her immediate control. If the occupant of a car is arrested, the entire passenger compartment is viewed as the area where the person could reach to obtain a weapon and/or to destroy evidence or contraband (*New York v. Belton*). The person arrested can be removed from the vehicle prior to the search; this does not change the requirement that the search be contemporaneous with the arrest.

The passenger compartment is easily identified in a sedan. It includes the area around the front and back seats, the glove box, and the console. The area that can be searched is the same, no matter how many people are in the car. It does not extend to the trunk, the area under the hood, or other parts of the vehicle. Vans, station wagons, and other models that do not have a physical barrier separating the seating area from

---

New York v. Belton
453 U.S. 454, 69 L.Ed. 2d 768, 101 S.Ct. 2860 (1981)

Issue: Search of Car Incident to an Arrest

"Accordingly, we hold that, when a policeman has made a lawful custodial arrest of the occupant of an automobile, he may, as a contemporaneous incident of that arrest, search the passenger compartment of that automobile.

"It follows from this conclusion that the police may also examine the contents of any containers found within the passenger compartment, for if the passenger compartment is within reach of the arrestee, so also will containers in it be within his reach. Such a container may, of course, be searched whether it is open or closed, since the justification for the search is not that the arrestee has no privacy interest in the container, but that the lawful custodial arrest justifies the infringement of any privacy interest the arrestee may have."

---

storage spaces require a factual determination of what is equivalent to the passenger compartment.

Everything within the passenger compartment may be thoroughly searched. This includes items, such as briefcases, that would normally fall under the Closed Container Rule. Locked storage areas, such as the console, may be opened. Since evidence other than weapons may be seized, areas too small to hide a gun or knife may also be searched.

4-5c Vehicle Search Based on Probable Cause

Primarily due to the mobility of cars and other vehicles, the Supreme Court in *Chambers v. Maroney* (399 U.S. 42, 26 L.Ed. 2d 419, 90 S.Ct. 1975 [1970]) authorized searches without a warrant if the police have **probable cause** to believe evidence is in the vehicle. It is now clear that these searches do not require any type of emergency as justification (*Michigan v. Thomas,* 458 U.S. 259, 73 L.Ed. 2d 750, 102 S.Ct. 3079 [1982]). In fact, a probable cause search may be conducted after a car has been towed to a guarded storage area for unrelated reasons. The search can include opening closed containers found in the car if the facts establish probable cause that they conceal contraband or evidentiary items.

The scope of a probable cause search is directly tied to the facts: officers may search anywhere there is probable cause to believe the evidence will be found. This includes items belonging to the person who is a suspect and things that belong to passengers in the vehicle. For example, if an officer saw someone grab a woman's purse, run from the scene, throw what appeared to be a wallet into the trunk of a car, and then flee the area on foot, there would be probable cause to believe evidence may be in the trunk of the car. Based on this probable cause, items in the trunk (whether belonging to the driver or a passenger) may be searched immediately.

United States v. Ross

456 U.S. 798, 72 L.Ed. 2d 572, 102 S.Ct. 2157 (1982)

Issue: Search of Car Based on Probable Cause

"In this case, we consider the extent to which police officers—who have legitimately stopped an automobile and who have probable cause to believe that contraband is concealed somewhere within it—may conduct a probing search of compartments and containers within the vehicle whose contents are not in plain view. We hold that they may conduct a search of the vehicle that is as thorough as a magistrate could authorize in a warrant 'particularly describing the place to be searched.'"

These facts, however, do not provide any justification to search the passenger compartment or under the hood of the car.

Sometimes probable cause searches and searches incident to arrests overlap. For example, if police pursue a car leaving the scene of a drive-by shooting with occupants matching the description of the suspects, they will have probable cause to arrest the occupants and probable cause to search the car. On the other hand, if a records check reveals that a person stopped for an illegal turn has an outstanding warrant, there will be a valid reason to make an arrest but no probable cause to search the car.

There is no time limit on when a probable cause vehicle search must be conducted. It can be done at the scene. Officers also have the option of towing the car to a storage yard, the police station, or some other convenient location before searching it. One evidentiary issue must be considered, however. If the search is not done immediately, the prosecution will have the burden of showing that no one tampered with the vehicle or "planted" the evidence between the time the car was impounded and the search was conducted.

4-5d Inventory of Impounded Vehicles

Whenever a car is legally impounded, it may be inventoried. The reason for impounding the vehicle has no bearing on the right to conduct an inventory. The Supreme Court, in *South Dakota v. Opperman,* based the right to conduct the **inventory** on the need to protect both the owner of

---

South Dakota v. Opperman

428 U.S. 364, 49 L.Ed. 2d 1000, 96 S.Ct. 3092 (1976)

Issue: Inventory of Impounded Vehicle

"When vehicles are impounded, local police departments generally follow a routine practice of securing and inventorying the automobiles' contents. These procedures developed in response to three distinct needs: the protection of the owner's property while it remains in police custody, the protection of the police against claims or disputes over lost or stolen property, and the protection of the police from potential danger. The practice has been viewed as essential to respond to incidents of theft or vandalism. In addition, police frequently attempt to determine whether a vehicle has been stolen, and thereafter abandoned."

* * *

"On this record, we conclude that, in following standard police procedures prevailing throughout the country and approved by the overwhelming majority of courts, the conduct of the police was not 'unreasonable' under the Fourth Amendment."

---

the vehicle and the police. The owner is protected by accounting for every-thing that is present and removing valuable items. The police are protected against unfounded claims of theft because a detailed report is available, stating exactly what was in the vehicle at the time it was taken into custody.

Any evidence found during the inventory is admissible. The primary question is whether the police were searching for evidence or conducting a legitimate inventory. In general, the courts are satisfied that an inventory was being conducted if the police systematically went over the entire vehi-cle. The inventory is more likely to be considered a pretext for a search if the officers stopped as soon as evidence was located. Department policies that require all impounded cars to be inventoried are usually considered on this issue. Closed containers may be opened during an inventory if the department's policy authorizes this procedure (*Florida v. Wells*, 495 U.S. 1, 109 L.Ed. 2d 1, 110 S.Ct. 1632 [1990]).

Another important issue is the intrusiveness of an inventory. It usually involves merely itemizing things that could be removed from the car. This commonly includes opening the glove compartment and trunk. It does not involve inspecting the inside of the spare tire or removing rocker pan-els or cutting the upholstery to see if they contain drugs. Such acts would be considered searches.

4-5e Search of Outside of Car

Officers are allowed to look for vehicle identification numbers (VIN) dur-ing routine traffic stops. The outside of a car parked in a public place falls under the plain view doctrine (*Cardwell v. Lewis*, 417 U.S. 583, 41 L.Ed. 2d 325, 94 S.Ct. 2464 [1974]); *New York v. Class*, 475 U.S. 106, 89 L.Ed. 2d 81, 106 S.Ct. 960 [1986]). What is seen may be used to establish probable cause for further action. For example, damage to a car may indicate that it has been in a collision; if this plus other facts known to the officers estab-lish probable cause, paint samples may be taken, either at the original loca-tion or later at the impound lot, and sent to a laboratory for testing.

4-5f Search of Car for Reasons Not Related
to Investigating Criminal Activity

Searches as part of non-criminal investigations were authorized by the Supreme Court if done as part of the "community caretaking function" of the police (*Cady v. Dombrowski*, 413 U.S. 433, 37 L.Ed. 2d 706, 93 S.Ct. 2523 [1973]). For example, when a wrecked car was taken to a storage lot after a traffic accident, it was searched for a gun the driver had the legal right to possess; evidence of a previously unreported murder that was discovered during this search was admissible at trial. The officer's actions were considered justified because they were done to prevent vandals from stealing the gun.

4-5g Stopping of Vehicles at Roadblocks

Roadblocks are frequently used to conduct inspections of safety equipment, such as brakes and taillights. They are not allowed, however, merely to check for outstanding arrest warrants (*Delaware v. Prouse*, 440 U.S. 648, 59 L.Ed. 2d 660, 99 S.Ct. 1391 [1979]). The Supreme Court approved the use of roadblocks for sobriety checkpoints after balancing the need to prevent drunk driving against the minimal intrusion roadblocks make on the rights of individual motorists (*Michigan Department of State Police v. Sitz*, 496 U.S. 444, 110 L.Ed. 2d 412, 110 S.Ct. 2481 [1990]). The Supreme Court refused to extend the right to use roadblocks to narcotics detection situations.

4-5h Closed Containers Found in Cars

The Supreme Court has ruled on several cases that considered the applicability of the Closed Container Rule to vehicles. Officers may open **closed containers** found in vehicles without a search warrant in many situations: during a vehicle stop based on reasonable suspicion; as part of a search incident to an arrest of a person in the vehicle; during an inventory of impounded vehicle; and during a search of a vehicle based on probable cause.

4-6 Blood, Breath, and Urine Tests

When a drunk driver is arrested, it is customary to conduct laboratory tests to show the level of alcohol in the body. Blood, breath, and urine tests are frequently used for this purpose, as well as in other situations where intoxication or drug usage is an issue. The Fifth Amendment privilege against self-incrimination applies to testimonial evidence, but not to body fluids and other physical evidence from the suspect's body. There are, however, important Fourth Amendment and due process issues involved.

The Supreme Court recognized that the breakdown of alcohol in the bloodstream by the body's metabolic processes cannot be stopped. Once the suspect has been arrested for an alcohol-related offense, officers are authorized to take the suspect to a medical facility for the tests without a search warrant (*Schmerber v. California*, 384 U.S. 757, 16 L.Ed. 2d 908, 86 S.Ct. 1826 [1966]).

Winston v. Lee

470 U.S. 753, 84 L.Ed. 2d 662, 105 S.Ct. 1611 (1985)

Issue: Obtaining Blood Alcohol and Other Evidence from Suspect's Body

"Schmerber v. California (1966), held, inter alia, that a State may, over the suspect's protest, have a physician extract blood from a person suspected of drunken driving without violation of the suspect's right secured by the Fourth Amendment not to be subjected to unreasonable searches and seizures. . . . In this case, the Commonwealth of Virginia seeks to compel the respondent Rudolph Lee, who is suspected of attempting to commit armed robbery, to undergo a surgical procedure under a general anesthetic for removal of a bullet lodged in his chest. Petitioners allege that the bullet will provide evidence of respondent's guilt or innocence. We conclude that the procedure sought here is an example of the 'more substantial intrusion' cautioned against in Schmerber, and hold that to permit the procedure would violate respondent's right to be secure in his person guaranteed by the Fourth Amendment."

Tests on other evidence may be useful for the prosecution of the case. These range from DNA to recovery of bullets lodged in the suspect's body. Due process prohibits procedures that are unduly painful, such as "pumping" the suspect's stomach to recover drugs that were swallowed to prevent officers from seizing them (*Rochin v. California*, 342 U.S. 165, 96 L.Ed. 2d 183, 72 S.Ct. 205 [1952]).

Surgical procedures are authorized only if there is minimal risk to the suspect's health and a compelling need for the evidence that would be produced. A court order is required for all surgical procedures performed for the purpose of obtaining evidence for the prosecution (*Winston v. Lee*, 470 U.S. 753, 84 L.Ed. 2d 662, 105 S.Ct. 1611 [1985]).

4-7 Misplaced Reliance Doctrine

The Supreme Court has placed the burden on the speaker to make sure that he/she can trust everyone who may hear what is said. It applies to the person spoken to as well as to other people who are close enough to overhear the conversation. This **Misplaced Reliance Doctrine** applies even though tape recorders and/or radio transmitters are used.

The facts from two leading cases help explain this doctrine. When Jimmy Hoffa was on trial in what is called the "Test Fleet" cāse, the Justice Department had another union official named Partin released from prison. Partin was instructed to join Hoffa's entourage and report on Hoffa's out-of-court activities. Partin frequented Hoffa's hotel room and overheard conversations about plans to tamper with the jury. No

---

Hoffa v. United States
385 U.S. 293, 17 L.Ed. 2d 374, 87 S.Ct. 408 (1966)

Issue: Misplaced Reliance on Another Person

"What the Fourth Amendment protects is the security a man relies upon when he places himself or his property within a constitutionally protected area, be it his home or his office, his hotel room or his automobile. There, he is protected from unwarranted governmental intrusion. And when he puts something in his filing cabinet, in his desk drawer, or in his pocket, he has the right to know it will be secure from an unreasonable search or an unreasonable seizure. . . .

* * *

"Neither this Court nor any member of it has ever expressed the view that the Fourth Amendment protects a wrongdoer's misplaced belief that a person to whom he voluntarily confides his wrongdoing will not reveal it."

---

electronic monitoring equipment was used. The "Test Fleet" case ended with a hung jury. Evidence supplied by Partin was used in a subsequent prosecution where Hoffa was charged with attempting to bribe jurors. The Supreme Court found that this was a case of misplaced reliance. Hoffa knew Partin was present and took the risk that Partin might report the jury tampering to the authorities. The fact that the Justice Department had "planted" Partin had no legal significance (*Hoffa v. United States*, 385 U.S. 293, 17 L.Ed. 2d 374, 87 S.Ct. 408 [1966]).

Federal narcotics agents used concealed radio transmitters in *United States v. White* (401 U.S. 745, 28 L.Ed. 2d 453, 91 S.Ct. 1122 [1971]). They recorded conversations between agents and the defendant that took place in public places, restaurants, the defendant's home, and an informant's car. The informant also allowed an agent to hide in a kitchen closet and transmit conversations between the informant and the defendant. All of these recorded conversations were found admissible under the Misplaced Reliance Doctrine. Defendant White should have been more careful in deciding whom he could trust. This even applied to the agent in the closet. White should not have relied on his friend, who allowed the agent to hide there.

It is important to understand the distinctions between misplaced reliance and electronic surveillance. Conversations that fall under the Misplaced Reliance Doctrine are made in front of one or more people who the suspect believes are trustworthy. One of these "friends" (including "planted" informants) or someone else who was close enough to overhear the conversation relays the information to the police. Electronic devices, such as radio transmitters and tape recorders, may be used without obtaining a warrant. Electronic surveillance, on the other hand, requires a specialized search warrant. Modern technology makes it possible to eavesdrop electronically without intruding on the physical privacy of the people involved. Electronic listening devices (wiretap or other monitoring equipment) relay the conversation without having an informant present. The suspect and all parties to the conversation are unaware that anyone is listening; none of them discloses the information. The Supreme Court ruled that this is an invasion of the reasonable expectation of privacy. Very strict laws apply to electronic monitoring. Anyone working with this type of equipment must be familiar with the unique rules that must be followed. They are not covered here because patrol officers are rarely involved.

4-8 Closed Containers

In 1977, the Supreme Court created the **Closed Container Rule** (*United States v. Chadwick,* 433 U.S. 1, 53 L.Ed. 2d 538, 97 S.Ct. 2476 [1977]). See also *Arkansas v. Sanders,* 442 U.S. 753, 61 L.Ed. 2d 235, 99 S.Ct. 2586 [1979]). Several exceptions have been made to this rule. Distinctions have also been made between closed containers that are opened by police and those that are opened by other people and then turned over to the police.

4-8a Police Seizure of Closed Containers

The original rule stated that closed containers could be seized by police without a warrant if there was probable cause that they contained contraband or other items of evidentiary value. The officers were allowed to retain custody of them long enough to obtain a search warrant. A search could legally be performed only after the warrant had been obtained.

Two clear exceptions to the Closed Container Rule have emerged. One involves cars (*United States v. Ross,* 456 U.S. 798, 72 L.Ed. 2d 572, 102 S.Ct. 2157 [1982]; *New York v. Belton,* 453 U.S. 454, 69 L.Ed. 2d 768, 101 S.Ct. 2869 [1981]; *Michigan v. Long,* 463 U.S. 1032, 77 L.Ed. 2d 1201, 103 S.Ct. 3469 [1983]; *Colorado v. Bertine,* 479 U.S. 367, 93 L.Ed. 2d 739, 107 S.Ct. 738 [1987]; *California v. Acevedo,* 500 U.S. 565, 114 L.Ed. 2d 619, 111 S.Ct. 1982 [1991]). Closed containers found in vehicles may be opened without a warrant if they are found incident to an arrest, as part of a searched based on reasonable suspicion that weapons are in the vehicle, during a probable cause search, or as part of an inventory.

The second exception allows searches of any closed container in the possession of a person being booked (*Illinois v. Lafayette,* 462 U.S. 640, 77 L.Ed. 2d 65, 103 S.Ct. 2605 [1983]). The routine inventory of everything confiscated during booking usually includes itemizing what was inside closed containers.

4-8b Reopening of Containers

There are a variety of situations in which the police may legally open a package. For example, customs officials may open it at the border; police may open it during the search of a car based on probable cause; or it may be searched pursuant to a warrant. A totally different rule relates to containers that have already been opened legally. Once legally opened, any expectation of privacy vanishes. Common carriers, such as airlines and freight companies, are frequently involved in cases where a box was legally opened and then turned over to the police. In these situations the police may reopen the box and search it (*Illinois v. Andreas,* 463 U.S. 765, 77 L.Ed. 2d 1003, 103 S.Ct. 3319 [1983]; *United States v. Jacobsen,* 466 U.S. 109, 80 L.Ed. 2d 85, 104 S.Ct. 1652 [1984]).

Sometimes the officers intentionally reseal the package and maintain surveillance while it is delivered to the addressee. This is called a **controlled delivery.** Constant surveillance is crucial for two reasons. First, if the package is allowed out of the sight of the officers, the contents may be changed. This greatly reduces the evidentiary value of the contents. Second, and very important from a constitutional standpoint, the Supreme Court found that the recipient may develop a privacy interest in the contents if there is a substantial likelihood that he/she has altered the contents of the package.

Chapter Summary

The basic rule that officers must follow while investigating criminal activity is that a search warrant is required *unless* there is an established exception to the Fourth Amendment that applies to the circumstances. There is no automatic right to enter and/or search a crime scene without the consent of the resident. Knock notice must be complied with when entering a residence to serve warrants, to make arrests, or to engage in other phases of the investigation of a crime.

Items left in plain view do not require search warrants if the officer can observe them from a place where he/she has the legal right to be. The officer does not have the right to pick up things and examine them in order to determine if they are stolen or contraband. Probable cause is a prerequisite to the right to seize each item. The rule for abandoned property is much easier. No one can claim a privacy interest in abandoned items; therefore, officers can seize them without probable cause.

Consent for a search is valid if it is voluntarily given by a person with apparent authority over the area. The person giving the consent controls the area that may be searched and the length of time involved. Consent may be withdrawn or expanded at any time.

Numerous exceptions to the warrant requirement exist for vehicles. If a vehicle is stopped based on reasonable suspicion and the officer reasonably believes that a weapon is in the vehicle, the passenger compartment may be searched for weapons, whether or not the suspect will be released at the scene. When an officer arrests a person who is in a vehicle, the officer may thoroughly search the passenger compartment. If an officer has probable cause to believe that there is evidence in a vehicle, the relevant portion of the vehicle may be searched at the scene or later at an impound lot or a police station. The contents of any vehicle legally impounded for storage may be inventoried. Closed containers found in a vehicle under any of the previously mentioned circumstances may be opened and inspected.

A search warrant is not required prior to obtaining a blood sample to determine if the suspect is intoxicated. This rule also applies to breath and urine tests. Other tests may be ordered by the court, but requests for surgical procedures to recover evidence will rarely be granted.

The Misplaced Reliance Doctrine applies to conversations relayed to law enforcement by an informant. It does not matter whether a tape recorder, a radio transmitter, or only unassisted human memory was used to recover what was said. This rule applies to anyone who was a party to the conversation as well as eavesdroppers. Electronic eavesdropping, however, requires a specialized search warrant.

Closed containers may be seized, but not searched, without a warrant. Many exceptions to this rule permit warrantless searches: an inventory of an impounded car; a search of a car during a *Terry* stop; a search of a car incident to the arrest of the driver or a passenger; a probable cause search of a vehicle; and jail booking searches. Packages opened legally by private parties may be reopened by the police without a warrant.

Study Questions

1. When is a search warrant required to enter a building during a criminal investigation of a crime believed to have been committed inside? Explain.
2. List three situations where officers must comply with knock notice.
3. Explain the Plain View Doctrine. Give three examples of situations where it would apply.
4. When may police officers seize abandoned property? Explain.
5. Who can give valid consent for a police officer to search an apartment? Is the officer required to tell the person that he/she has the right to refuse to consent?
6. Explain the search that an officer may conduct when stopping a vehicle based on reasonable suspicion that an occupant of the vehicle is involved in criminal activity.
7. Explain the search that an officer may perform after arresting a person who was in the car.
8. Explain the search that is allowed if there is probable cause that illegal drugs are concealed in a car.
9. Describe what an officer is allowed to do when conducting an inventory of a car that has been impounded when no search warrant has been obtained.
10. Is a search warrant required prior to taking a sample to be used by the lab when performing a blood alcohol test? Explain.
11. When is a judge likely to issue a warrant granting the prosecution's request that the suspect submit to laboratory testing? to minor surgery? Explain.
12. When are conversations reported by a police "snitch" admissible in evidence? Explain.
13. When may an undercover officer wear a "body mike" that transmits conversations to a backup team during a drug deal? Explain.
14. Give two examples of situations currently covered by the Closed Container Rule.
15. List four situations no longer covered by the Closed Container Rule.

True or False Questions

1. Police officers who are investigating crimes immediately after the crimes occurred do not need to obtain search warrants to enter homes.

2. The Plain View Doctrine applies only if the officer is legally at the scene.

3. The Plain View Doctrine does not allow officers to physically examine objects in order to determine if there is probable cause to seize them.

4. No probable cause is needed to seize abandoned property.

5. Police officers are not required to advise suspects of their right to refuse to give consent for a search.

6. Consent is valid only if the person giving consent has legal authority over the area to be searched.

7. A thorough search of the passenger compartment of a car may be performed at the time that a person in the car is arrested.

8. An officer is allowed to search a car based on probable cause only if there is an emergency that prevents the officer from obtaining a search warrant.

9. Police must obtain an electronic surveillance warrant prior to tape recording any conversation.

10. If the police have probable cause to seize a portable container, they automatically have authority to search the container.

Chapter 5

Interrogation and Identification Procedures

Outline

Key Terms

custody
interrogation
knowing, intelligent,
  and voluntary waiver
line-up
Miranda warnings

photographic line-up
right to have an attorney
  present during
  questioning
right to counsel
right to remain silent

self-incrimination
show-up
testimonial communication
unduly suggestive
volunteered statements
waiver of *Miranda* rights

Learning Objectives

Learning Objectives

After reading this chapter, the student will be able to

- Explain when the protections of the Fifth Amendment apply to police activities.
- Explain when officers must give a suspect the *Miranda* warnings.
- Accurately paraphrase the *Miranda* warnings.
- Describe the criteria for a valid waiver of *Miranda* rights.
- Explain the process police must follow to initiate interrogation after a suspect has invoked the right to remain silent.
- Explain the precautions that must be taken prior to initiating interrogation after a suspect has invoked the right to have an attorney present.
- Explain the constitutional rights that apply during identification procedures.
- Explain when the Sixth Amendment right to counsel applies.

A confession can be a vitally important piece of evidence in a criminal case, but the police must safeguard the suspect's constitutional rights when conducting an interrogation. The *Miranda* warnings, designed by the Supreme Court for this purpose, will be thoroughly covered in this chapter. Important restrictions on procedures used when eye witnesses are asked to identify the person they believe committed the crime will also be covered. Finally, the right to counsel will be discussed.

5-1 Self-Incrimination

The privilege against **self-incrimination** is based on the Fifth Amendment. It applies only to statements that would result in criminal liability for the person making them and cannot be used to refuse to give answers that would incriminate a friend. The Supreme Court has interpreted this privilege as applying only to **testimonial communication.** For this reason the suspect cannot refuse to participate in nontestimonial procedures, even though they are incriminating. Physical evidence is not protected, except for items, such as diaries, that contain statements which incriminate the person who wrote them.

Taking specimens of blood, breath, urine, or semen for laboratory analysis does not involve testimonial evidence; neither does obtaining a tissue sample for DNA testing. A person's physical appearance is not testimonial; therefore, the suspect can be photographed, fingerprinted, and required to stand in a line-up. Voice and handwriting exemplars are not testimonial because the person is told what to say or write. Videotapes of sobriety tests are admissible because they show physical characteristics (lack of coordination, unsteady gait, slurred speech, etc.). Questions asked during the sobriety test that elicit incriminating details—such as "How many drinks did you have?"—are admissible only if *Miranda* has been complied with (*Pennsylvania v. Muniz*, 496 U.S. 582, 110 L.Ed. 2d 528, 110 S.Ct. 2638 [1990]).

Self-incrimination means subjecting oneself to criminal prosecution. If statements cannot be used against a person in a criminal trial, there is no Fifth Amendment right to refuse to answer questions. This legal distinction comes into play in three situations: immunity, double jeopardy, and the statute of limitations. If a person is given immunity he/she cannot be prosecuted; hence, someone with this protection cannot claim the Fifth Amendment. The scope of the immunity is important. Formal documents conferring immunity explicitly state what it covers (for example, prosecution for robbery on July 5, 1998, at 123 Main Street, Ourtown). The suspect can be compelled to answer questions only within the scope of the immunity. If statements about other crimes are voluntarily made, they can be used against him/her.

Double jeopardy prevents a new trial if the person has been convicted or acquitted on the same charges. The fact that the person cannot be brought to trial again would preclude use of the Fifth Amendment as a reason not to testify. This rule becomes important in cases where multiple defendants are not tried together. Once one or more defendants have been convicted or acquitted, the prosecution can call them to testify against the others.

Each state legislature enacts statutes of limitations, which set deadlines for filing charges. Cases that could result in the death penalty frequently are not covered by the statutes of limitations; this means these cases can be filed at any time, even many years after the crime. Felonies usually have longer filing periods than misdemeanors. The statutes of limitations can be tolled (stopped) if a suspect flees the jurisdiction to avoid prosecution. The result of these rules is that the time to file charges may have expired against one, but not all, of the co-conspirators. For example, one suspect fled but another was caught, or one defendant can be charged with a more serious offense than the other. The suspect for whom the statutes of limitations has expired cannot claim the Fifth Amendment as grounds to refuse to testify against others who are standing trial for the same crime spree.

The Fifth Amendment applies only to criminal proceedings. A person involved in a civil case cannot use this constitutional right to avoid making statements that would result in financial liability. Litigants can claim the Fifth Amendment as grounds to refuse to answer questions during civil proceedings that could result in criminal liability. The defendant can invoke the Fifth Amendment only if his/her testimony could be used against him/her in criminal court (*Allen v. Illinois*, 478 U.S. 364, 92 L.Ed. 2d 296, 106 S.Ct. 2988 [1986]). Hence, the defendant cannot use the Fifth Amendment in civil proceedings seeking involuntary commitment to a mental hospital or during proceedings for civil commitment based on the allegation that the defendant is a sexually violent predator unless the statements relate to criminal charges that could still be filed against him/her.

5-2 Interrogation

Miranda v. Arizona (384 U.S. 436, 16 L.Ed. 2d 694, 86 S.Ct. 1602 [1966]) is one of the best known Supreme Court cases. The prosecution cannot use confessions obtained in violation of *Miranda* to prove the defendant's guilt.

5-2a When *Miranda* Warnings Are Required

Two key words summarize when *Miranda* warnings must be given: "custodial interrogation." The suspect must be in custody at the time, *and* the police must be interrogating him/her.

Custody, for the purposes of *Miranda*, is the equivalent of a custodial arrest. This does not include traffic stops where citations are issued and the violator is released at the scene. Field interviews based on reasonable suspicion do not require *Miranda* warnings (*Berkemer v. McCarty,* 468 U.S. 420, 82 L.Ed. 2d 317, 104 S.Ct. 3138 [1984]); *Pennsylvania v. Bruder,* 488 U.S. 9, 102 L.Ed. 2d 172, 109 S.Ct. 205 [1988]); neither does questioning at the police station if the suspect is not under arrest (*Oregon v. Mathiason,* 429 U.S. 492, 50 L.Ed. 2d 714, 97 S.Ct. 711 [1977]).

On the other hand, it does not matter why the suspect is in custody. Warnings are required if a suspect was arrested for one crime but questioned regarding a different one. Questioning by a different law enforcement agency while the person remains in custody necessitates the warnings. *Miranda* admonitions are also required if the suspect is questioned while in jail, serving time on a totally unrelated offense.

The Supreme Court has defined **interrogation** as the process of questioning or its functional equivalent. Asking questions about a crime or an alibi is clearly interrogation. So is requesting a narrative statement. The Court has also included indirect attempts to obtain information (*Rhode Island v. Innis,* 446 U.S. 291, 64 L.Ed. 2d 297, 100 S.Ct. 652 [1980]; *Brewer v. Williams,* 430 U.S. 387, 51 L.Ed. 2d 424, 97 S.Ct. 1232 [1977]). For example, two officers engage in a conversation in the presence of a suspect, intending the suspect to overhear them and hoping to elicit a response.

Custodial interrogation triggers the mandate to advise the suspect of his/her rights, even though the police are not conducting the interview. *Miranda* warnings are required when expert witnesses who will testify for the prosecution conduct custodial interviews with a suspect. Polygraph examiners and psychiatrists assessing sanity or competency to stand trial must give appropriate warnings (*Estelle v. Smith,* 451 U.S. 454, 68 L.Ed. 2d 359, 101 S.Ct. 1866 [1981]). Questioning by jailhouse informants and undercover officers before charges are filed may proceed without *Miranda* warnings; the Court reasoned that the lack of coercive police presence made the warnings unnecessary (*Illinois v. Perkins,* 496 U.S. 292, 110 L.Ed. 2d 243, 110 S.Ct. 2394 [1990]). Due process may require suppression of a confession obtained by an informant, however, if coercive tactics were used with or without the knowledge of the police (*Arizona v. Fulminante,* 499 U.S. 279, 113 L.Ed. 2d 302, 111 S.Ct. 1246 [1991]).

Rhode Island v. Innis

446 U.S. 291, 64 L.Ed. 2d 297, 100 S.Ct. 1682 (1980)

Issue: *Miranda* Required during Indirect Questioning

"We conclude that the *Miranda* safeguards come into play whenever a person in custody is subjected to either express questioning or its functional equivalent. That is to say, the term 'interrogation' under *Miranda* refers not only to express questioning, but also to any words or actions on the part of the police (other than those normally attendant to arrest and custody) that the police should know are reasonably likely to elicit an incriminating response from the suspect. The latter portion of this definition focuses primarily upon the perceptions of the suspect, rather than the intent of the police. This focus reflects the fact that the *Miranda* safeguards were designed to vest a suspect in custody with an added measure of protection against coercive police practices, without regard to objective proof of the underlying intent of the police. A practice that the police should know is reasonably likely to evoke an incriminating response from a suspect thus amounts to interrogation. But, since the police surely cannot be held accountable for the unforeseeable results of their words or actions, the definition of interrogation can extend only to words or actions on the part of police officers that they should have known were reasonably likely to elicit an incriminating response."

Volunteered statements are admissible even though *Miranda* warnings were not given (*Miranda v. Arizona*, 384 U.S. 436, 16 L.Ed. 2d 694, 86 S.Ct. 1602 [1966]). As used in this context, "volunteered" means the suspect came forward on his/her own initiative and made a statement. Follow-up questions about the volunteered information are considered interrogation.

5-2b Content of *Miranda* Warnings

Many police departments give their officers "*Miranda* cards" with the warnings stated in language quoted from Supreme Court opinions. Reading these warnings helps establish that they were given correctly but is not conclusive evidence that the suspect understood them. In fact, merely reciting quotes is frequently inadequate if a suspect with limited English ability or severe mental impairment is unable to comprehend their meaning. The Court has allowed paraphrasing of the *Miranda* warnings but has been quite intolerant of misleading the suspect. Officers must fully understand the Court's intent in *Miranda* in order to give the warnings correctly and to answer any questions the suspect asks.

Prior to custodial interrogation, the suspect must be given **Miranda warnings,** which cover four points:

Miranda v. Arizona

384 U.S. 436, 16 L.Ed. 2d 694, 86 S.Ct. 1602 (1966)

Issue: Interrogation of Suspect Who Is in Custody

"Our holding . . . it is this: the prosecution may not use statements, whether exculpatory or inculpatory, stemming from custodial interrogation of the defendant unless it demonstrates the use of procedural safeguards effective to secure the privilege against self-incrimination. By custodial interrogation, we mean questioning initiated by law enforcement officers after a person has been taken into custody or otherwise deprived of his freedom of action in any significant way. As for the procedural safeguards to be employed, unless other fully effective means are devised to inform accused persons of their right of silence and to assure a continuous opportunity to exercise it, the following measures are required. Prior to any questioning, the person must be warned that he has a right to remain silent, that any statement he does make may be used as evidence against him, and that he has a right to the presence of an attorney, either retained or appointed. The defendant may waive effectuation of these rights, provided the waiver is made voluntarily, knowingly and intelligently. If, however, he indicates in any manner and at any stage of the process that he wishes to consult with an attorney before speaking, there can be no questioning. Likewise, if the individual is alone and indicates in any manner that he does not wish to be interrogated, the police may not question him. The mere fact that he may have answered some questions or volunteered some statements on his own does not deprive him of the right to refrain from answering any further inquiries until he has consulted with an attorney and thereafter consents to be questioned."

- You have the right to remain silent.
- Anything you say can and will be used against you in a court of law.
- You have the right to have an attorney present during questioning.
- If you cannot afford an attorney, one will be provided at no charge to assist you during questioning.

The **right to remain silent** includes the right to refrain from making both oral and written statements. A corollary is the rule that the fact that a suspect invoked *Miranda* cannot be used at trial to imply guilt. Even if the suspect agreed to talk at the beginning of the interview, he/she has the right to stop the interrogation at any time. As will be discussed in section 5-2d, the suspect also has the right to waive the rights after initially invoking them.

Anything that the suspect says can be used against him/her in court. This includes all admissions that may be incriminating in any way, false alibis, attempts to blame another person, and anything which could be used to attack credibility during impeachment. An attempt to talk to the police "off the record" indicates that the suspect does not understand the warnings.

The suspect has the **right to have an attorney present during questioning.** Law enforcement officers may not continue questioning a suspect after an attorney has been requested. The police have two alternatives: to provide an attorney for the suspect and then continue the interrogation or to stop questioning. Failure to provide an attorney violates the suspect's rights *only if* there is further questioning.

Determining whether the suspect has invoked the right to an attorney may be complicated by the suspect's failure to give precise answers. The basic rule is clear—if the suspect indicates in any manner that he/she wants an attorney, the questioning must stop. Once the suspect has made such a request, officers may not try to convince the suspect that requesting an attorney is not a wise decision. A problem arises when a suspect makes an equivocal statement, such as "Well, yes, maybe I need an attorney." At this point, it is appropriate to ask questions to clarify what exactly the suspect wants (*Smith v. Illinois,* 469 U.S. 91, 83 L.Ed. 2d 488, 105 S.Ct. 490 [1984]). Officers must not yield to the temptation to tell the suspect what they personally think if the suspect asks, "What do you think I should do?"

Last, if the suspect cannot afford an attorney, one will be provided at no cost to the suspect. The purpose of this warning is to inform the indigent suspect that a lack of money will not prevent him/her from having an attorney present during questioning. It is not the duty of the police to review the financial status of the suspect. If the suspect requests an attorney, the police have only one option, regardless of the suspect's apparent wealth (or lack thereof): questioning must stop. Most attorneys tell their clients not to answer questions; therefore, the police usually forego further questioning and do not provide the suspect with an attorney. This is a practical application of the *Miranda* ruling and does not violate the suspect's rights.

Merely reciting the Court's language is not enough. The warnings must be given so that the suspect can understand them. This may mean using simplified language or calling for an interpreter. The prosecution bears the burden of convincing the judge by a preponderance of the evidence that the warnings were correctly explained to the suspect (*Colorado v. Connelly,* 479 U.S. 157, 93 L.Ed. 2d 473, 107 S.Ct. 515 [1986]). A signed waiver is helpful but does not rebut a defense claim that the suspect did not understand the warnings. Tape recordings of the entire interrogation are frequently helpful if the suspect alleges that the warnings were not given correctly or that a request to terminate the interrogation was ignored.

5-2c Waiver of *Miranda* Rights

Once *Miranda* warnings have been correctly given to a suspect who is in custody, the police may try to obtain a **waiver of *Miranda* rights.** There must be a **knowing, intelligent, and voluntary waiver.** To have a knowing waiver, the suspect must have been correctly advised of his/her rights. This includes any necessary explanations to accommodate language deficiencies, an inability to understand specific words, or a lack of education. The courts have uniformly required that the police show that they have done this. It is not presumed that anyone knows the *Miranda* warnings.

An intelligent waiver, as used in this context, means that the person has the basic intelligence necessary to understand his/her rights. This may be a problem if a juvenile is involved. Only the most extreme cases involving adults with mental impairments or intoxication (due to alcohol or other drugs) qualify for suppression due to the lack of an intelligent waiver.

A voluntary waiver is one that was given without coercion. Physical force or the threat of violence cannot be used to obtain a confession. Deprivation of food and/or sleep for long periods is not allowed. Neither are false promises of leniency, such as offers to drop charges or assurances that the suspect will get a shorter sentence if he/she makes a confession.

Coercive acts by the police, or anyone acting on behalf of the police, are not tolerated. Confessions that are the result of coercion from other sources are admissible (*Colorado v. Connelly,* 479 U.S. 157, 93 L.Ed. 2d 473, 107 S.Ct. 515 [1986]). For example, a man who had committed a murder began having audio hallucinations, during which he heard voices telling him that he had two choices: confess to the crime or commit suicide. He went back to the city where the crime had occurred and confessed. A defense argument that the confession was inadmissible because it was coerced was rejected by the Supreme Court.

Absent one of these obviously coercive acts, the courts look at the totality of the circumstances. The key concept is that the police are not allowed to overbear the will of the suspect. This balances the acts of the police against the vulnerability of the defendant. What is coercive when done to a naive teenager may be acceptable when applied to a streetwise ex-convict.

Lies and half-truths may be permitted. The police do not have to tell the suspect all of the crimes being investigated (*Colorado v. Spring,* 479 U.S. 364, 93 L.Ed. 2d 954, 107 S.Ct. 851 [1987]). Neither do they have to inform him/her that a friend has arranged for an attorney to come to the jail to provide assistance (*Moran v. Burbine,* 475 U.S. 412, 89 L.Ed. 2d 410, 106 S.Ct. 1135 [1986]). Statements such as "We found your fingerprints at the scene" and "Your friend confessed and blamed it all on you" have been allowed, even though they were not true.

The last issue involving the waiver of *Miranda* rights is the procedure used to obtain the waiver. The Supreme Court has not established a specific protocol. Express waivers are preferred, but in one case the Court found a valid waiver was implied by the suspect's conduct (*North Carolina v. Butler*, 441 U.S. 369, 60 L.Ed. 2d 286, 99 S.Ct. 1755 [1979]). The suspect had responded in the affirmative when asked if he understood his rights, but he did not reply when asked if he wished to waive them. The indication that he understood the warnings, coupled with the fact that he answered the questions, was enough to convince the Court that a valid waiver had been obtained. In another case, the Court decided that an oral confession was admissible, even though the suspect told police that he would talk to them but would not make a written confession without an attorney present (*Connecticut v. Barrett*, 479 U.S. 523, 93 L.Ed. 2d 920, 107 S.Ct. 828 [1987]).

5-2d Subsequent Interrogations

It is not uncommon for the police to interrogate a suspect more than once. The procedures that should be followed at the subsequent interrogation depend largely on what was done at the prior one(s).

Miranda *Error at Prior Interrogation Session*

Statements made by an inmate who is in custody during an interrogation session that was not preceded by a valid waiver of *Miranda* rights are not admissible as substantive evidence. They can be used for impeachment (*Harris v. New York*, 401 U.S. 222, 28 L.Ed. 2d 1, 91 S.Ct. 643 [1971]; *Oregon v. Haas*, 419 U.S. 823, 43 L.Ed. 2d 570, 95 S.Ct. 1215 [1975]). The impeachment exception to *Miranda* would be used during cross-examination of a defendant who testifies in a manner inconsistent with the statements made to the officers. Defendants frequently refuse to take the witness stand in order to avoid having the jury told about these statements.

Failure to correctly give *Miranda* warnings does not automatically make all of the suspect's subsequent statements inadmissible. It is possible, by correctly administering the *Miranda* warnings at a later interview, to obtain an admissible confession. There must be a significant time lapse before attempting to obtain a valid waiver. The courts look at the totality of the circumstances to see if the taint of the original *Miranda* error has been dissipated (*Oregon v. Elstad*, 470 U.S. 298, 84 L.Ed. 2d 222, 105 S.Ct. 1285 [1985]).

Valid Miranda *Waiver at Previous Session*

If the suspect has already waived the *Miranda* rights, subsequent interrogations can be conducted rather routinely. The Supreme Court has not required a new set of *Miranda* warnings at the beginning of each interrogation session. The warnings need to be repeated only if there is a possibility that the suspect does not remember his/her rights. If any doubt exists, officers should take the time to advise him/her again, rather than risk the suppression of any statements obtained. Agreeing to continue the interrogations does not deprive the suspect of the right to invoke *Miranda* at any time.

Valid Miranda *Warnings at Previous Session—Suspect Invoked Right to Remain Silent*

Interrogation must be stopped immediately if the suspect invokes the right to remain silent. This does not mean, however, that questioning may never be resumed. The Supreme Court has insisted that the suspect's right be scrupulously honored (*Michigan v. Mosley,* 423 U.S. 96, 46 L.Ed. 2d 313, 96 S.Ct. 321 [1975]). Police may not badger the suspect with frequent attempts to get the suspect to talk, but after a reasonable time they may ask if he/she would like to continue the interrogation. A new waiver of *Miranda* is mandatory prior to resuming questioning. In the leading case, there was a two-hour gap between the interrogation sessions; the second interview was conducted by different officers on a different floor of the police building and focused on a different crime.

Michigan v. Mosley

423 U.S. 96, 46 L.Ed. 2d 313, 96 S.Ct. 321 (1975)

Issue: Questioning after Suspect Invokes *Miranda* Rights

"A reasonable and faithful interpretation of the *Miranda* opinion must rest on the intention of the Court in that case to adopt

'fully effective means . . . to notify the person of his right of silence and to assure that the exercise of the right will be scrupulously honored. . . .'

The critical safeguard identified in the passage at issue is a person's 'right to cut off questioning.' Through the exercise of his option to terminate questioning, he can control the time at which questioning occurs, the subjects discussed, and the duration of the interrogation. The requirement that law enforcement authorities must respect a person's exercise of that option counteracts the coercive pressures of the custodial setting. We therefore conclude that the admissibility of statements obtained after the person in custody has decided to remain silent depends under *Miranda* on whether his 'right to cut off questioning' was 'scrupulously honored.'"

Valid **Miranda** *Warnings at Previous Session—Suspect Invoked Right to Counsel*

A different rule applies if the suspect asked to speak to an attorney rather than merely demanding that the questioning stop. In these situations, an attorney must be present at subsequent interrogation sessions unless the suspect voluntarily initiates a request for an interview (*Minnick v. Mississippi*, 498 U.S. 146, 112 L.Ed. 2d 489, 111 S.Ct. 486 [1990]). The fact that the subsequent interrogation is about a different crime does not alter this rule; neither does the fact that a different police agency is conducting the interview. The fact that the new interrogator acted without knowledge of the prior request for an attorney is not an acceptable excuse (*Arizona v. Roberson*, 486 U.S. 675, 100 L.Ed. 2d 704, 108 S.Ct. 2093 [1988]). The police must carefully record the request for an attorney and communicate this fact to all officers who may have contact with the suspect.

Minnick v. Mississippi
498 U.S. 146, 112 L.Ed. 2d 489, 111 S.Ct. 486 (1990)

Issue: Interrogation after Suspect Invokes Right to Counsel

"Edwards [*Edwards v. Arizona* (1981)] does not foreclose finding a waiver of Fifth Amendment protections after counsel has been requested, provided the accused has initiated the conversation or discussions with the authorities; but that is not the case before us. There can be no doubt that the interrogation in question was initiated by the police; it was a formal interview which petitioner was compelled to attend. Since petitioner made a specific request for counsel before the interview, the police-initiated interrogation was impermissible."

5-3 Identification Procedures

A variety of procedures may be used to allow victims and eye witnesses to identify the person who committed the crime. At a **line-up** a person who saw the crime is asked to view a group of people and indicate if one of them committed the crime. A **show-up** is a much simpler procedure. One suspect is shown to the person who is to make the identification. This can be done in the field, at a police facility, or elsewhere. A **photographic line-up** involves showing pictures. It may be done by handing the witness a few carefully selected photographs or allowing him/her to look through "mug books." The suspect is not present when this is done.

Constitutional rights must be protected during these identification procedures. There is no special exception to the Fourth Amendment which gives police the right to detain a suspect solely to conduct a line-up or show-up. A suspect may be detained based on reasonable suspicion and a show-up quickly conducted at the location where he/she was stopped. These show-ups usually occur shortly after the crime when a suspect has been detained near the scene. Probable cause to arrest is necessary in order to transport the suspect to the police station (*Dunaway v. New York,* 442 U.S. 200, 60 L.Ed. 2d 824, 99 S.Ct. 2248 [1979]). Once there, either a line-up or show-up may be conducted for any crime in which the arrested person is a suspect, or he/she may be used as an "extra" in a line-up for crimes committed by someone else. There is no Fifth Amendment right to refuse to participate in a line-up (*United States v. Wade,* 388 U.S. 218, 18 L.Ed. 2d 1149, 87 S.Ct. 1926 [1967]). The suspect can be required to walk, take a particular stance, wear designated clothing or disguises, make gestures observed during the crime, or repeat what witnesses reported the suspect said. While none of these requests violates the Fifth Amendment, due process demands fundamental fairness. Any special effects or actions that are done by one person in a line-up must be performed by each of the participants.

The suspect has a **right to counsel** during a line-up or show-up if it is conducted *after* arraignment or indictment (*Kirby v. Illinois,* 406 U.S. 682, 32 L.Ed. 2d 411, 92 S.Ct. 1877 [1972]). The attorney acts as an observer and does not have the right to tell the police how to conduct the identification procedure. Most attorneys carefully take notes and, if they believe errors were committed, make a motion in court to suppress testimony about the identification of the defendant. There is no right to counsel during an identification procedure if the suspect is not present. For this reason, photographic line-ups can be done before or after arraignment without notice to either the suspect or the defense attorney (*United States v. Ash,* 413 U.S. 300, 37 L.Ed. 2d 619, 93 S.Ct. 1568 [1973]). The defendant has the right to have counsel present during in-court identification procedures. This applies whenever a witness is asked if the person who committed the crime is present. It does not matter whether the identification is made before, during, or after the court hearing (*Moore v. Illinois,* 434 U.S. 220, 54 L.Ed. 2d 424, 98 S.Ct. 458 [1977]).

In the area of identification procedures, due process means that the police must not use **unduly suggestive** techniques. If there is a substantial likelihood of mistaken identification, the evidence will not be admissible in court (*Kirby v. Illinois,* 406 U.S. 682, 32 L.Ed. 2d 411, 92 S.Ct. 1877 [1972]). Line-ups and photographic line-ups have many of the same

---

Kirby v. Illinois

406 U.S. 682, 32 L.Ed. 2d 411, 92 S.Ct. 1877 (1972)

Issue: Right to Counsel during Line-ups

"The initiation of judicial criminal proceedings is far from a mere formalism. It is the starting point of our whole system of adversary criminal justice. For it is only then that the government has committed itself to prosecute, and only then that the adverse positions of government and defendant have solidified. It is then that a defendant finds himself faced with the prosecutorial forces of organized society, and immersed in the intricacies of substantive and procedural criminal law. It is this point, therefore, that marks the commencement of the 'criminal prosecutions' to which alone the explicit guarantees of the Sixth Amendment are applicable.

"In this case, we are asked to import into a routine police investigation an absolute constitutional guarantee historically and rationally applicable only after the onset of formal prosecutorial proceedings. We decline to do so.

* * *

"What has been said is not to suggest that there may not be occasions during the course of a criminal investigation when the police do abuse identification procedures. Such abuses are not beyond the reach of the Constitution. As the Court pointed out in Wade itself, it is always necessary to 'scrutinize any pretrial confrontation. . . .' The Due Process Clause of the Fifth and Fourteenth Amendments forbids a lineup that is unnecessarily suggestive and conducive to irreparable mistaken identification."

---

problems. Nothing in the way these procedures are conducted should point to the person who the police believe committed the crime. There must be a good selection of individuals with similar characteristics; five to seven are usually recommended. Each person in the line-up must match the general description of the perpetrator of the crime. The goal is to have participants who are sufficiently similar, so that there is no indication which one is the suspect. Anything that makes one person stand out is unduly suggestive. If one participant is asked to do or say something, all others in the line-up must do equivalent acts. This applies whether the police or a viewer initiated the request. Police must be cautious, so that they do not say anything in the presence of the people viewing the line-up that would suggest which one is the suspect. A prepared statement, including a warning that the person who committed the crime may not be in the line-up, is usually read to the witnesses. Care must also be exercised to prevent witnesses from conferring or in any way indicating to other viewers whom they selected.

Many of the protections against unduly suggestive line-ups do not apply to show-ups because there is usually only one person for the witness to identify. While the court will expect a rational explanation for using a show-up rather than a line-up, it is not necessary to establish that an emergency (e.g., the only eye witness is about to die) necessitated the show-up.

When evaluating show-ups, the United States Supreme Court focused on the reliability of the identification. Factors considered include the opportunity the witness had to view the suspect at the time of the crime (including the lighting and the length of time the witness was with the suspect); the degree of attention the witness paid to the suspect while the crime was in progress; the level of certainty of the witness when identifying the suspect; the accuracy of the description that was initially given to the police; the prior inaccurate identifications made by the witness; and the length of time between the show-up and the crime (*Neil v. Biggers*, 409 U.S. 188, 34 L.Ed. 2d 401, 93 S.Ct. 375 [1972]).

The prosecution cannot introduce testimony about inappropriately conducted identification procedures as part of its case-in-chief, but it may want to have the witness take the stand and identify the suspect during the trial. This will only be allowed if the prosecutor can show that the taint of the improperly conducted procedure has not infected the in-court identification (*Gilbert v. California*, 388 U.S. 263, 18 L.Ed. 2d 1178, 87 S.Ct. 1951 [1967]). If the witness is sure that the point of reference for the in-court identification is what transpired at the crime scene, not recollection of the line-up, the judge frequently allows the witness to point out who he/she believes committed the crime.

5-4 Right to Counsel

The right to counsel is guaranteed by the Sixth Amendment. Most of the case law has focused on when the government must provide attorneys for indigent defendants. It is now settled that counsel must be provided for the poor in all criminal cases, except minor offenses, such as infractions and misdemeanors that will not result in jail sentences (*Scott v. Illinois*, 440 U.S. 367, 59 L.Ed. 2d 383, 99 S.Ct. 1158 [1979]; *Nichols v. United States*, 511 U.S. 738, 128 L.Ed. 2d 745, 114 S.Ct. 1921 [1994]). The basic rule is that these services extend from arraignment through sentencing. A court appearance to enter a guilty plea is also covered (*Brady v. United States*, 397 U.S. 742, 25 L.Ed. 2d 747, 90 S.Ct. 1463 [1970]; *McMann v. Richardson*, 397 U.S. 759, 25 L.Ed. 2d 763, 90 S.Ct. 1441 [1970]; *Parker v. North Carolina*, 397 U.S. 790, 25 L.Ed. 2d 785, 90 S.Ct. 1458 [1970]). Providing an attorney to handle the first appeal is mandated, but subsequent appeals and *habeas corpus* proceedings do not require a government-funded lawyer for the defendant (*Pennsylvania v. Finley*, 481 U.S. 551, 95 L.Ed. 2d 539, 107 S.Ct. 1990 [1987]; *Ross v. Moffitt*, 417 U.S. 600, 41 L.Ed. 2d 341, 94 S.Ct. 2437

[1974]). The judge has the responsibility of advising the defendant of this right and reviewing any claim of financial need.

After ruling on many cases arguing that the government must provide attorneys, the Supreme Court heard a case in which the defendant wanted to represent himself at trial, even though the state had insisted on providing an attorney. The case was decided in the defendant's favor. The only factors that can be considered are the defendant's awareness of the right to counsel and whether a voluntary waiver was made by a mentally competent defendant (*Faretta v. California*, 422 U.S. 806, 45 L.Ed. 2d 562, 95 S.Ct. 2525 [1975]).

Police need to be aware of the right to counsel because special precautions must be taken in dealing with a defendant who has an attorney. Section 5-2, "Interrogation," explained that, once a suspect invokes the *Miranda* right to have an attorney present, the police may not question him/her about any crime without an attorney present. This applies to all subsequent custodial interrogations. Once the suspect is released from custody, a different rule applies.

Massiah v. United States (377 U.S. 201, 12 L.Ed. 2d 246, 84 S.Ct. 1199 [1963]) was decided two years before *Miranda*. *Massiah* involved the use of an informant to question a suspect who had been indicted and released from custody. The Supreme Court ruled that this violated the right to counsel. Note that this rule applies to all interrogations, not just those done while the suspect is in custody. Passive listening, without asking questions, is not covered (*Kulhman v. Wilson*, 477 U.S. 436, 91 L.Ed. 2d 364, 106 S.Ct. 2616 [1986]). Later cases indicate that a waiver of the right to counsel must be obtained prior to questioning, but if the suspect is not in custody the waiver can be obtained without an attorney present. *Miranda* warnings can be used for this purpose (*Patterson v. Illinois*, 487 U.S. 285, 101 L.Ed. 2d 261, 108 S.Ct. 2389 [1988]). The right to counsel that is triggered when the defendant asks the court to appoint an attorney, unlike the *Miranda* one, applies only to charges that have been filed in that case (*McNeil v. Wisconsin*, 501 U.S. 171, 115 L.Ed. 2d 158, 111 S.Ct. 2204 [1991]; *Texas v. Cobb*, 532 U.S. 162, 149 L.Ed. 2d 231, 121 S.Ct. 1335 [2001]). It covers all future proceedings in the case, whether in court or police interrogation (*Michigan v. Jackson*, 475 U.S. 625, 89 L.Ed. 2d 631, 106 S.Ct. 1404 [1986]). Out-of-custody questioning about crimes not included in the charges that were filed can be done by officers or surreptitiously by informants without notice of the right to counsel.

Interaction with the defendant in the courtroom or halls of the courthouse raise right to counsel issues. Once the arraignment has begun, the defendant must have an attorney present during any type of confrontation unless a specific waiver has been obtained. This applies to questioning the defendant as well as attempting to have witnesses identify him/her as the perpetrator of the crime (*Moore v. Illinois,* 434 U.S. 220, 54 L.Ed. 2d 424, 98 S.Ct. 458 [1977]). It also applies to psychiatric evaluations and other procedures done at the behest of the prosecution (*Estelle v. Smith,* 451 U.S. 454, 68 L.Ed. 2d 359, 101 S.Ct. 1866 [1981]; *Powell v. Texas,* 492 U.S. 680, 106 L.Ed. 2d 551, 109 S.Ct. 3146 [1989]).

Chapter Summary

The Fifth Amendment applies to testimonial communications that can result in criminal liability of the person who makes the statements. No Fifth Amendment rights can be asserted if the person has been granted immunity on the charges, the statute of limitations has run, or double jeopardy would prevent a new prosecution. A suspect can be compelled to provide nontestimonial evidence, such as blood, breath, or urine samples; fingerprints or DNA specimens; and voice or handwriting exemplars.

Miranda warnings must be given prior to custodial interrogation. Officers must make sure that the suspect understands his/her rights. Questioning will be admissible by the prosecution *only if* there is a knowing, intelligent, and voluntary waiver. If there is a waiver but questioning is interrupted, interrogation may be resumed at any time. After a suspect invokes the right to remain silent, questioning may be resumed after a sufficient time lapse to indicate that the suspect's rights were scrupulously honored *and* there is a new *Miranda* waiver. If the suspect requests an attorney, police may resume custodial interrogation *only if* there is an attorney present *and* a new waiver is obtained.

Suspects cannot use the Fifth Amendment privilege to refuse to participate in identification procedures. Photographic line-ups are usually done without the suspect present; because of this, neither the right to counsel nor any Fourth Amendment issues are involved. Police cannot compel a person to participate in a show-up or line-up unless there are legal grounds to detain him/her. Reasonable suspicion is sufficient to stop a person and conduct a show-up at that location; probable cause is required to transport a suspect to the police station for identification. A suspect has the right to have an attorney present at a line-up or show-up *only if* the event occurs after arraignment or indictment. Due process forbids line-ups, whether in person or photographic, that are unduly suggestive. Nothing about the selection of suspects or the way the procedure is conducted should point to one individual. Show-ups are judged by the credibility of the person making the identification.

Miranda warnings inform the suspect of the right to have an attorney present during questioning. These rules cover questioning about any crime while the suspect remains in custody. The Sixth Amendment right to counsel focuses on court proceedings. From the time of the arraignment through the first appeal, the suspect has a right to counsel at government expense if he/she cannot afford to retain one. During this time period, a waiver of the right to counsel is required in order to question the suspect about charges that have already been filed, *even if* he/she has been released from custody. Attempts to have eye witnesses identify the suspect also involve the right to counsel, whether done at a line-up, at a show-up, or during a court appearance.

Study Questions

1. List three situations in which a suspect cannot claim the Fifth Amendment as grounds to refuse to answer questions.
2. List three types of evidence that the suspect can be compelled to give without violating the Fifth Amendment.
3. State the *Miranda* warnings and explain each one.
4. Explain the standard for a valid waiver of the *Miranda* rights.
5. If a suspect has already invoked the right to remain silent, when can police renew attempts to interrogate him/her? Explain.
6. If a suspect has already invoked the right to have an attorney present during questioning, when can police renew attempts to interrogate him/her? Explain.
7. When can statements obtained in violation of *Miranda* be used in court? Explain.
8. Explain how to conduct a valid line-up and a valid show-up.
9. When does a suspect have the right to have the government pay for his/her attorney? Explain.
10. What procedures must the police follow if they wish to question a person *after* he/she has been arraigned on the charges to be discussed? Explain.

True or False Questions

F 1. A suspect can use the Fifth Amendment as a valid reason to refuse to participate in a show-up.

T 2. A suspect who has been given immunity cannot invoke his/her *Miranda* rights to avoid answering questions that relate to the crime for which immunity was given.

T 3. *Miranda* warnings are required prior to custodial interrogation.

T 4. A wavier of *Miranda* rights obtained by using coercion on the suspect is not valid.

T 5. An oral waiver of *Miranda* rights is valid.

F 6. Once a suspect invokes the right to remain silent, all subsequent statements the suspect makes to the police will be inadmissible in court.

F 7. A suspect's constitutional rights are violated if the suspect requests an attorney during custodial interrogation and the police do not immediately provide an attorney for the suspect.

T 8. The right to have an attorney present during questioning is the same before and after arraignment.

T 9. Photographic lineups that are unduly suggestive violate due process.

F 10. Suspects have the right to have their attorneys present at all lineups.

Chapter

6

Authority of Other Investigative Agencies

Outline

Key Terms

administrative hearing
alcoholic beverage control
attorney general's office
Bureau of Alcohol, Tobacco,
  and Firearms (ATF)
Central Child Abuse Index
Children's Protective
  Services
contract cities
coroner

coroner's jury
criminal history
Department of Justice
Department of Motor
  Vehicles
Drug Enforcement
  Administration (DEA)
exclusive jurisdiction
Federal Bureau of
  Investigation (FBI)

implied consent
inquest
joint jurisdiction
mutual aid agreements
"off-sale" license
"on-sale" license
Secret Service
sheriff's department
wants and warrants

Learning Objectives

Learning Objectives

After reading this chapter, the student will be able to

- Explain the types of cases handled by each of the following federal agencies: Federal Bureau of Investigation; Drug Enforcement Administration; Bureau of Alcohol, Tobacco, and Firearms; and Secret Service.
- Diagram the interaction between local law enforcement and the state agency which regulates sales of alcoholic beverages.
- Describe the interaction between local law enforcement and the state agency which regulates motor vehicle registration and drivers' licenses.
- Describe the interaction between local law enforcement and the state attorney general's office.
- Explain mutual aid agreements.
- Compare and contrast the relationship between city police and the sheriff's department.
- Explain the role of the coroner.
- Outline the role of Children's Protective Services.

Local police officers handle a wide variety of cases. Most other law enforcement agencies are more specialized. A police department may seek assistance from the experts in these specialized agencies. Sometimes the law gives only one agency the authority to handle certain types of cases; this is called **exclusive jurisdiction.** When such a crime occurs, the case must be transferred to that agency. More commonly, the law gives two or more enforcement agencies jurisdiction over the same event. This is referred to as **joint jurisdiction.** The people in both agencies must reach an understanding regarding the handling of these types of cases. This chapter describes the roles of a variety of investigative agencies.

6-1 Federal Agencies

There are many federal agencies with law enforcement responsibilities. Some are widely known. Others, such as the Securities and Exchange Commission, primarily regulate civil transactions but have small law enforcement units, which are highly specialized. Good working relationships between federal and local law enforcement are important. All law enforcement officers need to know which crimes are within the exclusive jurisdiction of specialized agencies. Information on these crimes should be transmitted to the appropriate personnel immediately. When two agencies have authority to handle a case, they must be able to reach agreement rapidly on what each will do. Prior arrangements for making these decisions are necessary in order to investigate crime effectively. A poorly coordinated response can result in failure to do a thorough investigation, loss of important pieces of evidence, needless duplication of efforts, and unpunished criminals.

6-1a Federal Bureau of Investigation

The **Federal Bureau of Investigation (FBI),** which is part of the Justice Department, is the general law enforcement agency for the federal government. All federal crimes not assigned to other agencies are investigated by the FBI. Its jurisdiction over espionage and treason gives it authority to act as an intelligence-gathering agency. The FBI National Academy at Quantico, Virginia, provides management courses for police chiefs and other management personnel, as well as classes on specialized techniques for investigators.

The list of crimes the FBI handles changes as Congress enacts new criminal laws and redefines the jurisdiction of other federal agencies. Criminal violations of the federal Civil Rights Act are investigated by the FBI. Some of the crimes handled by the FBI are also covered by state law. For example, robbing a bank is a federal crime if the bank is insured by the Federal Deposit Insurance Corporation (FDIC) and is robbery under state law; taking stolen vehicles across state lines comes within the FBI's jurisdiction because it violates the Dyer Act but can also be charged as grand theft auto in the state where the vehicle was stolen.

The FBI has offices in most major cities. Resident agents are located in many smaller cities and rural areas. Each police department needs to keep a list of crimes handled by the FBI and know how to contact FBI agents who are assigned to their area. Both patrol officers and detectives should know when to notify the FBI of criminal activity.

Another function assigned to the FBI is operation of the National Crime Information Center (NCIC). This is a computerized data bank on wanted persons, vehicles, and other items. Data are forwarded to the FBI by local agencies for inclusion. Modern communications equipment enables officers in the field and dispatchers to query the system.

The Uniform Crime Report (UCR) system is maintained by the FBI. *Crime in the United States,* a book published annually giving statistics on offenses reported, arrests, and clearances by police departments, is the main product of this system. Originally information was submitted to the FBI in tabular form monthly by local agencies. Many states now have a centralized agency, which collects the data from the police departments and sends summaries to the FBI. The UCR is not a report on investigations conducted by FBI agents.

6-1b Drug Enforcement Administration

Drug Enforcement Administration (DEA) is responsible for enforcing federal laws regulating controlled substances. The United States is a signatory to the Single Convention on Narcotic Drugs, signed in New York on March 30, 1961, and the Convention on Psychotropic Substances, signed in Vienna, Austria, on February 21, 1971. Title 21 of the United States Code contains the federal laws restricting controlled substances. Title 21 also mandates that the attorney general cooperate with local, state, and other federal agencies concerning trafficking in controlled substances and drug abuse. Upon the request of the attorney general, it is the duty of all federal agencies to furnish assistance, including technical advice, to the drug enforcement activities of the Justice Department. The combination of these laws gives the DEA authority to act worldwide and with all levels of law enforcement within the United States.

DEA has authority in two main areas: the prevention of controlled substances originating with legitimate pharmaceutical manufacturers from reaching inappropriate distributors and the investigation of traffic in illicit drugs. Many pharmaceutical firms manufacture drugs with legitimate medicinal value which are on the controlled substances list. DEA is authorized to inspect factories, wholesalers, retailers, pharmacies, and doctors' offices where controlled substances are stored. DEA's rights include copying and verifying all records these firms are required to keep, as well as inspecting the premises for finished and unfinished drugs, containers, and labels. DEA is not involved with financial records, sales figures unrelated to shipments, or pricing information.

Title 21 provides for the issuing of administrative warrants if necessary to conduct these inspections. No warrant is required if there is imminent danger to health or safety, reasonable cause to believe that the mobility of a vehicle makes it impracticable to obtain a warrant, or other emergency circumstances.

DEA is also heavily involved in preventing sales of drugs that are illicitly manufactured or smuggled into the United States. The international agreements give DEA the authority to enter foreign countries that have signed these conventions in order to prevent smuggling into the United States. Their authority to request assistance from other federal agencies has been used to involve the military in these activities. Equally important is cooperation with local law enforcement agencies. DEA usually investigates large-scale drug sales and smuggling operations, while local law enforcement handles cases involving smaller quantities. Information obtained during any type of investigation should be passed on to the appropriate agency. What initially appears to be a small drug ring may turn out to be an international operation.

6-1c Bureau of Alcohol, Tobacco, and Firearms

Bureau of Alcohol, Tobacco, and Firearms (ATF) was originally a unit of the Internal Revenue Service but has been a separate bureau in the Treasury Department since 1972. It enforces the following laws: Title XI (Explosives) of the Organized Crime Control Act of 1970; Gun Control Act of 1968 as currently amended; Anti-Arson Act of 1982; Federal Alcohol Administration Act of 1935; alcohol, tobacco, and firearms provisions of the Internal Revenue Code; Contraband Cigarette Law of 1978; and provisions of the Arms Export Control Act of 1976 relating to importation of firearms, ammunition, and implements of war.

ATF is concerned with compliance as well as law enforcement. The compliance function is designed to ensure that the firearms, explosives, alcohol, and tobacco industries comply with federal law, pay federal excise and occupational taxes, and obtain required licenses and permits. Illicit production of alcohol ("moonshine") is now infrequent, but ATF investigates and prosecutes bribery, kickbacks, and payoffs within the alcohol industry. False labeling and product contamination in the wine industry are within ATF's jurisdiction. It also assists states experiencing problems with smuggling of cigarettes and counterfeit tax stamps on cigarettes.

ATF investigates criminal bombings and thefts of explosives. Criminal use of explosive materials, as well as unsafe storage, are also its concern. A computerized Explosives Incidents System (EXIS), which contains information on all explosives incidents reported to and/or investigated by ATF, is used to match targets and motives of suspected bombers as well as identify those who use similar explosive devices. ATF shares information from this system with local law enforcement and has an agreement with the Defense Department for reciprocal exchange of information regarding thefts and recoveries of military ordinances. The National Explosives Tracing Center (NETC), operated by ATF, is used to trace the source of recovered, stolen, or abandoned explosives. It can also trace foreign commercial and military explosives.

The National Firearms Act of 1934 regulates machine guns, sawed-off shotguns, and some other "gangster-type" weapons. ATF's enforcement powers over firearms has been expanded, so that it now has task forces which target armed career criminals and violent gangs for prosecution in federal court. These activities require coordination with a variety of other federal and local agencies, particularly the DEA and the FBI. Stolen firearms transported in interstate commerce are under ATF's jurisdiction. ATF also works to combat international traffic in illegal firearms and ammunition. The National Tracing Center is operated by ATF to assist law enforcement authorities from all over the world in locating the source of recovered firearms.

Major arson-for-profit crimes involving commercial and industrial interstate activities are investigated by ATF. National Response Teams provide 24-hour response to any major arson, explosive, or explosives-related incident in the geographical United States. ATF provides assistance if a major arson problem exists which exceeds the local agency's resources or involves multiple jurisdictions. Laboratories operated by ATF analyze arson debris for local law enforcement agencies, and ATF Audit Staff assist in analyzing financial information on suspects in arson-for-profit cases.

Numerous training courses are offered to local law enforcement agencies on arson, explosives, firearms, and the smuggling of contraband cigarettes. Gang-related information-sharing conferences are hosted yearly. Advanced courses are given at the Federal Law Enforcement Training Center in Glynco, Georgia. A training course on arson-for-profit investigation is offered for insurance investigators.

6-1d Secret Service

Secret Service is a branch of the Treasury Department. It has two distinctly different functions: provide protection for the president of the United States and other dignitaries and investigate crimes involving federal obligations (currency, bonds, etc.) and certain other crimes assigned to it by Congress.

Secret Service provides protection for the president and vice president of the United States (and president-elect and vice president-elect) and immediate members of their families; former presidents and their spouses for life, except that protection for a former president's spouse stops if he/she remarries; children of a former president who are under 16 years of age; visiting heads of state or foreign governments; other distinguished foreign visitors to the United States; official representatives of the United States performing special missions abroad when the president directs that protection be provided; and major presidential and vice presidential candidates and, within 120 days of the general presidential election, the spouses of such candidates. Secret Service relies heavily upon local law enforcement and fire departments for assistance whenever any of the people it protects travel. Threats to kill or kidnap the president, president-elect, vice president, or vice president-elect are investigated by the FBI, not Secret Service.

The best known investigative function of Secret Service involves counterfeit money. Title 18, Section 3056, of the United States Code authorizes it to investigate violations of federal law involving "coins, obligations and securities" of the United States and foreign governments. "Obligations" include currency, stamps, bonds, passports, immigration papers, and food stamps. The same section empowers Secret Service to handle a variety of crimes against the Federal Deposit Insurance Corporation, federal land banks, and federal land bank associations.

The most recent additions to Secret Service's agenda involve fraudulent forms of financial transactions: electronic fund transfer, credit and debit cards, and false identification documents or devices. Interaction with other federal agencies, particularly the Postal Inspectors, is common. Secret Service frequently obtains information from local law enforcement to start these investigations. They work closely with local agencies to complete many cases.

6-1e Other Agencies

There are many other federal agencies with law enforcement responsibilities. The following list, which in no way covers all the federal agencies and regulatory commissions, illustrates those with investigative powers: Civil Aeronautics Board; Commission on Civil Rights; Commodities Futures Trading Commission; Consumer Product Safety Commission; Environmental Protection Agency; Equal Employment Opportunity Commission; Farm Credit Administration; Federal Communications Commission; Federal Deposit Insurance Corporation; Federal Elections Commission; Federal Trade Commission; General Services Administration; Interstate Commerce Commission; National Aeronautics and Space Administration; National Labor Relations Board; National Transportation Safety Board; Occupational Safety and Health Administration; Securities and Exchange Commission; Small Business Administration; U.S. Postal Service; and Veterans Administration. Some of these agencies do the complete investigation in cases involving laws within their jurisdiction; others use FBI agents if there is evidence of criminal wrongdoing.

6-2 State Agencies

There are many state-level agencies which are involved in law enforcement. Some, such as the Highway Patrol, are very visible. Others, such as the Department of Fish and Game, may be well known but not generally thought of as law enforcement agencies. A smooth working relationship between each police department and state agencies is important. First, it is necessary to determine what each agency is authorized to do. Laws creating specialized agencies may have a uniform purpose, but the legislative process results in minor differences among the laws of the various states. Officers cannot safely assume that they have the authority to act because police in another state do. For example, in some but not all states, laws regulating junkyards give the city police the right to inspect junkyards, without probable cause, to look for parts taken from stolen vehicles.

Second, local police departments and state agencies need to establish good working relationships. This is particularly important where the law gives both agencies the authority to act. Patrol officers need to know whether to handle the call or wait for personnel from a state agency to arrive. This involves policies of both agencies. It also requires a cooperative arrangement between the state agency's local office and the police department. Other factors, such as the distance each officer needs to travel to reach the crime scene, may also be important. Coordination of responses is crucial. The case may be lost if officers from both agencies assume the other agency is going to complete important parts of the investigation. Petty jealousies about who will get credit for the case also lead to improperly conducted investigations. The end result of these problems is unprofessional conduct and loss of the public's respect.

6-2a Alcoholic Beverage Control

Nearly every state has an agency charged with **alcoholic beverage control.** The exact name varies from state to state; it will be referred to in this chapter as ABC. The functions of this agency usually involve issuing licenses to sell alcohol and conducting inspections of premises which are licensed or should be licensed.

The licensing function is usually performed exclusively by ABC personnel. They verify that the applications have been completed properly. Investigations are usually conducted to determine if the owners have criminal backgrounds or ties to organized crime that would disqualify them. The investigation may be more extensive for **"on-sale" licenses** (bars, etc., where drinks will be consumed at the location where they are sold) than for **"off-sale" licenses** (liquor stores, etc.). State laws may also differentiate between private clubs and bars open to the public and bars that primarily sell liquor as opposed to "beer bars" and restaurants which serve drinks with meals. Special permits may be available for a limited time, such as for the day of a company picnic. Information on the number of alcoholic beverage licenses already issued for the immediate area may be considered.

Proximity of the licensed premises to churches and schools is frequently factored in. Sometimes public hearings are held to determine if people in the neighborhood object. If the application successfully passes the investigation, the license is usually issued for a specific length of time, such as five years. An application for renewal must be made when the license expires and another investigation is conducted.

State licensing laws usually provide that establishments serving alcohol may be inspected at any time. Records and other items may be checked to confirm that the establishment is selling only what is allowed by its license. Record inspections are normally done by ABC personnel.

State law usually allows officers to verify that regulations are followed when selling alcoholic beverages. "Bar checks"—going into "on-sale" establishments and checking the ages of people present or verifying that drinks are not sold after the legally mandated closing time—are frequently done by local police as well as ABC personnel. This may also be true for conducting surveillance to make sure liquor stores are not selling to minors.

Violations of laws regulating the sale of alcoholic beverages, such as selling beer to a minor, are grounds to revoke or suspend the license. Police officers who observe violations of these laws may be called as witnesses. The licensee is usually entitled to an **administrative hearing,** at which ABC personnel must present evidence to establish that there are legal grounds for the action. The hearing, which is usually conducted before a hearing officer or an administrative law judge, may be less formal than a court hearing. Due process requirements, such as notice prior to the hearing and a chance to respond, must be met. Administrative hearings frequently use more lenient rules of evidence, particularly as to hearsay. The standard of proof is usually a preponderance of the evidence. Some states make revocation of a license appealable to the civil court system; others require administrative appeals to be taken first. Charging the licensee with violating criminal laws and simultaneously attempting to revoke the license does not violate double jeopardy because license revocation is not a criminal proceeding.

6-2b Department of Motor Vehicles

States regulate the registration of vehicles and licensing of drivers. One state agency, **Department of Motor Vehicles,** referred to in this chapter as DMV, usually handles both of these functions. Local law enforcement officers interact with them less directly than with ABC.

DMV handles a complex system of vehicle registration ranging from passenger cars to commercial trucking. It may also license mobile homes

T A B L E   **6-1 Comparison of Criminal Trial and Administrative Hearing**

	Criminal Trial	Administrative Hearing
Who files complaint	District attorney or city prosecutor	Agency seeking to enforce its rules
What can be charged	Violation of criminal law	Violation of agency regulations
Where hearing will take place	Courthouse	Hearing room (several agencies may share hearing room)
Who presides over hearing	Judge	Hearing officer or administrative law judge
Who presents case	District attorney or city prosecutor	Officer of agency bringing action
Use of jury	At request of prosecution or defense	No jury
Rules of evidence	Strictly enforced	May admit hearsay and some other types of evidence not allowed in court
Use of precedence	Judge bound by decisions in prior cases	Hearing officer not bound by decisions in prior cases
Atmosphere	Formal	Less formal
Sanctions imposed	Conviction of crime—prison, jail, etc.	Suspend/revoke license, fines
Appeal	Next higher level court	Usually to higher administrative court and then civil court

and a variety of other conveyances. Part of this function is performed through car dealers who prepare the necessary forms when cars are bought and sold. DMV may make special arrangements, so that dealers collect registration fees and perform other functions. When problems arise, such as failure to forward fees to the state or falsification of registration, DMV personnel usually have sole responsibility for handling them. Local law enforcement rarely becomes involved in the registration functions, although they may issue citations for expired registration, take stolen vehicle reports from car dealers, and be called to a dealership when a dissatisfied customer becomes unruly.

Driver's licenses are normally issued directly from DMV. Testing, whether written or "behind the wheel," is usually done by DMV examiners. Too many traffic tickets for hazardous violations is usually grounds for suspension or revocation of the license. Violation of rules, such as being involved in a collision when not covered by insurance, may also be grounds for suspension or revocation of the license.

Traffic citations written by police are processed through the local court. DMV is notified by the court when a driver is convicted. Data on the conviction are entered into an automated data bank maintained by DMV. The computer generates notices to the driver when a certain quota of convictions has been reached, such as three moving violations in 12 months. The person whose license is about to be suspended or revoked has the right to request a hearing. Sometimes officers who wrote the tickets are called to testify. As with ABC hearings, the revocation or suspension is usually handled through an administrative process rather than the courts. There may be an appeals process within the administrative framework; it may also be possible to make a final appeal to the state's courts. The outcome of the administrative hearing does not change the action taken in traffic court. Double jeopardy is not violated because DMV actions are not considered criminal proceedings.

Most states have **implied consent** laws, which make a suspected drunk driver's refusal to take a chemical test for intoxication grounds for suspending his/her license. The vehicle code makes consent to take these tests a condition of issuing the driver's license. Specific tests, such as blood alcohol, breathalyzer, and urine analysis, are usually specified. Many states require that the driver be given a choice of tests. Procedures for the police to follow are mandated. License suspension is authorized only if the implied consent rule applies to the administrative process used by DMV to suspend licenses. It does not regulate the admissibility of evidence of intoxication at a trial for driving under the influence (DUI). These separate rules for the two procedures can lead to the following results: a driver can successfully challenge the attempt to suspend his/her license because a blood test was taken without offering the variety of tests specified in the vehicle code; the same driver may be convicted of DUI because the rules at trial permit the test to be used as relevant evidence on the DUI charge. It is also possible to suspend the license of a person who refused to take a mandated test, even though the DUI prosecution resulted in an acquittal.

6-2c Attorney General

Each state has an attorney general, who normally heads the state's Department of Justice. There is a great deal of variation among states, but the following functions are typically handled by the state **Department of Justice,** frequently referred to as the **attorney general's office:** investigate certain types of crimes; provide assistance to local law enforcement agencies; operate a data bank containing names of wanted persons; maintain criminal histories ("rap" sheets); compile statistics on crimes committed in the state; represent the state when defendants appeal felony convictions; and perform a variety of non-criminal functions. The Department of Justice frequently takes over criminal investigations when there would be a conflict of interest if a local agency handled the case. An example would be allegations that the chief of police is involved in criminal activity. The Department of Justice may also have experts available to assist small agencies. Department of Justice personnel may staff criminalistics laboratories. In some states, the Department of Justice operates task forces, which investigate drug dealers, gang activity, and other problems. Each police department needs to be aware of the services provided by the Department of Justice, so it can use them effectively.

Maintaining **criminal history** information is a database operation. A system is established so that the courts notify the Department of Justice when a person is convicted. Depending on the state's record-keeping system, arrest information may also be maintained even though a conviction does not occur. Information is entered into a computerized data bank. Police departments query the system to find out if a suspect has prior convictions. Laws regulating the right to privacy have restricted access to this data bank except when necessary as part of a criminal investigation, in the preparation of a pre-sentence investigation report, or for required records checks prior to employment in specified jobs.

A database on wanted persons, often called **wants and warrants,** is frequently operated at the state level by the Department of Justice, in addition to the National Crime Information Center (NCIC) operated by the FBI. The Department of Justice establishes criteria for entering into and removing names from the database. Each police department must pay close attention to the procedures for adding and deleting information in order to keep the system up-to-date. All law enforcement agencies in the state usually have access to this database. The equipment is now available, so that officers can query the system directly from their patrol cars. This is invaluable for the officer making a stop of a suspicious person in the field.

Other specialized databases may also be operated by the Department of Justice. A common one is the **Central Child Abuse Index,** which is a key component of many states' mandatory reporting systems. This index provides information on prior reports of physical and sexual abuse as well as criminal neglect. It can usually be searched by the name of either the suspect or the victim. Some states have recently started computerized databases on protective orders issued in domestic violence cases. Any police department in the state can use this system to verify that a valid order is in effect, even though they do not have a copy in their own files. Two problems frequently encountered in domestic violence cases make the statewide file particularly important: victims may be accosted by their abusers at unanticipated locations as they travel, and verifying the expiration date of the protective order is critical in order to determine whether it can be enforced.

Two types of criminal statistics can be generated by the Department of Justice: incident statistics and offender-based statistics. Incident statistics give the frequency with which specific events (e.g., murders, robberies, rapes, burglaries, and grand thefts) are reported to the police. Other information may also be tabulated, such as the number of arrests and/or clearances for each crime. Incident statistics are tabulated by the local agency, usually by computer, and forwarded to the Department of Justice monthly, quarterly, or annually. The state Department of Justice forwards copies of some of these reports to the FBI for inclusion in the Uniform Crime Reports. The data may also be used at the state level to generate a variety of reports.

Offender-based statistics are tabulated from information sheets that follow the offender through the system from arrest to sentencing. Law enforcement typically initiates the paperwork on the offender and then forwards it to the courts. After disposition of the case (dismissal, acquittal, or sentencing), the form goes to the Department of Justice, where the data are analyzed and reports are made available to law enforcement and the public. Offender-based statistics provide better information on how the criminal justice system is operating because they make it possible to see the disposition of cases. Due to delays among arrest, trial, and sentencing, the final statistics produced do not match the incident reports for the year in which the crimes occur.

6-2d Other State Agencies

Many other state-level law enforcement agencies exist, frequently as small units within departments not usually associated with investigating criminal activity—for example, Bureau of Consumer Affairs; Department of Fish and Game; Board of Medical Examiners; State Bar; Department of Forestry; Insurance Commissioner; Department of Corporations; and many more. It is important that each police agency be familiar with these agencies for two reasons: their investigators frequently have expertise that is invaluable to officers who rarely handle specialized cases, and state law may require participation by state-level investigators in some cases.

6-3 Local Agencies

Cooperation among local agencies is as important, if not more so, than cooperation among federal, state, and local agencies. Patrol officers, in many instances, interact with other local agencies on a daily basis. Sometimes the role assigned some of these agencies appears to conflict with that of the police department. This makes it doubly important that personnel on both sides try to understand each other's duties and work together in a professional manner.

6-3a Mutual Aid Agreements

State law normally gives local police officers jurisdiction to perform law enforcement functions within the city that employs them and to go to other areas of the state when necessary to investigate a crime that occurred within their city. Unusual events, such as riots and natural disasters (fires, earthquakes, hurricanes, etc.), leave a city in need of additional law enforcement personnel. Many cities enter into **mutual aid agreements** with other cities and/or counties, so that they can ask for help when an emergency arises. In effect, the mutual aid agreement gives the officers sent to help in another city the same powers as police officers employed by that city. Mutual aid agreements are formal documents, similar to contracts, and vary from city to city. They may cover all emergency services (police, fire, ambulance) or only one type of service. The agreement may specify the number of personnel who will be sent. More general language calling for "available personnel" is common; this permits a city to refuse to send aid in cases where sending personnel to another city would seriously impair services in the city that employs the officers. Some agreements call for the city requesting assistance to pay for the cost of services rendered, but it is common for the agency that employs the officers to pay their salary. Mutual aid agreements may be more symbolic than truly mutual. For example, an extremely large city may have a mutual aid agreement with a tiny city in its suburbs; it is unlikely that the large agency would benefit from such an agreement, although it could be of enormous benefit to the small department.

6-3b County Sheriff's Department

The role of the **sheriff's department** varies a great deal in the United States. Different functions are performed due to state laws that govern the sheriff; duties may also be different within a state due to agreements among local agencies.

One of the most common roles for the sheriff's department is operating the county jail. Officers working at the jail may be sworn peace officers or have correctional officer status. Some cities also operate jails. Usually the city jails are for presentenced inmates while the county jail houses those serving sentences. New York City Department of Corrections, which operates a large jail on Rykers Island, is an example of a city jail which houses both presentenced and sentenced inmates.

Bailiffs (also called "court services officers" and some other titles) maintain order in courtrooms and may be responsible for the custody of inmates who are in the building for a court appearance or trial. These services are provided by the sheriff's department in some areas and by separate agencies, sometimes called the Marshals, in other locations. The laws in some states, such as California, allow the local counties or judges to decide which agency will provide these services. Bailiffs are employed directly by the courts in some states.

Other court-related functions may be performed by the sheriff's department. These include serving legal papers, such as subpoenas and civil complaints. They may be responsible for carrying out evictions, garnishments, and other court orders.

Many states give the sheriff's department law enforcement duties. Probably the most common is to provide all police services for people who live in unincorporated areas. Depending on the size of the county and its population density, this ranges from serving a few people to over a million inhabitants. Agreements between a city and the county may result in the sheriff's department's providing the police services for an incorporated city. Cities which do this are frequently called **contract cities.** Depending on state law, a contract city can purchase all or part of its police services from the sheriff's department. Contracts may also be permitted between two or more cities.

Larger sheriff's departments provide specialized services, such as a centralized records bureau, criminalistics laboratory, or bomb squad, to cities within their jurisdiction. Sometimes these must be contracted for. Less formal arrangements also exist, such as calling someone in the homicide bureau and asking for advice.

6-3c Coroner

The basic role of the **coroner** is to determine when deaths are the result of criminal conduct. Autopsies are performed for this purpose. Some coroners also have investigators who look for clues outside the medical realm; others rely on local law enforcement agencies to perform these duties.

State laws identify the types of cases which must be referred to the coroner. Deaths under the following circumstances usually require notification of the coroner: deceased had not seen a doctor recently (law usually states a specific period, such as within 10 days); deceased's personal physician was unable to state cause of death; suspected homicide or suicide; death following accident or from gunshot, stabbing, or poison; death occurring shortly after the patient entered the hospital or while the patient was under anesthetic; death in prisons and other custodial facilities; and death of unidentified persons. Patrol officers and hospitals need to be familiar with the list in their state.

The coroner's office must be called when death occurs under the circumstances listed in the local state's laws. What the coroner will do varies with state law and local practice. The coroner's pathologist usually performs the autopsy if criminal activity is suspected. Consent of the deceased's family is not required. Some states permit the coroner to authorize another person, such as the hospital's pathologist, to perform the autopsy if no suspicious circumstances are evident.

Coroners are usually authorized to hold an **inquest.** This is a hearing, similar to a trial, to determine whether the death was by criminal means. The focus of the inquest is on *whether* a criminal homicide occurred, not who committed it or the type of offense (first-degree murder, voluntary manslaughter, etc.). The prosecutor is responsible for filing charges and handling the criminal case after the coroner has ruled that the death was by criminal means. The law may also provide for an inquest to determine whether a person committed suicide. This ruling may be important in determining how much money beneficiaries may collect under the deceased's life insurance policies.

Many states allow the coroner to empanel a jury, commonly referred to as a **coroner's jury,** for the inquest. A preponderance of the evidence is usually required for a finding of death by criminal means. Whether an inquest will be held is determined by local policy and state law. Some states make the inquest mandatory, while others leave it to the discretion of the coroner's office. The result of this discretion is that inquests are very common in some locales but done only rarely in others.

6-3d Children's Protective Services

All states now have laws mandating reporting of child abuse. This includes physical abuse, sexual abuse, and neglect. Law enforcement officers, probation officers, teachers, day care workers, and medical personnel are usually required to report suspected abuse. Other people may report it but are not held criminally liable for failing to do so. Each police officer should know the local law on what must be reported, when, to whom, and on what forms. Typically a report must be made by telephone immediately, with a written report following within one or two days.

Children's Protective Services (referred to in this chapter as CPS, although the exact name varies from state to state) is the social welfare agency that handles abuse cases. Local policing agencies frequently work with CPS if there is suspicion of criminal activity. The goals of law enforcement and CPS are not the same. Police focus on arresting and prosecuting the abuser. CPS's duties center on protecting the abused child. Keeping the family intact is usually a high priority with CPS. In many states CPS handles the civil court proceedings to remove a child from an abusive home. In these cases CPS functions as a placement agency and is usually responsible for locating and overseeing foster care and/or adoption. It is important to coordinate the responses between the police department and CPS. State law may require sharing reports.

6-3e Other Local Agencies

A wide variety of enforcement agencies exist at the local level. For example, some prosecutors employ investigators to help prepare cases for court; airports and school districts may have their own police forces; consumer fraud may be investigated by a local agency. Each police department needs to have a complete list of the investigative agencies that operate within its jurisdiction; policies should be developed, so that officers know when to notify these agencies of possible criminal activity. The police department's job is made easier if there is a coordinated response; failure to work harmoniously can result in criminals eluding apprehension and conviction.

Chapter Summary

The structure of American government has resulted in law enforcement agencies at the federal, state, and local levels. Local law enforcement officers need to understand the jurisdiction of other agencies in order to work effectively. Each police department should have policies describing the crimes handled by other agencies and when they should be notified of criminal activity. Cooperation between all agencies is imperative. While the law may give one agency jurisdiction, information gathered by others is frequently essential to solving the crime. Poorly coordinated activities involving multiple agencies—whether acting together or separately—can result in injuries to law enforcement personnel and innocent people. The end result may be that the suspect flees the scene and ultimately escapes without punishment.

The FBI is the best known federal law enforcement agency. It has jurisdiction over all federal felonies that are not specifically assigned by Congress to other federal agencies. DEA investigates the pharmaceutical industry's handling of controlled substances as well as the illicit manufacture and smuggling of drugs. ATF oversees regulation of the alcoholic beverage industry and investigates violations of federal firearms laws. It also handles cases involving bombings and thefts of explosives. In addition, AFT investigates the tobacco industry to enforce the tax provisions that apply. One of Secret Service's functions is to provide protection for the president, vice president, and other designated officials. It investigates counterfeiting of government documents and has recently been assigned bank fraud involving electronic transfers, credit cards, and ATM cards.

Numerous state-level law enforcement agencies exist. ABC regulates the sale of alcoholic beverages. It frequently has exclusive jurisdiction over licensing establishments that sell alcohol. It also does inspections of licensed premises to verify that state laws are being complied with. Patrol officers for the local police department may also do "bar checks" and conduct surveillance to make sure that stores do not sell liquor to minors. Violations of these laws may be used to suspend or revoke the license to sell alcohol. Police officers may be called to testify at administrative hearings held for this purpose.

DMV handles registration of vehicles and drivers. Testing and registration are normally handled by DMV personnel. Citations for vehicle code violations result in trials in traffic court. Convictions are usually recorded in the DMV computer. Excessive violations result in suspension or revocation of the driver's license. Refusal to take a chemical test for intoxication when stopped on suspicion of driving under the influence may also result in suspension of the driver's license. The officer who wrote the citation may be called to testify at an administrative hearing if the driver contests DMV's action.

The state Department of Justice may provide investigators to assist local law enforcement in some situations. Experts may be available to assist a police department; special services, such as a criminalistics laboratory, may be available. Criminal history information is usually maintained by the Department of Justice. The Central Child Abuse Index is also located there. Criminal statistics are compiled and sent to the FBI from this department.

Cooperative interaction among local agencies is necessary. Mutual aid agreements are frequently established, so that a city can request assistance from neighboring jurisdictions in case of an emergency. The sheriff's department usually operates the county jail; it may also provide a variety of other services for cities within the county.

The coroner is responsible for determining whether a death is by criminal means. This is usually done immediately after death; there may be no suspect at the time. Pathologists or other qualified personnel are employed to do autopsies. An inquest, sometimes with a jury, may be held to hear evidence regarding the cause of death. Once the coroner has determined that the death was caused by criminal means, it is the prosecutor's duty to decide how to proceed with the criminal case.

CPS investigates child abuse. The police department will usually handle the part of the case that goes to criminal court. CPS handles the civil proceedings to remove abused children from a home, establish foster care, or place the children for adoption.

Many other agencies exist with law enforcement duties. The expertise of their investigators can greatly assist local law enforcement. Every effort should be made to identify these agencies and to establish good working relationships with them.

Study Questions

1. Describe the interaction among law enforcement agencies at the federal, state, and local levels.
2. Explain the jurisdiction of the following federal agencies and how they work with local police departments:
   a. FBI
   b. ATF
   c. DEA
   d. Secret Service
3. Name five federal agencies (other than those listed in question 2) with law enforcement responsibilities.
4. Differentiate between a criminal trial and an administrative hearing.
5. Describe the functions of the following agencies in your state:
   a. ABC
   b. DMV
   c. Department of Justice

6. Name five state-level agencies in your state (other than those listed in question 5) that have law enforcement responsibilities, and explain
  a. what laws they enforce.
  b. the crimes over which they have exclusive jurisdiction.
  c. how they interact with your local police department.

7. Describe the role of the sheriff's department in your county.

8. Describe the role of the coroner. List the circumstances under which the coroner must be notified of a death under the laws of your state. When are inquests held by your local coroner?

9. Describe the role of Children's Protective Services in your area:
  a. What cases must be reported to CPS?
  b. How do CPS and your local police department divide responsibilities for investigation of child abuse cases?
  c. What types of cases are handled exclusively by CPS?

10. Other than those mentioned in questions 7, 8, and 9, name five other local agencies in your area that have law enforcement responsibilities, and explain
  a. what laws they enforce.
  b. the crimes over which they have exclusive jurisdiction.
  c. how they interact with your local police department.

True or False Questions

1. The Federal Bureau of Investigation has jurisdiction to investigate all federal crimes.

2. The Uniform Crime Reports contain information about cases investigated by federal law enforcement agencies.

3. The federal Drug Enforcement Administration's primary function is to train local police officers on how to investigate illegal drug sales.

4. The federal Bureau of Alcohol, Tobacco, and Firearms has the authority to investigate illegal gun sales.

5. The Secret Service has authority to investigate counterfeiting of foreign currency done in the United States.

6. State alcohol beverage control agencies have the authority to revoke a license to sell alcohol if the licensee is selling alcohol to minors.

7. Revocation of a driver's license is handled in administrative courts by the state's Department of Motor Vehicles.

8. The state's Attorney's General staff is not involved in investigating crimes.

9. A coroner's jury has the authority to mandate that the prosecutor file murder charges.
10. Children's Protective Services has jurisdiction in a case only if a child is physically injured.

The Criminal Complaint and Arraignment

Outline

Key Terms

arraignment	double jeopardy	probable cause hearing
citation	fact pleading	redacting a confession
citing out	filing the complaint	right to a speedy trial
code pleading	joinder	severed
complaint	jurisdiction	statute of limitations
continuance	nolo contendere	tolling the statute
count	plaintiff	of limitations
defendant	plea bargain	venue

Learning Objectives
Learning Objectives

After reading this chapter, the student will be able to

- Explain the prosecutor's role in filing criminal charges.
- Illustrate how the police interact with the prosecutor during the early stages of a case.
- Explain the decision-making process for selecting the charges that will be filed against a defendant.
- List what must be included in a criminal complaint.
- Describe what occurs at an arraignment.

Once the police have arrested a person, the case must be prepared for entry into the court system. The prosecutor's office usually drafts the necessary legal papers. The first court appearance on the charges is called the **arraignment.**

7-1 Role of the Prosecutor

Prior to making an arrest, the police frequently conduct the investigation on their own unless a warrant is needed. Key decisions on how much manpower to devote to the case, how thoroughly to investigate, and when there is enough information to justify an arrest are usually made by police officers. During the investigation the prosecutor may provide legal advice. The extent of this involvement is primarily governed by local custom and staffing levels. When the prosecutor's office has an excessive workload, there may be little interaction with the police, except on major cases. Some police departments employ their own legal advisors to fill this void.

The prosecutor serves as gatekeeper of the criminal courts. Except for independent grand jury investigations, no criminal charges can be filed without the prosecutor's approval. After the arrest, most of the key decisions will be made by the prosecutor. Although local practices vary, the following decisions are usually made by the prosecutor: whether or not to file charges; what charges to file; and whether or not to enter into plea bargains. Many prosecutors consult with the police when making these decisions.

Another important role of the prosecutor is to seek the truth on who is guilty and who is not. Law enforcement officers at times become too emotionally involved in an investigation: "catching the criminal" becomes the goal, even though not all the facts are known. Incentives, such as consideration of the number of arrests an officer has made when promotions are awarded, may also cloud objectivity. The prosecutor should be objective. It is important that the prosecutor review all the facts and not merely file charges against the person that the police arrested for the crime. Care must be taken not to give undue weight to factors such as the prior criminal record of the suspect and the fact that he/she was uncooperative with the police or has a very abrasive personality. Public outcries about the crime must not lead to a rush to file charges when there are too few facts to establish a suspect's guilt.

The available evidence is a primary concern in determining which charges to file. A variety of other considerations may influence the prosecutor's decision to file charges. One is whether the case can be prepared for trial in a timely manner. The Sixth Amendment **right to a speedy trial** gives the defendant the right to have the case dismissed if the period from arraignment to trial is too long. Two key factors usually influence the length of time it will take a case to go to trial: the staffing level of the prosecutor's office and court backlog. Screening of cases becomes necessary if either the prosecutor has insufficient staff or the court becomes overloaded. This screening process usually results in refusal to file weak cases and/or relatively minor charges.

Prosecutors also try to judge the attitude of the public. Filing cases the general public feels are insignificant frequently results in jury verdicts of acquittal. For example, while sex with a juvenile is against the law in most states, in many communities it is improbable that a conviction would result if charges were filed against an 18-year-old high school student for having sex with a very willing 17-year-old sweetheart. Sometimes the reverse is also true. Public outcry may result in the prosecutor's filing charges even though the case is weak.

Most prosecutors are elected officials. The performance of their personnel is an election issue. Win-loss records are used to support reelection or for attack by opponents. Some decisions to prosecute are related to these considerations.

7-2 Police Interaction with the Prosecutor

The prosecutor's office is normally the preliminary stop when the police want a warrant. Most jurisdictions require that the prosecutor screen the application before the request is taken to the judge. A prosecutor usually reviews the facts and assists with the drafting of affidavits and other necessary paperwork. If it appears that probable cause is lacking, the prosecutor will inform the police that additional information must be obtained prior to seeking the warrant.

How the police interact with the prosecutor to obtain the complaint is usually the result of two things: local custom and the types of charges. Three scenarios are common after the suspect is booked: the arresting officer takes the case to the prosecutor; detectives handle follow-up investigations and obtain complaints from the prosecutor; or a court liaison officer takes police reports to the prosecutor's office and seeks complaints. More than one of these may be used in the same police department; for example, detectives may handle felonies while a court liaison officer handles misdemeanors. Different procedures may be used if the suspect is released on a promise to appear instead of being booked.

In some cities, the police officer who makes the arrest takes the case to the prosecutor. This may be due to a team approach used by the police department. It is also commonly used when local court rules require the testimony of the arresting officer at the arraignment, which is held very shortly after arrest. One advantage of this approach is that the officer discussing the case with the prosecutor has firsthand knowledge of the facts. Lengthy delays at either the prosecutor's office or the courthouse result in inefficient use of patrol officers and inadequate patrol coverage. Excessive overtime may also be incurred.

Patrol officers rarely seek criminal complaints in some cities because detectives are assigned this function. This makes good communication between patrol officers and detectives crucial. Reports must be thorough, easily understood, and timely. Channels for transmitting the report from one officer to the other must be clearly established. The detectives may conduct an additional investigation and/or ask the patrol officer for more information. In either case, the detective who goes to the prosecutor's office for the complaint must have access to all the facts in the case. One advantage of this approach is that the detectives develop expertise in seeking complaints and may establish rapport with the prosecutors they see frequently. A disadvantage is that the detective may not be able to answer questions about the case as well as the person who was present at the scene of the crime.

Court liaison officers are used to take numerous cases to the prosecutor at once. This approach is used more often with misdemeanor cases than with felonies. The liaison officer is usually not involved in investigating cases. He/she frequently takes the crime reports to the prosecutor, waits for a decision, and transmits requests for additional information to the appropriate police officer. Additional duties may include taking subpoenas to the police department and maintaining records, so that concerned officers know when cases have been dismissed or settled by a plea bargain. The chief advantage of the court liaison officer approach is that it efficiently uses police personnel and reduces the number of officers waiting at the prosecutor's office and courthouse. A disadvantage is that the person dealing with the prosecutor can rarely provide information not included in the written reports.

Many offenders receive citations. A **citation** lists the charges the person was arrested for; the offender is released if he/she signs a promise to appear in court. Identification showing a local address is usually required. The court date is normally listed on the form given to the offender. The release may occur either before or after booking, depending on local practice and the severity of the offense. Failure to appear in court as directed on the citation is a separate offense, for which an arrest warrant may be issued. This process, referred to as **citing out,** is most commonly used for traffic violators. A growing number of other criminal offenses, including felonies, are being handled this way in some states. For traffic violations and some misdemeanors, the citation is designed so that it takes the place of a complaint. In non-traffic cases it is more common for a copy of the police report to accompany the citation when the case is given to the prosecutor. The advantage of this system is that it cuts down on the paperwork and time expended by both the police department and the prosecutor. A disadvantage is that the court may receive inadequate information on the case.

In some cases the offender is not arrested at the scene or is arrested but released prior to filing the criminal complaint. Arresting the suspect as soon as possible may be deemed important if the charges are serious or if the offender is believed to be likely to flee the jurisdiction. In less serious cases, such as traffic accidents, the police department may seek the complaint without trying to arrest the suspect. When the complaint is filed, the court may issue an arrest warrant for the police to serve. Sometimes the court will mail a notice to appear directly to the suspect, and no attempt will be made to make an arrest before the court date.

7-3 Decision to Charge

Criminal charges may be filed whenever there is *prima facie* evidence that the suspect committed the crime. In practice, this means there must be admissible evidence to establish probable cause that the defendant committed the crime. The prosecutor will go over the crime reports and try to determine what evidence can be used to establish each element of the case. While the complaint can withstand legal challenges as long as a *prima facie* case has been established, the prosecutor usually views the case with the goal of establishing guilt beyond a reasonable doubt at trial. Sometimes the complaint will be filed but the police will be directed to complete the investigation before trial.

7-3a Complaint

A **complaint** is a legal document which states the charges against the **defendant.** It is the first document filed with the court in cases where no arrest warrant or indictment was previously obtained. An arrest warrant contains similar information; therefore, some states do not require a complaint if one has already been obtained. Other states require that the police obtain an arrest warrant simultaneously with seeking the complaint if a warrantless arrest was made.

The complaint can be amended to add or delete charges or to make technical corrections, such as inserting the defendant's true name. Other documents, such as the indictment or information, may replace the complaint later in the case. The complaint must give sufficient facts to establish three things: the offense occurred within the jurisdiction of the court; the statute of limitations has not expired; and the defendant is charged with a particular crime or crimes.

7-3b Jurisdiction

Most states give a local court (municipal court, justice court, city court, etc.) jurisdiction to handle the initial proceedings for both misdemeanors and felonies. **Jurisdiction** is usually based on geography: the crime must have occurred within the boundaries of the court district. In some other situations, such as when the arrest was made on a warrant from another locale, the defendant may be arraigned in the court district in which the arrest was made, even though the crime occurred elsewhere.

7-3c Venue

Venue literally means neighborhood. The legal definition is the county in which the crime occurred. There is frequently more than one court district in a large county. A court district may contain more than one city; this is common in areas where population growth resulted in cities incorporating after the court district was formed. The officers responsible for seeking complaints must be aware of these boundaries, so that the case will be filed in the court district with both jurisdiction and venue to hear the case. Maps with the boundaries clearly marked should be available for officers who deal with more than one court district. Filing the case in the wrong court district results in dismissal of the charges and refiling of them in the correct court. Refiling is not allowed if the statute of limitations expires during the delay.

Police departments in metropolitan areas and counties with large geographical areas have one additional concern when filing a complaint. These larger districts may have more than one courthouse where criminal cases are handled. Assignment of a case to a particular courthouse is usually based on the location where the crime occurred. Once again, clearly marked maps are needed. As long as the court district is correct, cases filed in the wrong courthouse are usually transferred to the appropriate one, rather than being dismissed.

7-3d Statute of Limitations

A **statute of limitations** establishes the maximum length of time during which a complaint can be filed against an individual. The statutory period normally starts to run on the day the crime was committed. The statute of limitations is established by state law. Two main reasons for having statutes of limitations are: it is unfair to have a criminal prosecution hanging over a person indefinitely and permitting the prosecution to unduly delay a case interferes with the defense's ability to locate witnesses and produce relevant evidence.

Statutes of limitations exist for both criminal and civil matters. Most states have at least three different statutes of limitations in criminal cases: misdemeanors, felonies, and cases that can be filed at any time. Misdemeanors have the shortest statute of limitations—typically, one to three years. Felonies have statutes that are longer, with three to six years being common. Some states set the statute of limitations in proportion to the maximum sentence for the crime. There is usually a group of crimes for which no statute of limitations applies. Murder is universally in this group. State laws vary, but embezzlement of public funds and malfeasance in elected office frequently have no statute of limitations. Each law enforcement officer should know the various statutes of limitations for crimes he/she will be required to investigate.

The statute of limitations may be stopped (referred to as "tolled") if the suspect leaves the state in order to avoid prosecution. Intentionally evading the police may also toll the statute. The result of **tolling the statute of limitations** is that the statute of limitations becomes longer. For example, if the suspect left the state for six months in order to avoid arrest on a crime with a three-year statute of limitations, the charges could be filed up to three years and six months from the day the crime was committed.

The trend is to have longer statutes of limitations in cases involving sexual abuse of children. The statute may extend until the child becomes an adult. Recent cases in which victims have repressed memory of a crime are raising new issues. In a few states, the statute of limitations is tolled until the victim's memory of the event is restored.

7-3e Number of Charges to File

There are usually no limits on the number of charges that can be in a complaint, as long as the court has jurisdiction, the statute of limitations has not expired, and the offenses are related. Each charge is referred to as a **count.** The counts in the complaint do not have to match the charges for which the suspect was arrested. Crimes occurring in two different court districts cannot be combined in the same complaint.

Suspects are frequently arrested for more than one crime. Part of the charging decision involves determining how many charges to file and for what. Local custom also enters into the way charges are filed. In some cities the prosecutor files all possible crimes. This is done even though convictions cannot be obtained on all of them due to **double jeopardy.** For example, separate counts would be listed in the complaint for robbery and theft, even though the theft was a required part of the robbery; if the jury convicted on both, the theft (lesser included offense) would be dismissed by the judge because double jeopardy prohibits multiple punishments for the same criminal act.

Other courts may require that only the most serious count be listed in the complaint and the jury be instructed on all lesser included offenses. In the robbery example, a robbery charge would be filed but the jury would be instructed that it can convict on either robbery or theft (the lesser included offense). If the jury misunderstood the instructions and convicted on both, the judge would dismiss the less serious offense.

Many offenses can be charged in various degrees—for example, first- and second-degree murder as well as simple and aggravated assault. The one with the shortest sentence is treated the same as a lesser included offense. Depending on local custom, the complaint will list either the most serious charge or all possible degrees of the crime. Charges cannot be refiled on a degree of the crime on which the jury acquitted the defendant, although a lesser degree may be filed if the jury considered that offense and could not reach a verdict on it. For example, if the jury acquits the defendant on first-degree murder but is "hung" on second-degree murder, the prosecutor can refile the second-degree murder charge. The same rule applies if the jury unanimously rejects the death penalty in a murder case but cannot reach a decision on what degree of murder was committed: the prosecution cannot seek the death penalty at a subsequent trial.

Complaints frequently contain allegations that the defendant committed several crimes. Most courts require a logical connection among the crimes listed in one complaint. This connection is usually established in one of two ways: either the crimes were similar or the crimes occurred in one transaction. Numerous burglaries believed to have been committed by the defendant within the court district can be charged in the same complaint. The fact that the crime is the same (burglary) and the defendant is alleged to have committed all of them is a sufficient connection. Crimes committed during a "crime spree" are considered to be in the same transaction and are usually charged in the same complaint. Some states make it mandatory that crimes from one transaction be filed in the same complaint; failure to do so bars filing the remaining charges at a later time. Most court rules permit filing multiple counts even though some of the crimes are misdemeanors and the others felonies. Under these circumstances the case would be processed through the court which handles felonies.

Defendants who are alleged to have committed a crime together are normally tried together. Combining the cases against two defendants is known as **joinder.** If the defendants were initially charged in one complaint but asked for and received separate trials, it is said the cases were **severed.** When one complaint is used to specify charges against more than one defendant, there must be separate counts, so that each defendant knows exactly what crimes he/she is charged with. For example, Count I would charge John Jones with robbery; Count II would charge Bill Smith with the same robbery. Having one trial is more efficient, especially where the same evidence will be used against more than one defendant.

Occasionally joining the cases for one trial is not possible because evidence that can be used against one defendant is not admissible against the other. A good example of this is a confession made by Defendant Jones that implicates Defendant Smith. The confession is admissible against Jones as long as *Miranda* was complied with. Smith, on the other hand, has a Sixth Amendment right to confront and cross-examine Jones. If Jones exercises the Fifth Amendment right not to testify, Smith's Sixth Amendment rights will be violated. One solution is separate trials. Another is to "sanitize" the confession (called **redacting a confession**) to eliminate references to Smith; this may not work if the references to Smith are so intertwined with the statements about Jones that the sanitized version does not make sense. A novel solution was used in the highly publicized *Menendez* case: the judge ordered separate juries for each defendant. If evidence was to be admitted against only one defendant, only the jury for that defendant was allowed in the courtroom while that evidence was introduced.

Another problem with joint trials arises if charges against one defendant do not apply to the other defendant. For example, several burglaries could normally be listed in one complaint, but this may not be permissible unless both defendants are alleged to have participated in every burglary charged. The legal question is whether one defendant would be prejudiced by evidence admitted against the other defendant. Trial judges use their discretion when deciding whether to sever the trials.

Encouraging plea bargaining is another reason for filing numerous charges. Negotiations between the prosecutor and defense attorneys usually precede a **plea bargain.** As with most negotiations, each side enters the process demanding more than he/she is willing to settle for. By filing additional charges, the prosecutor sets the stage for offering to drop some counts in exchange for a guilty plea. The same can be said for filing a more serious crime, such as felonious assault, and accepting a plea to misdemeanor assault. The prosecutor is usually aware of the judge's sentencing practices. If concurrent sentences are likely, the prosecutor may be able to drop several of the charges and still have the defendant receive the same sentence as if convictions were entered on all charges. The need to drop or lower charges while negotiating a guilty plea frequently leads to over-charging in the complaint in order to obtain what the prosecutor believes is an appropriate sentence for the defendant's criminal behavior. Plea bargaining is discussed in more detail in section 9-2, "Plea Bargaining."

Many other factors enter into the decision to file charges. The prosecutor will review the reports and look for inadmissible evidence. The police are allowed to make decisions in the field on hearsay and other kinds of evidence that may not be admissible at trial. Evidence may have been obtained in violations of search and seizure rules, or a confession may have been obtained without properly giving *Miranda* warnings.

The likelihood of obtaining a conviction is also important. A weak case may not merit the time it takes to prepare it for trial. Further investigation may be requested if it appears this would help correct problems in the case. Credibility of the witnesses is a crucial consideration. No matter how obvious it is to the police that the crime occurred, the case may be doomed if victims and/or witnesses lack credibility on the witness stand. The prosecutor will consider such things as prior criminal histories of potential witnesses; ability of the victim to identify the defendant; level of certainty of the victim and/or witnesses when reporting the crime; and inconsistent statements made by the victim and/or witnesses.

Unfortunately, many young children make poor witnesses because they are frequently unable to distinguish clearly between their imaginary world and reality. Children also complicate a case because they become confused easily during cross-examination. The number of times a child victim has been interviewed by police, Children's Protective Services, doctors, and therapists adds to the problem because each interview makes it easier for the defense to allege that ideas were planted in the child's mind. For these reasons, many cases involving sexual abuse of young children are not filed.

7-4 Drafting and Filing of the Complaint

The complaint formally initiates the legal proceedings. Several items must be included in the complaint: name of the court; names of the plaintiff and defendant; and, for each charge, the date it was committed, the location, and a description of the charge. Information must be available to establish each of these when the case is taken to the prosecutor for filing. Failure to include any of these items gives the defense the right to have the complaint dismissed. The prosecutor's staff will usually draft and type the complaint.

The formal name of the court is given in the heading of the complaint. It usually gives both the name of the state and the court. If the court has multiple branches, the one where the case was filed must be indicated. This information is usually in a centered caption near the top of the first page. The **plaintiff** is the person who files a lawsuit. In criminal cases, the plaintiff is the government. Depending on local custom, the complaint will be worded "People of the State of . . .," "State of . . ., Commonwealth of . . .," and so on. A defendant is a person against whom a lawsuit is filed or an indictment has been returned. A criminal suspect is referred to in the complaint and subsequent legal papers as the defendant; he/she technically becomes a defendant when the complaint is filed with the court clerk.

Where possible the full name of the defendant will be listed; complaints against a defendant with an alias frequently list all known aliases. If the defendant's name is not known or there is reason to believe that the name given is an alias, the case may be filed listing the defendant as John Doe or Jane Doe. An amended complaint may be filed later to correct the name. If there are multiple suspects, the full name of each will be listed. Defendants whose true names are known will be listed before those with only aliases or no known names. The case will frequently be called by the last name of the defendant in the case (first defendant, if there are multiple defendants): *People v. Jones, State v. Jones,* or *Commonwealth v. Jones.*

The date the crime occurred must be listed for each charge in order to show that the statute of limitations has not expired—for example, "on or

---

T A B L E **7-1 Criminal Complaint**

IN THE SUPERIOR COURT OF THE STATE OF CALIFORNIA
FOR THE COUNTY OF LOS ANGELES, SOUTHWEST DISTRICT

People of the State	
of California	
Plaintiff,	CRIMINAL COMPLAINT
vs.	No. 123 456
John E. Doe	
Defendant.	

about the third day of January 2002." This gives sufficient information to satisfy the statute of limitations. At the same time, it provides room for minor errors in that date—the complaint would still be valid if the crime occurred on January 2, 2002. More than a few days' discrepancy between the date listed and the one established at trial gives the defendant the right to have the charge dismissed for lack of notice, as required by due process. The charges must be dismissed if the date established was after the statute of limitations had expired, even though due process was not violated.

A court's jurisdiction is geographical; therefore, the complaint must establish that the crime occurred within the boundaries of the court district. Listing the address is an easy way to satisfy this requirement. Other methods will be used in rural areas. Officers working in such areas must be aware of what information the prosecutor will need.

Each count must give sufficient information, so that the defendant knows what crime is charged. There are two ways to specify this information: fact pleading and code pleading. A combination of state law and local custom determines which method of pleading is used.

Fact pleading requires that a brief statement of the facts be given. Every element of the crimes must be shown by the facts stated. The following is an example of fact pleading:

> COUNT I: JOHN JONES is hereby charged with burglary in the first degree in violation of Penal Code Section 460(a) because on or about June 12, 2002, he broke a window and entered a residence located at 1234 W. Main Street, Anytown, CA, with the intent to steal a stereo.

Note that this count gives the name of the defendant, as well as the location and date of the crime. It then gives enough facts to establish first-degree burglary: breaking, entering, dwelling, intent. Fact pleading is more difficult to draft because it must be worded to closely match the facts of each case. Due to the greater detail that must be given, it is easier for the defendant to find errors inadvertently made by the prosecutor.

Code pleading uses the language of the penal code to give notice of the charge. The following is an example of code pleading for burglary:

> COUNT I: JOHN JONES is hereby charged with a felony to wit, Burglary in the First Degree, in violation of Section 460(a) of the California Penal Code in that on or about June 12, 2002, he entered a dwelling at 1234 W. Main St., Anytown, CA, with the intent to commit a felony or petty theft therein.

Although the preceding examples have only minor variations in wording, in complicated cases the differences between code pleading and fact pleading may be substantial. Code pleading enables the prosecutor to insert certain details, such as date, location, and offense charged, into a word processor which uses standardized wording. There are fewer chances for careless errors resulting in dismissal of the charges. The defendant may request more information, usually by asking for a Bill of Particulars, if needed.

The prosecutor usually is required to sign and date the complaint. It is then taken to the court clerk's office, where it is stamped "Filed" and the date it is filed is indicated. This delivery of the forms to the clerk is called **filing the complaint.**

7-5 Arraignment

The arraignment is a court hearing at which the defendant is informed of the charges against him/her. It is also referred to as the "first appearance" or other descriptive terms. An arraignment must occur without unnecessary delay if the defendant is in custody. State laws take two approaches: the defendant must be taken before a judge without undue delay, or the code sets a specific time period—for example, the arraignment must be within 48 hours after arrest.

7-5a Procedures at Arraignment

In most states the following occur at arraignment: the defendant is formally notified of the charges; appropriate inquiries are made to verify that the defendant's right to counsel is protected; the defendant enters a plea; and the next court date is set. Bail may be set if it has not already been established. The judge handling arraignments frequently hears a large number of cases each day. Detailed inquiries into the facts are not usually made during this court hearing.

The defendant has the right to be present at the arraignment, although he/she can waive this right. Transporting inmates to court is time-consuming and presents a risk that inmates will escape. It also is expensive if the jail is not located near the courthouse. One solution to this problem is to have a courtroom located in the jail facility. A judge is assigned to this courtroom, and prosecutors and defense attorneys are present. The inmate is present at the arraignment but does not go outside the jail.

Another alternative is conducting arraignments by two-way closed-circuit television. Television equipment is installed at the courthouse, and a studio is constructed at a convenient location, usually inside the jail. The defendant and defense attorney will view the court proceedings from the studio. Simultaneously the judge will view what is occurring at the studio. Audio communications will be maintained in both directions. Depending on local custom, the prosecutor will be located either at the studio or at the courtroom. The judge will conduct the arraignment in much the same manner as if the defendant were present in the courtroom. Documents can be FAXed back and forth as necessary.

A copy of the complaint serves as notice of the charges that have been filed. In some courts the defendant receives a copy of the complaint, and it is read aloud during the arraignment. It is more common, particularly if the defendant is represented by an attorney, to give the defendant a copy of the complaint and dispense with reading it aloud. Either procedure satisfies the due process requirement of notice of the charges. If the complaint is amended at a later time, the defendant will have to be given a copy and may need to be arraigned on the amended complaint.

The United States Supreme Court has interpreted the Sixth Amendment right to counsel to mean that a defendant in a criminal case has the right to have counsel from the arraignment through first appeal. Any actions that might alter the outcome of the case during this time period cannot be done without an attorney present or a waiver of that right by the defendant. Entering a plea is such an event. Therefore, the judge must verify that the defendant is represented by an attorney, or waives that right, prior to proceeding with the arraignment.

If the defendant attends the arraignment without an attorney, the judge must inquire into the reasons for this. Arraignments may be postponed if the defendant wishes to hire an attorney but has not been able to do so. A defendant who wishes to act as his/her own attorney may do so as long as the decision is made voluntarily with knowledge that there is a right to an attorney. If the defendant wants an attorney, but cannot afford to hire one, the government must provide one in all cases in which the defendant is sentenced to time in jail or prison. The judge must find the answer to three questions in order to determine if an attorney must be appointed: Does the defendant want an attorney? Does the defendant lack the money to hire an attorney? Does the prosecution intend to seek a sentence that will include incarceration? If there is an affirmative answer to each of these questions, a defense attorney must be appointed. A public defender is usually present at most arraignment courts to consult with indigent defendants, so that they can be arraigned without lengthy delays.

A plea is normally entered at the arraignment. Most cases require either "guilty" or "not guilty." "*Nolo contendere*" may be used in some cases; the effect is the same as a guilty plea in criminal cases, but it does not admit guilt for the purpose of later civil cases. If the defense wishes to raise the insanity issue, pleas of "not guilty" *and* "not guilty by reason of insanity" are usually entered. The defense may wish to wait to enter the "not guilty by reason of insanity" plea until after a psychiatrist has had an opportunity to examine the defendant. State law usually establishes how long the defense can delay this decision; some courts grant a **continuance,** so that the plea can be entered at an arraignment, which will be held at a later date. Continuances are used to reschedule a wide variety of court hearings.

The Supreme Court requires that the defendant waive the following rights prior to entering a guilty plea: speedy trial, ability to confront and cross-examine accusers, jury trial, and proof beyond a reasonable doubt. The record must show that the defendant voluntarily waived each of these rights. A waiver of counsel must also appear as part of the record if the defendant enters a guilty plea when not represented by an attorney. State law and local customs vary on procedures for accepting guilty pleas at arraignments. Many courts have preprinted forms, listing all the required warnings. The judge will read the list and the defendant must respond to each. Even when there is a guilty plea the imposition of sentence may be delayed until a later date to allow time for the preparation of a presentence investigation report. Some courts will not accept a guilty plea to a felony unless the defendant has consulted with an attorney.

The arraignment is the best time to set the next court date because all necessary parties—judge, defendant, prosecutor, and defense attorney—are present and can object if there is a conflict. For felonies, the next court date frequently is the preliminary hearing. Trial dates may be set in misdemeanor cases. Dates for other issues to be decided may also be established.

7-5b Probable Cause Hearing

The Supreme Court, in *Gernstein v. Pugh* (420 U.S. 103, 43 L.Ed. 2d 541, 95 S.Ct. 854 [1975]), stated that a defendant who is held in custody pending trial has the right to a **probable cause hearing.** A subsequent Supreme Court case ruled that the probable cause hearing must be held within 48 hours of the arrest. At this hearing a judge reviews the facts of the case to determine if there is probable cause to support the charges. Failure to establish probable cause results in the defendant's release from custody; charges do not have to be dismissed.

A probable cause hearing is required only if requested by a defendant who is in custody. No probable cause hearing is necessary if a judge has already reviewed the facts when issuing an arrest warrant. The defendant does not have the right to be present and is not entitled to have an attorney present when the judge makes the determination of probable cause. Sworn statements may be used, rather than calling witnesses to the hearing.

Several approaches to the probable cause hearing have been used. One is to make the procedure for filing a criminal complaint equivalent to that for obtaining an arrest warrant: a judge must review sworn affidavits and determine that there is probable cause. Another approach is to attach sworn statements to the complaint and have the judge review them at the arraignment. Waiting for the defendant to request the hearing also meets constitutional standards but is more disruptive of the court system. Officers must be familiar with how the probable cause hearing is handled in their area and be prepared to present the necessary information in an appropriate format.

Chapter Summary

Once the arrest is made, the prosecutor will make many of the important decisions regarding the case. Prior to filing a criminal complaint, the prosecutor will review the case to determine what charges can be supported by the facts the police have obtained. Other factors that will be considered when determining what charges to file include the workload of the prosecutor's office; the congestion of the court calendar; the credibility of potential witnesses; the possible inadmissibility of evidence at trial; and the likelihood of obtaining a conviction.

The process for obtaining the complaint varies with local laws and customs. Either the arresting officer, a detective, or a court liaison officer will take the case to the prosecutor. In addition to verifying that the facts support the charges, the prosecutor will check the statute of limitations and make sure that the offense occurred within the geographical boundaries of the court district. Local practice will govern whether all possible offenses are filed or whether the highest charge is filed with lesser included offenses being included in the jury instructions. Multiple counts can usually be included in one complaint if there is a connection among the crimes. Sometimes the prosecutor will file multiple counts, with the hope of inducing the defendant to plead guilty to at least one. A complaint may list more than one defendant if both participated in the same crimes.

The complaint must contain sufficient facts to establish the court's jurisdiction. At a minimum, this includes the name of the court, the defendant's name (if known), date the crime occurred, the location, and what code section was allegedly violated. States that use code pleading give little more information than this and rely on other documents, such as the police report, to give detailed information. Fact pleading, which requires the complaint to give more information about how the offense was committed, is used in other states.

The complaint is taken to the court clerk's office and filed. After this point the suspect is referred to as the defendant. The arraignment is held to officially notify the defendant of the charges. Several things are usually accomplished at the arraignment: the defendant receives a copy of the complaint and is thereby given notice of the charges; when the defendant is not represented by an attorney, the judge determines if a public defender should be appointed; a plea is entered; bail is set; and the next court date is set.

A probable cause hearing is necessary in warrantless arrest cases if a defendant who is in custody requests one. At this hearing a judge reviews affidavits containing the facts and determines whether there is probable cause to support the charges. Neither the defendant nor the defense attorney needs to be present at this hearing. If probable cause is not established, the defendant must be released from custody but the charges do not have to be dismissed. Some states design the arraignment so that it includes a probable cause hearing.

Study Questions

1. Describe the role of the prosecutor as the gatekeeper of the criminal court system.
2. How does the police department in the city where you live interact with the prosecutor's office for
   a. filing felony charges?
   b. filing misdemeanor charges?
3. How are traffic tickets written by your local police department filed with the court? If your city uses the citing out method for non-traffic offenses, describe how the citations are processed by the police and prosecutor at the filing stage of the case.
4. Select a case in which charges were filed that received extensive coverage in your local news media.
   a. What was the suspect arrested for?
   b. What charges did the prosecutor file?
   c. What do you think influenced the prosecutor to file these charges?
   d. What additional charges could have been filed?

5. Obtain a copy of a criminal complaint for a crime which occurred in your city.
   a. How are the plaintiff and defendant identified?
   b. Identify facts that establish the court's jurisdiction and facts that show the statute of limitations has not expired.
   c. Does your court use code pleading or fact pleading?
   d. Did the prosecutor file both the greater and lesser included offenses?
   e. If there were multiple defendants committing the same crime, will they be tried jointly or were their cases severed?
6. Draft a complaint for a case you selected out of a recent newspaper account of a crime.
7. Check with your local court and determine
   a. the name of the court where arraignments are held for crimes committed in the city where you live.
   b. the address where arraignments are held.
   c. whether arraignments are held in the courthouse, a special courtroom in jail, or some other facility.
   d. when arraignments are held.
8. How soon after arrest must the arraignment be held in your state?
9. Go to court and watch an arraignment court in action. Explain
   a. how defendants are notified of charges.
   b. the process for determining if the public defender will represent the defendant.
   c. the entry of pleas in felony and misdemeanor cases.
   d. what future court hearings are scheduled at the arraignment.
   e. the average time to arraign a case on the day you observed court.
10. Describe how probable cause hearings are handled in your local court.

True or False Questions

1. The prosecutor must file criminal charges if the police provide sufficient evidence to establish probable cause that the suspect committed the crime.
2. The criminal complaint is a legal document that is used only if misdemeanor charges are filed.
3. The criminal complaint must establish geographical jurisdiction of the court.

4. Venue is established in the complaint by stating the location where the crime was committed.
5. A criminal complaint can contain charges for more than one crime.
6. If more than one person committed a crime, a separate complaint must be filed against each person.
7. In states that use fact pleading, the complaint must state sufficient facts to establish each crime charged.
8. If a suspect is given a citation at the scene and released, the citation usually serves as the complaint.
9. A probable cause hearing must be held within 10 days of an arrest.
10. A defendant is not allowed to enter a plea until the preliminary hearing.

Chapter 8

Indictments and Preliminary Hearings

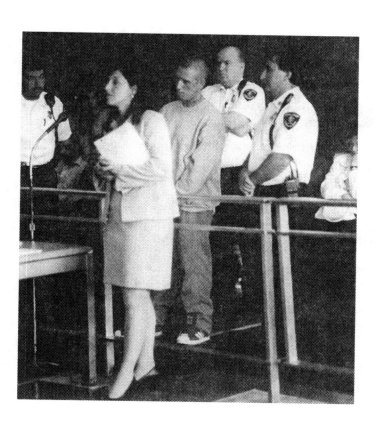

O u t l i n e

Key Terms

access of press to
   preliminary hearing
arraignment on information
   or indictment
chain of custody
   (chain of possession)
Contemporaneous
   Objection Rule

dismissed with prejudice
First Amendment
grand jury
   number of grand jurors
   number of votes to indict
held to answer
indictment
information

leading questions
no bill
preliminary hearing
right to counsel
serve a subpoena
Sixth Amendment
subpoena
true bill

Learning Objectives

Learning Objectives

After reading this chapter, the student will be able to

- Explain the prosecutor's role in filing criminal charges.
- Explain the defendant's right to be represented by an attorney from arraignment through preliminary hearing and grand jury proceedings.
- List the factors considered when the prosecutor decides between using a preliminary hearing and taking the case to a grand jury.
- Identify the rights of the press and public to be present at preliminary hearings.
- Describe what occurs at a preliminary hearing.
- Explain the function of the grand jury in criminal cases.
- Describe the process used by the grand jury when an indictment is sought.
- Explain what occurs at the arraignment that occurs after the preliminary hearing or indictment.

If a felony has been committed, the case against the defendant must be submitted to additional review before the case can proceed to trial. This is done at a grand jury hearing or by a judge at a preliminary hearing. This chapter discusses the procedures for both hearings as well as the filing of charges and arraignment that follow this review.

8-1 A Defendant's Right to Counsel

A defendant's **right to counsel** begins at the arraignment on the criminal complaint and applies to all court proceedings thereafter. A defendant may waive this right as long as this is done voluntarily after being informed of the right to counsel. The Supreme Court has interpreted the **Sixth Amendment** to mean that defendants who cannot afford to hire an attorney have the right to have one appointed to represent them at government expense from arraignment until the first appeal is completed. This right to free counsel is limited to cases in which the defendant is sentenced to serve time in jail or prison.

In addition to court appearances, the right to counsel applies to all questioning by government agents regarding the charges. This covers police officers as well as informants whom the police use to obtain information from the defendant. All questioning that occurs after the arraignment must comply with this rule, *whether or not* the defendant is in custody at the time. The defendant may agree to talk to the officers, but such statements may be taken only after obtaining a waiver of the right to counsel. *Miranda* warnings may be used to obtain a valid waiver.

The case is more complicated if the defendant invoked the right to counsel after being given *Miranda* warnings at an interrogation session after being arrested. Under these circumstances, the right to counsel can be waived only *with an attorney present*. This right to counsel, which is part of *Miranda*, is broader than the Sixth Amendment right to counsel: it applies to subsequent custodial interrogation even if the questions relate to different crimes. The police are expected to establish a system, so that all officers know that *Miranda* has been invoked; it is not a defense that an officer did not know about the defendant's invocation of *Miranda*. Fortunately, *Miranda* applies only to custodial interrogation: if the defendant has been released from custody, this rule no longer applies.

These rulings regarding the right to counsel during interrogation are summarized in Table 8-1.

T A B L E **8-1** Comparison of *Miranda* and Sixth Amendment
Right to Counsel

Questioning before Arraignment

Suspect is *not* in custody.

- *Miranda* is not required.
- Suspect can have an attorney present if he/she pays for it.

Suspect is in custody.
  Suspect must be given *Miranda* warnings
  1. If suspect asks for attorney.

- Questioning can continue *only* if attorney is present
- Waiver valid *only* if attorney present when waiver made
- Applies to questions about any crime by any police officer

  2. If suspect does not ask for an attorney.

- Questioning can continue if suspect waives *Miranda* rights
- Do not need an attorney present when suspect waives rights

Questioning after Arraignment

Suspect is in custody.
Suspect is *not* in custody.

- *Miranda* applies.
- *Miranda* does not apply.
- Sixth Amendment right to counsel applies.
- Defendant must waive right to counsel.
- Applies *only* to questioning about crimes the suspect has been arraigned on.
- *Miranda* warnings can be used to obtain a waiver.

8-2 Choice of Preliminary Hearing or Indictment

Felony charges must be reviewed by an independent source before a case can proceed to trial. This evaluation is done by either a judge at a preliminary hearing or the grand jury. The prosecutor's decision to file misdemeanor charges is ordinarily not subject to this type of review. Both law and local customs affect the decision to take the case to the grand jury or to proceed by preliminary hearing. The name used for the preliminary hearing varies from state to state. To avoid confusion, the term "preliminary hearing" is used in this book to refer to the court hearing held in front of a judge where evidence is presented and a decision is made on whether there is enough evidence to warrant taking the case to trial.

The Fifth Amendment begins:

No person shall be held to answer for a capital, or otherwise infamous crime, unless on a presentment or indictment of a Grand Jury, except in cases arising in the land or naval forces, or in the Militia, when in actual service in time of War or public danger; . . .

The Supreme Court held that this right to have a case taken before a grand jury applies only to criminal charges filed by the federal government. States are free to pass laws providing for preliminary hearings instead of mandating grand jury proceedings.

Some states have laws that require every felony case to be presented to a grand jury. Even among these states there are variations in procedures. For example, some require that the grand jury indict on at least one charge but permit prosecution on other crimes listed in the complaint, even though the grand jury did not hear evidence on these counts; others require counts to be dismissed if the grand jury does not return an indictment on them.

The more common procedure is to allow the prosecutor to decide whether to take the case to the grand jury or to hold a **preliminary hearing.** A variety of factors will influence this decision. One is privacy of the proceedings. Preliminary hearings must be open to the press and the public unless there is a specific showing of trauma to a witness. Grand jury proceedings are held behind closed doors. Two types of cases are frequently taken to the grand jury because of this confidentiality: (1) crimes in which the suspect has not been apprehended and there is reason to fear flight to avoid prosecution if the suspect learns charges are being sought and (2) situations where public review of the evidence would cause irreparable harm to the suspect's reputation, even though the charges are rejected. Major drug smuggling rings are examples of the former situation; a child molestation case exemplifies the latter. Charges against local elected officials are frequently handled by a grand jury.

Speed is another consideration. Depending on local practice, a case may be processed by the grand jury much faster than in the court proceeding required for the preliminary hearing. Grand jury proceedings are usually faster because there is neither cross-examination nor an opportunity for the defense to call witnesses. Some states allow the grand jury to return an indictment if any one of the charges listed is established by the evidence reviewed; most states require that every charged felony be established at a preliminary hearing. Where this is true, the grand jury is much faster if there are multiple charges.

A few states permit a defendant to request a preliminary hearing even though the grand jury has heard the case. This is done to compensate for the fact that grand jury proceedings do not allow the defendant the right to present a defense. Both having a preliminary hearing and taking the case before the grand jury slow the proceedings and create extra work for the prosecutor; therefore, the grand jury is seldom used in these states.

The main differences between grand jury proceedings and preliminary hearings are presented in Table 8-2. Procedural differences that have not been discussed in this section will be covered in section 8-6, "Obtaining an Indictment."

8-3 Rights of the Public and Press to Be Present

The **First Amendment** and Sixth Amendment both apply to criminal proceedings. Freedom of the press, a First Amendment right, is used to justify media access to court proceedings. The Sixth Amendment specifically guarantees the defendant's right to a "public trial" in criminal cases.

T A B L E **8-2** Comparison of Grand Jury Proceedings and Preliminary Hearing

Grand Jury Proceedings	Preliminary Hearing
They are held in private—the press and public are not allowed.	It is held in open court—the press and public have the right to be present.
The decision to indict is made by a group of citizens.	The decision to allow the case to go to trial is made by a judge.
The defendant does *not* have the right to be present.	The defendant has the right to be present.
The defendant can be required to testify but may invoke the Fifth Amendment to specific questions.	The defendant has the right to refuse to testify.
The defense attorney is *not* present when the defendant testifies or at any other time.	The defense attorney is present during the entire proceeding.
There is no cross-examination of witnesses.	All witnesses are subject to cross-examination.
The defense is *not* allowed to present evidence.	The defense may present evidence.
Some states require indictment on only one charge in the complaint.	The prosecutor usually must establish every felony in the complaint.
The exclusionary rule does *not* apply.	The exclusionary rule applies.
The prosecution has no duty to present evidence that may exonerate the defendant.	The defense has the right to discovery for any evidence the prosecutor has that would exonerate the defendant.
Hearing can be held prior to arrest without notice to the suspect.	Hearing can be held only after the suspect has been arrested and arraigned.

Another Sixth Amendment right, the right to an impartial jury, can be impaired by prejudicial press coverage.

The Supreme Court has used the historical function of the grand jury as a basis for permitting some practices that otherwise conflict with modern procedures. Media access to the grand jury is one of these. Since its inception in English common law, the grand jury has heard evidence in secret. Only in relatively recent times has the defense even had access to transcripts of what occurred. There is no duty to inform the press that an indictment is being sought. The media have access to what occurred in a grand jury proceeding in three ways: reporters may wait outside and observe witnesses who are leaving; in some jurisdictions, they may ask witnesses about their testimony; and, if transcripts are unsealed, the press may report on what is contained in them.

Preliminary hearings have been treated much like trials as far as the First and Sixth Amendments are concerned. The basic rule is that they must be held in open court. Even though the Sixth Amendment refers to the defendant's right to a public trial, a law permitting the defendant to have the press excluded was declared unconstitutional. The media may report on anything that occurs in open court.

A limited restriction on holding preliminary hearings in open court applies if it is established that testifying in public would cause severe psychological damage to a child witness. Even in these types of cases, the Supreme Court has required a case-by-case showing of potential injury to the child: broad rules that close the proceedings whenever a victim of child molestation testifies have been held unconstitutional.

Within these guidelines, the judge may close the courtroom in some instances. Witnesses, except the defendant, may be excluded except when testifying. This is done to prevent witnesses from altering their testimony because of what has already been said. The judge can clear the courtroom of unruly and/or boisterous people. Even the defendant may be excluded for disruptive behavior.

Occasionally, legal arguments pertaining to the admissibility of evidence can be heard without the press or public present. A good example is a defense motion to suppress the defendant's confession because *Miranda* warnings were not given correctly. The judge may close the courtroom while the issue is being discussed if press coverage about the inadmissible confession is likely to result in extremely prejudicial publicity. The key to the judge's decision is whether there is a strong likelihood that the publicity will so inflame public opinion that it will interfere with the defendant's right to have impartial jurors. Once the evidentiary ruling has been made, the courtroom must again be opened to the public and media.

8-4 Preliminary Hearing

Most states hold the preliminary hearing in the same level court where arraignments occurred (municipal court, justice court, city court, etc.). It will be in the court district for the location where the crime occurred. Typically this means the arraignment and preliminary hearing will be held in the same courthouse; if the defendant was arrested on a warrant while in another city, this may not be true.

The timing for the preliminary hearing is set by state law. Ten days to two weeks is usually the maximum time allowed between arraignment and preliminary hearing when the defendant is in custody. A longer delay may be allowed if the defendant is not in custody. The statutory deadline must be carefully considered when scheduling the preliminary hearing, but the defense can waive this limit by requesting a later date.

A judge or magistrate will preside over the preliminary hearing. The court administrator will estimate the number of judicial days each month that must be devoted to preliminary hearings. This will take into consideration the average number of cases and the usual length of preliminary hearings. In busy court districts, several judges may do nothing but handle preliminary hearings. They may remain in this assignment for six months, one year, or more. Some districts have all judges who are assigned to criminal cases hold preliminary hearings on one or two days a week, rather than making it a permanent assignment. Courts with a lower volume of preliminary hearings usually have one judge who hears preliminary hearings on specific days of the week.

The date for the preliminary hearing is usually set at the arraignment. After the arraignment the prosecutor reviews the case and decides which witnesses to call and what, if any, physical evidence to introduce. Witnesses are usually subpoenaed to appear at the preliminary hearing. A **subpoena** is a court document ordering a person to appear to testify at a specified date and time. Failure to appear can be charged as contempt of court. While victims and witnesses may say they will cooperate, subpoenaing them gives the court the power to compel their testimony if they change their minds. Many prosecutors even subpoena police officers; this is done more as a formal reminder of the court date than as a threat of contempt of court. The prosecutor's office prepares the subpoenas, sometimes after consultation with the officers to determine which witnesses will be needed. It may not be necessary to use all potential witnesses at the preliminary hearing because the burden of proof is lower than it will be at trial.

Police officers usually serve the subpoena on the witness. To **serve a subpoena** means to deliver it to the person; state law may require that this be done in person or may allow it to be left with any adult at the residence. The officers are also responsible for checking necessary items out of the evidence locker and taking them to court at the appropriate time. Subpoenas and requirements for serving them are discussed in more detail in Chapter 10, "Preparation of a Case for Trial."

Court personnel who are present for the preliminary hearing usually include judge, bailiff, clerk, and, in many jurisdictions, a stenographic reporter. The defendant will be present and usually sits at the counsel table with his/her attorney. The prosecutor will be at the other counsel table. Frequently, the officer in charge of the investigation will sit beside the prosecutor. If the defendant is in custody, a bailiff or custodial officer will be responsible for transporting him/her to and from the courtroom and for preventing escape. There is no jury; occasionally the jury box will be used for seating witnesses waiting to testify. Spectators are permitted in the courtroom, but frequently there are few, except for the immediate family of the defendant. The media are also permitted; local court rules regulate where they will be seated and what camera equipment may be used while court is in session. In high-profile cases, the court may limit the number of reporters who can attend at one time and may establish a system for determining which ones will be excluded.

A bailiff usually calls the court to order immediately prior to the entry of the judge from his/her chambers (the judge's office). The name of the first case will be read, and the attorneys will state their names for the record. The fact that the defendant is present is usually stated orally, so that it can be included in the transcript. The complaint is usually read aloud. Opening statements are not made because there is no jury. It is assumed the judge can follow the case as it is presented.

The prosecution presents evidence first because it has the burden of proof: it must establish probable cause (sometimes called a *prima facie* case) that the defendant committed each felony listed in the complaint. All evidence must be presented through testimony of sworn witnesses. The prosecutor does this by calling witnesses and asking questions. An item of physical evidence is admitted into evidence only after a sworn witness identifies it. The rules of evidence used at trial normally apply to preliminary hearings, although some states have modified the hearsay rule, the best evidence rule, and occasionally other rules, to expedite preliminary hearings.

Part of the prosecutor's preparation includes deciding which witnesses to call, in what order to call them, and what questions to ask. Sometimes the prosecutor goes to court with a written list of questions; other prosecutors use notes but phrase the questions more extemporaneously. The case can never be totally scripted in advance because witnesses sometimes give unexpected answers or have memory lapses. Every prosecutor has to be ready to ask appropriate questions in these circumstances; sometimes this requires quick action to subpoena another witness.

The prosecutor usually calls each witness by stating his/her name aloud. The witness comes forward, is seated in the witness stand, and takes the oath to tell the truth. The clerk may ask the witness to spell his/her full name, so that the record will be accurate. The witness may be required to give a home address and an occupation. Questioning usually begins with the background information necessary to set the scene. Facts are established to place the witness at the necessary location where relevant observations were made. This is usually done with pointed questions such as "Where were you at 9:30 P.M. on July 5, 2002?" The questions that follow are usually specific, asking for as complete detail as possible. Wording is important: leading questions cannot be asked at this stage. **Leading questions** are questions that imply the correct answer—for example, "You saw a gun in the defendant's hand, didn't you?" They are reserved for cross-examinations and a few other situations. Other restrictions on the types of questions that are impermissible include two questions in one statement (e.g., "Did you see him hit the man and shoot the lady?"); questions calling for speculation (e.g., "Why do you think he did that?"); questions assuming facts that have not been introduced into evidence yet; repeated questions that have already been answered; and argumentative questions.

The defense attorney may object to any question asked by the prosecutor. The **Contemporaneous Objection Rule** applies: the objection must be made at the time the question is asked. Witnesses are frequently instructed to pause briefly before answering each question to permit objections to be made. If an objection is made, the judge will ask the grounds for the objection. Some legal rule—usually a rule of evidence, such as the hearsay rule—will be given. The person who asked the question is then allowed to give a reason the question should be allowed. After hearing both sides, the judge will make a ruling: (1) objection sustained, which means the witness should not answer the question in its present form or (2) objection overruled, which means the witness should answer. If the objection is obviously correct, the judge may grant it without permitting discussion from the other side. Many times a skillful attorney can reword a question in a manner that avoids the technicality which caused the objection to be sustained; if so, the evidence will still be introduced. For example, the following dialog might occur in a drunk driving case:

PROSECUTOR: Where were you at 9:30 P.M. on July 5, 2002?
WITNESS: I was on duty as an ambulance attendant. We were called to the scene of a traffic accident at First and Flower.

PROSECUTOR: Did you see the defendant at that location?
WITNESS: Yes.
PROSECUTOR: Did he appear to be intoxicated?
DEFENSE: Objection, your honor.
JUDGE: On what grounds?
DEFENSE: Calls for an opinion by the witness.
PROSECUTOR: Your honor, I am asking for what the witness observed.
JUDGE: Objection sustained.
PROSECUTOR: How close did you get to the defendant?
WITNESS: About three feet.
PROSECUTOR: Did you notice any odors?
WITNESS: Yes.
PROSECUTOR: What odors did you notice?
WITNESS: Alcohol.
PROSECUTOR: Was the defendant able to walk?
WITNESS: He staggered and then fell down.
PROSECUTOR: Did you observe the defendant's eyes?
WITNESS: Yes. They were watery and bloodshot.
PROSECUTOR: Did you hear the defendant speak?
WITNESS: Yes. His speech was slurred.

By careful questioning, the prosecutor established that the witness smelled alcohol; saw the defendant stagger; and observed that the defendant had watery, bloodshot eyes and slurred speech: taken together, the statements allowed the jury to conclude the defendant was drunk, even though the witness was not allowed to give an opinion on the issue.

Testimony must establish that physical evidence is relevant to the case, identify the item as the one seized during the investigation of the case, and account for what has happened to the item since it was seized. This is called the **chain of custody or chain of possession.** The purpose is to make sure that the item has not been tampered with. The defense can object if any of these facts have not been established by testimony:

PROSECUTOR: Officer Smith, was a weapon recovered at the scene?
OFFICER SMITH: Yes.
PROSECUTOR: What weapon was recovered?
OFFICER SMITH: A knife.
PROSECUTOR: Where did you find the knife?
DEFENSE ATTORNEY: Objection, your honor, assumes facts not in evidence.
JUDGE: Objection sustained.
PROSECUTOR: Who found the knife?

OFFICER SMITH: I did.

PROSECUTOR: Where did you find the knife?

OFFICER SMITH: It was in the suspect's pocket.

PROSECUTOR: Please describe that knife.

OFFICER SMITH: It was a switchblade knife with a 6" blade and a white bone handle.

PROSECUTOR: What did you do with the knife after you located it?

OFFICER SMITH: I marked my initials on the base of the handle, attached an evidence tag with pertinent information, and put it in a brown 9" × 12" envelope, on which I wrote the case number. I then sealed it and wrote my name over the seal.

PROSECUTOR: What did you do with the envelope?

OFFICER SMITH: I placed it in the evidence locker at the police station.

PROSECUTOR: Is this the envelope?

OFFICER SMITH: Yes. It has my signature on the unbroken seal.

PROSECUTOR: Please open the envelope. Can you identify the knife in the envelope as the one you found at the crime scene on the night of July 5, 2002?

OFFICER SMITH: Yes. If you look right here at the base of the handle you will see my initials, ABS.

PROSECUTOR: Your honor, please admit the knife into evidence as People's Exhibit Number 1.

JUDGE: Defense counsel, do you have any objections?

DEFENSE ATTORNEY: No, your honor.

JUDGE: The knife is admitted as People's Exhibit Number 1.

Sometimes it requires more than one witness to establish all of these facts. For example, if a patrol officer found a gun at the crime scene and the gun was sent to a ballistics laboratory for comparison with bullets taken from the victim, testimony of both the patrol officer and the person conducting the tests would be needed.

When the prosecution has presented all of its evidence, it will rest its case. A motion to dismiss the charges is typically made by the defense attorney at this point, based on an argument that the prosecution has failed to establish all the elements of the crime or that there is not enough credible evidence to establish probable cause to believe that the defendant committed the crime(s). If the judge denies the motion, the defense then has the opportunity to present evidence. Witnesses may be called and items of physical evidence introduced. Many times, however, the defense does not present any evidence at the preliminary hearing. This is a tactical decision, usually made when it appears certain that the judge will rule that there is ample evidence to hold the defendant for trial. Rather than disclose the defense's case to the prosecution this early in the case, the defense uses cross-examination of the prosecution's witnesses as its main tool at the preliminary hearing.

After the defense completes its case, the judge will make a ruling on whether or not there has been sufficient evidence presented to warrant taking the case to trial. The judge usually makes an oral declaration before the parties leave the courtroom. If the judge finds the evidence is sufficient, the defendant will be **held to answer** on the charges. The judge must also sign a declaration, the wording of which is usually established by state law—for example,

> It appears to me that the offense in the within complaint mentioned has been committed, and that there is sufficient cause to believe that the within named Jane Smith is guilty, I order that she be held to answer to the same.

If there are multiple charges, a separate ruling and declaration will be needed for each count. Charges for which the judge did not find probable cause will be dismissed. Some counts may be dismissed while the defendant is held to answer on others.

The judge must also sign a declaration if the defendant is not held to answer—for example,

> There being no sufficient cause to believe the within named Jane Smith guilty of the offense within mentioned, I order that the complaint be dismissed and that she shall be discharged.

Dismissal of a charge at this stage does not give the defendant double jeopardy protection against the charges being refiled. State law may allow the judge to indicate whether charges can be refiled: charges that are **dismissed with prejudice** cannot be refiled; other charges can be refiled if the prosecution believes it can establish the case at another preliminary hearing. If the prosecution was unable to establish the case due to unavoidable circumstances, such as sudden illness of a key witness, the judge will usually allow the case to be refiled. Any refiling of the charges must be within the statute of limitations.

8-5 Filing of the Information

If the judge holds the defendant to answer on the charge(s), the prosecution must complete additional paperwork. An information must be drafted. An **information** is a formal document which states the charges against the defendant and contains acknowledgment that the judge found probable cause to proceed on the charges. The format and content requirements are very similar to those of the complaint: the name of the court must be included; geographical jurisdiction must be established; facts must show that the statute of limitations has not expired; and the specific charges must be stated.

In many jurisdictions the prosecutor has the discretion to drop charges at this point by not including them in the information, even though the judge held the defendant to answer. This decision may be based on the strength of the testimony of key witnesses at the preliminary hearing, an inability to locate potential witnesses, or other factors that make the prosecutor believe that proceeding on a charge is not merited at this point. Since misdemeanor charges do not have to be presented to the judge at the preliminary hearing, the prosecutor can usually add misdemeanor charges to the information that was not previously considered.

8-6 Obtaining an Indictment

An **indictment** is returned by a grand jury after investigating a case brought to it by a prosecutor. An indictment is a formal charging document, which will be filed with the court. If the grand jury investigates the case on its own accord, a document called a presentment will be prepared. In some states, the presentment merely asks the prosecutor to investigate the case, possibly including taking the case back to the grand jury at a later time for an indictment; in other states, it is filed with the court and initiates criminal charges against the defendant.

Historically the grand jury protected citizens from malicious prosecution by the government: felony charges could be filed against a person only if the grand jury held that they were warranted. Apparently the grand jury also served as a trial jury during its earliest history, but this function is not considered part of our common law. The role of the grand jury in protecting citizens from government resulted in rules which made grand jury proceedings secret. The secrecy was to protect the grand jurors, not the persons being investigated for criminal conduct. Most jurisdictions still regard grand jury proceedings as secret, some to the extent that, even after indictment, the defendant does not have the right to receive a copy of the minutes of the grand jury or a transcript of the testimony presented. Some states even prohibit individuals who appear before the grand jury as witnesses to disclose what they were asked or testified about.

The Supreme Court has held that the Fifth Amendment right to a grand jury applies only to federal felonies. The states have been free to enact their own laws regulating grand juries. This section will present general rules on grand jury proceedings, but you should investigate your own state's laws on the issues because there is substantial variation across the nation.

Grand juries are normally appointed by the court of general jurisdiction of the county and must represent the demographics of the population. A grand jury usually serves for a term. This will coincide with the court's term, if the court divides its time this way. Many states provide that the grand jury serve for one year or 18 months. Some states permit more than one grand jury to be empaneled at the same time. The grand jury has jurisdiction to hear cases where the crime was committed within the court's jurisdiction. If a hearing is being held on a case when the term expires, the grand jury is usually empowered to continue until the case is complete.

The method of selecting grand jurors must not discriminate on the basis of race, gender, religion, or political affiliation. A defendant can challenge the indictment if the selection process is discriminatory, even though he/she is not a member of a group discriminated against. The challenge is to the selection process, not the composition of a single grand jury. For example, a white male could challenge the grand jury if Hispanics had been systematically excluded from grand juries for the past 10 years, but not based on the fact that there were no Hispanics on the grand jury that indicted him.

Grand jurors do not have to be selected in the same manner as trial jurors. Some states use a sponsor system, whereby judges or other officials provide names for a list of individuals to serve on the grand jury. Names are drawn from this list to make the grand jury. A person is usually disqualified for grand jury duty if he/she is not a citizen, cannot speak English, or is currently serving as a trial juror. Economic hardship caused by missing work for extensive service on the grand jury is usually grounds for exemption. There is usually no process whereby a defendant can remove individual grand jurors for personal prejudice or by peremptory challenge.

At common law, a **grand jury** consisted of 23 people, and a positive vote of 12 was required to indict. Many states still use these numbers. Those that do not typically require a vote of one more than half of the grand jurors in order to indict. The combination of the majority vote and the lengthy term served by grand jurors has led to rules that permit indictment even though not all members were present to hear the evidence: a majority of the grand jurors must have heard all of the evidence and statutory minimum must vote to indict. For example, if only 20 of the 23 grand jurors heard the evidence of Jane Smith's guilt, the indictment would still be valid as long as 12 members who heard all the evidence voted for the indictment.

All states empower grand juries to hear felony cases brought to them by the prosecutor. Unlike trial jurors, grand jurors are usually allowed to consider facts in their personal knowledge when making decisions. Some states authorize grand juries to initiate criminal investigations on their own and return indictments. Government corruption is frequently an area the grand jury is authorized to investigate without the prosecutor's cooperation. Some states provide investigators and legal counsel to assist the grand jury; others prohibit these forms of assistance.

Grand juries frequently are also required to make a variety of reports on government functions. They may tour all custodial facilities and report on their conditions. Some states go so far as asking the grand jury to make recommendations for improving the efficiency of local government.

The judge may charge the grand jury with investigating a specific crime, but in most cases the prosecutor presents the case to the grand jury. An experienced prosecutor will have prepared the case by making a list of potential witnesses and questions to be asked. Relevant physical evidence will be ready for presentation. Taking testimony by the grand jury is usually less formal than in court. Most of the rules of evidence do not apply, but confidential and privileged communications cannot be obtained. Grand jurors are usually allowed to ask questions and request that additional witnesses be subpoenaed. The exclusionary rule does not apply: the grand jury can base its decision on evidence seized in violation of the Fourth Amendment. A person who has been summoned does not have to be told what crime is being investigated or who is suspected of criminal wrongdoing. Refusal of a subpoenaed witness to testify, except when invoking the self-incrimination clause of the Fifth Amendment, is grounds for holding the witness in contempt of court and can result in incarceration for the remainder of the grand jury's term.

The defendant's rights are vastly different before a grand jury than when a preliminary hearing is held (review Table 8-2). The defendant does not have to be told that he/she is the focus of a grand jury investigation. Neither does the defendant have the right to cross-examine witnesses or present evidence to exonerate him-/herself. Unsolicited attempts to communicate such information to the grand jury are considered contempt of court and, in some states, can also be charged as misdemeanors. If the grand jury decides to call the defendant to testify, most states do not give him/her the right to refuse to testify, but the Fifth Amendment can be invoked as grounds to refuse to answer specific questions. A common practice is to allow the defense attorney to wait in the hallway and consult with the defendant when the defendant so requests. This works to the disadvantage of the defendant who does not know his/her rights well enough to anticipate when legal advice is needed prior to answering a question.

The length of time a grand jury devotes to one case varies enormously. Sometimes the prosecutor can present a fairly simple case in less than an hour. Complicated cases take longer. Sometimes a grand jury hears evidence for several months. Unlike a trial jury, which ordinarily meets daily or at least four days a week, a grand jury may devote only one day a week, or sporadic meetings, to the investigation.

A vote will be taken after all the evidence has been heard. Some states use the *prima facie* case standard for grand jury proceedings. Others ask the grand jurors to consider whether all the evidence before them, if unexplained or uncontradicted, would warrant a conviction. State law specifies how many grand jurors must agree in order to indict: it is usually a simple majority or slightly more. If the requisite number of grand jurors vote to indict, the indictment will be endorsed a **true bill** and must be signed by the foreperson. A variety of terms are used to endorse an indictment if there are insufficient votes to indict: "ignoramus" (Latin for "we are ignorant" of the facts); **no bill,** and "not a true bill." Most states make the failure of a grand jury to indict a bar to seeking an indictment on the charges against the same suspect in the future.

The indictment serves as an arrest warrant for the defendant if he/she was not in custody at the time of the indictment. Sometimes law enforcement is poised to act as soon as the indictment is returned, in order to prevent the suspects from fleeing the state to avoid prosecution. In some cases the defense attorney will make arrangements for the suspect to appear for arraignment on the indictment without being arrested.

8-7 Arraignment on Indictment or Information

An **arraignment** is held **on** the **information,** presentment, or **indictment.** The rights afforded the defendant at the arraignment on the complaint apply: the defendant has the right to be present and represented by an attorney; the charges will be read or a copy of the formal pleading entered into the record and given to the defendant; a plea will be entered; future court dates will be set; and a bail hearing will be incorporated into the proceedings, if necessary.

This arraignment has legal significance for several reasons. In states with a two-tier court system for felonies and misdemeanors, the original arraignment is usually held in the lower court, but the arraignment on the indictment or information is held in the higher court. This second arraignment is necessary to establish the jurisdiction of the higher court. The charges filed originally may be different from those that will be brought to trial. Providing the defense with a copy of the indictment or information fulfills the due process notice requirement. Some cases are presented to the grand jury before the defendant is arrested so there has been no previous arraignment. Due process mandates the arraignment on the indictment under these circumstances.

Chapter Summary

The defendant has the right to be represented by an attorney at all proceedings from the arraignment through the first appeal. Law enforcement officers are not allowed to question the defendant after arraignment without a waiver of this right to counsel.

All felonies tried under federal law must be taken to the grand jury. State legislatures have the option of authorizing proceedings by preliminary hearing or grand jury. The need for secrecy prior to arresting the suspect as well as the amount of time required for a preliminary hearing versus grand jury proceedings are considerations for the prosecutor when deciding which avenues to pursue.

The defendant has the right to a public hearing. Even if the defendant wishes to waive this right, the press has the right to attend preliminary hearings. The judge may close the preliminary hearing during the testimony of a child victim if testifying before the public would cause severe emotional trauma. Grand jury proceedings are held in secret, and the press has no constitutional right to attend. Some states also prohibit grand jury witnesses from discussing their testimony with the press.

The preliminary hearing proceeds much like a trial, except that there is no jury and usually no opening or closing statements. A judge hears the case. The prosecution has the burden of proving that there is probable cause to take the case to trial. Witnesses will be called, questioned, and cross-examined, much as at trial. Some rules of evidence may be modified to expedite the preliminary hearing. The defense has the right to present evidence, including the defendant's testimony. At the end of the preliminary hearing, the judge will determine if sufficient evidence has been presented on the charges. If so, the defendant will be held to answer. The prosecutor will draft an information stating the charges.

Grand juries have traditionally been considered a protection against government harassment. Their proceedings are held in secret to protect the grand jurors from outside pressures. Today the prosecutor prepares most cases for the grand jury, although the right of jurors to conduct independent investigations still exists. Many of the constitutional rights afforded the defendant at the preliminary hearing and trial do not apply to grand jury proceedings. Statutes establish how many grand jurors must vote for the indictment. If sufficient votes are obtained, the indictment is endorsed a true bill. Warrants will be issued if no one is in custody on the charges and arrests made where possible.

The defendant must be arraigned on the indictment or information. This establishes the jurisdiction of the court which will try the case. It also complies with due process notice requirements by informing the defendant of the charges against him/her and when the trial is scheduled.

Study Questions

1. Explain the defendant's right to counsel after indictment
   a. if the defendant is in custody and previously invoked the *Miranda* right to counsel.
   b. if the defendant is in custody and has *not* previously invoked the *Miranda* right to counsel.
   c. if the defendant is not in custody.
2. Explain when it is mandatory that the prosecutor take a criminal case to a grand jury.
   a. if charges were filed in federal court
   b. if charges were filed in state where you live
3. List 10 ways grand jury proceedings differ from those of a preliminary hearing.
4. How soon after arraignment must a preliminary hearing be held in your state
   a. if the defendant remains in jail?
   b. if the defendant has been released from jail?
5. At a preliminary hearing
   a. who has the burden of proof?
   b. what level of proof is required?
   c. who has the right to subpoena witnesses?
   d. who has the right to present evidence?

6. Determine the following facts about preliminary hearings for crimes committed in the town where you live.
  a. the location where preliminary hearings are held
  b. the days of the week when preliminary hearings are held
  c. how judges are assigned to preliminary hearings
  d. the average court time needed for a preliminary hearing
7. What does the law in your state require for service of a subpoena?
  a. How is the subpoena initiated?
  b. Who may serve the subpoena?
  c. Are there restrictions on when the subpoena may be served?
  d. Are there restrictions on how long a subpoena is valid?
  e. When can subpoenas be served out of state?
8. How is the grand jury selected in your county?
  a. How are names selected for grand jury service?
  b. How many members are there on a grand jury?
  c. How many members must vote in favor of bringing charges against the suspect in order to indict?
  d. How long do members of the grand jury serve?
  e. How often does the grand jury meet?
  f. Can more than one grand jury be empaneled at the same time?
9. What are the local rules regarding grand jury proceedings?
  a. Can a suspect refuse to testify?
  b. Does the suspect have the right to have an attorney present?
  c. Are witnesses before the grand jury sworn to secrecy?
  d. What level of proof is required to indict?
  e. How many grand jurors must vote in favor of indictment?
  f. Is the suspect entitled to a transcript of the grand jury proceedings after he/she has been indicted?
  g. Is the press entitled to see a copy of the transcript of the grand jury proceedings after the suspects have been arrested?
10. What are the local practices for arraignment on the information or indictment?
  a. In what court are the arraignments held?
  b. When are they held?
  c. Are there time limits on how long after the preliminary hearing or indictment the arraignment must be held?

True or False Questions

1. The right of an indigent defendant to have counsel appointed at government expense only applies to trials.
2. States have the option to use a grand jury in felony cases or to design an alternate method of reviewing cases.
3. Grand jury proceedings are open to the public.
4. The defendant has a constitutional right to have his/her preliminary hearing closed to the public.
5. Both the prosecution and defense have the right to subpoena witnesses to testify at the preliminary hearing.
6. The prosecutor will file an indictment if the judge at the preliminary hearing rules that the defendant should be "held to answer."
7. If the preliminary hearing is held in a court with limited jurisdiction, the trial will be held in the same court.
8. The selection of members for the grand jury is done in the same manner as the selection of members of the trial jury.
9. An indictment is used if a criminal case is taken to the grand jury.
10. A defendant is arraigned after the preliminary hearing only if he/she was not arraigned previously on the charges.

Pretrial Court Proceedings

O u t l i n e

Key Terms

bail	Fruit of the Poison Tree	plea bargaining
bail bond	Doctrine	points and authorities
cash bail	geographical jurisdiction	pretrial conference
challenge to the pleadings	good faith exception	public safety exception
charge bargaining	house arrest	question of fact
discovery	independent source	speedy trial
diversion	inevitable discovery	statute of limitations
double jeopardy	insufficient evidence	subject matter jurisdiction
electronic monitoring	lack of jurisdiction	suppression hearing
Exclusionary Rule	non-cash bail	suppression motion
failure to state a	own recognizance release	*voir dire*
cause of action	personal bond	

Learning Objectives

Learning Objectives

After reading this chapter, the student will be able to

- Explain the process used to determine if a defendant will be released from custody before trial.
- Describe the plea bargaining process.
- Explain the use of pretrial diversion in criminal cases.
- Explain at least four types of legal challenges that can be made to a complaint, an indictment, or information.
- Explain the pretrial proceedings to obtain rulings on the admissibility of evidence.
- Describe the discovery process in criminal cases.
- Explain the purpose of pretrial conferences in criminal cases.

Many legal maneuvers occur before trial. The defendant may be released from custody. Many cases are resolved by a plea bargain, while others are diverted from the criminal justice system. The defense frequently attempts to have specific items of evidence ruled inadmissible and/or have the charges dismissed. Many states now require that the prosecutor and defense attorney share evidence rather than disrupt the trial with surprise witnesses. One of the final steps is a pretrial conference with the attorneys and judge present to settle administrative matters.

9-1 Pretrial Release

Defendants in capital cases are nearly always kept in custody from the time of their arrest until trial. The death penalty is considered to be sufficient motivation to cause these inmates to flee the jurisdiction if allowed to leave the jail. Most other defendants are eligible for release prior to trial. Traditionally the decision to release has focused on the likelihood that the person will appear in court as scheduled; many jurisdictions now consider other factors, such as the likelihood the person will commit additional crimes or will threaten potential prosecution witnesses if released from custody. The most common device used to assure that the defendant will appear for trial is to require the posting of **bail** or a bond. **Own recognizance release** (commonly referred to as OR) has become common during the past 30 years. **Electronic monitoring** is now being used to verify that the defendant has not violated the conditions of release.

9-1a Bail

Bail can be defined as setting an inmate free when security has been posted for his/her appearance at a specific location on the date indicated. It is commonly used before trial, and, under some circumstances, defendants are released on bail while appealing a conviction. The amount of the bail is set high enough so that a person will appear for trial in order to have the bail returned. Bail is set higher in felony cases because a defendant facing a prison sentence is more likely to flee to avoid conviction and sentencing. Since the consequences of a misdemeanor conviction are less serious, a lower bail is considered adequate to obtain the defendant's attendance at trial.

At one time, bail was routinely set at the arraignment. If the defendant wanted an earlier release, the defense attorney filed a *habeas corpus* petition requesting a bail-setting hearing. This process was both time-consuming for the courts and expensive for the defendants. Today many courts have bail schedules: a list stating the bail for specific offenses. At the time of booking, the person who has been arrested is told the amount of bail. Arrangements for posting bail can be made without waiting for a court appearance.

Sometimes the amount stated in the bail schedule is not appropriate for the case. Two opposite reasons result in deviation from normal bail: a poor defendant who cannot afford the normal bail but is likely to appear at trial and a rich defendant who is not likely to be deterred from fleeing by the normal bail for the offense. In either of these cases, a bail hearing may be held to review the personal situation of the defendant and determine what is reasonable bail under the circumstances. Excessive bail is considered a violation of the Eighth Amendment.

Traffic court is the most common example of posting bail. Many states permit the person who receives a traffic ticket to post bail in the amount of the fine for the offense. If the person does not appear for trial, a conviction is entered and bail forfeited. In practice, many people believe they are paying the fine and do not even think of it as bail (see Table 9-1).

Bail can be posted in several forms. **Cash bail** is deposited with the court clerk or at another designated location, such as the jail or police station. Cash, money order, or cashier's check is required. The entire amount of the bail is usually returned if the defendant appears in court as ordered. Cash bail is not costly for the defendant who keeps the scheduled court date because the entire amount is returned: all that is lost is interest that would have been earned on the money used for bail.

Many defendants cannot afford to post cash bail. A **bail bond** may be posted instead. This bond functions as an insurance policy: the person

T A B L E **9-1** Pretrial Release on $10,000 Bail

Type of Release		Cost to Defendant Who Appears in Court as Scheduled
Bail		
Cash	Deposit:	$10,000 with court
	Refund:	$10,000
	Net cost:	0
Non-cash	Deposit:	$20,000* worth of deeds, stock certificates, etc., with court
	Refund:	All items deposited
	Net cost:	0
Bail bond	Pay:	$1,000** to bail bond company
	Refund:	0
	Net cost:	$1,000
Personal bond	Deposit:	$1,000** with court
	Refund:	$900
	Net cost:	$100
OR release	Deposit:	0. Must show ties to community indicating likelihood defendant will appear for trial
	Refund:	Not applicable
	Net cost:	0

*Estimate based on posting twice cash bail.
**Based on estimate of 10 percent. Actual amounts vary.

needing bail pays a premium, usually ranging from 10 percent to 25 percent of the bail, depending on the risk to the bonding company; in return, the bonding company gives the court its guarantee that the person will appear for trial. If the person does not go to court as scheduled, the bond company must pay the court the full amount of the bail. On the other hand, if the defendant appears as scheduled, the bond company keeps the premium and owes the court nothing. Bond companies employ investigators to locate people who do not appear as scheduled. Court rules frequently permit the bond company a period of time, such as 10 days, in which to bring the defendant to court, rather than paying the full amount of the bail. The bond company frequently has the option of returning a person to jail before the court date if it believes there is likelihood he/she will leave the jurisdiction.

Some jurisdictions use an intermediate device, referred to as **personal bond,** when the defendant cannot afford cash bail but appears likely to keep the court date. The defendant posts an amount equivalent to what would be paid to a bail bond company. A processing fee may be charged, perhaps 10 percent of the amount posted, but the remainder of the money is returned to the defendant when all court dates have been kept. This provides a less expensive way for low income people to post bail.

Non-cash bail may also be posted. Deeds to real estate can be used for this purpose. State law usually specifies the ratio of property value to bail. For example, a person may have to post deeds to property appraised at twice the dollar amount of bail. The reason for requiring more than face value is that the price received at forced sales is usually below market value. Only equity in property can be used as bond; the amount of outstanding mortgages will be deducted when determining if sufficient property has been posted. A lien is usually filed against the property, so that the amount of the bail can be recovered if the property is sold.

9-1b Own Recognizance Release

An inmate may be released on his/her promise to appear in court as scheduled. OR releases are usually given to inmates who are believed to be very likely to attend trial. The inmate is usually asked to complete a questionnaire, and the facts given are verified. Factors usually considered favorable for OR release include: is currently employed; has a stable job record; has lived in the community for some time; has family in the community; may receive a relatively short sentence; and has few prior arrests or convictions. There may be points assigned to each of the factors involved, and an inmate who has a specified number of points will be released OR. As with bail, a person who has been released OR may be returned to jail if there is evidence of plans to flee the jurisdiction, rather than stand trial, or if the person has committed another crime.

9-1c Electronic Monitoring

A variety of electronic devices are currently being used to monitor activities of defendants released pending trial, as well as to supervise those on probation and parole. Pretrial monitoring can be done as a condition of being released either on bail or OR. Two basic types of devices are in use: an electronic device that must be inserted into a receiver attached to a telephone and one that sends a radio signal that can be used to determine where the transmitting device is located. Both procedures rely on having tamper-proof equipment that the defendant wears, usually as a bracelet or leg band, and that the defendant cannot remove. Many jurisdictions require the person being released to pay the cost of the monitoring equipment; some also permit the court to assess the cost of supervision.

House arrest occurs when the defendant is released but ordered to stay at home, or some other location, and wear electronic monitoring equipment. Frequently the defendant wears an electronic bracelet, which must be inserted into a device attached to a telephone in order to verify where the wearer is. The person is directed to activate the monitor at specific times and verify his/her presence whenever the probation officer calls. By calling at unpredictable times, the probation officer attempts to maintain surveillance of the defendant's activities. Other identifying techniques, such as asking for specific personal data, may be requested to ensure that the defendant has not transferred the device to another person.

More mobile tracking devices are used for defendants who are not required to stay at one location. By transmitting a honing signal, the device can send information on where it is currently located. This gives the probation officer the ability to monitor the defendant's movements without voice or visual contact. The defendant is deterred from committing additional crimes because he/she knows his/her movements can be traced to the crime scene.

9-2 Plea Bargaining

The prosecutor and defense attorney frequently reach an agreement on the charges the defendant will plead guilty to. Bargaining done before the arraignment is technically called **charge bargaining.** The same type of negotiations done later in the case is called **plea bargaining.** Both are frequently called plea bargaining; that practice is followed in this book. Plea bargaining may occur at any time from arrest until the jury returns a verdict. The key questions usually are "On which charges will the defendant enter guilty pleas?" and "What sentence will be imposed?" State law and local practice may set limits on plea bargaining. In some states the judge retains the power to sentence; therefore, the plea bargain cannot guarantee a maximum sentence. The defendant can usually withdraw the plea if the judge will not honor the conditions the prosecutor agreed to when making it.

An experienced prosecutor can usually make a reasonable estimate of the case's chances of success and the sentence the judge is likely to give. Based on this estimation a plea bargain may be offered to the defendant. In other cases, the defense attorney approaches the prosecutor and initiates the bargaining process. Lengthy negotiations may be involved before the deal is completed. A variety of inducements are used: drop one or more of the charges; do not use enhancements that would increase the sentence, such as use of a weapon or prior felony conviction; recommend shorter sentence; or dismiss charges in this case if the defendant will assist the prosecution on other cases. The Supreme Court has upheld the prosecutor's right to file additional charges if the defendant refuses to plead guilty provided there is a factual basis for each new charge. Refusal to admit guilt can also be considered as an aggravating factor when sentencing the defendant.

There is no trial when all the charges are settled by plea bargaining. The agreement will be formalized before a judge. This is frequently done in the court that handles arraignments. The proceedings include the defendant's waiver of the rights associated with a trial as well as the entry of the guilty plea. The judge usually asks the defendant to affirm the following items: the plea is entered voluntarily and without coercion; the defendant is represented by an attorney or has voluntarily waived the right to counsel; the defendant waives trial rights, including public trial, confrontation of witnesses against him/her, right to present a defense, and a jury of peers deciding the case. The judge may sentence the defendant immediately after the plea is accepted or order a presentence investigation report and schedule a sentencing hearing for a later date.

Many ask if plea bargaining is fair. Does it give the victim justice? Is it fair to society? At its best, plea bargaining reaches a conclusion that is fair in that the defendant receives a sentence similar to those of other defendants with similar charges. To the extent that plea bargaining has driven down the "cost" of crime for all defendants, this result is not fair to society. Some victims are well served by plea bargaining because it reduces the number of court sessions they must attend and the trauma of testifying and facing grueling cross-examination. This is particularly so if they believe the defendant receives a "fair" sentence. Other victims are outraged by the plea bargaining process because it reduces their case to a commodity to be bartered away by the attorneys. The greatest anger is voiced when a very lenient punishment is the result of the process.

A less often asked question is whether plea bargaining is fair to defendants. Some defendants benefit greatly by plea bargains that substantially reduce the sentence they receive. Some unscrupulous defense attorneys who take cases for a flat fee see plea bargaining as a way to increase their incomes and avoid time-consuming trials. These attorneys pressure their clients to enter a plea that may not be much of a bargain. A few innocent defendants, frequently at the prompting of their attorneys, weigh the cost in time, money, and emotional energy of a trial to vindicate their reputation plus the uncertainty of a jury verdict against probation or a short sentence and plead guilty. These defendants may claim plea bargaining is not fair. Plea bargaining as practiced in many courts has little to do with these concerns. Judges with too many cases to handle are inclined to make "moving the calendar" a high priority. Prosecutors who face having cases dismissed because the statutory time between arraignment and trial is about to expire frequently decide that a plea bargain, however favorable to the defense, is better than no conviction at all. Experienced defense attorneys understand the pressures on the system and use these problems as leverage to achieve the best possible results for their clients. Habitual criminals also know how the process works and take advantage of its weaknesses.

9-3 Diversion

Some cases can be best handled outside the criminal justice system. **Diversion** is the process used to send these cases to resources outside the court system. Diverted cases typically involve first offenders with misdemeanor charges when there appears to be a high potential for rehabilitation through counseling. The main problem may be alcoholism or drug abuse, lack of parenting skills (child abuse cases), and poor anger control and communication skills (domestic violence cases). Many states have established programs to divert these cases. Each is governed by specific state laws, but general patterns will be discussed in this section.

Defendants are usually screened prior to entering the program; only those who were not diverted into the program previously and have no serious criminal record are usually accepted. The screening criteria are usually stated in the state statute. The probation department or other court officers verify eligibility. In addition to meeting the entry criteria, the defendant must consent to be in the program. Conditions of diversion usually include attending counseling sessions for six months to two years, committing no new crimes similar to the one which triggered diversion, and refraining from other specified conduct. Many states require the defendant to pay for the cost of counseling and any other services used.

Some programs divert the defendant before the charges are filed. The prosecutor will keep the complaint, so it can be filed if the offender does not satisfactorily complete the program. When prefiling diversion is used, the case can be held only until the statute of limitations has expired. The defendant who successfully completes the program has no record because the case was never filed in court.

A more typical pattern is to file the criminal charges and then have the defendant agree to diversion. The judge obtains the defendant's waiver of speedy trial, agreement to attend counseling for a specific period, and acknowledgment that charges can be prosecuted if the defendant does not perform satisfactorily during the diversion program. A court hearing is usually required to obtain a ruling that the defendant has failed diversion so prosecution may be reinstituted. Charges are dismissed against defendants who satisfactorily complete the program, and their arrest records are expunged.

There are several problems with diversion. One is the level of supervision provided. Counselors frequently feel that their therapeutic role is compromised by reporting violations to the court. A probation officer or another person assigned by the court is needed to ensure that the defendant is attending the counseling sessions and to determine if the defendant has been arrested and, if so, for what charges.

Finding appropriate counseling programs can be another problem. Most combine formal instruction with a group therapy format. They need to be focused on specific problems. Defendants from child abuse cases need to go to parenting classes; permitting them to attend counseling for drunk drivers is inappropriate. Some defendants, however, may have more than one problem and need to be involved in multiple counseling programs: for example, an alcoholic parent who abuses his/her children may need a program for alcoholics as well as one to teach parenting skills.

Prosecuting the case after the defendant fails diversion may also be a problem. If the defendant was on diversion for a lengthy period of time, it may be difficult to locate witnesses needed for the trial. Even when located, some may not want to testify. While the case can be prosecuted whenever the defendant fails diversion, many cases ultimately are dismissed because of uncooperative or missing witnesses. This is particularly true in spousal abuse cases. Even when the case is tried immediately, many victims do not want to testify. When the victim has tried to start a new life, facing the abuser again after one to two years and going over the old incidents are often traumatic. Another problem is that some victims continue their relationship with their abusers and are fearful of testifying.

9-4 Challenges to the Pleadings

There are a variety of technical challenges that defense attorneys make prior to trial. Many are based entirely on the content of the complaint, indictment, or information. The challenge can be to the entire document or to only one of the counts. A formal motion is usually made to the court and a hearing held. This procedure is called a **challenge to the pleadings.**

TABLE **9-2 Challenges to Pleadings**

Challenge	Defense Must Show
Double jeopardy	Official court records indicating prior conviction or acquittal on the same offense or a greater/lesser included offense
Lack of subject matter jurisdiction	The state law that this court does not have the authority to handle the charges in the case
Lack of geographical jurisdiction	An official map of the court district and testimony showing the crime occurred outside its boundaries
Statute of limitations	The time between the date the crime occurred and the date of filing the case in court exceeding the statute of limitations for the crime charged
Speedy trail, Sixth Amendment	Evidence that the defendant's right to a fair trial was violated, requiring a combination of lengthy delay, the fact that the defendant asserted the right to speedy trial, no valid reason for delays, and prejudice to the defendant caused by delays
State law	Evidence that the time between filing the charges and the first day of trial, excluding continuances requested by the defendant, exceeds the time limit specified in state law

State court rules frequently mandate that the defense make these motions before trial. Failure to make a timely motion waives the right to raise the issue later. If the motion is made at the appropriate time but the judge denies it erroneously, the issue can be raised again on appeal or through some other procedure (see Table 9-2).

9-4a Double Jeopardy

The Fifth Amendment protection against **double jeopardy** applies in state court. A defendant cannot be convicted for an offense after being acquitted on it. A conviction on a lesser included offense is void if the defendant has already been convicted of a crime which includes the lesser offense. The opposite is also true: a defendant who has been convicted of the lesser offense cannot be convicted for the greater one. For an offense to be considered a lesser included offense, all elements of the lesser offense must be included in the definition of the more serious one. For example, theft is a lesser included offense in robbery.

Many times the judge will not know that there has been a prior prosecution for the crime. Procedurally it is up to the defense to bring double jeopardy to the court's attention. This is usually done with a motion to dismiss the case on grounds of double jeopardy. A certified copy of the prior conviction must be presented to the judge in order to establish double jeopardy. Even with this in hand, dismissal of the charge may not be required if the prosecution successfully demonstrates that the two offenses are not the same: for example, what the defense claims is a lesser included offense may not qualify. If the prosecution is able to demonstrate that the two prosecutions are by separate sovereigns (for example, state and federal governments), double jeopardy does not apply.

Either a conviction or an acquittal on the charge must have occurred to qualify for pretrial dismissal based on double jeopardy. It is not a defense that the complaint lists a crime and its lesser included offense. Neither does it apply to pretrial dismissal of charges filed previously—for example, the judge's ruling that there was insufficient evidence to hold the defendant to answer at the end of the preliminary hearing. If the jury finds the defendant guilty of crimes to which double jeopardy applies, the judge should dismiss the lesser one at the time of sentencing, or the appellate court will make a similar ruling.

9-4b Lack of Jurisdiction

A challenge based on **lack of jurisdiction** raises the issue of whether the court is authorized to hear the case. It can be based on lack of either subject matter or geographical jurisdiction. In a two-tier court system, it is possible to allege that the court does not have jurisdiction over certain offenses; for example, a lower-level court may not have jurisdiction to proceed on felony charges after the preliminary hearing, or a higher-level court may not have jurisdiction to hold a trial on misdemeanors unless at least one felony is charged in the same complaint. These technical challenges to subject matter jurisdiction are based on intricacies of state law. Legal maneuvers, such as suppression hearings, that caused some of the charges to be dismissed may affect the **subject matter jurisdiction** of the court on the remaining charges.

The court also lacks jurisdiction if the offense occurred outside the geographical boundaries of the court district or, in the case of large districts, outside the boundaries of the particular subdivision of the district that the court hearing the cases services. Challenges to **geographical jurisdiction** are more mechanical: the exact location where the crime occurred must be established, and the boundaries of the court district must be proven. Proof of the court's geographical jurisdiction is established by introducing the official map. Testimony of eye witnesses may be required to establish where the offense occurred. For example, if the defense can show that the offense occurred 30 feet outside the judicial district's boundary, the court does not have geographical jurisdiction to try the case. The analysis may be complicated by the fact that some crimes, such as kidnapping, can occur in more than one court district.

9-4c Statute of Limitations

Much like challenges based on geographical jurisdiction, the statute of limitations is a combination of very specific rules and the facts. State law establishes a **statute of limitations,** the maximum length of time during which a prosecution can be begun, for most crimes. Capital offenses and a few other crimes usually have no statute of limitations. For all other cases it is a matter of checking the code for the applicable period. Many states consider the statute of limitations satisfied as long as an arrest warrant is issued within the limitation period. In such cases the code specifies how long the warrant is valid; an arrest after the expiration date has a similar effect as one after the statute of limitations has expired.

The factual question is determining whether the time period from the day the crime occurred until the date the complaint was filed exceeds the statute of limitations. For example, the defense could successfully challenge a misdemeanor battery charge with a statute of limitations of one year if the complaint alleges the offense occurred on August 1, 2000, and the complaint was stamped "Filed" on August 3, 2001. At the pretrial stage, the date given in the pleadings is considered correct. If at trial it appears that the crime was committed on an earlier date, the challenge can be renewed. The defendant is entitled to the statute of limitations that was in effect on the date the crime was committed; changes by the legislature that go into effect at a later date cannot be used to defeat a motion raising this issue.

9-4d Lack of a Speedy Trial

The Sixth Amendment gives defendants the right to a **speedy trial.** This refers to the period from arrest to the first day of trial. The Supreme Court has identified four factors that must be considered in evaluating this issue: length of the delay; reasons for the delay; the defendant's assertion of the right to a speedy trial; and prejudice to the defendant. No one factor is determinative. The defendant must show that the combination of these factors resulted in the denial of a fair trial. The longer the delay, however, the less evidence there needs to be of actual prejudice.

Defendants cannot ignore the issue during lengthy delays and then claim that their right to a speedy trial has been violated: timely objections must be made. A defendant who requests a continuance waives the right to claim a denial of speedy trial for the time consumed by the continuance;

lengthy delays by the prosecution after the defense has requested that the trial begin can be considered. Pretrial appeals taken in good faith by the prosecution cannot be used as grounds for claiming denial of speedy trial. An example of a successful challenge based on denial of speedy trial is a case that did not go to trial for four years because the prosecution repeatedly asked for continuance on the grounds it was not ready while the defense was demanding that the trial begin; during this lengthy delay, the defendant's key witness died.

Most states have statutes which establish time lines for bringing the case to trial. It is usually easier for the defense to win motions based on these statutes than based on the Sixth Amendment because the codes normally state specific time periods, such as 120 days. Demonstrating violation of such rules is easier than showing prejudice to the case: the judge counts the calendar days from the last relevant proceeding, such as the judge's holding the defendant to answer at the end of the preliminary hearing, to the first day of trial.

9-4e Other Challenges to the Pleadings

Failure to state a cause of action is a challenge to pleadings. It claims that the information given on one or more counts does not adequately describe a crime. The judge must review the wording of the complaint and determine if every element of the crime charged is included in the pleading. Motions based on careless drafting, typographical errors, or words omitted when typing the documents are successful. Challenges on this ground are more common in fact-pleading states because the documents must show facts for each element of the crime. In code-pleading jurisdictions, a cause of action can be stated by merely referencing the code section. The judge will usually allow the prosecution to correct the error and refile the charges if the statute of limitations has not expired.

A variety of other technical challenges can be made, depending on local court rules. Failure to have the correct signatures on the documents is one. The fact that the code section being charged has been repealed or ruled unconstitutional is another. Defense attorneys keep abreast of local rules, so that they can make any challenge that is feasible.

9-5 Challenges to the Evidence

Pretrial motions are used to obtain a judge's ruling on whether evidence can be admitted at trial. In criminal cases the defense is likely to utilize these procedures to activate the **Exclusionary Rule** and thereby suppress evidence that was obtained in violation of the defendant's constitutional rights. A hearing is held; both sides have the opportunity to present evidence and argue the law on the issues. If the defense succeeds in having evidence suppressed, a motion is usually made to dismiss the charges. The outcome of this tactical maneuver depends on how much credible evidence remains after inadmissible evidence is suppressed (see Table 9-3).

9-5a Exclusionary Rule and Fruit of the Poison Tree Doctrine

The Exclusionary Rule was imposed on federal courts in *Weeks v. United States* (232 U.S. 383, 58 L.Ed. 652, 34 S.Ct. 341 [1914]) and extended to state courts in *Mapp v. Ohio* (367 U.S. 643, 6 L.Ed. 2d 1081, 81 S.Ct. 1684 [1961]). The early cases focused on Fourth Amendment issues; since that time the rule has been used for *Miranda* violations as well as a variety of other infringements of constitutional rights. Basically the rule states that evidence obtained in violation of the defendant's constitutional rights cannot be used at trial to establish his/her guilt. Many states have similar rules that prevent the use of evidence obtained in violation of their statutes in addition to constitutional errors.

T A B L E **9-3 Challenges to Evidence**

Challenge	Evidence Considered	Legal Issue
Warrant not valid, no probable cause	Facts in affidavits submitted to judge when warrant issued	Do all facts in affidavit, taken together, establish probable cause?
False information in affidavit	Testimony to establish what facts were known to be false or included with reckless disregard of truth	Judge reviews affidavit after excluding known falsehoods and lies included with reckless disregard of truth: do facts that remain show probable cause?
Search and seizure violation	Transcripts of preliminary hearing and grand jury plus sworn testimony at suppression hearing	Determine what law applies to the search that was conducted; then determine if facts show that the search violated that law.
Confession obtained in violation of *Miranda*	Transcripts of preliminary hearing and grand jury plus sworn testimony at suppression hearing	Determine if *Miranda* warnings were required; if so, were warnings given correctly and did defendant make a knowing, intelligent, and voluntary waiver?

Closely related to the Exclusionary Rule is the **Fruit of the Poison Tree Doctrine** (*Wong Sun v. United States,* 371 U.S. 471, 9 L.Ed. 2d 441, 83 S.Ct. 407 [1963]). The Exclusionary Rule prevents the use of unconstitutionally obtained evidence at trial. The Fruit of the Poison Tree Doctrine is invoked if other evidence (sometimes called derivative evidence) is discovered *as a result of* evidence that falls under the Exclusionary Rule.

Example 1   A police officer arrested Dan *without* probable cause. At the time of the arrest, the officer searched Dan and found cocaine in his pocket and the key to a storage locker in his wallet. When the storage locker was searched, officers discovered 10 kilograms of marijuana.

√ An arrest without probable cause is a violation of the Fourth Amendment—the Exclusionary Rule can be used to prevent testimony about the arrest.
√ Cocaine was seized during the search incident to the illegal arrest. This search is so closely related to the arrest that it will probably be considered under the Exclusionary Rule.
√ Marijuana was not discovered during the arrest and search of Dan, but it was found *as a result of* the illegal search. It will be excluded under the Fruit of the Poison Tree Doctrine.

Example 2   Denise was legally arrested and taken to the police station. *Miranda* warnings were *not* administered properly. She confessed to committing a burglary and selling a stolen TV to Sally. The police arrested Sally. At the time Sally was arrested, Denise's statement was the only evidence the police had, indicating that Sally was involved in criminal activity.

√ Denise's confession is inadmissible because of the *Miranda* violation; it cannot be introduced at Denise's trial to prove that she is guilty. This is an application of the Exclusionary Rule.
√ Sally's arrest is based on information illegally obtained while questioning Denise; it is therefore inadmissible under the Fruit of the Poison Tree Doctrine.

Evidence that would normally fall under the Fruit of the Poison Tree Doctrine may be admitted if there are sufficient intervening events involved to remove the taint of the original illegal activity. Whether this has occurred is determined by reviewing the facts of the case; frequently considered are the length of time between the illegal act and discovery of the evidence; whether a person voluntarily cooperated with the investigation after being illegally arrested and/or interrogated; whether new

Miranda warnings administered after a confession was improperly obtained helped restore the person's ability to exercise his/her rights; and whether a person whose *Miranda* rights were violated was released from custody prior to the attempt to obtain the confession which the prosecution now wants to introduce at trial.

When defending a suppression motion based on the Exclusionary Rule or the Fruit of the Poison Tree Doctrine, the prosecution's first line of defense is to prove that no constitutional violation occurred. If this is successful, the judge will deny the suppression motion. When the judge rules that the defendant's rights were violated, the prosecution will try to show that an exception to the Exclusionary Rule applies. If the prosecutor is successful, the result will be that the evidence will be admitted, *even though* it was seized in violation of the defendant's constitutional rights.

The **good faith exception** to the Exclusionary Rule applies when officers honestly believe they are complying with all of the suspect's constitutional rights. This is a much narrower rule than the name implies because the Supreme Court has allowed it to be used only in a few situations: reliance on a search warrant that appeared to be valid on its face (*Massachusetts v. Sheppard,* 468 U.S. 981, 82 L.Ed. 2d 737, 104 S.Ct. 3424 [1984]; *United States v. Leon,* 468 U.S. 897, 82 L.Ed. 2d 677, 104 S.Ct. 3405 [1984]); enforcement of a statute that at the time of the arrest was believed to be valid but was later ruled unconstitutional (*Illinois v. Krull,* 480 U.S. 340, 94 L.Ed. 2d 364, 107 S.Ct. 1160 [1987]); and information in the court's computerized database that erroneously indicated that a warrant had been issued for the suspect's arrest (*Arizona v. Evans,* 514 U.S. 1, 131 L.Ed. 2d 34, 115 S.Ct. 1185 [1995]).

The **inevitable discovery** exception requires the prosecution to convince the judge that the evidence would have been discovered *even if* the illegal acts were never performed (*Nix v. Williams,* 467 U.S. 431, 81 L.Ed. 2d 377, 104 S.Ct. 2501 [1984]). For example, there were so many detectives assigned to the case that one of them would have discovered the victim's body even if the suspect had not told them where to look.

A more difficult rule to establish is referred to as the **independent source** exception (*Murray v. United States,* 487 U.S. 533, 101 L.Ed. 2d 472, 108 S.Ct. 2529 [1988]). It is based on the rationale that, although the police performed acts during the investigation that were unconstitutional, the item was found without relying on tainted evidence. The difficult part of the proof is showing that the inadmissible information was not used by the officer(s) who discovered the items that the prosecution wants to use at trial.

In emergencies officers are allowed to ask a few quick questions at the time the suspect is apprehended in order to retrieve weapons or rescue victims. This is called the **public safety exception** to the Exclusionary Rule (*New York v. Quarles,* 467 U.S. 649, 81 L.Ed. 2d 550, 104 S.Ct. 2626 [1984]). *Miranda* applies if there is an attempt to prolong questioning or to obtain a confession.

The Exclusionary Rule can be used only when government activity resulted in a violation of the defendant's rights. If the acts were done by a private person, there is no violation of constitutional rights; therefore, the Exclusionary Rule cannot be used by the defense. For example, if a neighbor took drugs from the suspect's house and gave them to the police, there is no Fourth Amendment issue, as long as the neighbor had not been recruited by the police or encouraged to engage in acts that violated the suspect's reasonable expectation of privacy.

9-5b Suppression Motion

Most states permit the defense to ask for a hearing on the issue of admissibility of evidence before the trial starts. Trial time is saved by settling these issues before trial. Knowing what evidence cannot be used at trial makes trial preparation more efficient for both sides. The pretrial hearing on whether evidence will be admissible is called a **suppression hearing** because one party is asking the court to suppress evidence. Some states permit an appeal of the admissibility ruling before trial. This gives the prosecution the opportunity to appeal it might not otherwise have: if the case went to trial and the defendant was acquitted, double jeopardy would prevent the prosecution from appealing an incorrectly granted suppression motion.

The normal procedure used to schedule the hearing is to file a **suppression motion** with the court. This written document states what evidence the moving party believes should be suppressed and is accompanied by **points and authorities,** a legal document, prepared by the attorney, requesting the court to take action; it cites statutes, case law, and legal arguments supporting the request. A court date is obtained for the hearing, and a copy of the motion, points and authorities, and notice of time and place for the hearing are served on the opposing side. The opposition then has time, frequently a minimum of 10 days, to prepare points and authorities to support its view of the law. Both sides may present relevant testimony and oral arguments at the hearing.

Suppression Motion Challenging the Validity of the Warrant

Both arrest warrants and search warrants are issued by judges based on the affidavits accompanying the warrant application and any other sworn testimony given before the judge at that time. Therefore, the validity of the warrant is evaluated based on the affidavits and transcripts of the sworn testimony. No other evidence can be introduced to support probable cause. Facts the police were aware of but did not include in the affidavits are irrelevant because the judge did not consider them when making the determination that probable cause existed. For this reason, no witnesses testify at a hearing which decides if the warrant was based on probable cause.

If an arrest warrant is being challenged, the issue is whether the facts in the affidavit, and any other sworn testimony the judge heard, are sufficient to cause a reasonable person to believe it is more probable than not that the person named in the warrant committed the crimes indicated. The judge is allowed to make reasonable inferences from the facts stated. To win the suppression motion, the defense must establish that the facts are so weak that it was erroneous to conclude that probable cause existed. Two types of attacks are typical: (1) the facts, even if believed, do not establish every element of the crime and (2) the facts are from sources, such as unreliable informants, that lack credibility. Both of these are questions of fact: the judge must weigh the facts and inferences reasonably drawn from them and make a decision. The same process is used to challenge search warrants: the affidavits must show that there was probable cause to believe that evidence which may legally be seized was at the location where the search was to be conducted and that the information came from credible sources.

Another avenue for attacking a warrant is to allege that the facts presented to the judge are untrue. The Supreme Court has ruled that falsehoods the police knowingly included in the affidavits, and statements included in reckless disregard of the truth, cannot be used to support probable cause. False information given to the police, which they had no reason to suspect was untrue, can be used to establish probable cause. The procedure at the suppression hearing starts with taking testimony on the question of whether the officers knew, or should have known, that they were including falsehoods in the affidavit. The officers may be called by the defense. Sources named in the affidavit may be called to testify that they did not provide the information stated or that the officers never questioned them. The judge must be convinced that the officers intentionally included lies, or included information they should have known was not true without checking the validity of the source.

Once the judge is convinced the officers violated this constitutional standard, the affidavit must be reconsidered. All facts that the officers knew were false, or included in reckless disregard of their truthfulness, must be deleted from the affidavit. The judge reviews the revised affidavit to determine if probable cause can be established based on the remaining facts. If there is still probable cause, the warrant is considered valid: appropriate actions taken pursuant to the warrant are constitutional. If probable cause cannot be established based on the remaining facts, the warrant is not valid; therefore, actions taken in reliance on it are unconstitutional. If the warrant was sought to search for several objects, it is possible that there is now probable cause for some, but not all, of the items sought.

The prosecution is not allowed to bring in additional facts to support the warrant. It can, however, show that the actions were valid under an exception to the warrant requirement. For example, even though it is determined that an arrest warrant was not valid, the arrest would be legal if it were made under circumstances that did not mandate the use of an arrest warrant.

Suppression Motion for Police Actions Taken Without a Warrant

The majority of suppression motions are not based on warrants. In these cases the suppression motion summarizes the facts, and the points and authorities discuss the legal issues involved. Witnesses may be called to testify at the suppression hearing, and the judge may also consider transcripts of the preliminary hearing and/or grand jury proceedings. The opposing side has the right to present its own points and authorities, to call witnesses, and to make oral arguments. If the witnesses at the suppression hearing testify in an unanticipated manner, oral arguments will attempt to explain what law applies to the facts that were introduced at this hearing. If necessary, the court may grant a continuance, so that both sides can prepare additional arguments.

Most suppression motions focus on either search and seizure violations or confessions. The focus is on the procedures used, not on the item to be introduced into evidence. For example, the issue may be whether *Miranda* warnings were given properly; the defendant's confession is not admitted at the hearing because the contents of the confession are not relevant at this stage of the proceedings. If the defendant claims a car was searched unconstitutionally, the court addresses the issue of how the Fourth Amendment rules apply to the search, not whether drugs or stolen credit cards were found in the car.

Both sides have the right to call witnesses at a suppression hearing and to cross-examine those testifying for the other side. The testimony of police officers is frequently needed to establish details about the event in question. Due to the intricacies of the laws in this area, both direct examination and cross-examination are usually very detailed and focus on minute details and the sequence in which events occurred. Many states make the defendant's testimony at the suppression hearing inadmissible at trial. This is done to allow the defendant to exercise Fourth Amendment rights without waiving the Fifth Amendment.

Sometimes testimony introduced at the preliminary hearing or before the grand jury reveals that evidence was obtained illegally. For example, testimony may not establish probable cause for the arrest; testimony may indicate that an item of evidence was seized without legal justification; or the officers may have testified to obtaining a confession without giving *Miranda* warnings. These statements were made under oath and usually are recorded in a verbatim transcript. The defense need only cite the transcript as grounds for requesting suppression of the item involved.

The prosecutor usually combines two tactics when defending against a suppression motion: presenting points and authorities to show that the item was legally obtained and arguing that the facts do not merit suppression of the evidence. There are hundreds of cases dealing with search and seizure, many of which will not be relevant to the case. The defense points and authorities cite those believed to justify suppression of the evidence. The prosecutor will look for cases that hold differently. The variations of facts that are present during police activity result in each case being unique. Arguments will be made using analogies to convince the judge which case should be applied to the facts in the present case.

Most search and seizure rules are based on reasonable police conduct. Once the correct rule of law is determined, the judge must address the **question of fact:** an individualized determination must be made on how the law applies to the events that occurred in this case. The defense attorney presented the evidence in the light most favorable to the defendant; therefore, the prosecutor needs to convince the judge that what the police did in the case was reasonable. Many times the transcripts do not provide enough information to make this decision. Testimony of police officers and other witnesses who were present when the search was performed may be used at the suppression hearing to fill these gaps.

9-5c Motion to Dismiss for Insufficient Evidence

If the defense is successful in suppressing evidence, it will frequently make a motion to dismiss the charges based on **insufficient evidence.** Success with this tactic depends on how important the evidence was that the judge ruled should be suppressed. If key items of evidence, such as the murder weapon and the defendant's confession, were suppressed, it is likely that the charge will be dismissed. On the other hand, if there is ample evidence left after something was suppressed, the motion to dismiss will be denied. In cases with multiple counts, it is possible to dismiss one or more counts but allow the prosecution of others to continue.

9-5d Other Challenges to the Evidence

A variety of other reasons exist for suppressing evidence. One is that the testimony relates to privileged conversations. Some courts will consider this issue before trial if the questioned statements are key parts of the case. The hearing relates to two distinct legal issues: if the conversation occurred under circumstances covered by the evidentiary privilege and, if so, if any exceptions to the privilege apply to the facts. Testimony regarding the circumstances under which the conversation occurred, but not the content of the conversation, is presented at the hearing.

Another challenge might be to the use of scientific evidence. One of the requirements for expert testimony is that there be an established body of knowledge in the field. Newly developed scientific tests may not meet this test. As long as the test is considered experimental, the courts will not permit testimony about the test results. For example, DNA testing (genetic fingerprinting) has been used to establish that body fluids recovered at the crime scene are from the defendant. While this type of testing is now well recognized, prior to 1990 nearly all courts rejected it because the newly developed tests were not considered "established science." Even when scientific tests are accepted, there is always the secondary issue of whether they were conducted properly in the current case.

9-6 Discovery

Discovery is the pretrial process of learning what evidence the other side has. Long ago, and in some mystery movies today, one side wins the case by producing a surprise witness. Modern court procedures require the pretrial disclosure of much of the evidence in the case. Formal discovery motions can be made in court. Frequently local practice is to give some items, such as the police reports, without waiting for a motion in court because the court automatically grants such requests. Discovery enables both sides to prepare for trial and encourages settlement of the case without going to trial. Both of these results facilitate more efficient operation of the court system.

Discovery operates somewhat differently in criminal cases than in civil cases. This is due primarily to the defendant's Fifth Amendment privilege against self-incrimination. This privilege has been interpreted to mean that the defendant does not have to reveal information that would assist the prosecution in establishing the elements of the crime.

9-6a Discovery Requests by the Defense

The Supreme Court ruled that due process requires the prosecution to disclose any information it has that would exonerate the defendant. Information requested by the defense under this rule is frequently called *Brady* material because the case that established this right was *Brady v. Maryland* (373 U.S. 83 10 L.Ed. 2d 215, 83 S.Ct. 1194 [1962]). Later cases clarified the extent of the prosecution's duty to disclose information: evidence that either obviously tends to show that the defendant is not guilty (such as a confession by someone else) or appears to be helpful to the defense (such as the statement of a person who claims to have seen the defendant at a different location at the time the crime occurred) should be given to the defense, even though the attorney did not ask for it; items that, on their face, do not appear to show the defendant's innocence have to be revealed only if the defense makes a discovery motion to obtain them. Intentional failure to reveal evidence the court deems valuable to the defense is grounds for reversing a conviction. All evidence known to the police department is considered to be in the prosecutor's file for the purpose of this rule: sanctions, including dismissing the case, can be applied based on the fact that the police had the information, even though the prosecutor did not know it existed.

Most states have rules which require either side to provide the other with a list of witnesses before trial begins. During trial an attorney is allowed to choose not to call a person whose name appears on the list. Intentional failure to include a person on the witness list in order to gain unfair advantage over the other side can be grounds for refusing to allow the person whose name was left off to take the witness stand.

Prior statements made by a witness are important tools for cross-examination. They may be crucial for impeaching the credibility of the witness. Timing of the release of these statements varies from state to state. Some statements, such as testimony at the preliminary hearing, are public record. Police reports are usually subject to discovery; therefore, statements included in them are available to the defense. Testimony made before the grand jury is released before trial in some states but remains sealed in others. Federal courts, and some state courts, require that a witness's statement be given to the opposing side, but permit disclosure to be delayed until the person takes the witness stand.

Lists of physical evidence are usually part of the discovery process. The defense has the right to examine evidence before trial and to have its own experts perform relevant tests. There is no duty, however, for police departments to preserve evidence for the sole purpose of enabling the defense to do these tests. The Supreme Court ruled, for example, that breathalyzers used in DUI cases do not have to be modified to save a breath sample for independent testing. Some states also permit the discovery of reports by experts who will be called to testify. Normally the factual content of the report is given to the other side (such as the fact that the blood found at the scene was human type B blood), but conclusions made for the benefit of the attorney (such as a recommendation that the defense not enter a plea of not guilty by reason of insanity because the defendant has no history of mental illness) are considered privileged and not subject to discovery. Reports by experts who examined the evidence but will not be called to testify are not usually subject to discovery, although some states permit the discovery of the names of all experts employed by the other side.

Names of police informants used in the case may be requested by the defense. Many states make such information privileged. The Supreme Court has ruled that it must be disclosed pretrial only if it is crucial to the defense. A showing that the informant was the only eyewitness to the crime would meet this requirement. Names of people who provide information to the police are not discoverable if the police conducted an investigation and observed the key events in the case themselves.

9-6b Discovery Requests by the Prosecution

Discovery by the prosecution must not interfere with the defendant's Fifth Amendment rights. Some states have gone to the extent of prohibiting all discovery by the prosecution for this reason. Such an approach is not constitutionally mandated. For example, the Supreme Court ruled that requiring the defendant to file a list of witnesses and to give notice that an alibi defense would be used does not violate the privilege against self-incrimination. Statements made by the defendant, however, cannot be obtained. State laws and local court rules vary a great deal on what other items the defense is permitted to withhold.

9-7 Pretrial Conferences

Settlement conferences are used in civil cases to help the parties reach an agreement on the issues of liability and how much compensation is justified. Plea bargaining serves the purpose of settlement conferences in most criminal cases. Judges are usually prohibited from being involved in negotiating a guilty plea.

Pretrial conferences are used to make the trial more efficient. They normally consider administrative matters rather than issues relating to the defendant's guilt or innocence. The number and timing of pretrial conferences vary, based on local practice as well as the type of case involved. Many simple misdemeanor cases do not have any pretrial conferences. Complex felony cases in which lengthy trials are anticipated may require several conferences. Pretrial conferences are usually held within 30 days of the anticipated trial date; a final one may occur on the day the trial is scheduled to begin.

Prosecutors and defense attorneys meet with the judge at the pretrial conference to discuss such issues as the expected length of the trial; the equipment that may be needed by expert witnesses; the need for interpreters for the defendant and/or witnesses; and any other special needs of the case. The discussions are frequently informal and may occur in the judge's chambers rather than in the courtroom. Verbatim stenographic notes are usually made only if disagreement on an issue might lead to an appeal.

Details concerning selecting the jury also are discussed. The number of potential jurors that need to be available for *voir dire* is estimated. A decision is made on how many alternate jurors to seat. Whether the jury should be sequestered (kept in a hotel rather than allowed to go home each night) is decided. Transportation for the jury must be arranged if either side is requesting that the jury view the crime scene.

Some courts use questionnaires to obtain information from prospective jurors in controversial cases. Pretrial conferences will be used to determine what will be included in these questionnaires. Questions may focus on potential prejudice due to pretrial publicity. In death penalty cases both direct and indirect questions attempt to determine if jurors have objections to capital punishment that will interfere with their ability to apply the law in the case.

In high-publicity cases a pretrial conference may be used to decide how to handle the press: how many reporters will be allowed in the courtroom and, if space restrictions make it necessary, what methods will be used to decide which reporters will be allowed to attend. If the court policy is to permit the press to bring audio and/or video equipment into court, decisions will be made on how much equipment will be permitted and where it will be located.

Chapter Summary

Defendants in non-capital cases are usually eligible for release on bail. The bail is set high enough to motivate the defendant to return for the trial rather than forfeit bail. Cash can be posted as bail and so can non-cash items, such as deeds to land, stock certificates, and other valuable items. A bail bond company will post bond for a fee. Defendants in misdemeanor cases who are not considered likely to flee before trial may be released on their own recognizance without posting bail.

Plea bargaining can occur at any time between arrest and trial. The prosecutor considers the strength of the case and the likely sentence. Some charges may be dismissed in order to induce the defendant to plead guilty. Additional charges may be filed if the defendant refuses to enter a guilty plea if there is probable cause to support each charge.

Some misdemeanor cases are diverted from the court system. Typically these cases involve alcohol abuse, spousal abuse, or child abuse. The defendant must attend counseling; upon successful completion of the program, the charges are dismissed and the defendant has no criminal record for the charge.

The defense may challenge the legal sufficiency of the pleadings before the trial begins. Motions may be filed based on double jeopardy, the court's lack of either geographical or subject matter jurisdiction, expiration of the statute of limitations, or a violation of the right to a speedy trial. Depending on the error, success by the defense will result in dismissal of the charges with or without prejudice. The prosecution can refile charges dismissed without prejudice if the statute of limitations has not expired.

Some evidentiary issues, particularly those related to unconstitutionally obtained evidence, can be settled before trial. Among the issues the defense can raise by making a suppression motion are a warrant not supported by probable cause; an affidavit in support of warrant that contained false information; police who violated the Fourth Amendment in obtaining evidence; and *Miranda* warnings that were not properly given before obtaining a confession. The defense will argue that the Exclusionary Rule and the Fruit of the Poison Tree Doctrine mandate the suppression of evidence in question. The prosecutor will try to establish that the police did not make errors; when this fails, there may be an attempt to show that the case falls under an exception to the Exclusionary Rule. The most common exceptions are good faith, inevitable discovery, independent source, and public safety. It may also be possible to show that the time and intervening acts dissipated the taint of the original constitutional error. If evidence is suppressed, the defense will likely make a motion to dismiss for insufficient evidence. The success of this motion depends on what evidence remains in the case that is admissible.

The modern trend is to permit either side to discover what evidence the other has before trial. Opinions of lawyers and experts do not have to be released. Lists of witnesses to be called to testify may be required. Statements made by witnesses who testify usually must be given to the opposing side no later than the time when cross-examination begins. Physical evidence in the other side's possession may be examined by opposing experts. The Fifth Amendment privilege permits the defendant to refuse to disclose his/her own statements.

Plea bargaining in criminal cases generally replaces settlement conferences. Pretrial conferences may be held to settle issues related to the trial, such as jury selecting; the arranging for interpreters; preparing for the press; and meeting any other unique needs of the case. These conferences are usually held during the last month before trial.

Study Questions

1. Define bail, and explain how it operates in your local jail.
   a. Is a bail schedule used? If so, what is the bail on
      1. misdemeanor battery?
      2. robbery?
      3. the sale of cocaine?
   b. Where is bail posted?
   c. Does your court permit posting a personal bond instead of paying for a bail bond?
   d. What are the procedures for posting
      1. cash bail?
      2. non-cash bail?
      3. bail bond?
2. Define own recognizance release.
   a. For what crimes may an inmate in your local jail be released OR?
   b. How does an inmate initiate a request to be released OR?
   c. Who processes requests for OR releases?
   d. What factors are used in making the decision to release an inmate OR?

3. Is electronic monitoring used for pretrial release in your area? If so,
   a. what type of equipment is used?
   b. how does a defendant qualify for electronic monitoring?
   c. what fees must the defendant pay?
4. What is plea bargaining? Explain how it operates in your local court.
   a. Do state laws restrict plea bargaining?
   b. Does the prosecutor's office have policies that restrict plea bargaining?
   c. Approximately what percentage of cases is settled by a plea bargain?
5. Do laws in your state provide for pretrial diversion? If so,
   a. what types of cases may be diverted?
   b. what are the conditions of diversion?
   c. how long does diversion last?
6. Explain how the defendant can raise each of the following issues before the trial:
   a. double jeopardy
   b. court's lack of jurisdiction
      1. subject matter jurisdiction
      2. geographical jurisdiction
   c. expired statute of limitations
   d. violation of right to a speedy trial
      1. under the Sixth Amendment
      2. under state law
7. Explain the process used to obtain a pretrial ruling on the admissibility of evidence.
   a. What is a suppression motion?
   b. What are points and authorities?
   c. What occurs at a suppression hearing?
   d. What issues may be raised at pretrial suppression hearings in your state?
   e. Does your state allow pretrial appeal of the ruling on a suppression motion?

8. Explain how a defendant in a case filed in your local court can make a pretrial challenge to the legality of police conduct.

   a. How can the probable cause supporting a search warrant be attacked?

   b. How can the defense attack the warrant based on false information contained in the affidavits?

   c. How can the defense have evidence excluded from trial based on the fact it was seized in violation of the Fourth Amendment?

   d. What process can the defense use to have the defendant's confession suppressed on grounds that *Miranda* was not correctly followed?

9. How is discovery conducted in criminal cases under the laws of your state?

   a. What items does the prosecutor routinely give the defense attorney without the defense making a formal motion for discovery?

   b. How does the court handle discovery motions?

   1. What judge hears them?

   2. When are they heard?

   c. What must the defense disclose to the prosecution?

   d. Does your local court require

   1. filing a list of anticipated witnesses? If so, when is it filed?

   2. the defense to file notice that an alibi defense will be used? If so, when is it filed?

   3. giving opposing sides statements made by witnesses who testify at trial? If so, when are they given?

10. Check with the clerk of your local court.

   a. What types of pretrial conferences, if any, are held in misdemeanor cases?

   b. What types of pretrial conferences, if any, are held in felony cases? If they are held,

   1. when are they held (length of time between pretrial conference and the beginning of the trial)?

   2. who normally presides over them?

   3. what issues are addressed?

True or False Questions

1. Bail can be posted only by a bail bond agency.
2. A person is released on his/her own recognizance only if the judge has ordered that the charges must be dismissed.
3. A person who enters a plea bargain may withdraw the plea if the judge does not agree to the sentence recommended by the attorneys.
4. If a person enters a diversion program, the criminal charges are dropped immediately.
5. The defense of double jeopardy must be entered before the trial begins.
6. All evidence that is seized in violation of the Fourth Amendment is inadmissible at a criminal trial.
7. Most states allow the defense to make suppression motions prior to trial.
8. The defense can refuse all attempts at discovery because the Fifth Amendment protects everything in the defense files.
9. The prosecution has the right to pretrial notice of the names of the defendant's alibi witnesses.
10. The main purpose of the pretrial conference is to settle administrative details about the trial.

Chapter
10

Preparation of
a Case for Trial

Outline

Key Terms

case management system	past recollection recorded	rehabilitation
chain of custody	physical layout	reputation for dishonesty
chain of possession	of the crime scene	serving the subpoena
impeachment	physical limitations	subpoena
inability to perceive events	of the witness	subpoena duces tecum
inconsistent statements	present memory refreshed	trial brief
motive, bias, or prejudice	prior convictions	
"on call" subpoena	proof of service	

Learning Objectives

Learning Objectives

After reading this chapter, the student will be able to

- Identify what steps must be taken to prepare physical evidence for trial.
- Describe what must be done to subpoena witnesses for trial.
- Explain what can be done to refresh the memory of a witness before trial.
- Give examples of what can be introduced into evidence if a witness cannot recall events related to the crime.
- Explain five things that can be done to attack the credibility of a witness at trial.
- Describe how the prosecutor evaluates the strengths and weaknesses of a case.
- Interpret how the prosecutor anticipates the defense strategy.
- Describe the trial brief.

The final trial preparation requires attention to details. The physical evidence must be assembled and be ready for delivery to the courtroom. Witnesses must be subpoenaed. Attorneys usually test the memory of potential witnesses and assess the strengths and weaknesses of their case. Good attorneys anticipate the strategy of the opposing side. Many attorneys prepare a trial brief to assist the judge in evaluating the issues in the case.

10-1 Assembling the Physical Evidence

As the trial date approaches, the police officer in charge of the case must assemble the items that will be needed in court. This includes evidence recovered at the crime scene, such as weapons, ammunition, demand notes, and bloodstained clothing. Other items, such as diagrams and pictures of the crime scene and photographs taken through a comparison microscope in the ballistics laboratory, may also be needed. A list should be made identifying each item that will be needed. It is better to include items that may not be introduced at trial than to have a judge refuse to admit evidence because the prosecutor did not have it ready when needed.

Each police department should use a **case management system** to keep records on all aspects of the case: reports that have been filed; the status of the court case; physical evidence; and potential witnesses. By using one system throughout the department, it is possible for officers to assist one another and, if necessary, prepare the evidence and subpoenas, even if the officer initially handling the case is unavailable.

It is particularly important to know the location of physical evidence, so that each item can be retrieved quickly and the facts needed as a foundation for its admissibility can be easily established. File cards can be used for this purpose, but computerized systems make it easier to keep track of the case and update information. A computerized system can cross-reference all entries and update common items, such as court dates, whenever new information is added. It can also alert the person in charge of evidence storage that items will be needed for court or can be released to the owners. The case management system might include the screen depicted in Table 10-1 for each piece of evidence in the case.

Knowing how each item fits into the case is important. Of equal legal significance is the list of everyone who has had access to the item. The side introducing the item must lay the foundation and establish the **chain of possession** (also called the **chain of custody**) before an item can be introduced into evidence. The foundation establishes the relevance of the evidence to the case. For example, the gun was taken from the defendant at

T A B L E **10-1** Case Management System:
Physical Evidence Information

Police department file number: Court file number:

Defendant's name:
Names of other defendants:
File numbers of related cases:

Next scheduled court date:

Evidence locker tag number:

Description:
  Who found this item:
  Where was it found:
  Witnesses needed to establish chain of possession:
     Witness   Date   Reason for Possession
  1.
  2.
  3.
  Currect location of item:
  Tests performed on this item:
  Results of tests:
  Use of this item at trial:
  Weaknesses of this item:

Remarks:

---

the crime scene. Establishing that the gun looks like one a witness claims the person who committed the crime had is not enough.

The chain of custody establishes what has been done with an item of evidence since it was taken into police custody. The purpose of this requirement is to verify that the item has not been tampered with and is in the same condition it was in when found. Testimony will be needed from every person who had possession of the item from the time it was taken into police custody until it is introduced into evidence at trial, including from evidence technicians and personnel from the criminalistics laboratory. Information on transporting items to and from the evidence locker must be included.

Questions will be asked to establish a description of the item (e.g., man's blue plaid shirt, size medium); identifying marks on the item (e.g., officer's initials—JS—written on the underside of the collar); the condition of the item when found (e.g., covered with dirt and caked with dark red, dried material); how it was packaged (e.g., air dried and placed in a brown 8″ × 12″ envelope, "Case No. 94-5678" written in upper left corner of the envelope, envelope sealed, and Officer J. Smith's signature placed across seal); what was done with it (e.g., taken to criminalistics laboratory by Officer J. Smith for test to determine if human blood was present and, if so, what blood type); what was done with it after processing was complete (e.g., returned to the envelope it came in, envelope sealed with tape, and "A. B. Cowan"—signature of laboratory technician—written across seal and envelope taken to evidence locker by A. B. Cowan); and what was done with it after it was checked into the evidence locker (e.g., Officer J. Smith checked envelope out of evidence locker, took it to court, and kept it in his possession until he opened it while testifying). If the test altered the appearance of the item, it is necessary to inform the jury what was done, so that they will understand why the item does not match the description of the one recovered at the crime scene.

A similar process is involved if fingerprint comparisons were made. The person who dusted for prints at the crime scene will be needed to testify about lifting the prints. A latent print expert must testify about the match that was (or was not) made. It will be necessary to have latent prints and fingerprint cards available for introduction at trial. The prosecutor may want enlargements to show to the jury. It may also be necessary to call the officer who rolled the prints used for the comparison. The case management system can be used to keep track of where latent prints and fingerprint cards can be found and whose testimony will be needed to introduce them.

The same case management system can be used for diagrams, photographs, and other items that were made to assist at the trial. The person in charge of assembling the evidence should check local court rules for restrictions on the size of such items. For example, some courts required that all photographs be 8″ × 10″; others permit enlargements of any size. No chain of custody is needed for most of these items, but other details will be necessary. Diagrams prepared in advance for use at trial normally must be made to scale. The scale should be indicated on the diagram. Testimony must be given regarding all facts used as a basis for the diagram. Information about photographs is usually given through the testimony of the photographer: when and where pictures were taken; lighting; enlargement factor (frequently satisfied by reference to an item, such as a ruler, placed in the picture for this purpose); and factors that might cause visual distortion, such as angle used to shoot the picture. In controversial cases, the negative may be needed to establish that the picture has not been tampered with. Digital pictures present a greater problem because of the ease with which alterations can be made after the picture is taken.

10-2 Subpoenaing Witnesses

Keeping track of witnesses is also the responsibility of the officer in charge of the case. Information on all potential witnesses should be kept in the case management system. Addresses should be kept current. The prosecutor will need to know both the potential strengths of the witness, such as being six feet away from the victim at the time the crime was committed, as well as possible weaknesses, such as having memory loss due to recent severe head trauma. Information on witnesses who do not appear to be useful for the prosecution should also be kept in the system: if they are called by the defense, the prosecutor will need to know as much as possible about them in order to cast doubt on their credibility. A screen from the case management system for witnesses might look like the one depicted in Table 10-2.

Police officers whose testimony may be needed at trial should be included in the case management system as witnesses. It is best to include all officers involved with the case, not just the ones who wrote reports. Vacations, retirements, and illnesses may make it necessary to call officers whose testimony was not originally anticipated. Names of officers from other law enforcement agencies, firefighters, and emergency medical personnel who were at the scene or otherwise involved should be included. This list will be more accurate if made at the time the investigation is begun and if routinely updated.

Occasionally there will be a material witness who is uncooperative and believed to be likely to flee the jurisdiction. Many states give the judge discretion to require such witnesses to post a bond or written undertaking as security under these circumstances. The amount of the security is left to the discretion of the judge. A person who refuses to post the required security or appears ready to flee the jurisdiction rather than testify usually can be taken into custody and held in jail until called to testify. Immediate review of these cases is provided in order to prevent abuse of judicial discretion.

Victims and eyewitnesses normally receive little, if any, compensation for testifying. State law may give the court discretion to pay them; if so, they normally receive about the same compensation as jurors. Expert witnesses are normally paid for their services by the side calling them. Expert witnesses who work for indigent defendants in criminal cases are usually paid by the government. Witness fees frequently must be posted in

T A B L E **10-2** **Case Management System:
Witness Information**

Police department file number: Court file number:

Defendant's name:
Names of other defendants:
File numbers of related cases:

Next scheduled court appearance:

Name of witness:
   Home address:
   Business address:
   Daytime telephone:
   Evening telephone:
   What this witness can testify about:
   Physical evidence this witness can identify:
   Strengths of witness:
   Weaknesses of witness:
Subpoena issued for: Date: Time:
   Served: Yes   No
   Proof of service filed: Yes   No
   Witness on call: Yes   No
If witness on call:
   Telephone number to contact witness:
   How long will it take witness to come to court?

Remarks:

advance when government employees are subpoenaed by private attorneys to testify as expert witnesses or regarding events not involved in criminal trials.

10-2a Obtaining Subpoenas

Once the trial date is set, the prosecutor and officer handling the case usually meet and decide which witnesses need to be subpoenaed to testify at trial. Subpoenas must be typed, signed, and served on each witness. A **subpoena** is a court order directing a person to appear at a specific date and time at the location stated in the subpoena; a person who fails to appear when subpoenaed can be held in contempt of court (see Figure 10-1). If documents are to be taken to court, a *subpoena duces tecum* is required.

Figure 10-1
Typical Criminal Subpoena

SUPERIOR COURT OF THE STATE OF CALIFORNIA FOR THE COUNTY OF ORANGE

☐ Courthouse — 700 Civic Center Drive West   Santa Ana, California 92701
☐ Courthouse — 1275 N. Berkeley Avenue   Fullerton, California 92632
☐ Courthouse — 8141 13th Street   Westminster, California 92683

THE PEOPLE OF THE STATE OF CALIFORNIA, Plaintiff | **SUBPOENA — CRIMINAL**
vs. | Case No.

Defendant(s)

THE PEOPLE OF THE STATE OF CALIFORNIA

TO:

YOU ARE COMMANDED to appear in the above entitled court to testify as a witness in a criminal action prosecuted by the People of the State of California against the above named defendant(s) at the following time and place:

Date: _____

Time: _____

Department: _____

AND YOU ARE REQUIRED, also, to bring

with you the following:

Michael R. Capizzi

MICHAEL R. CAPIZZI, DISTRICT ATTORNEY
COUNTY OF ORANGE, STATE OF CALIFORNIA

Given under my hand this date: _____   Telephone: (714) 834-3600

Disobedience to this subpoena may be punishable as contempt of court. (Penal Code Sec. 1331)

You may be entitled to witness fees, mileage, or both, in the discretion of the court. After your appearance contact Victim-Witness Office in the courthouse.

CERTIFICATE OF SERVICE

I hereby certify that on _____, 20 _____, I served the within subpoena on the person(s) named hereafter by personally delivering a true copy thereof to said witness(s). (1) _____

(2) _____ (3)_____ (4)_____

Not Served (name and reason): _____

I declare under penalty of perjury that the foregoing is true and correct.

Executed at _____ , California, on _____ , 20 _____ .

By: _____

VICTIM NOTIFICATION OF DEFENDANT'S RELEASE

"If the Defendant in a case is sentenced to State Prison, the victim or next of kin of the victim- - may request notification prior to the release of the Defendant from State Prison, by writing the Director, Department of Corrections, 630 K Street, Sacramento, CA 95814. As defined, a victim is any person sustaining physical or financial injury to person or property."

(C.P.C.11155)

F 0232-425.7 (R1/90)

When a witness is to testify and take documents, both types of subpoenas should be issued. The court clerk and judge have the authority to issue subpoenas; in criminal cases, the district attorney and public defender are usually authorized to sign subpoenas. Private defense attorneys obtain blank subpoenas from the court clerk and complete them in the same manner as public defenders.

Subpoenas are usually preprinted forms identifying the document as a subpoena in a criminal case and stating the name of the judicial district and address of the court, as well as other relevant information, such as the penalty for failing to appear. Blanks are provided for the following information to be inserted: name of the case; case number; whether prosecution or defense is subpoenaing the witness; date, time, and courtroom where witness is to appear; documents to be produced in court; and signature of the person issuing the subpoena. A copy of the completed subpoena is filed with the court.

Many subpoenas list the time and date the trial is scheduled to begin as the time the witness must appear. This can be very inconvenient for witnesses who must wait at the courthouse during a lengthy trial. Giving the witness an **"on call"** subpoena means that the witness does not have to wait in the courthouse as long as it is possible to call the witness and have him/her appear when needed. This is done only if the prosecutor is sure the witness can be depended on to come quickly when called. Failure of an "on call" witness to be present when it is time to take the witness stand can result in sanctions, including refusal to allow that witness to testify later, against the side that subpoenaed the witness. This may ultimately lead to failure to sustain the burden of proof.

The normal rule is that a person served with a subpoena must appear in court as directed. Many states have placed distance limitations on this; for example, a witness cannot be compelled to attend court more than 150 miles from home or place of business unless there is a special showing that the witness has material evidence in the case. A judge's signature, rather than that of the prosecutor or defense attorney, is typically required to certify that there has been a preliminary showing that the witness's testimony meets this requirement.

The Uniform Act to Secure the Attendance of Witnesses from without the State in Criminal Cases is a compact signed by most states. As the name indicates, it is used to subpoena witnesses who are outside the state. It can be used to subpoena witnesses before the grand jury or for criminal trials. A judge in a court where the person is to testify must determine that the person is a necessary and material witness and must sign a certificate indicating how many days the person is needed and the time and place where the witness must appear. The state requesting the witness must agree to protect the witness from arrest and service of civil or criminal process while he/she is in the state. This protection also applies to travel through other states while going to and from court. The certificate is presented to a judge in the county where the person being subpoenaed resides. This judge will hold a hearing to review the determination that the witness has material testimony; undue hardship to the witness will also be considered. If the request is granted by the local court, the witness must be given travel expenses and per diem fees prior to going out-of-state. Uncooperative witnesses may be taken into custody and transported to the out-of-state court.

10-2b Serving Subpoenas

Most states permit anyone over 18 who is not a party to the case to serve subpoenas, but it is more common to have peace officers serve them in criminal cases. Delivering the subpoena in person qualifies as **serving the subpoena.** Some states provide for mail service, but if this is done it is usually valid only if the person receiving it cooperates and returns a document acknowledging service. The person who serves the subpoena must complete a form called a **proof of service,** which gives the name of the document; the name of the case and the case number; the date, time, and location where the subpoena was served; and the signature of the server. The law frequently specifies alternate procedures when a police officer must be subpoenaed regarding events that occurred in the line of duty. Delivering two copies of the subpoena to the police department is usually adequate; the department becomes responsible for forwarding one copy to the officer.

10-3 Assessing the Ability of Witnesses to Recall Relevant Events

No one is expected to have perfect recall. A witness in court is asked to testify regarding his/her recollection of facts relevant to the case. This current recollection is important; how the person's memory was refreshed is not. Officers may help the witness recall key events: this is called **present memory refreshed.** Memorizing facts for the purpose of repeating them on the witness stand is prohibited. Prior to calling a witness to testify at trial, the prosecutor will need to know if there are any recall problems. Under some circumstances the hearsay exception for past recollection recorded can be used if the witness cannot recall enough details.

10-3a Present Memory Refreshed

Witnesses are allowed to use any device available, with the exception of hypnosis, to refresh their memories. Attorneys at trial may ask what was used to refresh the witness's memory, but the important thing will be what was recalled. A wide variety of things help people remember events. If a person memorized facts in sequence, recalling the first fact usually triggers memory of the second. Memory is also triggered by sights, sounds, and people associated with the main event; for example, hearing a song on the radio may cause a person to remember what he/she was doing when that song was popular.

Written documents may be used to refresh memory. These can be anything from a formal report to notes written on a scrap of paper. Two things are important: whatever was written down was accurate and it refreshed the memory. Police officers frequently refer to their field notebooks both before trial and while on the witness stand. An experienced prosecutor will ask appropriate questions when this is done: "What are you looking at?" "Does it contain notes regarding this case?" "When did you make those notes?" "Has looking at those notes refreshed your memory?" "Can you now testify from memory of the event, or are you merely repeating what your notes say?"

Witnesses should be told that they have the right to refresh their memories but that they may be asked, during cross-examination, about what they did to help recall the events in question. The judge will usually permit the opposing side to see notes or other documents used to refresh memory. If, during cross-examination, it can be shown that the witness's testimony was nearly verbatim from the notes, the attorney can cast doubt on the witness's memory. This is damaging to the witness's credibility, particularly if testimony has been given claiming an exceptionally good memory.

10-3b Past Recollection Recorded

The **past recollection recorded** exception to the hearsay rule is used when a witness has unsuccessfully attempted to refresh his/her memory but there is a written report stating the facts. In most states the requirements for using this rule include all of the following:

1. The statement made in the report would have been admissible if the witness had made it while testifying from memory.
2. The witness has insufficient present recollection to testify fully and accurately.

3. The statement is contained in a writing which
   a. Was made at time when the facts were fresh in the memory of the person making the report
   b. Was made by the witness personally or by another person at his/her direction for the purpose of recording the witness's statement
   c. The witness testifies that written document is a true and accurate statement of the facts
   d. The written document is authenticated as an accurate record of the statement

Portions of the report will be inadmissible if they were not based on firsthand observations of the witness, unless some other evidence rule applies. For example, statements of an eyewitness to the crime telling of a conversation overheard between two other people is inadmissible hearsay.

The report will be used at trial if testimony establishes that it is covered by past recollection recorded. Local practices vary, but it is common to have the report read into evidence by the court clerk, the attorney introducing it, or the witness who made the report. Some courts permit a copy of the report to be introduced as an exhibit; others feel that this places undue weight on the report. Most states allow the report to be introduced by the opposing side if done to show inaccuracies or otherwise raise doubts about the report.

The attorney seeking to have the written document admitted will ask the witness pertinent questions to establish the required facts. The most contradictory fact that must be established is that the witness does not remember the facts but knows that the report is accurate. This is usually done by testimony that the report was reviewed immediately after it was completed and all errors were corrected. Officers are trained to sign reports only after the corrections have been made. When this is the normal practice, an officer can testify that the signature indicates that the report was accurate. The following is an example of a prosecutor's line of questioning in a case seeking to admit the police report as past recollection recorded:

PROSECUTOR: Did you make a written report about what you observed at the crime scene?
OFFICER: Yes.
PROSECUTOR: Did you write the report or dictate it to a secretary?
OFFICER: I typed it into my computer.
PROSECUTOR: When?
OFFICER: Before I went off duty that day.
PROSECUTOR: Were the facts fresh in your memory at that time?

OFFICER: Yes. It was only two hours after I saw the fight.

PROSECUTOR: Did you use any notes to help you make the report?

OFFICER: Yes—the notes I made in my field notebook while talking to witnesses.

PROSECUTOR: Did you review the report after it was printed out?

OFFICER: Yes. I always do.

PROSECUTOR: Is this a copy of that report?

OFFICER: Yes.

PROSECUTOR: Is it accurate?

OFFICER: Yes.

PROSECUTOR: How do you know the report is accurate?

OFFICER: I was trained to read my reports carefully, make needed changes, and never sign one until it is totally correct. I have made this a habit. I never sign a report that is not accurate.

PROSECUTOR: Is this your signature on the report?

OFFICER: Yes.

PROSECUTOR: Do you believe that this report is accurate?

OFFICER: Yes. My signature is on this report, so I know I reviewed it and determined that it was accurate.

The report can be read into evidence based on this dialog between the prosecutor and the officer and proof of authenticity. It may be necessary to call someone from the police Records Bureau to testify that the document referred to is a true copy of the report filed by the officer on the day of the crime. This authenticates the report. Some courts allow the officer to identify his/her handwriting in order to authenticate the report; others accept a certified copy of the report without calling a witness to authenticate it.

Opposing counsel will be allowed to cross-examine the person whose report is being admitted into evidence. The cross-examination may attempt to show that there is sufficient current memory to require the officer to testify rather than use the report. The legal test is that the witness has insufficient present recollection to testify fully and accurately. This is a question of fact. It does not require total memory lapse: the judge will use his/her discretion based on the facts introduced at trial to determine whether there is sufficient memory to permit the person to testify. The fact that the report contains more details than the witness can now recall is not sufficient grounds to introduce the report.

Another approach taken on cross-examination is to point to inaccurate facts (such as listing the wrong color for the vehicle involved or giving the wrong time or date) and other errors (grammatical, spelling, etc.) in the report. This challenges the officer's statement that the report was proofread and determined to be correct. The content of the report remains in evidence, but the attorney is trying to raise doubt in jurors' minds about its accuracy and the officer's ability to record facts correctly.

10-4 Evaluating Strengths and Weaknesses of a Case

Prior to trial, the prosecutor must develop a strategy for handling the case. This requires assessment of the strengths and weaknesses of each witness and every piece of physical evidence. The officer in charge of the case should be prepared to discuss this realistically with the prosecutor. Providing overly optimistic analysis can be very damaging because the prosecutor will be unprepared for serious challenges by the defense. If a witness cannot be located or if a witness is hostile and may not testify as anticipated, the prosecutor must try to find alternate means of presenting the desired evidence to the jury.

10-4a Physical Evidence

An objective review of each item of physical evidence is necessary. The case management system should contain information needed to establish the chain of custody. Evaluation at this point needs to focus on the strengths and weaknesses of each item. Strengths include positive identification as the weapon used in the crime; eyewitness who can connect item to crime; conclusive laboratory tests establish point in question. Weaknesses might be: eyewitness description of item does not match physical evidence; item recovered damaged and no tests could be performed to establish that this was item used in crime; inconclusive laboratory tests; fingerprints recovered at scene were smeared and no match could be made. The prosecutor needs to be prepared for any challenge the defense attorney might make.

10-4b Witnesses

Information in the case management system should describe what each witness can testify about. The strengths and weaknesses of each potential witness should be reviewed. Prosecutors consider a person to be a strong witness if he/she has important information and can testify in a manner that will impress the jury that he/she is telling the truth. Weak witnesses may possess important information but the prosecutor believes the jury might not believe them. Questions considered when deciding if the witness is strong or weak include the following: Was the witness in a position to clearly observe the events? Is the witness able to communicate effectively? Does the witness have behavior traits, such as nervousness or failure to make eye contact, that may cause the jury to doubt the truthfulness of the testimony? Can the witness's credibility be attacked? If there are numerous witnesses available, it may be possible to establish guilt beyond a reasonable doubt without calling the weaker ones. In cases with few witnesses, the prosecutor may need to call all of them.

Each witness will be subject to impeachment during cross-examination. **Impeachment** is the process of showing that the witness lacks credibility. It is an attempt to imply that the witness is not telling the whole truth; rarely will a witness admit outright to lying. While the attorney may use voice inflections, gestures, and dramatic pauses to make this point during cross-examination, the argument that the witness should not be believed comes during closing statements. The testimony on direct examination remains part of the evidence even if the witness is impeached: the witness is not barred from testifying. Jurors are told it is their duty to decide whom to believe.

There are a variety of reasons for impeaching a witness. Some of the most common include the witness's inability to observe what he/she testified about; **inconsistent statements;** motive, bias or prejudice for distorting the truth; **prior convictions;** and **reputation for dishonesty.** The prosecutor needs to be aware of any potential problems. Facts that can be used to rehabilitate the witness should also be in the file. **Rehabilitation** is the process of showing that the witness should be believed in spite of the opposing side's efforts to cast doubt on the testimony. For example, if the defense establishes that the eyewitness is very nearsighted, the prosecution can introduce testimony that, on the night in question, the witness was wearing glasses and was able to see 20/20.

Attacks on the witness's **inability to perceive events** testified to fall into two categories: inability to observe due to the **physical limitations** he/she has of the witness, and inability to observe because physical barriers made the observation impossible. Facts such as poor eyesight and bad hearing are in the first group. Rehabilitation could focus on the witness's wearing corrective lenses or a hearing aid. It may also be possible to show that the victim was able to make the same observation an unimpaired person would have; for example, the parties were shouting so loudly that anyone could have heard them.

The second attack on the ability to observe focuses on the **physical layout of the crime scene** at the time the observation was made. For example, the witness testified that he/she had a clear view of the intersection and observed the car enter on the red light, but a photograph taken at the location where the witness claims to have been standing shows a large tree blocking the line of vision, so that the traffic light could not be seen, or someone may claim to have looked out a window and observed the shooting, but an officer, standing at the same location at the same time of day, discovered that the lighting was so poor that a positive identification was impossible. The key to impeachment and rehabilitation on these items is a detailed knowledge of the scene *as it was at the time in question*. Merely going to the scene a few days before trial is not enough: bushes grow and can be trimmed, walls may have been built or torn down, and so on between the day of the crime and the trial. Detailed descriptions in police reports made on the day or night of the crime are very helpful for this purpose.

Prior inconsistent statements made by the witness can be used to impeach. The statement made during direct examination is evidence in the case: the inconsistent statement is introduced to attack the credibility of the witness and is not evidence that can be used to meet the burden of proof. These statements range from totally contradictory, such as recanting a confession, to minor inconsistencies; they can also be oral or written. The statement which is inconsistent with what is said on the witness stand can be made to anyone. It does not have to be recorded in a written document or on tape. One key question will be the credibility of the person who claims to have heard the prior statement: Is that person honest? Did he/she hear the statement clearly? Was there a chance that what was said was taken out of context or misinterpreted? The jury is likely to be impressed by statements that differ on important aspects of the testimony; time spent on minor discrepancies is usually wasted and may irritate the jury.

Most courts require that the witness be given the date the inconsistent statement was made, the name of the person it was made to, and the content of the statement and then be allowed to explain. For example, if the witness testified that she saw the defendant rob the victim, defense counsel might try to impeach as follows:

DEFENSE ATTORNEY: You have testified that you saw the defendant at the crime scene; is that correct?
WITNESS: Yes.
DEFENSE ATTORNEY: Describe the person you saw take the victim's purse.
WITNESS: The guy looked just like the defendant—about 6′ 4″ tall, about 225 pounds, stringy brown hair. I'd recognize him anywhere.
DEFENSE ATTORNEY: Did you make a statement to a police officer immediately after you saw the crime?
WITNESS: Yes.
DEFENSE ATTORNEY: Did you tell the officer everything you saw?

WITNESS: Yes.

DEFENSE ATTORNEY: Did you say, and I'm quoting from the police report, "I didn't get a good look at the guy because I was hiding from him, but he was skinny and couldn't have been over 6′ tall."

WITNESS: I may have said that. I don't remember. I was really scared that night—he shot my best friend.

Some judges allow the police officer who took the statement to be called to testify about what the witness said on the night in question. This is more likely to be done if the witness denies making the statement. Rehabilitation will follow, usually by showing the statement was taken out of context or was not reported accurately. Sometimes it can be shown that the witness was too emotional to make an accurate report at the time but, after calming down, recalled the events more clearly.

Exercise of the Fifth Amendment privilege against self-incrimination cannot be used to attack the defendant's credibility. The jury may not be urged to conclude that invocation of *Miranda* rights indicates guilt. No argument may be made that an innocent defendant would have taken the witness stand. A defendant who does take the witness stand, however, can be cross-examined. Any voluntary pretrial statements made by such a defendant can be used to impeach. This includes statements obtained under circumstances that would not satisfy *Miranda* as long as there was no coercion. In cases where the defendant has taken the witness stand and for the first time has claimed to be innocent, some lower courts have permitted questioning on why no attempt was made to explain this earlier. Most states permit defense witnesses to be asked to reconcile their testimony regarding the innocence of a friend with the fact that they have made no previous effort to obtain the defendant's release from custody.

A witness can be impeached if there are conscious or unconscious reasons to distort the facts. This is known as impeachment on **motive, bias, or prejudice.** It includes any reason a person would be less than objective. The more obvious examples are people motivated by personal dislike for the defendant or by racial prejudice against the defendant's ethnic group. The opposite also is grounds for impeachment: someone who likes the defendant may see things in a light more favorable toward him/her; racism can cause the witness to believe that what the defendant did was right. It is this type of favorable prejudice that makes a mother a poor alibi witness: she may be unable to see the faults in her children and, some would assume, may be willing to lie to protect them.

Financial motives may cause a person to testify less than objectively. Being the beneficiary of an insurance policy is one illustration. Another is testifying on behalf of an employer: if the defendant is convicted, the witness may be fired. While it is occasionally possible to show that the witness was threatened, it is more common to merely imply that potential financial hardship has subconsciously influenced the witness. Financial rewards for testimony can also be considered. Attempts to bribe the witness would be relevant. Questions about the fee paid an expert witness are used to show that the testimony may unduly favor the side that hired the expert.

Prior convictions are used to impeach: people may infer that a convicted criminal is less than honest. Many states place limits on what convictions can be used. The most common is to permit the use of felony convictions, but not those for misdemeanors. Some states require that the conviction relate to an offense that involves dishonesty or moral turpitude. Sometimes a conviction is not admitted because it occurred too long ago. There may be a specific policy, such as a conviction is inadmissible if the defendant has been out of custody for at least 10 years and has had no convictions during that time, or the judge may have discretion to exclude evidence of a conviction if the judge believes it is so old that it is not relevant.

A witness's reputation (sometimes called "character") for untruthfulness is always relevant for impeachment. If this method of impeachment is used, rehabilitation can be attempted by calling witnesses to testify about the witness's reputation for honesty. State rules vary on how reputation is established. The traditional approach is to use witnesses who can testify to the person's reputation in the community. Community, as used in this book, is the town or neighborhood where a person lives; many courts now accept the workplace as a community. This type of testimony focuses on what the witness has heard others say, not on the witness's own belief or observations. Some states also permit testimony about specific acts of dishonesty; others allow the reputation witness to give his/her own opinion of the person being impeached.

An example of reputation in the community is testimony by Mary that she has talked to many people who know Sam and that everyone says Sam is a liar and a thief. In states permitting the reputation witness to give personal opinion, Mary can testify that she has had business dealings with Sam and believes that Sam is a liar. If specific examples were allowed, Mary might testify that she had a conversation with Sam on September 9, 2002; during that conversation Sam told Mary that he had paid $2,000 for a stereo but wanted to sell it because he needed cash for medical bills; Mary later learned that Sam had stolen the stereo in question during a burglary.

10-5 Anticipating the Defense Strategy

Anticipating the defense strategy is almost as important as evaluating the prosecution's case. The approach is quite similar to assessing the strengths and weaknesses of the prosecution's case. All potential defense witnesses should be reviewed; methods of impeaching each must be considered. The prosecutor must plan to counter their testimony, either by cross-examination or by calling other witnesses.

Physical evidence the defense is likely to introduce must be considered. Necessary arrangements should be made to have prosecution experts examine this evidence and conduct relevant tests. The credibility of defense experts must be considered: Do they have the necessary education, training, and experience? Have they conducted appropriate tests? Can the equipment used for these tests be challenged? Does the witness testify in favor of defendants so often that he/she can be impeached for bias? Are the fees being charged so high the jury will believe the opinion has been influenced by them? The prosecutor must also consider whether the prosecution should call one or more experts to refute the opinions given by the defense experts. This decision will need to be made based on an evaluation of the evidence, the strength of the defense experts, and the allocation of burden of proof.

Possible legal challenges must be anticipated. Those related to the Fourth Amendment and *Miranda* may have been resolved before trial. Others, such as applicable exceptions to the hearsay rule and privileges, are usually raised at the time testimony is being given. Attorneys are expected to be able to spontaneously cite the rules, case law, and statutes supporting their arguments at trial. Research may be needed on these points before trial.

A growing trend is for defense attorneys to attack the personal credibility of prosecution witnesses, particularly police officers. Catching the officer lying under oath is classic impeachment; so is the use of earlier statements that are inconsistent with testimony given at trial. Other forms of untruthfulness that can be used include "padded" overtime and expense vouchers and exaggerated claims for worker's compensation benefits and disability retirements. Statements made while handling the present case are very damaging, but derogatory comments about members of the defendant's race, for example, may be admissible even though they occurred in the witness's personal conversations several years before the case began. These types of negative comments are used during cross-examination to impeach the witness. The prosecution needs to be aware of any conversations or written communications that can be used for this purpose.

10-6 Dismissing Charges

Part of the preparation of the case for trial is a serious review of the charges. Events after the arraignment may indicate that there is no longer a strong possibility that the prosecution can establish its case at trial. Two main reasons contribute to this decision: lack of admissible evidence and problems with the witnesses.

Pretrial suppression hearings frequently challenge many items of physical evidence as well as statements obtained from the defendant. As discussed in section 9-5, "Challenges to Evidence," the judge will determine what items the prosecution cannot use at trial. The impact of such rulings varies. Sometimes the loss of the use of one piece of evidence is so damaging to the case that it will be impossible to meet the burden of proof. Suppression of everything seized in a case charging possession of controlled substances is a good example: without the drugs and related laboratory tests there is no way to establish that the items in the defendant's possession were contraband. In other cases the suppressed evidence may not seriously affect the case; for example, the loss of the defendant's confession may not be important if there is overwhelming physical evidence.

Even though the prosecution may have won at a hearing on the defense's motion to *dismiss for insufficient evidence,* it may still be prudent to drop the charges before trial. The prosecutor may reassess all the evidence in the case and decide that the available evidence will not be sufficient to meet the burden of proof. One reason for this is that at trial the prosecution must convince a jury beyond a reasonable doubt that the defendant is guilty, but the burden at a pretrial hearing is lower. Other factors are accidental loss or destruction of evidence, and laboratory tests may not have produced the results originally anticipated.

One or more witnesses may have disappeared or died before trial. When this is a problem, records of the case should be reviewed for statements that can be admitted in court without the person's taking the witness stand. The most useful hearsay exceptions for this purpose are former testimony (usually from the transcript of the preliminary hearing) and dying declaration.

Uncooperative witnesses can also foil a prosecution. This category includes victims who are afraid to testify due to possible retaliation, hostile witnesses who have personal reasons to favor the defendant, and individuals who are generally antagonistic to law enforcement and the courts. The prosecutor must weigh the alternatives. Subpoenaing the witness may ensure that the witness attends the trial, but witnesses may change their testimony to be more favorable to the defense or repeatedly claim they cannot remember. A commonly cited example is the battered wife who has reconciled with her husband before trial and now tries to avoid saying anything negative about him. Other evidence may be available, such as eyewitnesses to the crime who can testify. Some forms of hearsay are admissible even though a witness refuses to testify.

The prosecutor reviews all of the factors when deciding when to dismiss the charges. The bottom line is will the evidence be sufficient to convince the jury of the defendant's guilt? If the prosecutor believes that the physical evidence and anticipated testimony of available witnesses will not meet this standard, one or more charges will be dismissed (also called dropping the charges).

Entries in the court record of "dismissed in the interest of justice" reflect the discretion that is inherent in the process. Factors ranging from a defendant who is suffering from a terminal disease to agreements to act as a police informant are in this category. In misdemeanor cases it is also common to see docket entries "dismissed because the victim did not appear in court." This is most likely to occur when the victim was the only eyewitness to the crime other than the defendant; therefore, there is no way to prove the case without the victim's testimony. Some prosecutors honor the victim's request to dismiss charges even if there is other evidence that could be used.

10-7 Preparing the Trial Brief

A **trial brief** is a written document that outlines the evidence and legal issues in the case. Points and authorities are included if the attorney believes they are necessary. The trial brief is presented to the judge, either on the first day of trial or a few days before, by an attorney. A copy must also be given to the opposing side. A trial brief is usually optional.

An attorney in the case or a member of his/her staff prepares the trial brief. Consultation with the officer handling the case may be necessary to outline the evidence. Some trial briefs include a list of witnesses who will be called to testify and a synopsis of the testimony anticipated from each. In lengthy and/or complex cases the trial brief is very helpful: the judge can refer to it to see the relevance of the testimony of each witness. It is beneficial if scheduling problems make it necessary to alter the normal sequence in which witnesses are called. The brief will also help the judge make rulings on the admissibility of questions and physical evidence. It serves as a guide to the trial; it is not evidence in the case.

Chapter Summary

Chapter Summary

The final case preparation for trial is usually shared by the prosecutor and the officer in charge of the investigation. One or more meetings is usually necessary to decide which witnesses to subpoena and what evidence to introduce. Complete candor is necessary in order for the prosecutor to prepare the case effectively. The strengths and weaknesses of each witness and item of physical evidence need to be considered. The officer will be responsible for making sure that the evidence is in the courtroom at the appropriate time and that the subpoenas have been served.

In criminal cases the subpoenas can usually be signed by the prosecutor, public defender, or court clerk. The subpoena must indicate where and when the witness is ordered to appear and must be served on the witness. A proof of service must be filed with the court for each subpoena. Special showings regarding the importance of the testimony are usually required to subpoena a witness from a substantial distance.

There is no legal barrier to refreshing the memory of a witness prior to trial. The witness must, however, be able to testify from memory. A witness can be discredited if it is shown that the testimony was memorized. The past recollection recorded exception to the hearsay rule can be used to introduce written reports made shortly after the event if the witness cannot remember enough to testify fully about them. The witness must be able to vouch for the accuracy of the report.

Objective evaluation of the physical evidence is important. The prosecutor needs to be prepared to meet defense challenges based on improperly handled evidence, inconclusive laboratory tests, and attacks on the credibility of the witnesses. The extent of each witness's knowledge of the case must be reviewed. Behavioral characteristics that either enhance or detract from credibility must be considered.

Potential impeachment of both prosecution and defense witnesses needs to be evaluated. Credibility can be attacked based on physical limitations of the witness that interfered with the ability to perceive the events in question; the fact that the layout of the location made the observation testified to impossible; prior inconsistent statements by the witness that indicate untruthfulness; motive, bias, or prejudice, which may influence testimony; prior convictions; and the witness's reputation for dishonesty.

Prosecutors need to go over every aspect of the defense's case and try to anticipate the defendant's strategy. Each possible piece of physical evidence needs to be considered. Every potential defense witness must be evaluated and methods of discrediting his/her testimony reviewed.

Each attorney may give the judge a trial brief. This document, prepared by the attorney's staff, summarizes the case and presents legal arguments. Its content is not evidence in the case, but it assists the judge in understanding why the attorney is calling each witness and asking specific questions. The trial brief is usually optional.

Study Questions

1. Explain how to establish the chain of custody for the following items:
   a. a gun found at the murder scene
   b. the body of the victim so the autopsy report will be admissible
   c. a ballistics test showing the gun found at the murder scene fired the bullet recovered from the victim during autopsy
2. Check your local court rules, and explain how to subpoena the following people:
   a. the police officer who took the crime report
   b. the pathologist from the coroner's office who conducted the autopsy
   c. the person believed to have been with the victim at the time of death—this person lives in your state but is 250 miles from the courthouse
   d. the person who can refute the defendant's alibi—this person is now an inmate serving time in another state
3. What can be done with witnesses who have memory problems?
   a. List three ways to refresh a witness's memory.
   b. Prepare a script for the prosecutor and defense attorney, in which the officer who wrote a report about the theft of a six-pack of soda from a grocery store cannot remember very many details of the case.

4. Prepare a script for the defense attorney to use when attempting to impeach Wendy, an eyewitness to a robbery, on each of the following:
    a. prior inconsistent statements—on the night the crime was committed Wendy gave police a description of the robber that does not match the defendant
    b. inability to observe—Wendy has bad eyesight and was not wearing glasses
    c. inability to observe—Wendy claims to have been able to see everything, but the officer's diagram shows there was a large bush between the victim and where Wendy was standing
    d. motive, bias, and prejudice—Wendy is the victim's sister, and Wendy recently broke off her romance with the defendant after a bitter fight
    e. prior convictions—Wendy was convicted of petty theft three years ago
    f. reputation—a person who works with Wendy claims everyone at work knows Wendy submits false expense account claims
5. Collect newspaper clippings on a major criminal case that occurred recently in your area. Make a report.
    a. List the strengths and weaknesses of each potential witness, including specific facts to be used for
        1. impeachment.
        2. rehabilitation.
    b. List the strengths and weaknesses for each possible item of physical evidence:
        1. How will the chain of custody be established?
        2. What witnesses are needed to introduce each item into evidence?

True or False Questions

1. Evidence retained for use at trial is normally stored in the police department's evidence locker.
2. Subpoenas are issued only if the judge who will hear the trial is convinced that the witness can testify to material evidence.
3. A *subpoena duces tecum* is used to subpoena a person who has information about documents that cannot be found.
4. All subpoenaed witnesses must appear in the courtroom on the first day of the trial.
5. Witnesses must be served with subpoenas at least 10 days before the trial begins.
6. A witness may testify only if he/she can pass the test for present memory refreshed.
7. The Past Recollection Recorded Rule applies only to police reports.
8. Police officers should collect information that could be valuable to impeach witnesses at trial.
9. The chain of possession must be established for each item of physical evidence that the police seized and plan to introduce at trial.
10. It is mandatory that each attorney submit a trial brief on the first day of trial.

Chapter 11

The Trial

O u t l i n e

Key Terms

alibi witness	hostile witness	relevant evidence
alternate jurors	hung jury	rest the case
bench trial	*in propria persona (pro per)*	Sixth Amendment rights—
case-in-chief	jury commissioner	assistance of counsel
challenge for cause	jury instructions	compulsory process
change of venue	jury pool	confront witnesses
character	lay witnesses	impartial jury
closing statements	leading questions	informed of the nature
confront witnesses	limited admissibility	and cause of the
Contemporaneous	mistrial	accusation
Objection Rule	narrative questions	speedy and public trial
continuance	objection overruled	stipulation
cross-examination	objection sustained	*sua sponte*
cumulative evidence	opening statements	*voir dire*
direct examination	peremptory challenges	
expert witnesses	poll the jury	

Learning Objectives

Learning Objectives

After reading this chapter, the student will be able to

- Identify six rights the Sixth Amendment guarantees for defendants in criminal trials.
- Describe the process used to select a jury.
- Explain the purpose of opening and closing statements in criminal trials.
- Explain what the prosecutor does during the case-in-chief.
- Explain the function of the defense's case-in-chief.
- Explain when an attorney may reopen testimony and/or present rebuttal.
- Describe how the jury is instructed on the law.
- Identify what the jury does during deliberations.
- Explain the process for entering a jury verdict.

Jury selection is the opening event at trial. Once this is complete, attorneys make opening statements. The prosecution presents its evidence first. After the prosecution has called all of its witnesses, the defense has the right to call witnesses. Closing statements are given after all witnesses have testified. The judge then instructs the jury on the law that applies to the case, and the jury deliberates the defendant's guilt or innocence. If the jurors vote to acquit or convict, the verdict is read in open court. A mistrial will be declared if there is serious misconduct during the trial or the jurors cannot agree on a verdict.

11-1 The Defendant's Constitutional Rights

The **Sixth Amendment** protects the criminal defendant's trial rights. It states:

> In all criminal prosecutions, the accused shall enjoy the right to a speedy and public trial, by an impartial jury of the State and district wherein the crime shall have been committed, which district shall have been previously ascertained by law, and to be informed of the nature and cause of the accusation; to be confronted with the witnesses against him; to have compulsory process for obtaining witnesses in his favor, and to have the Assistance of Counsel for his defense.

Streamlining the federal and state court systems cannot be done at the expense of these **Sixth Amendment rights.**

11-1a Speedy and Public Trial

The Sixth Amendment was designed to protect against the practices that were common at the time of the American Revolution: leaving the defendant to languish in jail for years without trial and conducting secret trials in which the government was able to obtain a conviction. The right to a speedy trial was discussed in section 9-4, "Challenges to the Pleadings": the delay between arrest and trial must not be so long as to be prejudicial to the defendant. Factors considered include the length of the delay; reasons for the delay; the defendant's assertion of the right to a speedy trial; and prejudice to the defendant. No one factor is determinative. The defendant must show that the combination of these factors resulted in the denial of a fair trial. The longer the delay, however, the less evidence there needs to be of actual prejudice.

The right to a speedy and public trial is in the Sixth Amendment's list of the defendant's rights, but the Supreme Court has ruled that it does not belong solely to the defendant. The right of the public to attend trials and to be informed about what occurs is also of constitutional dimension. First Amendment issues of freedom of the press are involved. The result of the confluence of these rights is that the trial must be open to the public and press, except when there is an urgent need to close it temporarily. Witnesses waiting to testify, except the defendant, may be excluded because listening to other witnesses may directly or indirectly influence their testimony. Unruly people, including defendants, may be removed from the courtroom to maintain decorum. Excluding the public and press en mass requires a showing of a more urgent need. The most common situation where this is allowed involves children who have been sexually assaulted. Closing juvenile court proceedings to the public has been permitted because this protects the juvenile defendant and encourages rehabilitation.

11-1b Impartial Jury

Despite the Sixth Amendment's reference to juries, there is no constitutional right to be tried by a jury if the maximum sentence is six months or less. The rule used by the Supreme Court parallels the United States Code's definition of "petty offenses" (18 U.S.C. §1). The defendant's constitutional right to a jury trial does not mean the opposite is true: the defense cannot have a trial without a jury if the prosecutor requests a jury. Trials by a judge without a jury, called **bench trials,** occur only if neither side requests a jury.

An impartial jury will be selected after *voir dire* examination. They can be questioned regarding any preconceived opinions and prejudices which would interfere with their ability to decide the case based on the evidence introduced at trial and the law given in the jury instructions. The system for excluding jurors who may be partial to one side is discussed in section 11-2, "Jury Selection." In high-publicity cases the media's coverage of the case may make it difficult to find impartial jurors. The courts have limited authority to restrain the media in order to protect potential jurors' neutrality. See section 8-3, "Rights of Public and Press to Be Present." A **change of venue**, which means a change in the location of the trial, is frequently used if the judge is convinced that the publicity has influenced so many people that finding an impartial jury is unlikely. A **continuance**, which is a postponement of the trial, may be granted so that inflamed public opinion may cool.

Traditionally the jury consisted of 12 members, who had to reach a unanimous verdict. Neither of these requirements is constitutionally mandated. The Supreme Court has approved 6-member juries but held that smaller ones are not acceptable. When using a 6-person jury, the verdict must be unanimous. State laws allowing convictions based on votes of 11 to 1, 10 to 2, and 9 to 3 have been accepted by the Supreme Court. This gives individual states flexibility in determining rules on juries in criminal cases. The jury used in each case must comply with the state law (i.e., a defendant cannot be convicted on a 10-to-2 vote if the state law requires unanimity).

11-1c Informed of the Nature and Cause of the Accusation

Prior to trial, the defendant must be given notice of the charges. This satisfies the defendant's Sixth Amendment right to be **informed of the nature and cause of the accusation.** The arraignment partially satisfies this requirement. Charges may be dropped after the arraignment for a variety of procedural reasons, as discussed in Chapter 9, or the prosecutor may decide there is insufficient evidence, due to the disappearance of witnesses or other reasons, to justify going forward on one or more of the charges. The result is that the charges to be adjudicated at trial may not be the same as those in the original complaint, the information filed after the preliminary hearing, or the indictment. The defendant usually has knowledge of the charges because the defense attorney was present in court when they were made. Even so, trials begin with a reading of the charges unless the defendant requests that this not be done. This gives official notice of the charges and informs the jury of the nature of the case.

11-1d Confronted with the Witnesses against Him/Her

The right to **confront witnesses** takes two forms: the accuser must testify at trial and the defense has the right to cross-examine each prosecution witness. Both have exceptions. There may be circumstances that justify not calling an eyewitness. For example, the witness may have died from natural causes, accident, or criminal means. Statements made by witnesses who are unavailable to testify at trial are hearsay, but the traditional exceptions to the hearsay rule are viewed as incorporated into the Sixth Amendment right to confrontation. In other words, the defendant's rights are not violated by admission of statements if there is a long-standing exception to the hearsay rule that permits the statement to be used at trial. Newer exceptions which are not based on the trustworthiness of the testimony have been viewed as violating the right to confront the accuser.

Normally the confrontation clause is interpreted to mean that the witness must testify in the presence of the defendant. The Supreme Court has allowed the use of closed-circuit television as an alternative to eye-to-eye contact when there was a specific showing that normal procedures would produce severe trauma to a sexually abused child testifying against the assailant. The Court made it clear that an individualized showing of trauma was necessary. Standing rules allowing all molestation victims to testify outside the presence of the accused were not acceptable; neither was a standing policy that allowed the prosecution to place a screen between the defendant and the victim, so that the victim would not have to look at the attacker.

Our adversarial system considers cross-examination the key to determining the truth. The defendant therefore has the right to cross-examine any witness who is called by the prosecution. Unreasonable restrictions on cross-examination violate the Sixth Amendment. Judicial discretion may be used to stop cross-examination that is irrelevant, repetitious, or is done solely to harass the witness.

The defense attorney must be allowed to question each witness. The ability to ask questions, not the witness's ability to answer them, is the heart of this right. The defendant's rights are not violated by prosecution witnesses who have limited memory. Tactical decisions are made by the defense on how extensive cross-examination will be or whether to waive cross. For example, the Supreme Court found no violation of this right when a prosecution witness testified to identifying the defendant as the assailant but, due to a head injury, could not recall all the facts relating to the crime. Neither are the defendant's rights violated by the use of testimony from the preliminary hearing where the defense attorney chose not to cross-examine the witness.

11-1e Compulsory Process for Obtaining Witnesses

Compulsory process means the right to subpoena witnesses. It would be grossly unfair if the prosecution could use the power of the court to compel witnesses to attend trial but the defense could not. The Sixth Amendment guarantees the defendant's right to use the authority of the court to compel witnesses to attend trial and testify. There is no provision for the defense to grant immunity to a witness. The defense must comply with appropriate procedures and deadlines when using the subpoenas. It is also the defense's responsibility to locate the people to be subpoenaed. See section 10-2, "Subpoenaing Witnesses," for details on how subpoenas are obtained and served.

11-1f Assistance of Counsel

The Sixth Amendment guarantees the defendant's right to have an attorney at any criminal trial. A series of cases starting with *Gideon v. Wainwright* (372 U.S. 335, 9 L.Ed. 2d 799, 83 S.Ct. 792 [1963]) interpreted this right to include appointing attorneys at government expense if the defendant cannot afford to hire private counsel. An indigent person cannot be sentenced to jail or prison as a result of a trial in which he/she was not represented by counsel or voluntarily represented him-/herself. The Supreme Court does not require appointment of an attorney in cases in which only fines or probation without time in custody is imposed.

Defendants who understand their right to counsel may act as their own attorneys, called being *in propria persona,* or *pro per.* The only test the judge may use when deciding whether to permit a defendant to be a *pro per* is whether there is a voluntary waiver of a known right. The defendant must be informed that there is a right to free counsel, and no coercion may be used. No questions may be asked regarding court procedures. *Pro per* defendants can be required to follow court rules the same as licensed attorneys. Some judges appoint an attorney to assist a *pro per,* but this is not constitutionally mandated. A defendant who is granted the right to be a *pro per* cannot appeal a conviction based on incompetent trial counsel.

One attorney representing more than one defendant raises questions of adequate representation. Frequently the best defense is to try to blame everything on the other defendant. This is impossible if there is only one attorney. Forcing defendants to share an attorney violates their Sixth Amendment rights if it interferes with their ability to present a defense. The judge must honor a request for separate representation if there is any reason to believe there is a conflict. The Supreme Court also held that the judge may deny joint representation if the judge believes it is impossible for one attorney to handle multiple defendants, even though the defendants have agreed to accept the same lawyer.

The right to counsel would be meaningless unless there were a right to a competent attorney. The constitutional standard is that the attorney's conduct is below the norm for defense attorneys in criminal cases and it is likely that this incompetence is a factor in the outcome of the case. The courts will not second-guess tactical decisions made at trial, as long as they were made with knowledge of the law. Acts done due to ignorance or failure to prepare the case properly are signs of incompetence. The standard is based on the average criminal defense attorney in the area. The second prong of the test is the effect of the incompetence on the outcome of the case. Appellate judges base their decisions on the likelihood that the defendant would not have been convicted if the defense attorney had performed competently. If the prosecution's evidence was strong, errors by the defense attorney may not merit reversal of the conviction; in close cases, the defense attorney's inadequacies give the defendant the right to a new trial with a better attorney.

11-2 Jury Selection

Our justice system uses juries as the conscience of the community. To do this, the jury panel must represent a cross section of the local population. The process of selecting a jury actually begins with the summonsing of people to jury duty. A government official, frequently called the **jury commissioner,** is in charge of selecting the people who will be called. Neither race, gender, nor religious affiliation can be used to exclude people from participating. Voter registration records were traditionally used for this purpose. Many states now combine voter registration with other sources, such as driver's license records, to make up the initial pool.

A formula derived from past experience is used to determine how many people should be summoned for jury duty. Factors considered are the percentage of people normally excused from jury duty; the number of trials anticipated; and the number of potential jurors usually questioned in order to select a jury. State law specifies who is exempt from jury duty. Minors, people who are not citizens, police officers, and people who do not speak English are usually exempt; convicted felons normally are disqualified. These people can notify the jury commissioner and be excused from appearing at the courthouse. In addition to automatic exemptions, there are usually a variety of personal circumstances that may be considered. For example, teachers and college students may be able to delay jury duty until school vacations; some states permit people who are the primary caregivers for preschool children to be excused. The summons to jury duty may include a form to be used to request exemption on these grounds.

A large group of potential jurors will be ordered to appear at the courthouse. This group is called the **jury pool**. A waiting room is provided and some form of orientation is usually given. When a judge is ready to start jury selection, the court clerk telephones the jury commissioner's office and requests a jury panel. A group of people will be selected from the jury pool. This may be done by drawing names each time a jury panel is needed; some jury commissioners place names on lists before the jurors arrive and send everyone on the list to the courtroom at the same time. When they arrive at the courtroom the potential jurors are given an oath to truthfully answer questions during *voir dire*. Names are randomly selected to make a jury. *Voir dire* follows. Local rules govern how *voir dire* is conducted. The attorneys may ask questions, the judge may ask the questions, or the judge and attorneys may share the responsibility. Sometimes questions are directed at all potential jurors; at other times jurors are queried individually.

There are two types of challenges that can be used to exclude jurors: challenges for cause and peremptory challenges. A **challenge for cause** excludes a juror because that individual is unable to base a decision on the evidence presented at trial and the law given by the judge. There is no limit on the number of potential jurors who can be challenged for cause. Either side may exercise a challenge for cause, but the judge must be convinced that there is a factual basis for the challenge. Questions used during *voir dire* as a basis for a challenge for cause include "Do you believe every person the police arrest is guilty?" "Can you base your decision in this case on the facts presented at trial and not what you already know about the case?" and "Do you understand that the prosecution must establish guilt beyond a reasonable doubt and that the defense does not have to disprove the charges?"

Peremptory challenges give an attorney the right to exclude a potential juror for subjective reasons. Neither race nor gender may be used as a reason for challenging a juror, but almost any other factor can. If the opposing side suspects that challenges are being made on the basis of race or gender, an objection must be made at that time. Once this objection has been made, the judge is required to ask the attorney for the reason for the challenge and determine if there is a permissible reason behind the challenge. General questions—such as "Do you have friends that are police officers?"—are used during *voir dire* to help the attorneys decide how to use peremptory challenges. Other questions frequently relate directly to the facts of the case. For example, in a drunk driving case jurors may be asked whether they believe driving while mildly intoxicated is wrong; in a domestic violence case they might be asked if they have ever had a violent argument with their significant other. The answers to these questions rarely establish grounds to exclude a juror for cause, but they help the attorneys judge the possible reaction of the juror to the evidence in the case. Body language and general demeanor are also considered. Attorneys try to exclude jurors they believe are likely to vote for the other side.

State law establishes how many peremptory challenges may be used in a case. The number is usually based on the severity of the case (misdemeanor, felony, death penalty case) and the number of defendants. For example, six peremptory challenges may be permitted in misdemeanor cases. If there is only one defendant, the prosecutor and defense attorney have the same number of challenges; the quotas may be different if there are multiple defendants.

The process of selecting the jury begins with challenging jurors for cause. An attorney asks the judge to excuse a specific juror. Opposing counsel may argue that the request should be denied. The judge gives a ruling after hearing arguments from both sides. If a juror is excused, another name is drawn. The new person undergoes *voir dire*. Additional challenges for cause are made and replacements drawn until enough people to make a jury are seated.

Peremptory challenges are used next. Local rules designate who starts; the attorneys then alternate. During this process jurors are frequently addressed by number: "The Prosecution would like to thank and excuse Juror Number Three." No grounds are given for exercising the peremptory challenge. Once a juror is excused, a name must be drawn for a replacement, who then undergoes *voir dire* and may be challenged for cause. Once the replacement juror has been seated, the other side exercises a peremptory challenge. The process continues, going back and forth between the prosecution and defense. An attorney may skip a turn, and thus save a peremptory challenge for later, by stating that he/she accepts the current jury; this does not forfeit future rights to use peremptory challenges. If both sides accept the jury, the panel is sworn in. If the attorneys cannot agree, the exclusion of jurors based on peremptory challenges continues until both sides have exhausted their peremptory challenges.

Extra jurors, called **alternate jurors,** are selected to hear the case and act as substitutes if one or more of the jurors become ill or otherwise unable to continue. They are needed because a mistrial must be declared if the number of jurors falls below the legal minimum. The judge decides on the number of alternate jurors, based on the estimated length of the case and past experience with the drop-out rate of jurors. Alternate jurors are selected last. They undergo *voir dire* and are subject to challenge for cause. Separate rules usually govern the number of peremptory challenges—for example, one peremptory for every two alternate jurors.

Once jury selection is complete, the jury is sworn in. The oath given at this point requires the jurors to decide the case on the evidence presented at trial and to follow the judge's instructions. The judge may give a brief speech, telling the jurors to take notes, to not discuss the case until it is time for deliberations, and to avoid discussion about the case with people who are not on the jury. Administering this oath officially starts the trial. Actions after this point are covered by double jeopardy. In a bench trial, double jeopardy attaches when the first witness is sworn.

11-3 Opening Statements

Trials usually begin with the reading of the charges, followed by opening statements. **Opening statements** are speeches made by the attorneys; they are not evidence in the case. The purpose of the opening statement is to provide an outline of the case. A good opening statement gives the jury a summary of the facts that will be presented. If there will be a large number of witnesses, the opening statement highlights how the testimony will fit together. It also points out things the jurors should watch for and explains things that may not be obvious, such as why experts will be called. Bench trials frequently do not have opening statements because it is assumed the judge will be able to understand the evidence.

Each side is entitled to make an opening statement in a jury trial. It is optional, but the prosecutor almost always makes one. The defense attorney has three choices regarding opening statements: make one immediately after the prosecutor; delay the opening statement until the defense is ready to call its own witnesses; or do not make an opening statement at all. This is a tactical decision. Many defense attorneys feel their statement has more impact if made when defense witnesses will be testifying. Waiting until this time also gives the defense attorney a chance to hear the prosecution's evidence and to tailor its opening statement accordingly. Postponing the opening statement also allows the defense to conceal its strategy until after the prosecution's case-in-chief is concluded. Waiving the opening statement is most common in cases in which the defense decides not to call any witnesses. When an opening statement is made, the defense usually summarizes the facts and emphasizes the rule that the prosecution has the burden of proof.

11-4 Presentation of Evidence at Trial

Testimony at trial must relate to something that is relevant to the case. Relevant means the evidence tends to prove or disprove any disputed fact in the case. In most cases it takes many pieces of evidence to establish guilt beyond a reasonable doubt. Each piece is relevant whether it relates to establishing an element of the crime, laying the foundation for admission of an item of physical evidence, or impeaching a witness. The entire case may be circumstantial; it is not necessary to have direct evidence.

11-4a What Is Admissible?

Anything tending to establish an element of the crime(s) charged (or a defense) is **relevant evidence** unless the point is no longer in dispute. What is relevant can be determined only from the facts of the case. For example, questions regarding the floor plan of a restaurant would be relevant if a robbery were committed there but totally irrelevant if all events related to the crime occurred somewhere else; questions regarding education may be relevant for an expert witness but irrelevant for an eyewitness to the crime.

Relevant evidence may be excluded for a variety of reasons. The exclusionary rule makes evidence seized in violation of the Fourth and Fifth Amendments inadmissible even though it is relevant. If both sides admit an event occurred, called a **stipulation,** facts that establish that event are no longer in dispute and testimony that would otherwise be admissible is irrelevant. Privileged information is relevant but not admissible: the strong policy favoring confidential communications between attorney and client, physician and patient, clergy and penitent, husband and wife and certain other relationships permits the parties to refuse to reveal relevant evidence at trial.

Judicial discretion can be used to exclude relevant evidence if it is highly inflammatory, is confusing, or would take an excessive amount of court time, compared with the probative value of the item in question. A balancing process is involved. For example, if a complicated scientific test were used that would require hours of testimony to explain to the jury, the judge would consider the importance of the test versus the time and possible confusion caused. If the test were a major factor in the prosecution's case, it might be allowed if it was extremely accurate, but if it were reliable in only 20% of the cases it would be excluded.

Some evidence is relevant for one purpose but not another. This is called **limited admissibility.** When such evidence is admitted, the jury is told that it can consider the item for one purpose but must not use it for another. Impeachment evidence is a good example. The fact that the witness made an inconsistent statement is relevant on the issue of the truthfulness of the witness, but the prior statement is not admissible as evidence to prove an element of the crime.

Lay witnesses (eyewitnesses, crime victims, and others) are allowed to testify to what they observed with their five senses: hearing, smell, taste, touch, and sight. Opinions are not usually allowed. The reason for this rule is that it is the jury's function to draw conclusions from the facts in the case. Some opinions are so ingrained in everyday life that many judges will permit lay witnesses to give them—for example, "he looked sick," "she seemed upset," "he walked as if he were drunk."

Patrol officers and detectives usually testify as lay witnesses. They can relate everything they observed at the crime scene and while investigating the crime. Statements made to them by victims, eyewitnesses, suspects, and other people are admissible *only if* covered by an exception to the hearsay rule. Other restrictions may apply—for example, a confession by the defendant must have been obtained in compliance with *Miranda*. Common opinions, such as "he was driving too fast," are usually allowed, but statements such as "the car was going 75 miles per hour" must be established by some other form of evidence, such as a radar gun.

Expert witnesses, on the other hand, are allowed to give opinions. In fact, they are called to testify specifically so the jury can hear their opinions. To introduce this type of testimony, the side calling the expert must show that the jury needs the help of an expert to understand the evidence, there is a recognized body of knowledge on the subject, and the expert has appropriate training and/or experience. *Voir dire* is done to determine if the expert is qualified. Once the expert is on the witness stand, questions can be used to determine whether tests were conducted correctly and the equipment used was accurate.

Some officers testify as expert witnesses. Special training is required to achieve this status and is usually combined with many years of experience. Examples include latent fingerprint examiners, those who conduct ballistics tests, and officers trained to calculate speed based on skid marks at an accident scene. These officers testify as experts only when providing information relating to their specialized knowledge and skills. If they testify regarding things observed when they were not using their expertise, they must testify as lay witnesses. The same is true for all expert witnesses.

Objections to a question must be made immediately after the question is asked—the **Contemporaneous Objection Rule.** The main reason for the rule is to exclude improper questions before the jury hears the answers. When an objection is made, the judge will hear arguments from both sides and then rule on the question: **objection sustained,** meaning that the question cannot be asked, or **objection overruled,** inferring the objection was meritless. The objections and arguments regarding them are normally made without leaving the courtroom. Sometimes the judge or attorneys wish to discuss the objections outside the hearing of the jury and/or witness. When this is desired, the discussion is usually done in muted voices at the sidebar, the side of the judge's bench farthest away from the jury box. The judge may tell the attorneys to "approach the bench" or refer to this as a bench conference. If lengthy debate is expected, the jury may be asked to leave the room.

11-4b The Prosecution's Case-in-Chief

During its case-in-chief, the prosecution must establish every element of each charge beyond a reasonable doubt. This is done by calling witnesses to testify and, when appropriate, using their testimony to introduce physical evidence of the crime. The prosecutor may ask the officer in charge of the investigation to sit at the counsel table. This makes it easier for the prosecutor to ask the officer for details needed to question witnesses. Arrangements must also be made to have each item of physical evidence in court when needed.

The process of questioning a witness begins with **direct examination.** This means that the side that called the witness asks questions. Questions should be phrased so that they are easy to understand and provide an opportunity for the witness to reveal what he/she knows. Many times questions are worded so that the answer need be only yes or no. **Narrative questions,** which ask the witness to give an unstructured response, are usually not allowed for two reasons: witnesses tend to ramble and waste court time and the witness may bring up information that the court has ruled is inadmissible. For this reason, the witness is rarely asked, "What happened on June 25, 2001?" Specific questions are used to focus the testimony: "Where were you at 3:00 P.M. on June 25, 2001?" "Did you see a person enter the building?"

Leading questions are usually not allowed on direct examination. A leading question is one that implies the answer—for example, "He had on a red shirt, didn't he?" Appropriate questions on direct examination to establish what the robber was wearing include the following:

PROSECUTOR: Where were you at 3:00 P.M. on June 25, 2001?
MS. JONES: At the Denny's restaurant on First and Main.
PROSECUTOR: Did anyone talk to the cashier while you were there?
MS. JONES: Yes. One man did.

PROSECUTOR: Please describe that man.

MS. JONES: He was about 25 years old and probably six feet tall. I think he weighed about 200 pounds.

PROSECUTOR: What was he wearing?

MS. JONES: Red shirt and blue jeans.

PROSECUTOR: Describe the shirt.

MS. JONES: It was red plaid, sort of dirty. It had short sleeves.

PROSECUTOR: What else was he wearing?

MS. JONES: Blue jeans and dirty white tennis shoes, no socks.

Sometimes leading questions are permitted on preliminary matters in order to save time. These relate to setting the scene as to date, time, and location.

An exception to the rule prohibiting leading questions is made for hostile witnesses. A **hostile witness** is a person who is unfriendly to the side that subpoenaed him/her. In a criminal case this is usually due to the witness's friendship with the defendant or the fact that the witness is being prosecuted for a related offense. A police officer subpoenaed by the defense would also be a hostile witness in most cases. Since the hostile witness is not willing to cooperate, leading questions are allowed in order to force answers to specific questions. Normally a motion must be made, asking the judge to consider the person a hostile witness. Being declared a hostile witness does not prevent the witness from claiming the Fifth Amendment as grounds for refusing to answer questions. In the following example, the prosecutor calls the defendant's brother as a hostile witness:

PROSECUTOR: Where do you work?

MR. SMITH: At the Denny's restaurant on First and Main.

PROSECUTOR: Were you working there on the afternoon of June 25, 2001?

MR. SMITH: Yes.

PROSECUTOR: Where were you at 3:05 P.M.?

MR. SMITH: I was cooking at the grill.

PROSECUTOR: Did you hear loud voices coming from the area near the cash register?

MR. SMITH: Yes.

PROSECUTOR: Describe what you heard.

MR. SMITH: Someone was yelling, "Give me the money!"

PROSECUTOR: Did you recognize the person who was shouting?

MR. SMITH: Ah, well, no, I don't wanna say.

PROSECUTOR: Mr. Smith, are you related to the defendant in this case?

MR. SMITH: Yes. He is my brother.

PROSECUTOR: Your Honor, the People request that Mr. Smith be declared a hostile witness.

DEFENSE ATTORNEY: We object, your honor. The People subpoenaed this witness. They should not be allowed any special privileges.

PROSECUTOR: He was an eyewitness to the crime. We should be allowed to question him about what he saw, but he is refusing to cooperate because the defendant is his brother.

JUDGE: Motion granted. Mr. Smith, you are under oath. You must answer the questions.

PROSECUTOR: Mr. Smith, did you have a clear view of the cash register?

MR. SMITH: Yes.

PROSECUTOR: Could you see the person who shouted, "Give me the money"?

MR. SMITH: Yes.

PROSECUTOR: Mr. Smith, you recognized the person who said, "Give me the money," didn't you?

MR. SMITH: Yes.

PROSECUTOR: Your brother said, "Give me the money," didn't he?

MR. SMITH: Uh huh.

PROSECUTOR: Please answer yes or no. Did your brother, who is the defendant in this case, say, "Give me the money"?

MR. SMITH: Yes.

PROSECUTOR: And what did he have in his hand when he said, "Give me the money"?

MR. SMITH: Something.

PROSECUTOR: He had a gun in his hand, didn't he?

MR. SMITH: Yes.

PROSECUTOR: Where was the gun pointed?

MR. SMITH: I didn't see nothin'.

PROSECUTOR: Mr. Smith, you testified that you had a clear view of the cash register. You said he had a gun in his hand. Now, you must have seen where it was pointing. Was it pointed at you?

MR. SMITH: No.

PROSECUTOR: Was it pointed at the ceiling?

MR. SMITH: No.

PROSECUTOR: It was pointed at the cashier, wasn't it?

MR. SMITH: Yes.

PROSECUTOR: Did you tell your brother where the cashier kept the extra money?

MR. SMITH: You can't ask me that! My public defender told me to take the Fifth.

Due to the fact that Mr. Smith was declared a hostile witness, the attorney conducting the direct examination was allowed to ask leading questions, just as on cross-examination. This does not mean that only leading questions may be asked.

The prosecution normally is allowed to call as many witnesses as it deems necessary. The judge does have the discretion to refuse to allow a witness to testify if it appears that the testimony will merely duplicate what has been said by several other witnesses. This is called **cumulative evidence.** For example, there may be numerous eyewitnesses to a crime and several have already given very similar descriptions of what occurred.

The defense attorney is entitled to conduct **cross-examination** after direct examination of each witness by the prosecutor. During cross-examination, the witness will be asked for additional details that were not previously included, questioned on discrepancies in the testimony, and possibly impeached. See section 10-4, "Evaluating Strengths and Weaknesses of a Case," for a detailed discussion of impeachment. Unlike direct examination, leading questions may be used during cross-examination to force the witness to answer specific questions. The defense might cross-examine Ms. Jones as follows:

DEFENSE ATTORNEY: Ms. Jones, on this diagram of the restaurant, I want you to put a *J* to indicate where you were sitting.
MS. JONES: I was right here.
DEFENSE ATTORNEY: Please put a *C* where the cashier was.
MS. JONES: She was right here, at the end of the counter.
DEFENSE ATTORNEY: How far were you from the cashier?
MS. JONES: About 20 feet, I guess.
DEFENSE ATTORNEY: Which direction were you facing when you were eating?
MS. JONES: Toward the window.
DEFENSE ATTORNEY: Were you facing the cashier?
MS. JONES: No. She was behind me.
DEFENSE ATTORNEY: So you couldn't see her?
MS. JONES: Only when I turned around.
DEFENSE ATTORNEY: What was in this square on the diagram?
MS. JONES: That was where they put the dirty dishes.
DEFENSE ATTORNEY: Was it out in the open, so you could see it?
MS. JONES: No. It had a little wall around it.
DEFENSE ATTORNEY: A little wall? What kind of wall?
MS. JONES: Sort of a partition, maybe four feet high, covered with carpeting.
DEFENSE ATTORNEY: Could you see through the wall?

MS. JONES: No.
DEFENSE ATTORNEY: What did you hear the man say?
MS. JONES: "Give me all your money."
DEFENSE ATTORNEY: Are you sure?
MS. JONES: Yes.
DEFENSE ATTORNEY: Are you sure it wasn't "Give me all my money?"
MS. JONES: Yes.
DEFENSE ATTORNEY: When was the last time you had your hearing tested?
MS. JONES: A year ago.
DEFENSE ATTORNEY: Did the doctor say you had perfect hearing?
MS. JONES: No.
DEFENSE ATTORNEY: Did the doctor say you needed a hearing aid?
MS. JONES: Yes.
DEFENSE ATTORNEY: Were you wearing a hearing aid on June 25, 2001?
MS. JONES: No, but . . . .
DEFENSE ATTORNEY: That will be all, Ms. Jones.

If the witness denies facts relevant to impeachment, the judge may permit another witness to be called to verify that the event used for impeachment occurred.

The credibility of every officer is important. Officers must avoid the temptation to alter their testimony to appear more competent, to conform testimony to what other officers will say, or to show compliance with the Fourth Amendment or *Miranda*. Defense attorneys zero in on any hint of dishonesty in the present case, as well as a prior allegation of untruthfulness. An officer's reputation for being a liar or for misstating facts is targeted. A law enforcement agency's negative reputation is brought up to insinuate that the officers who testified should not be believed.

Redirect examination follows cross-examination. This gives the attorney who called the witness a chance to follow up on testimony given during cross-examination. Using this stage to ask questions that the attorney forgot to ask during direct is not appropriate; the judge will sustain objections by the opposing side if this is attempted. Redirect examination is an attempt to rehabilitate a witness that has been impeached. This is usually done by showing that the statements introduced on cross were taken out of context or by specifically asking the witness about his/her objectivity. The prosecutor might try to rehabilitate Ms. Jones:

PROSECUTOR: Ms. Jones, you testified that there was a partition surrounding the area where they stored the dirty dishes. Was this partition between where you were sitting and the cashier?
MS. JONES: Yes.
PROSECUTOR: Could you see over the partition when you were sitting down?
MS. JONES: No.
PROSECUTOR: Were you sitting down when you first heard the man yelling?
MS. JONES: No. I had just gotten up to go to the rest room.
PROSECUTOR: From where you were standing, could you see the cashier clearly?
MS. JONES: Yes.
PROSECUTOR: You testified that you have a hearing loss. Is that true?
MS. JONES: Yes.
PROSECUTOR: How severe is the loss?
MS. JONES: The doctor said it was mild to moderate.
PROSECUTOR: Did you hear what the defendant said?
MS. JONES: Yes.
PROSECUTOR: Are you sure?
MS. JONES: Yes. He was shouting, and I was only a few feet away.

If impeachment took the form of attacking the witness's reputation for honesty, another person may be called to testify to that reputation.

The prosecutor must constantly evaluate the strength of the evidence that has been presented. It is not necessary to call all possible witnesses, but the defendant will be acquitted if there has not been enough evidence to meet the burden of proof. At some point, either after all potential witnesses have been called or when it appears that the charges have been established beyond a reasonable doubt, the prosecutor will **rest the case.** This means that a decision has been made not to call additional witnesses. This is usually done by stating, "The Prosecution rests," when it is time to call the next witness.

11-4c The Defense's Case-in-Chief

There is no requirement that the defense prove anything: the prosecution has the burden of proof. If the prosecution's case was not overwhelming and cross-examination went well, the defense may decide not to call any witnesses. This is a tactical decision. The attorney must consider the alternatives and know the relevant law; as long as this has been done, the appellate courts will not reverse on incompetent counsel, even though no evidence was introduced. The defense attorney does not have to inform the court of his/her decision to present a case until after the prosecution rests.

If the defense decides to present a case-in-chief, it will start after the prosecution rests. An opening statement may be made if one has not already been given. Witnesses with relevant testimony may be called. The defendant may testify. As with the prosecution's case-in-chief, there is no set limit on the number of witnesses who may be called or the length of time allotted. During its case-in-chief, the defense will attempt to do two things: present its side of the story and discredit the prosecution's version of the facts. The defense attorney will conduct direct examination of the witnesses, and the prosecutor will be entitled to conduct cross-examination.

Alibi witnesses may be called to testify that a person was at a different location at the time in question. In effect, when the defense calls an alibi witness, the defendant is claiming to be a victim of mistaken identification. Suppose a defendant's girlfriend were called to establish an alibi:

DEFENSE ATTORNEY: Ms. Green, please tell us where you live.
MS. GREEN: At 4321 Elm Street.
DEFENSE ATTORNEY: Is that near First and Main?
MS. GREEN: Oh, no. That's on the other side of town.
DEFENSE ATTORNEY: Where were you at 3:00 P.M. on June 25, 2001?
MS. GREEN: I was home, watching TV.
DEFENSE ATTORNEY: What were you watching?
MS. GREEN: The Yankees play the BoSox.
DEFENSE ATTORNEY: Were you home alone?
MS. GREEN: No, my boyfriend was there, too.
DEFENSE ATTORNEY: Was anyone else there?
MS. GREEN: No. It was just us two—the way we like it.
DEFENSE ATTORNEY: What is your boyfriend's name?
MS. GREEN: Matt Smith.
DEFENSE ATTORNEY: Is Matt Smith in the courtroom today?
MS. GREEN: Yes. That's him sitting beside you.

Alibi witnesses are vulnerable to impeachment for bias because they are usually friends of the defendant. More impartial witnesses, such as the receptionist in a doctor's office, are more likely to convince the jury.

The defense may put the defendant's **character** at issue. This means the defendant argues to the jury that he/she is a person of good character and therefore would not have committed the crime. Specific character traits may be introduced if they are relevant; for example, the defendant may claim to be mild-mannered in order to show that he/she would use force only in self-defense. Character is introduced by calling witnesses who testify about reputation. For example, defendant Matt Smith in our hypothetical robbery case might call Larry Wright as a character witness:

DEFENSE ATTORNEY: Mr. Wright, where do you live?
MR. WRIGHT: 5678 Lime Street.
DEFENSE ATTORNEY: Is Matt Smith, the defendant in this case, your neighbor?
MR. WRIGHT: Yes.
DEFENSE ATTORNEY: How long have you lived there?
MR. WRIGHT: Five years.
DEFENSE ATTORNEY: Do you know how long Matt Smith has lived there?
MR. WRIGHT: He rented the house next door to me about a year after I moved in.
DEFENSE ATTORNEY: Are you familiar with Matt Smith's reputation in the neighborhood?
MR. WRIGHT: Yes.
DEFENSE ATTORNEY: How did you learn about his reputation?
MR. WRIGHT: I have a large rose garden in my front yard. I work on it a lot, and, when I do, I frequently talk to the neighbors. I know just about everybody who lives around there.
DEFENSE ATTORNEY: What do those neighbors say about Matt Smith?
MR. WRIGHT: They like him, think he is a nice guy.
DEFENSE ATTORNEY: Specifically, do they think he is honest?
MR. WRIGHT: Yes. I've heard a lot of them say they think Matt is honest.
DEFENSE ATTORNEY: Does he have a reputation for being a thief?
MR. WRIGHT: Oh, no. There's another neighbor everyone thinks is a thief. A couple people mentioned that Matt returned things they accidentally left at his house.

The prosecution is not allowed to attack the defendant's character during its case-in-chief. If the defense raises the issue, the prosecution may attack the defendant's character either by cross-examining the defense's witnesses or by calling witnesses who have different views of the defendant's reputation.

The defense attorney must try to judge the cumulative impact of the testimony on the jury. When it appears the desired effect has been achieved or the defense has run out of witnesses, the defense rests. This is done by stating, "The Defense rests," when it is time to call the next witness.

11-4d Reopening and Rebuttal

Reopening the case is used to present evidence in response to facts introduced by the other side. Rebuttal is an attempt to refute what specific witnesses said. Witnesses who have already testified may be recalled to the stand, or new witnesses may be called. If the defense presented alibi or character witnesses, the prosecutor has an opportunity to call witnesses to refute their testimony. For example, the prosecutor may wish to impeach Ms. Green, Matt Smith's alibi witness, by calling Mr. Adams as a rebuttal witness:

> PROSECUTOR: Mr. Adams, where are you employed?
> MR. ADAMS: Handyman Hardware.
> PROSECUTOR: What is your job?
> MR. ADAMS: I am manager on the afternoon shift.
> PROSECUTOR: Do you post a schedule of when employees are scheduled to work?
> MR. ADAMS: Yes. We post one every Friday for the next week.
> PROSECUTOR: Is this the schedule for Handyman Hardware for the week of June 20 to 27, 2001?
> [The prosecutor shows a sheet of paper to the defense attorney and then hands it to Mr. Adams.]
> MR. ADAMS: Yes, that was our schedule.
> PROSECUTOR: Did Barbara Ann Green work at Handyman Hardware during the month of June 2001?
> MR. ADAMS: Yes.
> PROSECUTOR: What shift was she scheduled to work on June 25, 2001?
> MR. ADAMS: 3:00 P.M. to 6:00 P.M.
> PROSECUTOR: Are you responsible for keeping the time cards for employees who work on your shift?
> MR. ADAMS: Yes.
> PROSECUTOR: Did Ms. Green come to work as scheduled?
> MR. ADAMS: Yes.
> PROSECUTOR: Did you see her there?
> MR. ADAMS: Yes, I did. I talked to her in my office when she picked up her paycheck about 5:00 P.M.
> PROSECUTOR: Was she at Handyman Hardware at 3:00 on June 25, 2001?

MR. ADAMS: Yes.

PROSECUTOR: How can you be sure?

MR. ADAMS: Here is her time card. She clocked in at 2:58 P.M. and out at 6:00.

PROSECUTOR: Is it possible that someone else, maybe another employee, punched Ms. Green's time card?

MR. ADAMS: I don't think so. We're very strict about not letting employees clock in for each other.

If the prosecution reopens the case or presents rebuttal witnesses, the defense is entitled to attack the new testimony by conducting cross-examination and calling additional witnesses if necessary.

11-5 Closing Statements

Closing statements (also called closing arguments) are speeches the attorneys make to the jury at the end of the case. They are not evidence but merely attempts to persuade the jury to interpret the facts in the light most favorable to the side making the statement. They are tailor-made to fit the facts of the case. There are usually at least three speeches: a summation by the prosecutor; a summation by each defendant's attorney; and then a closing argument by the prosecutor. The prosecution goes first because it has the burden of proof. For the same reason, it is allowed to make a closing argument, a rebuttal speech, after the defense. No time limitations are placed on closing statements.

The closing statement must parallel the trial testimony. The factual summary presented in the closing statement may be different from the one given in the opening statement if the evidence produced at trial was not exactly what the attorney expected. The more important function of the closing statement is to persuade the jury how to interpret the facts. Attorneys argue how inferences drawn from the facts can be used to establish elements of the crime or defense. Attempts will be made to persuade the jurors to believe witnesses favorable to the attorney's side and to discount what other witnesses said. Any impeachment evidence that was introduced will be stressed by the attorney who elicited the testimony; opposing counsel will try to show the witness was completely rehabilitated. An attorney may not, however, argue that the jury should believe a witness because the attorney does, or that witnesses were called because the attorney could personally vouch for their truthfulness.

Prosecutors frequently inform the jury what the elements of the crime are and refer to specific testimony which supports each element. In complicated cases it may take testimony from several witnesses to establish one point. Prosecutors may give excerpts from the anticipated jury instructions and tell the jury what testimony may be used to establish the crime. Defense attorneys usually argue that the prosecution has failed to establish the elements of the crime and that the witnesses who testified are not worthy of belief. They normally make a major point of the burden of proof being beyond a reasonable doubt and stress that this is a very high standard.

The Fifth Amendment privilege not to incriminate oneself poses unique problems during closing statements. The Supreme Court held that there can be no reference to the defendant's invocation of this right. The prosecutor cannot ask the jury to infer that the defendant is guilty because he/she did not testify. Some defense attorneys feel that more is necessary: the jury should be told that it may not draw any negative inference from the defendant's failure to testify. Others feel that the judge merely draws the jurors' attention to the fact and may trigger suspicion. If the defense requests a jury instruction on this point, the judge must give it. The opposite is also true: the judge may not give such an instruction if the defense objects.

11-6 Jury Instructions

Jury instructions are statements made by the judge to inform the jurors of the law that must be applied to the facts of the case. Near the end of the defense's case-in-chief, the judge will meet with the attorneys to discuss jury instructions. The meeting is frequently held in the judge's chambers and is not open to the public. The court reporter is present to record any disagreements that might later be part of the appeal.

In some states there is an official book of jury instructions, frequently with each instruction given a number for easy reference. For example, Part 9 of *California Jury Instructions Criminal* contains instructions relating to crimes against the person. Instruction 9.01 gives the definition of simple assault; 9.03 relates to unlawful shootings and contains instructions for Discharging a Firearm at Unoccupied Motor Vehicle (Instruction 9.03.1) and Grossly Negligent Discharge of Firearm (Instruction 9.03.2). The content of the instructions usually comes from quotations in leading cases on the issue or directly from relevant statutes. Some instructions are in a "fill-in-the-blanks" format, so that facts from each case can be inserted. Attorneys and/or the judge may draft instructions if the case has unique issues that are not covered by published instructions. States without official jury instructions rely on the judge to draft the statements. Wording is discussed in the conference called to select jury instructions.

Attorneys usually go to the conference with a list of jury instructions that they want the judge to give. This may be merely a list of numbers, such as Instruction 9.01, 10.2, and so on, if the state has official instructions. The attorneys may draft instructions in advance and ask the judge to read them to the jury. The prosecutor frequently has a standard list for the burden of proof, ways to assess credibility of the witness, and other routine issues.

All proposed instructions are discussed at the conference, and the judge makes rulings on which ones to give. There may be mutual agreement on many of the instructions. Failure to request an instruction normally waives the right to appeal because the jury instructions on that issue were inadequate; so does failure to object to the judge's decision to give an instruction requested by the other side. The judge has the duty *sua sponte* to give some instructions. This means the judge has a duty to do it even though neither attorney requested it. For example, if no one specifically asked for an instruction defining proof beyond a reasonable doubt, the judge still has a duty to make sure the jury is instructed on this topic. Failure to include these types of instructions is grounds for reversal on appeal, even though the attorney forgot to raise the issue at the time.

Jury instructions are normally read to the jury after the closing statements. In states with officially approved instructions, this may literally be a reading of the instructions. Judges in other states may work the information into a speech admonishing the jury about its duty to decide the case. Some states that use standardized jury instructions provide printed copies for the jurors (see Figure 11-1).

11-7 Jury Deliberations

The judge instructs the jury on its duties: select a foreperson; deliberate on the evidence; consider the opinions of the other jurors; and vote on verdicts. The verdict forms are explained. Then the jury is sent to the jury room to deliberate. Prior to voting on the case, jurors should review the testimony and exhibits. All jurors should enter into a discussion of the evidence and their varying interpretations of what was said and inferences that arise from the testimony. Witnesses may not be called to clarify their testimony, but, if there are serious differences of opinion about what a witness said, the jurors may ask to have the court reporter read the verbatim transcript aloud to them.

Jurors may ask the judge to clarify the jury instructions. Prior to responding to this request, the judge usually holds a conference with the attorneys in the case to discuss what new instructions, if any, should be given. In states that do not give the jury written instructions, the jury may also ask to have instructions repeated.

Figure 11-1
Sample *California Jury Instructions Criminal*

Instruction 2.81   **OPINION TESTIMONY OF LAY WITNESS**

In determining the weight to be given to an opinion expressed by any witness who did not testify as an expert witness, you should consider [his][her] credibility, the extent of [his][her] opportunity to perceive the matters upon which [his][her] opinion is based and the reasons, if any, given for it. You are not required to accept such an opinion but should give it the weight, if any, to which you find it entitled.

Instruction 8.24   **MURDER BY TORTURE**

Murder which is perpetrated by torture is murder of the first degree.

The essential elements of murder by torture are:

1. One person murdered another person, and
2. The perpetrator committed the murder with a willful, deliberate, and premeditated intent to inflict extreme and prolonged pain upon a living human being for the purpose of revenge, extortion, persuasion or for any sadistic purpose.
3. The acts or actions taken by the perpetrator to inflict extreme and prolonged pain were a cause of the victim's death.

The crime of murder by torture does not require any proof that the perpetrator intended to kill his victim, or any proof that the victim was aware of pain or suffering.

The word "willful" as used in this instruction means intentional.

The word "deliberate" means formed or arrived at or determined upon as a result of careful thought and weighing of considerations for and against the proposed course of action.

The word "premeditated" means considered beforehand.

After the evidence has been thoroughly discussed, the jurors vote on the verdicts. Individual verdict forms are usually provided to facilitate the voting process. Each form states one charge and the possible verdicts, usually guilty and not guilty. For example, in a robbery case where petty theft is a lesser included offense, there would be two verdict forms: one for robbery and one for petty theft. When there are lesser included offenses, the jury is usually instructed to vote on the greater offense first and take a vote on the lesser one only if it does not convict on the greater charge.

Juries reach a verdict when the vote is sufficient to convict or acquit under the law of the state (federal law for federal courts). As mentioned in section 11-1b, "Impartial Jury," many states require a unanimous verdict but some accept 11-to-1, 10-to-2, or 9-to-3 votes. When the verdict cannot be reached the jury usually sends a note to the judge announcing this fact. The judge has the discretion to encourage the jury to try again to reach a verdict, rather than dismissing the jury at this point.

The last resort with a jury that cannot agree on a verdict is to declare a **mistrial.** The result is a trial with no legally binding conclusion. The trial did not occur, as far as double jeopardy is concerned.

11-8 Entry of Verdict

Verdicts are not official until they are read in open court. This must occur with the judge, prosecutor, defendant, defense attorney, and all jurors present. The judge usually formally asks the foreperson, "Have you reached a verdict?" Upon an affirmative reply, the foreperson reads the verdict or the verdict forms are handed to the court clerk, who reads them aloud. After the verdicts have been read, either side has the right to **poll the jury.** This means that each juror is asked if he/she agrees with the verdict. When the jury is polled, the verdict is not final until each juror has affirmed that he/she agrees with the verdict. Once the poll is complete, the judge tells the clerk to enter the verdict into the minutes. Jurors are dismissed by the judge after the verdicts are accepted. Death penalty and insanity cases are an exception to this because there is a second phase of the trial, which is heard by the same jury.

If a conviction was entered, the defense attorney usually makes a motion for a new trial. This is frequently only a formality, but a judge may grant it if he/she believes serious mistakes, whether involving admissibility of evidence or unreasonable decisions by the jurors, will result in reversal on appeal.

Sentencing may occur immediately after the entry of the verdict. Most felony cases, and some misdemeanors, require a presentence investigation report to provide background information for the judge to consider when imposing sentence. Some courts order the report before the verdict is entered, but many wait until after the conviction has occurred. This requires a delay before the sentencing hearing can be held. Local practice and the backlog of cases determine how long this delay will be; six weeks is not uncommon. The judge will hear arguments and make a ruling on whether the defendant will be free on bail, released OR, or remain in custody until this hearing.

11-9 Mistrials

Mistrial is the term used to describe any trial that ends without a verdict. The two main reasons for a mistrial are prejudicial misconduct during the trial and a jury that cannot agree on the verdict. The judge hears arguments from both sides before declaring a mistrial. Double jeopardy does not bar refiling charges after a mistrial because there has been neither a conviction nor an acquittal. State law may prohibit refiling the case if there was serious misconduct by the prosecutor; a limit may also be set on the number of times a case can be refiled.

Many errors occur in trials, but few result in mistrials based on prejudicial misconduct. The most common problems relate to the introduction
of testimony on a topic that the judge has already ruled should not be presented to the jury. Even so, a mistrial is justified only if the statements are
likely to adversely influence the jury's verdict. Most errors are not this serious. Comments by the attorneys while questioning witnesses or making
opening and/or closing statements may also be so inflammatory that the
judge considers the only available recourse to be starting over with a new
jury.

The defendant is entitled to a mistrial if there are insufficient jurors
remaining to decide the case. Alternate jurors are empaneled to avoid this
possibility but, occasionally, so many jurors become ill or must be excused
for other reasons that there are not enough alternates remaining. A new
trial is usually held when this occurs.

A **hung jury** occurs when the required number of jurors deliberated
on the facts of the case but were unable to reach a verdict. If there are multiple charges, there can be a hung jury on some charges and verdicts on
others. When an impasse occurs during deliberations, the jury foreperson
notifies the judge that it has not been able to reach a verdict on specific
count(s) but usually does not reveal the final vote. The judge holds a conference with the attorneys in the case to decide what admonitions should
be given to the jury. The judge usually calls the jurors back into the courtroom and asks if there is any possibility that further deliberation will
change anyone's opinion. If there is any indication that progress is possible, the judge will instruct the jurors to continue deliberations. Many
times additional jury instructions are given about the deliberation process.
Jurors can be urged to consider each other's viewpoints but cannot be told
that the opinions of other jurors should be weighed as evidence in the
case. The judge has discretion to send the jury back to continue deliberation more than once. At some point the judge will decide that a deadlock
has occurred and will declare a mistrial.

The prosecutor usually has the right to refile charges if there is a hung
jury, regardless of what the final vote was. Lopsided votes in favor of
acquittal (such as 11-to-1) may convince the prosecutor that the case
should not be refiled. A review of what occurred at trial and interviews
with cooperative jurors may give invaluable insight into how to win the
case when it is retried. Some states have laws that limit the number of
retrials, but these usually do not apply until the case has gone to trial at
least twice.

speedy and public trial; impartial jury for crimes with sentences over six months; pretrial information on the charges; in-court confrontation and cross-examination of prosecution witnesses; right to subpoena witnesses for the defense; and assistance of counsel.

A jury must be empaneled to hear the case if either the prosecution or defendant requests one. In these cases jury selection will be the first event in the trial. Potential jurors may be excused for cause if their personal biases make it impossible for them to objectively review the evidence and apply the law the judge tells them is applicable to the case. Peremptory challenges may be used to exclude jurors based on the attorney's subjective opinions, but never on account of race or gender. State law provides limits on the number of peremptory challenges each attorney may use.

The prosecutor's opening statement precedes the presentation of evidence. This speech provides an overview to help the jurors understand the big picture as each witness testifies. The defense may give an opening statement immediately following the prosecutor's, wait until the defense is ready to call its own witnesses, or waive the opening statement entirely. Opening statements are usually not made by either side when the case is heard by a judge without a jury.

Only relevant evidence is admissible at trial. Relevant evidence may be inadmissible under the Exclusionary Rule, if it is privileged, or if the judge decides it is too inflammatory, is confusing, or would take too much time in relation to its value. Some evidence may be relevant for one purpose but not another.

Lay witnesses may testify to what they observed with their five senses. Experts, on the other hand, are allowed to give their professional opinions. These witnesses are allowed only if the jury needs their expertise in order to understand the evidence. They are questioned on *voir dire* to establish their qualifications before they testify.

The prosecution calls its witnesses and attempts to establish the elements of the crime during its case-in-chief. Answers to the questions asked by the prosecutor become evidence. Objections to a question must be made immediately after the question is asked. Testimony is needed to show the relevance of each item of physical evidence and to establish the chain of custody. Defense attorneys are allowed to cross-examine each prosecution witness immediately after the prosecutor finishes questioning him/her. Leading questions may be used on cross-examination. The prosecutor rests after he/she believes all charges have been established beyond a reasonable doubt.

The defense's case-in-chief comes after the prosecutor rests. Due to the fact that the prosecution has the burden of proof, the defense is not required to present any evidence. Defense witnesses will be called if the defense attorney decides that it is necessary. They are subject to direct examination by the defense attorney, followed by cross-examination by the prosecutor. The defense may call alibi witnesses and have its own expert witnesses testify. It is the defense's option to call the defendant. Jurors may not infer guilt from the fact that the defendant does not testify. The defense rests after its last witness has been called.

Witnesses may be called for rebuttal or if the judge permits an attorney to reopen the case after both sides have rested. The prosecutor may rebut testimony given during the defense's case-in-chief. If a new line of defense was presented, the prosecutor may be allowed to reopen the case. The defense may cross-examine when the prosecutor calls new witnesses at this stage and may call additional witnesses in rebuttal.

The attorneys make closing statements after all witnesses have been called. These speeches summarize the evidence and argue what inferences the jury should draw. Defense attorneys usually emphasize the heavy burden of proof the prosecution must bear. The prosecutor gives the first summation, followed by the defense. A closing statement is made by the prosecutor.

Jury instructions are read to the jury after the speeches are finished. These instructions are prepared at a conference attended by the judge, prosecutor, and defense attorneys. Instructions must cover all elements of the case, including the specific elements of each crime charged; the duty of the jurors to deliberate; the weight of the evidence and credibility of the witnesses; and burden of proof. Some states have books of approved jury instructions; others allow the judge to draft the instructions with the approval of the attorneys. The wording of jury instructions is common grounds for appeal.

Jury deliberations take place in the privacy of the jury room. The jury is instructed to select a foreperson and to go over all the evidence before taking any votes. They are usually given forms with each possible verdict, so that they can vote on all possibilities. If questions arise during deliberations, the foreperson can write a note to the judge, explaining the problem. No new evidence may be introduced, but the jury is entitled to have the court reporter read the verbatim transcript to them. It may be necessary for the judge to give additional jury instructions to clarify the jury's legal questions. A conference must be held with the attorneys before this decision is made.

Deliberations continue until there is a verdict, or until the jurors decide a verdict is impossible, on each charge. The jury notifies the judge when it reaches a verdict. The verdict will be read in open court, with the defendant and attorneys present. The defense may request that the jury be polled to give jurors one last chance to change their minds. Once this is done, the verdict is officially accepted. A mistrial will be declared if the jurors are unable to reach a verdict.

If there is a conviction, the defense attorney usually makes a motion for a new trial. Sentencing may be done at the time the verdicts are accepted. Frequently sentencing is delay to allow time for the preparation of the presentence investigation report. Motions may be made to permit the defendant to be free on bail or released OR during this delay.

Study Questions

1. Check your local laws and procedures on jury selection:
   a. How many jurors are required for a criminal trial?
   b. Is a unanimous verdict required? If not, how many votes are required?
   c. What are the qualifications for jury service?
   d. How does the jury commissioner select the jury pool?
   e. How many peremptory challenges are permitted for a
      1. misdemeanor?
      2. felony?
      3. death penalty case?
2. How are jury instructions selected for criminal trials in your local court?
   a. Are standardized jury instructions available?
   b. Are jurors given a printed copy of the jury instructions?
   c. Draft a set of jury instructions for the robbery case in this chapter.

3. Go to court and observe a trial. Prepare a report describing the following.
   a. opening statements
   b. For each prosecution witness:
      1. relevant testimony
      2. impeachment
      3. rehabilitation
   c. For each defense witness:
      1. relevance
      2. impeachment
      3. rehabilitation
   d. For each piece of physical evidence:
      1. relevance
      2. witnesses required to establish the chain of custody
   e. closing statements
   f. jury instructions
   g. the verdict
4. Hold a mock trial on a case that is currently receiving publicity in your area. Have students play the roles of each person in the scenario, or ask the acting class to play these parts. Assign students to prepare and present
   a. the prosecution's opening statement.
   b. the defense's opening statement.
   c. the prosecution's case-in-chief.
   d. the defense's case-in-chief.
   e. the closing arguments.
   f. the jury instructions.
5. Rent a video of a movie that has major trial segments. Critique how accurately the movie portrays the proper handling of a trial, including
   a. the selection of the jury.
   b. the opening statements.
   c. the prosecutor's case-in-chief.
   d. the defense's case-in-chief.
   e. the closing statements.
   f. the jury instructions.
   g. the jury deliberations.
   h. the entry of verdict(s).

True or False Questions

1. The Supreme Court has interpreted the Sixth Amendment as giving anyone charged with a crime the right to trial by an impartial jury.
2. Peremptory challenges are used to exclude potential jurors who have already made up their minds about the guilt of the defendant.
3. A statement may be admitted at trial only if the person who originally made the statement testifies.
4. A person who cannot afford to hire an attorney has the right to a government appointed attorney only if charged with a felony.
5. The judge makes the opening statement.
6. Lay witnesses are not allowed to testify about their opinions.
7. The prosecution must establish the defendant's guilt on all charges during the prosecution's case-in-chief.
8. Only the defense can call the defendant to testify at trial.
9. The prosecution may base its case on the defendant's bad character.
10. The judge selects the jury instructions without input from the prosecutor and defense attorney.

Chapter

Chapter 12

Special Trials

265

Outline

Key Terms

aggravating circumstances	involuntary civil	petitioner
competency to stand trial	commitment	respondent
dependency court	jurisdiction hearing	sanity phase
dependent children	(adjudication hearing)	special circumstances
detention hearing	mitigating circumstances	*sua sponte*
disposition hearing	not guilty by reason	transfer a case
fitness hearing	of insanity	to adult court
guilt phase	penalty phase	ward of the court
intake	petition	

Learning Objectives

Learning Objectives

After reading this chapter, the student will be able to

- State the standard for determining if a defendant is competent to stand trial.
- Identify the procedures for determining if a defendant is competent to stand trial.
- Explain the procedures for determining if a defendant who entered a plea of not guilty by reason of insanity should be acquitted.
- Describe the procedures used in capital cases to determine if the death penalty should be imposed.
- Explain the procedures when a person is tried in juvenile court.
- Describe the procedures for determining whether a juvenile should be tried as an adult.
- Explain the court procedures for removing dependent children from an unfit home.

Several types of cases require special procedures. If the defendant's mental competency to stand trial is questioned, a separate hearing must be held on this issue. If, on the other hand, the issue is the defendant's mental state at the time of the crime, a separate portion of the trial will address evidence relevant to that issue. If the jury votes to convict in a capital murder case, a separate hearing will focus on determining whether the defendant should be executed. Juvenile court parallels adult proceedings, but there are unique features, which will be discussed in this chapter.

12-1 Competency to Stand Trial

The Supreme Court has held that a person must be mentally competent during all court proceedings. This rule also applies to the time of execution. This right is based on due process and is not waived if the defense fails to raise the issue: the prosecutor and judge also have an obligation to see that competency is determined if the defendant's conduct suggests a lack of competency.

12-1a Test for Competency

Competency is the defendant's ability to function during court proceedings. The test for **competency to stand trial** is composed of two separate parts: the defendant must understand the nature of the proceedings and the defendant must be able to assist in his/her defense. The defendant must pass both parts of this test.

Understand the Nature of the Proceedings

The defendant must have a general understanding of the court process. Specifically he/she must understand that the trial is being held to determine if punishment should be imposed upon him/her. Confusion about the roles of the participants in the proceedings, such as believing that a friendly prosecutor is looking out for the defendant's best interest, may also result in a ruling that the defendant does not sufficiently understand the nature of the proceedings.

Assist in the Defense

The defendant must be able to assist with the defense by conferring with his/her attorney and providing appropriate information; there is no requirement that the defendant understand the rules of evidence and criminal procedure. Two fairly common situations arise that involve this part of the competency test: lack of memory and refusal to cooperate with the defense attorney.

The courts are very suspicious of a defendant's claim of having no memory of the events in question. False claims of amnesia are easy to make and hard to disprove. In cases where amnesia is claimed, the court usually places the defendant at an in-patient mental health facility for treatment and waits for memory to return. The courts must honor permanent amnesia, however, if there is no other person available to provide details that the defense attorney needs. An example of a case where amnesia was successfully claimed involved a robbery in which the clerk, who was the only person present besides the robbers, was killed. A high-speed chase ensued, in which the car driven by the robbers struck a tree, killing one robber and resulting in serious head injuries to the other. Medical testimony established that amnesia resulted from head injuries sustained in the crash, and there was no foreseeable chance of recovery. The court held that permanent amnesia, coupled with the lack of eyewitnesses, made a trial a denial of the defendant's due process rights.

A more common problem is the defendant's failure to cooperate with his/her attorney. Paranoid defendants frequently refuse to believe that their attorney, especially a court-appointed defense attorney, represents their interests. As a result, the defendants refuse to disclose any information about the crime to the attorney; sometimes they refuse to talk to the attorney at all. A total lack of communication results in a defendant's being unable to assist with the defense. Judges frequently appoint a different defense attorney in hopes that the defendant will confide in the new one. If such procedures fail, the defendant may be declared incompetent to stand trial.

Occasionally the lack of communication is due to the defendant's physical or mental impairments. The case that was the basis for the television movie *Dummy* involved a deaf-mute who lacked the mental capacity to learn sign language. Transfer of the defendant to a training school resulted in no improvement. Finally, the case was dismissed.

12-1b Procedure for Determining Competency

The proceeding to determine competency is technically a civil hearing rather than part of the criminal trial. Once the issue of competency is raised, the criminal proceedings are suspended. The important consequence of this distinction is that it does not result in a violation of double jeopardy to return the defendant to court to face criminal charges after competency has been restored.

The question of the defendant's competency to stand trial is usually raised by a motion by the defense. If made during the pretrial proceedings, it will usually be a formal, written motion, with copies served on the prosecution before the hearing. When the issues arise during trial, an oral motion may be made in open court. The prosecutor may also make the motion; if both sides fail to notice signs of the defendant's incompetency, the judge has a duty to consider the issue *sua sponte* (on his/her own initiative without a motion from either side).

The judge must hold a competency hearing if there appears to be any evidence, including in-court behavior, in support of the motion. This normally requires the court to appoint mental health professionals to examine the defendant and report back to the court. The actual hearing usually does not occur immediately, due to the time needed to conduct these examinations and make reports. The defense may want to have the defendant examined by its own experts during this period. A six-week delay is not unusual. The defendant may be transferred to a mental health facility or held in jail during this period. Treatment may be ordered during this delay if he/she appears to be seriously disturbed.

The competency hearing usually proceeds much like a civil trial. The expert witnesses are subject to direct and cross-examination. While the crucial question is competency during the court proceedings, a history of mental illness, or lack thereof, may be important. Lay witnesses may be called to testify about the defendant's conduct, both before and during trial. Officers who made the arrest and those who had contact with the defendant at the jail testify as lay witnesses and may be asked about behavior they observed.

Some state laws require that a jury decide the issue of competency. The burden of proof is a preponderance of the evidence. The side raising the issue has the burden of proof; in most cases this is the defense.

The criminal trial will resume if the verdict is that the defendant is competent to stand trial. If the delay has been minimal, the same jury that was originally empaneled may hear the case. Lengthy delays may require starting the trial over with a new jury. If there is a verdict of not competent to stand trial, the defendant is transferred to the mental health system. Typically this means he/she will be confined in an in-patient facility for treatment; some states use out-patient facilities if the defendant's condition indicates this is appropriate.

State law establishes the procedures following the defendant's commitment to mental health authorities. Typically the court must review the defendant's progress at specified intervals, such as every six months. A maximum length of confinement is usually stated—for example, three years or the maximum sentence for the crimes charged, whichever is shorter.

Some defendants can be restored to competency by the use of antipsychotic drugs, such as thioridazine. Defendants may object to such treatment because the drugs have painful side effects, such as severe upper body spasms; overmedication may result in drowsiness, possibly to the extent of not knowing what is occurring in court. An additional reason for declining to take these medications is the potential impact on the jury of a defendant who appears to be "normal": the jury may consider the defendant's in-court appearance of normality as an indication that the defendant was not insane at the time the crime occurred. The Supreme Court has held that a defendant can be required to take these medications against his/her will only if they are medically necessary and there is no less restrictive means to prevent the patient from harming him/herself or others. Drugs may not be administered involuntarily merely to make the patient more "manageable."

A formal hearing is triggered by one of two events: a staff report by a mental health expert indicating that the defendant has recovered or the expiration of the maximum period for which the defendant may be held. The judge will review the staff reports and determine if the defendant has recovered sufficiently to stand trial. If so, a trial date will be set and the case returned to the criminal court calendar. If the maximum detention has elapsed without recovery, the judge must decide what to do: release the defendant or place him/her under a civil commitment. The minimum standard for a civil commitment is that the defendant is dangerous to him/herself or to others. The Supreme Court has held that a defendant may not be detained under involuntary civil commitment unless he/she is both mentally ill and dangerous.

12-2 Sanity Phase of a Trial

The plea of **not guilty by reason of insanity** is separate from the consideration of competency to stand trial. The two proceedings are based on different legal definitions; they also focus on the defendant's mental state at different time periods. The insanity plea alleges that the defendant was criminally insane at the time the crime occurred; competency proceedings focus on mental capacity at each court appearance. Three possible outcomes occur: the defendant was insane at the time the crime occurred and is also incompetent to stand trial; the defendant was insane at the time the crime occurred but has recovered competency by the time of the trial; and the defendant was legally sane when committing the offense but is now incompetent.

Unlike competency to stand trial, which has no double jeopardy implications, a verdict of not guilty by reason of insanity has all the consequences of any other not guilty verdict: the defendant may not be tried again on the charges, regardless of any bad faith in bringing the defense.

Procedurally the defense must plead not guilty by reason of insanity before trial. State court rules usually require that the insanity plea be entered early enough to enable the prosecution to prepare for trial on the issues of the defendant's sanity. The normal procedure is to enter two pleas: not guilty and not guilty by reason of insanity. A trial is held on the charges to determine if the defendant is guilty of committing the offense; this is referred to as the **guilt phase** of the trial. Another hearing, frequently called the **sanity phase,** is held to determine if the defendant was sane at the time the crime was committed. Some states hold the guilt phase first, while others conduct the sanity phase first. The verdict at the first phase will determine if the second phase is needed. For example, in a state that holds the guilt phase first, there will be a sanity phase only if the jury finds the defendant guilty of committing the crime.

12-2a Insanity Test

State law establishes the legal standard for insanity. The M'Naghten rule is the most commonly used. *Black's Law Dictionary* states that the M'Naghten rule requires proof that, at the time the crime was committed, the defendant was

> . . . laboring under such a defect of reason from disease of the mind as not to know the nature and quality of the act he was doing, or if he did know it that he did not know he was doing what was wrong.

Other tests—such as the American Law Institute rule, which requires that the defendant lack substantial capacity to conform his/her conduct to the law—are in use in some states. The Supreme Court declined a request to rule on whether Montana's abolition of the insanity defense is constitutional. This leaves individual states free to pass laws which refuse to allow defendants to use the insanity defense. An intermediate approach used by some states is a plea of guilty but mentally ill. A guilty verdict results in confinement to a mental health facility; upon recovery, the defendant is returned to prison to serve any time remaining on the sentence.

12-2b Procedure for Establishing Criminal Insanity

The law presumes the defendant is sane. If the defense does not raise the issue, it will be presumed the defendant is sane, no matter how irrational his/her behavior was. Some defendants refuse to enter an insanity plea, possibly due to the stigma society attaches to mental illness. This results in inmates being convicted and sentenced to jail or prison who are incapable of dealing with life in custody; many states maintain separate facilities for these types of inmates.

The defense must raise the issue of insanity. In addition to entering a plea of not guilty by reason of insanity, the defense must present some evidence showing that the defendant was not sane at the time the crime was committed. The burden of going forward with evidence on the issue of sanity then shifts to the prosecution. States may assign the burden of proof on the issue of insanity differently than the burden for other issues in a criminal trial. For example, some states require the defendant to establish insanity by a preponderance of the evidence.

In most states the sanity phase of the trial is held only after a verdict of guilty has been returned. The reason for this is two-fold: it saves the time of presenting evidence on insanity if the defendant is not guilty of committing the crime, and much of the evidence on sanity would be inadmissible, and potentially prejudicial, if presented at the trial on the issue of guilt. The sanity phase usually begins immediately after the guilty verdict is returned. Both sides have had ample notice that the issue will be considered, so there is no need for a continuance. The jury that decided guilt usually determines sanity.

The focus of the insanity defense is the defendant's mental state at the time the crime was committed. Eyewitnesses can be called as lay witnesses to provide information on how the defendant behaved, as well as any relevant statements he/she made. Police officers who were present when the crime occurred or who arrived shortly after the event may testify to what they observed. These lay witnesses may not state conclusions such as "He acted like a crazy person," but they may provide insight into whether the defendant's actions appeared to be rational and his/her speech coherent. The defendant's physical appearance and oral and written statements are relevant.

Both the prosecution and defense have the right to have experts examine the defendant prior to trial in order to testify in court. Prosecution experts must advise the defendant of his/her *Miranda* rights prior to such an interview. Therapists who have previously treated the defendant may be called to testify if the defendant has a history of mental-illness. While this testimony cannot establish the defendant's mental state at the time the crime was committed, jurors may infer that serious mental illness (or the lack thereof) immediately prior to the crime is indicative of the defendant's mental state at the time in question.

In many cases the sanity phase becomes a battle of the experts. More than one expert may be called by each side, but the judge has the discretion to limit the number testifying if it appears excessive. Each side may call expert witnesses to testify regarding their opinions of the defendant's mental state at the time the crime was committed. Many states permit the court to appoint more impartial experts as well. The normal rule that experts may be asked hypothetical questions applies. This means experts who did not personally examine the defendant may give opinions as to his/her mental state, based on a review of the evidence in the case. The jury is inundated by psychiatric opinions. Experts, including those called by the same side, frequently disagree on the seriousness of the defendant's mental disease. Diagnoses used by psychiatrists and psychologists do not directly relate to the legal definition of sanity.

Jurors, who usually have been screened by using peremptory challenges to exclude anyone with knowledge of psychiatry, are left to analyze the conflicting opinions and decide how to apply the law to the facts and opinions introduced. Jurors may conclude that a defendant is sane or insane based on the testimony of lay witnesses and may reject the opinions of the experts. Jurors may reject the experts' opinions if they find them implausible or if they are so technical that the jurors do not understand them. They may consider the background qualifications of each expert, the length of time the expert interviewed the defendant, whether the opinions appear to be logical, and any bias that the expert may have which might interfere with an objective analysis of the case. Two areas of impeachment frequently have major impacts: high fees paid to the expert for testifying and a witness's history of testifying for only one side—for example, having testified as an expert in 10 cases and concluding that the defendant was insane in all 10.

If the jury finds the defendant sane, the judge will proceed to sentencing, frequently after a delay to obtain a presentence investigation report. A verdict of not guilty by reason of insanity is treated as an acquittal. The defendant may not be sentenced for the crimes committed; nor may the charges be refiled when the defendant recovers. In many states the court has the power to order the defendant detained in a mental health facility under an **involuntary civil commitment** if he/she is a danger to him/herself or others. The defendant may be temporarily admitted to a mental health facility for an evaluation of the need for such a commitment. Defendants confined on these grounds must be released as soon as they recover sufficiently so that the danger is over. The Supreme Court has ordered periodic reviews of a patient's progress in order to satisfy due process when involuntary commitments occur.

12-3 Penalty Phase of a Death Penalty Case

The Supreme Court has spent the past 30 years trying to establish rules on the use of the death penalty. Well over 100 cases have been decided, and the rulings are not completely compatible with each other. Some basic rules have emerged: the death penalty may be imposed only in murder cases; it cannot be imposed if the defendant was under the age of 16 at the time of the crime; the jury must have controlled discretion to decide who receives the death penalty; state law must establish clearly defined "special circumstances" under which murder becomes a capital offense; jurors must be allowed to consider both aggravating and mitigating circumstances in all capital cases; the death penalty may not be automatically imposed without considering the possibility of mitigating circumstances.

These features of a capital murder case result in unique trial procedures. The prosecution must give the defendant notice before trial that the death penalty will be sought. Defendants in these cases have the right to additional assistance prior to trial; this usually includes hiring experts to examine the evidence and provide assistance to the defense attorney. Other issues, such as a not guilty by reason of insanity defense, may further complicate trial procedures.

Jury selection takes on added features: jurors may be excluded based on their personal opposition to the death penalty if their beliefs would make it impossible for them to vote in accordance with the law. Additional questions are used during *voir dire* of potential jurors. Many courts try to expedite the process by having potential jurors complete printed questionnaires prior to *voir dire*. The focus on the personal beliefs of the jurors requires extra time. Questions will be asked to try to distinguish between jurors who do not believe the death penalty is appropriate but will follow the law if the facts indicate the death penalty is legally required and those who have conscientious objections to capital punishment and would not vote for death, no matter what the facts are. A juror with the latter beliefs could be challenged for cause. Each side is usually given extra peremptory challenges in capital cases. The attorneys must make subjective determinations about each potential juror's reservations about the death penalty in order to exercise these challenges. Experts on jury selection may be employed to assist with this process. It may also be necessary to excuse more people than usual because the length of the trial imposes hardships beyond what jurors are normally expected to bear.

The trial is usually divided into two parts: the guilt phase, where the jury determines if the defendant committed the crime; and the **penalty phase,** where the jury determines if capital punishment should be imposed. The same jury normally hears both phases. In many states the guilty verdict can be affirmed on appeal even though the penalty phase must be retried because it was found to contain reversible error.

At the guilt phase of the trial, the prosecution must establish both guilt for the murder and at least one special circumstance. **Special circumstances** are listed in the capital murder statute. They can be divided into two major types: nature of the current crime (multiple murders, killing for hire, death of a peace officer the defendant knew was acting in the line of duty, gratuitous violent crimes causing excessive suffering, etc.) and the defendant's social history (prior murder convictions, history of extreme antisocial behavior, etc.). Accomplices who participate in a murder with the knowledge and intent that it be carried out under conditions amounting to special circumstances can also be given the death penalty.

Death penalty cases frequently result in the introduction of evidence that would normally be inadmissible at criminal trials. Some special circumstances relate to prior crimes, such as the defendant's conviction for a murder committed several years before the current offense. Other special circumstances—for example, sadistic torture—place the defendant's mental state in issue. Some states permit the consideration of future dangerousness to society. Expert witnesses, particularly psychiatrists and psychologists, are frequently called to testify on these issues.

The prosecution is allowed to show **aggravating circumstances** during the penalty phase, which justify the imposition of the death penalty— for example, the extreme brutality of the crime or the defendant's lack of remorse. The Supreme Court's holding that the defendant can submit any evidence he/she deems appropriate to show **mitigating circumstances,** which justify a more lenient punishment, has resulted in a wide variety of evidence being admitted—for example, the defendant's inadequate personality, deprived childhood, low intelligence, lack of prior criminal record, and youthfulness at the time of the crime.

The jury receives a potpourri of evidence as a result of the requirement that it determine both special circumstances and aggravating and mitigating circumstances. Appropriate jury instructions are given. Only two verdicts are usually allowed at the penalty phase: death or life imprisonment without possibility of parole. If no verdict is reached, some states impose life without parole; others permit the penalty phase to be retried before a different jury.

The trial judge is usually required to review the verdicts in capital cases. The death penalty verdict may be rejected if the judge finds that the evidence does not support it. Most states with capital punishment also provide for automatic review by the state's highest court, usually without prior hearings before intermediate-level appellate courts. These procedures are seen as reducing the chances of arbitrary imposition of the death penalty. A proportionality review is usually required. This means that the reviewing court compares the crime with others receiving the death penalty: if the crime appears substantially less heinous than others receiving the death penalty, the sentence should be reduced.

12-4 Juvenile Court

The juvenile court movement began in the 1890s with the purpose of rehabilitating wayward youth. A kindly, father-figure judge was seen as putting his arm around the delinquent and guiding him/her into a productive life. Over the years the juvenile courts became more crowded, and the informality envisioned by its founders resulted in denial of a fair hearing for many juveniles. Two Supreme Court cases, *Kent v. United States* (383 U.S. 541, 16 L.Ed. 2d 84, 86 S.Ct. 1045 [1966]) and *In re Gault* (387 U.S. 1, 18 L.Ed. 2d 527, 87 S.Ct. 1428 [1967]), require that juveniles be given many of the same procedural rights as adults: notice of charges, confrontation of witnesses, proof beyond a reasonable doubt, and so on. Juveniles also have the same right to be represented by an attorney as adults have. A few rights, particularly public trial, jury, and bail, have not been extended to juvenile court proceedings.

The defendant's chronological age at the time the crime was committed, not the trial date, places him/her under the jurisdiction of the juvenile court. Most states have provisions to send juvenile cases to adult court for the most serious crimes or when the minor has demonstrated, by prior court records, that he/she will not benefit from the services provided by juvenile court. The maximum age limit for juvenile court is set by state law and is not always the same as the age of majority: many states use 18, but some extend the jurisdiction only to those who are under 16 or 17. Juvenile court may be a branch of the court that tries felonies; some states make it a part of family court. Juvenile courts frequently handle both misdemeanors and felonies; some also handle traffic offenses committed by juveniles.

In addition to handling criminal cases involving minors, juvenile court usually handles cases of abused, neglected, and abandoned children (called **dependent children**) if it becomes necessary to remove them from the custody of their parent(s) or guardian(s). Sometimes this is done in a branch of the juvenile court referred to as **dependency court.** A social worker from Children's Protective Services (or a similar agency) usually conducts the necessary investigation in these cases. Court-ordered outcomes in these cases can range from leaving the child in the home while the caregivers take classes to improve their parenting skills, placement of the child in foster care, and severing parental rights so the child can be placed for adoption. Many states require a separate juvenile facility for children who are being detained pending disposition by the court in these types of cases. In some states juvenile courts also handle the trials of individuals accused of crimes in which children are the victims.

Another unique feature of juvenile court in most states is its authority over so-called status offenses: actions that make a juvenile in violation of the law but are not crimes if committed by adults. Truancy, running away from home, and curfew violations are typical examples; habitual refusal to obey reasonable commands of parents also fits into this category. Children who are under juvenile court supervision for these reasons are frequently referred to as "persons in need of supervision" (PINS), "minors in need of supervision" (MINS), or a variety of other similar titles.

12-4a Procedures When a Minor Is Tried as a Juvenile

The most obvious difference in juvenile court procedure is that the names of documents and court proceedings are frequently different from those used in adult court. Some of these differences are shown in Table 12-1. The terms used are more similar to those in civil court than in criminal court.

The process of completing the necessary paperwork for admission to a juvenile facility is frequently called **intake** (not booking) and is done by an intake officer. Officers are required to notify the minor's parents that he/she has been taken into custody. This must be done very soon after the arrest, usually within four to six hours. State law specifies the time limits for filing the petition against a minor who is being held in custody; they

T A B L E **12-1** Terms Commonly Used in Juvenile Court

Term Used in Adult Court	Term Used in Juvenile Court
Booking	Intake
Criminal complaint	Petition
Plaintiff	Petitioner
Defendant	Subject or respondent
Arraignment	Detention hearing
Trial	Jurisdiction hearing (also called adjudication hearing)
Sentencing hearing	Disposition hearing
Convicted	Adjudicated within the jurisdiction of the juvenile court
Sentenced	Made a ward of the court

are frequently shorter than for filing charges against an adult. For example, a state may require that an adult be arraigned within 48 hours, but the first court appearance for a minor must be within 24 hours. Officers are usually required to notify the minor's parents of the pending court action and to keep the juvenile informed.

A **petition** is filed to start the juvenile court proceedings. The petition serves the purpose of the complaint: it must satisfy the due process requirements of giving notice of the charges; other legal requirements include establishing the court's geographical jurisdiction and showing that the statute of limitations has not expired. The government may be called the **petitioner** and the juvenile referred to as the **respondent.** The prosecutor usually files the petition if the case involves criminal activity by a minor. In many states either a prosecutor or probation officer may file the petition if status offenses are involved. Social workers usually prepare the petition if the purpose of seeking court involvement is to take custody of dependent children.

The first hearing in the juvenile case is frequently called a **detention hearing:** its purpose is to determine if the child should remain in custody until the court hearing is held to determine if the alleged acts actually occurred. The judge reviews the charges to verify that juvenile court has jurisdiction and decides whether it is necessary to keep the child in custody. Options available to the judge usually include the release of the child to the parent(s) or guardian(s), placement in foster care, or detention in a secure juvenile facility. Attorneys will be appointed at the detention hearing. In dependency cases the court may appoint separate attorneys for the child and the parent because their interests may not be the same: the parents want to keep custody of the child, but the child's best interests may be to be removed from an unfit home.

The **jurisdiction hearing** (also called the **adjudication hearing**) serves the purpose of the trial: it determines whether the minor is within the jurisdiction of the juvenile court. This means the evidence must be sufficient to place the child under the authority of the court based on his/her age and behavior or, in the case of dependent children, the actions of a parent or guardian. The time between the detention hearing and the jurisdiction hearing is frequently shorter than for the corresponding hearings in adult court. Both sides have the right to call witnesses and conduct cross-examination. Depending on the state law, it is heard by a judge, commissioner, or referee; very few states permit juries in juvenile court. The result of the jurisdiction hearing is referred to as adjudication, not a conviction.

A child who has been found to be within the jurisdiction of the juvenile court may be made a **ward of the court,** literally meaning that a person is under the protection of the court. It gives the court the power to control the custody of the child. A decision will be made on whether to allow the child to stay in his/her home while on probation or to send him/her to a detention facility; foster care and adoption decisions may be made in the case of dependent children. The type of detention facility must also be decided. This is done at a **disposition hearing** (similar to a sentencing hearing in adult court). Later court hearings can be used to release the juvenile from wardship or to change the level of supervision.

State law may provide that the authority of the juvenile court for the purpose of punishment and rehabilitation extend past the age of majority. For example, a person who commits a crime as a juvenile may be held in the custody of the Youth Authority (or a similarly named agency) until the age of 21 or longer. Without this type of provision, juveniles near the upper age limit of the juvenile court's jurisdiction would escape with little or no punishment.

12-4b Transfer of a Case to Adult Court

Some states allow the prosecutor to file juvenile cases involving serious crimes directly in adult court. It is more common for the state to have provisions in its juvenile law permitting serious cases originally filed in juvenile court to be transferred to adult court. Many states specify minimum age limits so that juveniles younger than 14, for example, can never be tried as adults. The decision to **transfer a case to adult court** is usually within the discretion of the juvenile court judge. A hearing, frequently referred to as a **fitness hearing,** is held to determine which court will hear the case. Two factors are usually considered before a case is transferred: the nature of the current offense and the juvenile's criminal history.

State laws frequently include a list of serious offenses, such as murder, rape, arson, and armed robbery, that are presumed to be more appropriately heard in adult court. Even so, the defense may argue that there are mitigating circumstances justifying retention of the case in juvenile court. When this approach is taken, the defense has the burden of proof. The prosecution may argue that a juvenile belongs in adult court even though the offense is not on the list of serious offenses. Criteria for a transfer on these grounds are usually listed in the statutes and include such things as degree of criminal sophistication exhibited; possibility for rehabilitation, including consideration of success or failure of previous attempts to rehabilitate; criminal history; and gravity of the current offense. The prosecution usually has the burden of establishing that these cases should be transferred to adult court. Due to the consideration of many personal factors, it is possible for two juveniles who are the same age to commit an offense together but one is tried as an adult while the other remains in juvenile court.

Cases that are transferred to adult court usually are handled in the same manner as those for adults: public trial, jury, and so on. State law may provide, however, that a juvenile convicted in adult court be sentenced to prison facilities designed for serious juvenile offenders. When this occurs, the convicted person is sent to a juvenile facility; however, if the maximum age for detention in such a facility is met before the sentence is complete, the person will be transferred to an adult prison to serve the remainder of the sentence. Laws in each state designate the maximum ages involved.

12-4c Dependent Children as Wards of the Court

Children come under the jurisdiction of dependency court because they are victims of parental abuse, neglect, or abandonment. A child who has been beaten by a parent is a typical case; so is an incest victim. The law is usually broad enough to allow legal intervention when a parent intentionally permits the child to be abused by another person and does nothing to intervene. Abandonment cases range from the baby left on a stranger's doorstep to children whose parent(s) have been taken into custody and therefore cannot care for them.

A social welfare agency, such as Children's Protective Services, usually handles dependency cases. Sometimes they are the first agency called; other times law enforcement officers initially handle the case and turn the children over to the social workers for placement. Most social workers operate under the premise that they are there to protect the best interest of the children. They believe, contrary to the beliefs of many police officers, that keeping the family intact serves that interest. Terminating parental rights and placing the child for adoption is considered a last resort.

Legal proceedings in this area are very involved; the code usually requires numerous hearings at specified intervals. The burden of proof usually increases as more intrusive measures are considered: less evidence is necessary if the court is asked to make the child a ward of the court but to leave him/her in the home than is necessary to terminate parental rights. Adoption decisions typically cannot be made until two or more years after the wardship has been imposed. Parents are normally given the opportunity to redeem themselves by taking appropriate classes on child discipline and development and by otherwise demonstrating the ability to care for their children. Courts usually seek placement with relatives over foster care with strangers if the child is to be removed from the home.

Foster care is considered preferable to keeping the child in an institutional setting.

Dependency cases are considered civil rather than criminal. The rules of evidence involved are usually similar to those used in criminal court, but the burden of proof is usually lower. Many of the hearings in dependency court have names similar to those in juvenile court (detention hearing, jurisdiction hearing, disposition hearing). Police officers may be called to testify at the jurisdiction hearing if they witnessed any events relevant to the case. The officers will be subject to cross-examination by an attorney representing the parents and possibly another attorney who represents the child.

State law may permit the social worker to make an agreement with the parents that they will be under the informal supervision of the social worker while they try to improve their behavior. When this is done, a substantial delay may exist between the date when the officers handled the case and the date it goes to court. Dependency cases may not go to court immediately if someone had volunteered to take care of the children but later was unable to fulfill this responsibility. It is important that officers keep notes on these cases until the final disposition has occurred.

Chapter Summary

Due process requires that a defendant stand trial only if he/she is competent. This means the defendant must understand the nature of the proceedings and be able to assist with the defense. The defense, prosecution, or judge may raise this issue. Criminal proceedings are suspended while civil proceedings are used to determine if the defendant is competent. A defendant who is not competent will be sent to a mental health facility for treatment. This delay does not affect the statute of limitations or double jeopardy: the trial may resume when the defendant is declared competent.

A plea of not guilty by reason of insanity also triggers inquiry into the defendant's mental health. Only the defense can raise this issue. When this plea has been entered, the trial is divided into two parts: the guilt phase determines if the defendant committed the crime; then the sanity phase considers whether or not the defendant is legally sane. Many states use the M'Naghten rule to determine legal insanity. A defendant who has been found insane is acquitted and double jeopardy prevents a retrial.

Death penalty cases are usually tried in two phases: the guilt phase to determine if the defendant is guilty of the crime charged and the penalty phase to decide if the death penalty should be imposed. The prosecution must prove that special circumstances exist that make the case more serious than ordinary murder. State law cannot make the death penalty the automatic punishment upon conviction for certain crimes: the defendant always has the right to introduce evidence to show what he/she believes to be mitigating circumstances.

Juvenile court is usually considered part of the civil court system. Names of procedures may be different from those used in adult court. Juvenile court may handle delinquents (those who would be charged with crimes if they were adults), status offenders, and dependent children. Most of the procedural rights afforded adults now apply to juvenile court. The state sets age limits for minors to be brought before the juvenile court. Sanctions imposed by this court can range from probation to incarceration in a facility designed for young offenders.

Juveniles may be tried as adults for serious crimes. State laws designate the age groups that can be transferred to adult court and the reasons for such actions. Normally the transfer applies only to the most serious crimes or offenders who have a history of juvenile offenses without any showing of rehabilitation.

Dependency court, usually a branch of juvenile court, handles the placement of abused, neglected, and abandoned children. Law enforcement becomes involved in these cases when they handle reports of physical and/or sexual abuse of children. Action by this court may also be necessary when adults are taken into custody and no one is available to care for their children.

Study Questions

1. Find a case involving competency to stand trial in your local newspaper.
   a. Who brought the motion for a determination of the defendant's competency?
   b. At what phase of the criminal court proceedings was the motion made?
   c. What facts were used to establish the incompetency of the defendant?
   d. What procedures were used to postpone criminal proceedings while competency was determined?
   e. If the defendant was determined to be incompetent:
      1. what was done with him/her?
      2. was the defendant tried on the criminal charges at a later date?

2. Search local newspapers for a case involving a plea of not guilty by reason of insanity.
   a. When was the insanity plea entered?
   b. Was a proceeding held to determine competency to stand trial?
   c. Was the defendant found guilty of the substantive offense?
   d. What test for insanity is used in your state?
   e. What occurred at the sanity phase of the trial?
   f. Was the defendant found legally sane?

3. Use your local newspapers to follow a case in which the death penalty was sought by the prosecution.
   a. Under the laws of the state where the crime occurred, when may the death penalty be imposed?
   b. What procedures were used to select the jury?
   c. What special circumstances applied to the case?
   d. What facts were used to establish special circumstances?
   e. Was the defendant found guilty of capital murder? If so,
      1. what evidence did the prosecutor introduce at the penalty phase to show aggravating circumstances?
      2. what evidence did the defense attorney introduce at the penalty phase to show mitigating circumstances?
      3. what was the verdict from the penalty phase?

4. Check your state law and find the terminology used in your juvenile court for
   a. criminal complaint.
   b. arraignment.
   c. trial.
   d. sentencing hearing.
   e. status offender.
   f. a child who is under court supervision.
   g. a hearing to determine if juvenile will be tried as an adult.
   h. the court handling cases involving abused, neglected, or abandoned children.

5. Check the laws of your state for situations involving juveniles.
   a. What is the name of the court handling juvenile cases?
   b. What is the maximum age for treatment as a juvenile?
   c. What juveniles can be tried as adults?
      1. ages
      2. types of offenses
      3. other factors considered
   d. Where are children charged with crimes detained prior to trial?
   e. Where are abused and neglected children housed?
   f. What is the maximum age for detention as a ward of the court?
   g. Where do juveniles serve their sentences if they are convicted for offenses committed as juveniles but they receive sentences that extend past the time they reach the age of majority?
   h. Where are juveniles housed who are tried as adults
      1. while awaiting trial?
      2. when sentenced?

True or False Questions

1. The issue of competency to stand trial can be raised only at the beginning of the trial.
2. The criminal charges must be dismissed if a judge rules that a person is not competent to stand trial.
3. The insanity defense focuses on the defendant's mental state at the time the crime was committed.
4. The Constitution mandates that the defendant be acquitted if he/she was insane at the time the crime was committed.
5. Double jeopardy prevents a prosecutor from refiling criminal charges if the defendant perjured him/herself in order to obtain a verdict of not guilty by reason of insanity.
6. The prosecution has the discretion to ask for the death penalty in any first-degree murder case.
7. The defendant's right to introduce mitigating evidence at the penalty phase of a death penalty case can be restricted by the state legislature.
8. Juveniles have the same constitutional rights as adults.
9. The U.S. Constitution sets 18 as the maximum age for juvenile court.
    Dependency court handles cases involving children who have been abused by their parents.

The Sentencing Hearing

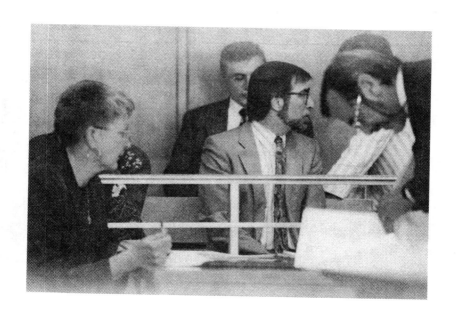

Outline

Key Terms

aggravating circumstances
allocution
community service order
concurrent sentences
consecutive sentences
determinate sentencing
enhancements
fine

indeterminate sentencing
intermittent sentences
mitigating circumstances
pre-sentence investigation
  report
presumptive sentence
  (base sentence)
probation

recidivist
restitution
sentencing guidelines
victim impact statement
work furlough

Learning Objectives

After reading this chapter, the student will be able to

- Differentiate between determinate and indeterminate sentencing.
- Explain the sentencing options normally available to a judge.
- Explain the factors the judge considers when deciding on a sentence for a person who has been convicted of a crime.
- Identify what is included in the presentence investigation report.
- Describe what usually occurs at the sentencing hearing.

After the jury votes to convict, the judge must impose sentence. In many cases a separate hearing is held for this purpose. The defendant's background, including prior criminal activity, is considered when the judge decides on the sentence.

13-1 Sentencing Laws

Sentencing is a function of the judiciary, but the sentencing laws are enacted by the legislature. This creates a delicate balance between the two branches of government: the legislature sets the sentences for specific crimes, but in most states the judiciary retains the discretion to consider other factors besides the current conviction when imposing sentence on an individual.

Each state has its own laws governing the sentencing of convicted defendants. Crimes prosecuted in federal court are governed by the United States Code and the Federal Sentencing Guidelines. A variety of sentencing systems are used. Some states use a combination. It is important to understand the sentencing system in use in the state where you live, so that appropriate information will be retained in police files for use by the prosecutor at the defendant's sentencing hearing.

13-1a Indeterminate Sentencing

Indeterminate sentencing laws do not give the defendant a specific number of years in prison. The statutes usually set minimum and maximum limits, but the judge is allowed to give any sentence within these ranges. For example, state law may provide that the sentence for robbery is from 4 to 15 years, but an individual convicted of robbery might be sentenced to serve 5 to 10 years in state prison. How long the person actually serves is left to the discretion of the prison authorities and the parole board. The idea behind indeterminate sentencing is twofold: (1) observations of the inmate's behavior in counseling and other prison programs provide the best indication of when the person is ready to be released; and (2) the opportunity for early release motivates inmates to rehabilitate themselves. It is fairly common to use determinate sentences for misdemeanors in states that have indeterminate sentencing for felonies.

13-1b Determinate Sentencing

Determinate sentencing systems require the judge to impose a specific sentence, such as 10 years in prison. State statutes may read like indeterminate sentencing laws (e.g., 5 to 10 years), but the judge imposes a fixed sentence (8 years). Some state statutes provide a more structured framework for use by the judge when deciding on the sentence. There usually is a **presumptive sentence** (sometimes called a **base sentence**): it is the sentence the legislature intended for the crime, but the judge can impose a shorter one if there are mitigating circumstances or a longer term if there are aggravating ones. For example, the penalty for robbery may be 10 years, but the judge can impose a different sentence if there are unusual circumstances. Or the penalty for burglary might be 2, 4, or 6 years, with 4 years being the presumptive sentence, 2-year sentences are imposed if there are mitigating circumstances, and 6-year sentences are imposed when aggravating circumstances are present. Even within a determinate sentencing system, there are usually options available to the correctional system, such as "good time," to motivate the inmate to comply with the prison rules. These are discussed in Chapter 15.

13-1c Length of Sentence

The judge starts with the length of sentence designated by the legislature. Two basic methods are used to indicate the baseline information. They can be used in both determinate and indeterminate sentencing systems.

Designating Crimes by Class

Some states organize their sentencing laws by constructing several classes for felonies and misdemeanors. When this approach is used, the definition of the crime states the class of the crime: robbery is a Class 2 felony. The code sections listing the sentences are usually in one place, frequently at the beginning of the penal code. Table 13-1 gives the sentencing ranges used in Virginia. For example, Class 1 felonies are the most serious and have sentences of life imprisonment or the death penalty; the judge can impose a 25-year sentence for a Class 2 felony and so on. Table 13-2 illustrates an indeterminate sentencing law. A Florida judge selects a minimum term from those stated, but the maximum term is set by law; for example, a person convicted of a second-degree felony could receive an indeterminant sentence of 4 to 15 years.

Designating Individual Crimes

Other states designate the sentence for each crime, or group of crimes, along with the definition. An example of this is a code that defines robbery and then states that the sentence for first-degree robbery is 15 years and second-degree robbery is punishable by 12 years in prison. There is frequently a section in the code stating the sentence for felonies and misde-

T A B L E **13-1** Determinate Felony Sentencing Laws

Code of Virginia Section 18.2-10

Punishment for conviction of felony. The judge must select a determinate sentence within the following authorized punishments; the judge has the discretion to impose any fine up to the maximum amount indicated in addition to the prison sentence:

Class of Felony	Length of Incarceration	Maximum Fine
Class 1	Death or imprisonment for life	$100,000
Class 2	Imprisonment for life or for any term not less than 20 years	$100,000
Class 3	Not less than 5 years or more than 20 years	$100,000
Class 4	Not less than 2 years or more than 10 years	$100,000
Class 5	Not less than 1 year or more than 10 years, or in the discretion of the jury or the court trying the case without a jury, confinement in jail for not more than 12 months	$2,500
Class 6	Not less than 1 year or more than 5 years, or in the discretion of the jury or the court trying the case without a jury, confinement in jail for not more than 12 months	$2,500

meanors when nothing is stated in the defining section. Table 13-3 shows sentences for some felonies in California. The judge has a choice of three terms for each crime; as discussed in section 13-1d, "Sentencing Guidelines." Enhancements may be applied to increase these sentences.

13-1d Sentencing Guidelines

Judges are given **sentencing guidelines** to use when imposing sentences. Some, like the sentencing guidelines used by the federal courts, contain a very complex point system, which the judges must use. Others involve a series of statutes which must be considered. Many states have worksheets, which are used to calculate the actual sentence once the judge has decided

T A B L E **13-2** Indeterminate Felony Sentencing Law

Florida Statute 775.082

★ ★ ★

b) For a felony of the first degree, by a term of imprisonment not exceeding 30 years or, when specifically provided by statute, by imprisonment for a term of years not exceeding life imprisonment.

c) For a felony of the second degree, by a term of imprisonment not exceeding 15 years.

d) For a felony of the third degree, by a term of imprisonment not exceeding 5 years.

T A B L E **13-3** California Felony Sentences for Selected Crimes

Punishment for felonies. The judge imposes one of the three sentences listed in the penal code. The middle sentence is the presumptive sentence; the lower one is imposed if there are mitigating circumstances. Imposition of the higher one requires aggravating circumstances. Additional enhancements may be added based on the facts of the case.

Crime	Sentence
Aggravated mayhem (PC 205)	Life with possibility of parole
Kidnapping for ransom (PC 209)	Life with possibility of parole, no parole if victim suffered bodily harm
Forcible rape (PC 261(a)(2))	3, 6, or 8 years
Arson of inhabited structure (PC 451(b))	3, 5, or 8 years
Kidnapping (PC 207)	3, 5, or 8 years
Robbery, first degree (PC 212.5)	3, 4, or 6 years
Burglary, first degree (PC 460(a))	2, 4, or 6 years
Mayhem (PC 203)	2, 4, or 8 years
Robbery, second degree (PC 211)	2, 3, or 5 years
Burglary, second degree (PC 459)	16 months, 2 or 3 years in prison, or 1 year in jail
Forgery (PC 470)	16 months, 2 or 3 years in prison, or 1 year in jail
Grand theft (PC 487)	16 months, 2 or 3 years in prison, or 1 year in jail

upon all the relevant factors. Some of these systems are very complicated. Figure 13-1 shows the California worksheet for felonies. Note the numerous items that must be considered. It is important for police officers to understand what facts can be used to impose longer sentences and to make sure that relevant evidence is available for the sentencing hearing.

Aggravating and Mitigating Circumstances

Nearly all criminal statutes permit the judge to consider **aggravating** and **mitigating circumstances** when imposing sentence. The judge considers all facts presented at the sentencing hearing when making this decision. It is not a question of showing more items on one list than the other; for example, the judge might impose the highest possible term, even though there were three mitigating circumstances (young, mentally impaired defendant who was a first offender) if one aggravating factor, such as the extreme level of violence used, outweighed them. State laws may establish aggravating and mitigating factors, or it may be left to the judge's discretion. Table 13-4 contains a partial list of the factors considered under Illinois law; it is typical of the laws in many states. Even when the law provides a list of factors to consider, the judge usually has the discretion to consider any facts that are unique to the case.

Figure 13-1
Fixed Term Worksheet

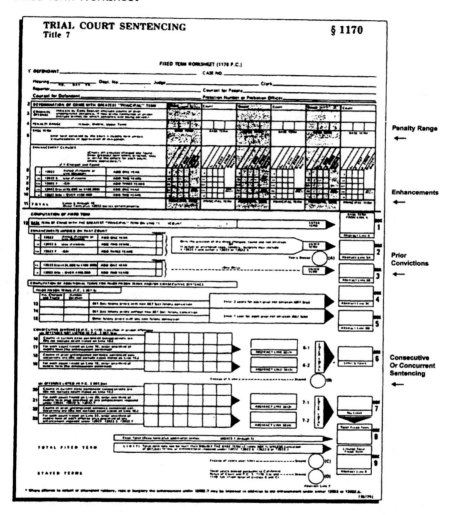

Enhancements

State laws frequently permit the enhancement of a sentence in addition to imposing a longer term because of aggravating circumstances. Usually **enhancements** are imposed due to prior criminal conduct, but sometimes they relate to factors involved in the crime itself. The distinction between aggravating circumstances and enhancements is not always clear. Facts used to show aggravating circumstances normally cannot be used for enhancements, but sometimes the legislature permits the use of certain facts for both purposes. This does not violate double jeopardy.

T A B L E **13-4** Factors Used as Aggravating
and Mitigating Circumstances

Partial List of Factors in Illinois Statutes 5/5-5-3.1 and 5/5-5-3.2

Aggravating circumstances that the judge may consider as grounds to impose a more severe sentence or extend the term of a sentence include

- The defendant's conduct caused or threatened serious harm.
- The defendant received compensation for committing the offense.
- The defendant has a history of delinquent or criminal activity.
- The defendant, by the duties of his office or by his position, was obliged to prevent the particular offense committed or to bring the offenders committing it to justice.
- The defendant held public office at the time of the offense, and the offense related to the conduct of that office.
- The defendant utilizes professional reputation or position in the community to commit the offense or to afford him an easier means of committing it.
- The sentence is necessary to deter others from committing the same crime.
- The defendant committed the offense against a person 60 years of age or older or such person's property.
- The defendant committed the offense against a person who is physically handicapped or such person's property.
- The defendant committed the offense by reason of another individual's actual or perceived race, color, creed, religion, ancestry, gender, sexual orientation, physical or mental disability, or national origin.
- The offense took place in a place of worship or on the grounds of a place of worship, immediately prior to, during, or immediately following services.
- The defendant was convicted of a felony committed while he was released on bail or his own recognizance pending trial for a prior felony and was convicted of such prior felony, or the defendant was convicted of a felony committed while serving a period of probation, conditional discharge, or mandatory supervised release for a prior felony.
- The defendant committed or attempted to commit a felony while wearing a bulletproof vest.
- The defendant held a position of trust or supervision, such as, but not limited to, family member, teacher, scout leader, baby-sitter, or day care worker, in relation to a victim under 18 years of age, and the defendant committed a crime listed in Sec. 5-5-3.2(14) against the victim.
- The defendant committed an offense related to the activities of an organized gang.

Mitigating circumstances that may be grounds for withholding or minimizing a prison sentence include

- The defendant's criminal conduct neither caused nor threatened serious physical harm to another.
- The defendant did not contemplate that his criminal conduct would cause or threaten serious physical harm to another.
- The defendant acted under strong provocation.
- There were substantial grounds tending to excuse or justify the defendant's criminal conduct, though failing to establish a defense.
- The defendant's criminal conduct was induced or facilitated by someone other than the defendant.

continues

- The defendant has compensated or will compensate the victim of his criminal conduct for the damage or injury that he sustained.
- The defendant has no history of delinquency or criminal activity or has led a law-abiding life for a substantial period of time before the commission of the present crime.
- The defendant's criminal conduct was the result of circumstances unlikely to recur.
- The character and attitudes of the defendant indicate that he is unlikely to commit another crime.
- The defendant is particularly likely to comply with the terms of a period of probation.
- The imprisonment of the defendant would entail excessive hardship to his dependents.
- The imprisonment of the defendant would endanger his or her medical condition.
- The defendant is mentally retarded.

A common enhancement is for the use of a firearm or other danger- ous weapon while committing the crime. This normally applies only if using the weapon involved is not part of the definition of the crime for which the defendant was convicted. For example, state law may provide a one-year enhancement for being armed; this could be used to increase the sentence of a burglar who carried a gun but not a person charged with *armed* robbery. For this reason, some states no longer have a separate crime of armed robbery; the enhancement is used to increase the sentence in much the same way as the older armed robbery code section did. The basic enhancement for being armed has been expanded due to the pro- liferation of assault rifles and other types of combat weapons. Table 13-5 shows a list of some of the enhancements used for this purpose in California.

Enhancements are also enacted to cover a wide variety of situations that make the crime more serious in the eyes of the legislature. Committing a crime while out on bail or free OR frequently is considered as an enhancement. Excessive property damage during vandalism may be handled this way; usually a dollar amount is specified—for example, dam- age over $10,000. Most states have both misdemeanor and felony theft statutes, but enhancements may be used to add punishment for an excep- tionally large loss; again, dollar figures are normally included in the enhancement—for example, in cases of theft over $25,000, the sentence should be enhanced by a two-year term.

Table 13-6 shows Florida's approach for assaults and batteries on sen- ior citizens. Some states use enhancements for "hate crimes," rather than enacting specific laws prohibiting criminal actions against a person on the basis of race, gender, sexual orientation, religion, and so on. For example, a sentence for battery might be one year in the county jail under ordi- nary circumstances; however, if the victim was abused primarily for racial

T A B L E **13-5** Sentencing Enhancements for Using
a Firearm during a Crime

Partial List from California Penal Code
Sections 12022 to 12022.5

Action by Defendant during a Crime	Years Added to Sentence
Armed with firearm during commission or attempted commission of a felony	1 year
Armed with assault weapon or machine gun during commission or attempted commission of a felony	3 years
Defendant personally used firearm during commission or attempted commission of felony	3, 4, or 10 years
Armed with firearm during commission or attempted commission of felony and had ammunition in possession that is designed primarily to penetrate metal or armor	3, 4, or 10 years
Personally used assault weapon or machine gun during commission or attempted commission of a felony	5, 6, or 10 years

T A B L E **13-6** Sentencing Enhancements for Battery
against a Person over 65

West's Florida Statutes Annotated Section 784.08

Mandatory minimum sentence for aggravated assault or aggravated battery on a person 65 years of age or older, and reclassification of assaults and batteries against victims in this age group:

(1) A person who is convicted of an aggravated assault or aggravated battery upon a person 65 years of age or older shall be sentenced to a mandatory minimum term of 3 calendar years and fined not more than $10,000 and shall also be ordered by the sentencing judge to make restitution to the victim of such offense and to perform up to 500 hours of community service work. Restitution and community service work shall be in addition to any fine or sentence which may be imposed and shall not be in lieu thereof.

(2) Whenever a person is charged with knowingly committing an assault or aggravated assault or a battery or aggravated battery upon a person 65 years of age or older, the offense for which the person is charged shall be reclassified as follows:

 (a) In the case of aggravated battery, from a felony of the second degree to a felony of the first degree.

 (b) In the case of aggravated assault, from a felony of the third degree to a felony of the second degree.

 (c) In the case of battery, from a misdemeanor of the first degree to a felony of the third degree.

 (d) In the case of assault, from a misdemeanor of the second degree to a misdemeanor of the first degree.

(3) Notwithstanding the provisions of s. 948.01, adjudication of guilt or imposition of sentence shall not be suspended, deferred, or withheld.

reasons, an enhancement of two years might be added to the one-year term. In other states the same case might be handled as a battery with aggravating circumstances, instead of using enhancements.

Recidivist Laws

A **recidivist** is a person who has a prior conviction. Recidivists frequently receive longer sentences. Depending on how the legislature worded these provisions, the prior convictions may be considered enhancements, aggravating circumstances, or a trigger for recidivist laws. Some states consider juvenile convictions for this purpose. Table 13-7 shows New York's approach to this problem. Note that the sentencing pattern is more severe for recidivists who have convictions for violent crimes.

Some states make a second conviction for selected misdemeanors a felony; this is common with petty theft. Another approach is to leave the offense a misdemeanor but increase the fine and/or make a minimum jail sentence mandatory if there is a second conviction; spousal battery is treated this way in some states. A few statutes recognize the fact that some defendants have been convicted more than twice for the same crime and include progressively longer mandatory minimum sentences for each subsequent conviction.

The legislature has a great deal of leeway in designing recidivist laws. They may require a prior conviction for the same offense or a similar group of offenses, such as violent sex crimes. Some are more general, such as those that impose a longer sentence if the defendant has any prior felony convictions. Sometimes these laws apply only if the person served a prison sentence for the prior conviction. Another approach is to give the longer sentence only if the current offense occurred within a stated period, such as 10 years, after the first conviction or the date the person was released from prison on the previous conviction. The sentencing guidelines used by the federal courts contain an elaborate combination of these approaches. The worksheet illustrated in Figure 13-2 is used to calculate the points that will be added to the federal defendant's "score" for purposes of deciding what sentence should be imposed.

"Three strikes and you're out" has become the catchy phrase for imposing life sentences on defendants with three felony convictions. This type of sentencing law was reviewed twice by the United States Supreme Court in the early 1980s. It held that such laws are constitutional, even if each prior felony was a non-violent property crime but that giving "life without parole" was too harsh. The statutes reviewed imposed a life term

T A B L E **13-7** Sentences for Recidivists

Persistent Criminal Laws

Penal Law 70.08 and 70.10 of McKinney's Consolidated Laws of New York

Persistent felony offender is defined as a person, other than a persistent violent felony offender, who stands convicted of a felony after having previously been convicted of two or more felonies. A previous felony conviction, as used for this purpose, is a conviction for a felony committed in New York or any other state, provided:

i)   That a sentence to a term of imprisonment in excess of one year, or a sentence to death, was imposed therefore; and

ii) That the defendant was imprisoned under the sentence for such conviction prior to the commission of the present felony; and

iii) The defendant was not pardoned on the ground of innocence.

Persistent violent felony offender is defined in a similar manner except that both prior convictions for which prison sentences were served must have been for violent felonies [code lists specific offenses that apply].

Authorized sentence:

Persistent Felon Judge has *discretion* to impose sentence the same as for Class A-1 felony (15 to 25 years in prison) upon findings that:

- Defendant is persistent felon AND
- The history and character of the defendant and the nature and circumstances of his criminal conduct indicate that the extended incarceration and life-time supervision will best serve the public interest

Persistent Violent Felon Judge is **mandated** to impose an indeterminate sentence:

- For a Class B felony, the minimum period must be at least 10 years and must not exceed 25 years
- For a Class C felony, the minimum period must be at least 8 years and must not exceed 25 years
- For a Class D felony, the minimum period must be at least 6 years and must not exceed 25 years.

on the third or fourth felony conviction. Due process requires states to clearly identify which crimes are eligible for treatment in this manner and to notify the defendant that the longer sentence will be sought. Case law on other recidivist laws has held that using convictions for crimes that occurred before the recidivist law was enacted does not violate the prohibition against *ex post facto* laws.

13-1e Other Sentencing Options

A wide variety of other sentencing options is usually available to the judge. Many of them can be combined, such as imposing a fine as well as a jail

Figure 13-2
Federal Worksheet C (Criminal History)

WORKSHEET C (Criminal History)

Defendant _____ Docket Number _____

Date Defendant Commenced Participation in Instant Offense (Earliest Date of

Relevant Conduct) _____

1. 3 POINTS for each prior ADULT sentence of imprisonment exceeding ONE YEAR and ONE MONTH imposed within 15 YEARS of the defendant's commencement of the instant offense OR resulting in incarceration during any part of that 15-YEAR period. (See §§4A1.1(a) and 4A1.2.)

2. 2 POINTS for each prior sentence of imprisonment of at least 60 DAYS resulting from an offense committed ON OR AFTER the defendant's 18th birthday not counted under §4A1.1(a) imposed within 10 YEARS of the instant offense; and

   2 POINTS for each prior sentence of imprisonment of at least 60 DAYS resulting from an offense committed BEFORE the defendant's 18th birthday not counted under §4A1.1(a) from which the defendant was released from confinement within 5 YEARS of the instant offense. (See §§4A1.1(b) and 4A1.2.)

3. 1 POINT for each prior sentence resulting from an offense committed ON OR AFTER defendant's 18th birthday not counted under §4A1.1(a) or §4A1.1(b) imposed within 10 YEARS of the instant offense; and

   1 POINT for each prior sentence resulting from an offense committed BEFORE the defendant's 18th birthday not counted under §4A1.1(a) or §4A1.1(b) imposed within 5 YEARS of the instant offense. (See §§4A1.1(c) and 4A1.2.)

   NOTE: a maximum of 4 POINTS may be imposed for the prior sentences in Item 3.

Date of Imposition	Sentence Status*	Offense	Sentence	Release Date**	Criminal History Pts.
_____	_____	_____	_____	_____	_____
_____	_____	_____	_____	_____	_____
_____	_____	_____	_____	_____	_____
_____	_____	_____	_____	_____	_____

*   Sentence status, juvenile (J) or adult (A), required on sentences if offense committed prior to age 18.

** A release date is required in only three instances:

   1. When a sentence covered under §4A1.1(a) was imposed more than 15 years prior to the commencement of the instant offense but release from incarceration occurred within such 15-year period;

   2. When a sentence counted under §4A1.1(b) was imposed for an offense committed prior to age 18 and more than 5 years prior to the commencement of the instant offense, but release from incarceration occurred within such 5-year period; and

   3. When §4A1.1(c) applies because the defendant was released from custody within 2 years of the instant offense or was still in custody at the time of the instant offense.

Total Criminal History Points for §4A1.1(a), 4A1.1(b), and 4A1.1(c) (Items 1, 2, 3)

Rev.   11/1/91

---

sentence. The penal code may contain a comprehensive provision, such as a statement that a judge may impose a fine of up to $1,000 for any misdemeanor conviction, or individual sections may specify what additional punishments may be imposed.

Probation

Probation was originally instituted to give first offenders convicted of minor crimes an opportunity to demonstrate that they could conform to society's norms. Probation officers supervised them, gave direction and counseling, and if necessary brought the case back to court because the defendant did not comply with the conditions of probation. Today probation is used in both misdemeanor and felony cases. State laws establish the maximum period of probation for a given offense. Defendants who do not comply with the conditions of probation may be required to serve time in jail or prison.

The judge normally tries to select defendants who are most likely to benefit from probation, but jail and prison overcrowding has resulted in many repeat offenders being placed on probation. Some legislatures have tried to control the judge's discretion in sentencing defendants to probation. Laws may be enacted making a person convicted of certain crimes ineligible for probation. "Use a gun, go to jail" laws deny the judge the option of giving probation if the defendant used a gun while committing the offense for which he/she was convicted. Judges sometimes avoid this consequence by striking the allegation that the defendant used a firearm. A less severe legislative approach to restricting the use of probation is to require the judge to state in open court the reasons for his/her choice of sentence.

Probation is normally considered an alternative to incarcerating a defendant. This is not always the case: a jail term may be made a condition of probation. Recent trends include requiring a mandatory minimum jail sentence, frequently 48 hours to 30 days, for persons placed on probation after conviction for driving while under the influence of alcohol.

A defendant who is placed on probation must comply with the conditions of probation imposed by the judge. These frequently include mandatory periodic meetings with a probation officer, attendance at counseling sessions, maintenance of a good job/school record, no association with known criminals, no substance abuse, and a curfew. Agreeing to abide by these conditions is a prerequisite to being placed on probation. The judge must select a different sentence if a defendant refuses. Procedures to remove a defendant from probation because of failure to comply with the conditions imposed are discussed in Chapter 15.

Work Furlough

Work furlough programs permit an inmate to maintain a job outside the jail facility. Typically the inmate goes to work on his/her normal schedule but spends the remaining hours in jail. This arrangement allows inmates to keep jobs and support their families. Frequently it keeps the family off welfare. It also makes the transition back into the community easier after the sentence has been served because the inmate is employed. Sometimes inmates are allowed to go to vocational or college classes under arrangements similar to work furloughs. Only defendants who are not considered escape risks are placed in this type of program because they are usually not accompanied by a guard from the time they leave for work until they return to the jail. Defendants convicted of drug use or drug dealing are usually not allowed on work furlough because of the potential risk they pose.

Operating work furlough programs requires a great deal of cooperation by the correctional facility staff. Schedules must be coordinated, so that the inmates can go to work on time. Meals at unusual hours and sack lunches to take to work may be required. Inmates returning from work must be searched to make sure that contraband does not enter the facility. Larger jails may house work furlough inmates in a separate area to make this special handling easier.

Intermittent Sentences

Another approach used to help persons with fairly short sentences retain their jobs is intermittent sentencing. When defendants are given **intermittent sentences,** they are allowed to serve their sentence a few days at a time. Intermittent sentences are frequently referred to as serving "weekends" because the defendant typically works at a job from Monday through Friday and spends the weekend in jail. Many jails can accommodate people with other days off. This approach can also be used for other reasons, such as allowing a defendant to continue going to school while serving a jail sentence.

In some states the judge sentences the defendant to a three-month intermittent sentence, which means every weekend for three months will be spent in jail; other states impose a sentence, such as 30 days, with the provision that the defendant can spend each weekend in jail until a total of 30 days has been served. Intermittent sentences, such as work furlough, require extra effort by jail personnel to handle the unique requirements of these inmates and the extra record keeping involved. Some state laws specifically provide for weekends. In other areas, jail and judicial personnel have made the necessary arrangements, so that it can be offered.

Fines

In most cases the judge has the authority to **fine** a defendant who is convicted. A fine can be combined with other sentencing options, or it can be the sole punishment for the crime. It is common to have standard fines, such as $1,000 for misdemeanors and $10,000 for felonies. Statutes may regulate the maximum and minimum amount that can be imposed. Judges usually have the discretion to impose fines based on the circumstances, including the income of the defendant. Some states also have laws raising the amount of the fine if the defendant profited financially from the crime; for example, in felony fraud cases the fine may be $10,000 or three times the victim's loss, whichever is greater.

Equal protection prohibits sending people to jail because they are unable to pay fines. This applies to making decisions at the sentencing hearing and to revoking probation because a defendant has not paid a fine. The rule applies only to a person who in good faith is unable to pay. A person who is unwilling to pay but has the financial ability, or one who refuses to look for a job so that he/she will not have the money, can be sent to jail for not paying a fine.

Restitution

A recent trend is to require the defendant to pay **restitution** to the victim. This is separate from imposing a fine: the fine goes to the government; restitution money goes to the victim. Fines are usually set by the legislature based on the severity of the offense (felony or misdemeanor), while restitution is based on the victim's financial losses. State laws regulate what types of losses are covered. Typically they include medical bills, lost wages, and damage to property. The actual amount of these losses must be established at the sentencing hearing. Table 13-8 shows the type of form a judge uses when determining the amount of restitution the defendant must pay.

Case law has not clearly established the point yet, but it appears that equal protection prohibits restitution orders against defendants who in good faith cannot pay. It is possible, however, to extend the time for payment to allow the defendant to find a job or otherwise obtain the funds needed; installment payments are also a common method used to facilitate the collection of court-ordered restitution.

Community Service Orders

Some states permit the sentencing judge to make a **community service order** that requires the defendant to perform volunteer work for the benefit of the community. Other states permit community service in lieu

TABLE **13-8** Restitution Order

Based on Florida Rule 3.986

By appropriate notation, the following provisions apply to the sentence imposed in this section:

____ Restitution is not ordered as it is not applicable.

____ Restitution is not ordered due to the financial resources of the defendant.

____ Restitution is not ordered due to _____.

____ Due to the financial resources of the defendant, restitution of a portion of the damages is ordered as prescribed below.

____ Restitution is ordered as prescribed below.

____ Restitution is ordered for the following victim. (Victim refers to the aggrieved party, aggrieved party's estate, or aggrieved party's next of kin if the aggrieved party is deceased as a result of the offense. In lieu of the victim's address and phone number, the address and phone number of the prosecuting attorney, victim's attorney, or victim advocate may be used.)

_____   _____

Name of victim   Name of attorney or advocate if applicable

Address _____

City, State and Zip Code _____

Phone number _____

____ The sum of $_____ for medical and related services and devices relating to physical, psychiatric, and psychological care, including non-medical care and treatment rendered in accordance with a recognized method of healing.

____ The sum of $_____ for necessary physical and occupational therapy and rehabilitation.

____ The sum of $_____ to reimburse the victim for income lost as a result of the offense.

____ The sum of $_____ for necessary funeral and related services if the offense resulted in bodily injury resulting in the death of the victim.

____ The sum of $_____ for damages resulting from the offense.

____ The sum of $_____ for _____.

It is further ordered that the defendant fulfill restitution obligations in the following manner:

____ Total monetary restitution is determined to be $_____ to be paid at a rate of $_____ per (check one) ____month ____week ____other (specify) ____ and is to be paid (check one) ____through the clerk of the circuit court, ____to the victim's designee, or ____through the Department of Corrections, with an additional 4% fee of $_____ for handling, processing, and forwarding the restitution to the victim(s).

____ For which sum let execution issue.

of paying fines. The code usually indicates the maximum number of hours that can be required. One thousand hours is the equivalent of working full-time for six months. The defendant usually works a few hours a week until the mandated total is reached.

A variety of approaches is used. The defendant may be allowed to select any non-profit agency that provides services to the public. There may be a local agency, such as a volunteer center, which matches the defendant's abilities with agencies in need of help. Sometimes the judge orders the work done at an agency that assists victims of crimes similar to those committed by the defendant; for example, a person convicted of spousal abuse may be required to do maintenance work at a shelter for battered women. The defendant may have to work for a government agency; an example of this is California's program which requires persons convicted for driving under the influence of alcohol who cannot pay their fines to help the Department of Transportation pick up trash along the freeway.

Court Costs

Court costs may be assessed against the defendant who is convicted. Usually there is a set schedule used rather than actually trying to calculate the time expended by the judge and other court personnel. The amount imposed needs to be related to the expense to the taxpayers.

The United States Supreme Court upheld an Oregon law that allowed the judge to require a convicted defendant, as a condition of probation, to pay the cost incurred by the county in prosecuting the case. The court mandated protection of the defendant from undue hardship and suggested that procedures similar to those used to protect a creditor from excessive wage garnishment be used. Some states have become innovative in this area and try to collect the cost of incarcerating the defendant and/or investigating the case.

13-1f Concurrent and Consecutive Sentences

When the defendant has been convicted of more than one crime, the judge is usually given the discretion to decide if the sentences will be concurrent or consecutive. **Concurrent sentences** can be served at the same time; for sentences imposed at the same time, this means that, when the longest sentence has been served, the defendant is released because the shorter ones are also complete. Sometimes a judge rules that a sentence can be served concurrently with one the defendant received in an unrelated case. Concurrent sentences may become important if one, but not all, of the convictions are reversed on appeal. When this happens, the defendant can be required to serve the sentences for the convictions that were affirmed.

Consecutive sentences are served in sequential order: the defendant serves all of the time imposed for one crime before starting to serve the sentence for another offense. This results in a longer prison term than would have been served if concurrent sentences were given. Factors frequently considered by the judge when deciding to impose consecutive sentences include whether the objectives of the crimes were predominantly independent of each other; whether the crimes involved separate acts of violence; and whether the crimes were committed so closely together that a single period of aberrant behavior is indicated. The criteria to be considered may be listed in the sentencing law or the court's rules.

Some states mandate consecutive terms for specific crimes. Extra time imposed for enhancements or recidivism may also be required to be served consecutively. A few states have mathematical formulas which require the defendant to serve part, but not all, of the normal sentence for crimes when consecutive sentences are imposed. For example, California requires the defendant to serve the full term for the first crime and one third of the presumptive term for each consecutive sentence.

13-2 Pre-sentence Investigation Report

The **pre-sentence investigation report** provides the judge with relevant background information about the defendant. It is usually prepared by a probation officer or another officer of the court. Most judges request the report after the verdicts are read. There are two main reasons for delaying the preparation of the report until this time: reports are prepared only for defendants who are convicted, thus saving the staff time required to investigate and write reports on defendants who are acquitted, and the person writing the report can interview the defendant and include his/her statements in the report because the defendant can no longer claim the Fifth Amendment as a grounds to refuse to discuss the case. When the pre-sentence investigation report is not requested until after the verdict is entered, a continuance is necessary before the sentencing hearing. Six weeks may be allotted for this purpose.

As section 13-1, "Sentencing Laws," demonstrated, many factors are considered by the sentencing judge in addition to guilt of the offense charged. For this reason, the pre-sentence investigation report must contain information on many things that were not introduced into evidence at trial. It contains a social history of the defendant. This includes a brief biographical summary of the defendant's success (or lack thereof) in school and his/her behavioral problems. Attention is focused on the defendant's prior convictions as either an adult or a juvenile. If the defendant has ever been on probation, the report indicates the outcome: revoked, revoked but reinstated, or successfully completed. The number of times probation has been imposed and the defendant's success are important considerations if probation will be an option when the judge imposes the current sentence. Prior convictions, particularly those for which the defendant served time in prison, frequently are grounds for imposing a more severe sentence.

The facts of the current case are summarized. The impact of the offense on the victim may be discussed, particularly if the victim was injured, left fearful of future harm, or suffered financial hardship due to the crime. Other aggravating and mitigating facts are included. Pre-sentence investigation reports usually end with a recommendation to the judge on the sentence to impose. If prison is recommended, the report suggests the length of the term. When probation is recommended, the report usually states the length of the probation and the conditions of probation that should be imposed. In states that have a sentencing worksheet for the judge to use to calculate the sentence, the pre-sentence investigation report usually contains a worksheet with the necessary computations completed.

The pre-sentence investigation report is submitted to the judge. Many courts consider the report confidential and do not make it part of the public record, but both the prosecutor and the defense attorney are usually entitled to copies. They may want to dispute facts stated in the report or urge the judge to draw different conclusions. This is normally done by oral argument, but documents, including a private pre-sentence investigation report prepared by a consultant for the defense, may be filed with the court. Any such documents must be served on the opposing side before the hearing to permit time to prepare to discuss them in court.

13-3 Procedures at the Sentencing Hearing

The sentencing hearing is a formal court hearing. The defendant, prosecutor, and defense attorney are present. It is usually presided over by the judge who accepted the guilty plea or heard the trial, and it is normally held in the courtroom where these events occurred. In states that allow the jury to recommend a sentence, the sequence of events may vary. Most sentencing hearings are brief and consist of little more than the presentation of the presentence investigation report and a statement by the defendant. In major cases, particularly death penalty trials, the hearing may last for a week or more.

The normal rules of evidence usually apply to the sentencing hearing, although the hearsay rule may be relaxed to admit evidence discussed in the pre-sentence investigation report. Evidence may be admissible at the sentencing hearing that was inadmissible at trial, since the issues are different; therefore, items that are relevant at the sentencing hearing may have been irrelevant at trial. For example, the defendant's prior criminal record is relevant when deciding if probation should be imposed, but it is not relevant in determining guilt for the offense; the amount of the victim's hospital bill is relevant when computing a restitution order but not relevant on the question of guilt for committing battery. Evidence that was not admissible at trial because of the exclusionary rule may be used at the sentencing hearing, except when it was seized specifically to enhance the sentence.

In many states the hearing begins with the testimony of the person who made the pre-sentence investigation report. The information in the report may be repeated from the witness stand and the prosecutor and defense attorney given the opportunity to ask questions. The judge is also allowed to ask questions.

Witnesses may be called if it is necessary to present evidence not introduced at trial. This is organized much as a trial, with one side, usually the prosecution, calling all of its witnesses before the opposing side presents testimony. All witnesses are subject to cross-examination. The judge decides what weight, if any, is to be placed on the testimony of each witness, except when a jury is assigned the task of deciding the sentence.

Three unique situations occur at sentencing hearings: the defendant has the right of allocution, private pre-sentence investigation reports may be introduced, and victims may make statements. *Black's Law Dictionary* defines **allocution** as "formality of court's inquiry of prisoner as to whether he has any legal cause to show why judgment should not be pronounced against him on verdict of conviction." In practice, the right of allocution is the defendant's opportunity to make a speech during the sentencing hearing. As with other rights, it can be waived if the defendant does not wish to exercise it. Defendants who exercise this right usually express remorse for their actions and ask the judge for a lighter sentence.

Some states allow the defense to introduce a private pre-sentence investigation report. Consultants usually prepare the reports. Many times, the consultant is a former probation officer or a psychologist. The purpose of this report is to summarize the facts, including the defendant's background and potential for rehabilitation, in a manner favorable to the defense. Normally, mitigating circumstances and ways to rehabilitate the defendant are stressed. A treatment program with little or no time in custody is usually recommended. The person who prepared the report frequently testifies. The testimony is usually handled much as an expert witness would be at trial. The prosecutor has the right to cross-examine on the person's professional qualifications, as well as on the facts and opinions expressed.

Many states now give the victim input at the defendant's sentencing hearing. This is frequently called a **victim impact statement.** Some states allow the victim to submit written material, and others require oral testimony; sometimes the victim is given a choice of either method of participation. Family members of a victim who died as a result of injuries inflicted during the crime are usually allowed to testify. Some states allow the victims to give their views on what sentence should be imposed. Two reasons buttress the use of the victim impact statements: they give crime victims a greater input into the criminal justice system, and they provide information for the judge on the mental, physical, and financial suffering caused by the defendant.

After all the evidence is admitted, the prosecutor and defense attorney present arguments regarding the sentence that should be imposed. As with the closing statements at trial, each side attempts to portray the evidence in a light most favorable to its view. If the state's sentencing laws are complex, this may include a very detailed analysis of what code sections are mandatory and which ones the judge has the option to ignore.

The judge must make the final decision on what sentence to impose. If the defendant is being placed on probation, it is also necessary to include the conditions of probation. Worksheets are frequently used to calculate the sentence. A standardized form is usually used if state law requires additions and/or subtractions for aggravating circumstances, mitigating circumstances, prior convictions, and enhancements. Some of the forms are very complicated (review Figure 13-1).

The final action at the sentencing hearing is usually the judge's oral pronouncement of sentence. Many states require the judge to give reasons for the sentence that is being imposed if it deviates from the base sentence. The judge usually gives a short speech, summarizing the facts that were considered as aggravating and/or mitigating and, if the defendant was convicted for committing more than one crime, stating whether the sentences will run concurrently or consecutively. This statement by the judge may provide the grounds for an appeal if the factors stated do not coincide with what the law allows the judge to consider or if the mathematical computations are not correct.

Chapter Summary

Sentencing laws vary a great deal from state to state and between the states and the federal system. It is important for an officer to understand what factors are considered when sentences are imposed, so that relevant evidence will be retained for presentation at the sentencing hearing.

Sentences are either determinate (the judge imposes a specific sentence) or indeterminate (the judge imposes a range and the parole board decides if the defendant's behavior in prison indicates he/she is ready for release; the nature of the crime and the defendant's prior record are also considered). Many states use determinate sentences for some crimes, while giving indeterminate sentences for others.

Statutes set the length of sentence for each crime, but many factors are considered when sentencing the defendant. Most states have a range of potential sentences for a crime, and the judge selects a sentence based on a combination of the crime charged, the aggravating and mitigating circumstances, the defendant's prior criminal record, and other enhancements approved by the legislature. If the defendant is convicted of more than one crime, it is also necessary to decide if the sentences will be concurrent (served at the same time) or consecutive (one starts after the prior sentence has been completed).

Judges usually have a variety of options available: prison, jail, probation, fines, community service, restitution, and the paying of court costs. The sentencing laws usually state which of these can be combined—for example, one year in jail plus a fine and restitution. There may be options available for those who will be incarcerated, such as intermittent sentences or work furlough.

Many judges request a pre-sentence investigation report to assist them in making sentencing decisions. The report summarizes the defendant's social history as well as facts relating to the current crime. It normally discusses the defendant's potential for rehabilitation and recommends a sentence. The issues will be further explored at the sentencing hearing, where both the prosecution and the defense have the right to call witnesses and make arguments in favor of their views of what is an appropriate sentence. After hearing all the evidence, the judge imposes the sentence. Many states require the judge to explain any deviations from the base sentence.

Study Questions

1. Which crimes in your state have determinate sentences? Which ones have indeterminate sentences?
2. Check the laws of your state.
   a. What aggravating circumstances may the judge consider when imposing sentences?
   b. What mitigating circumstances may the judge consider when imposing sentences?
   c. What, if any, other enhancements are authorized?
   d. What special sentencing rules apply to recidivists?
3. Check the laws of your state and explain the rules for including the following as part of a sentence.
   a. a fine
   b. restitution
   c. community service
   d. court costs
4. What are the rules in your state for imposing the following sentences?
   a. jail
   b. an intermittent sentence
   c. work furlough
   d. prison
5. Attend a sentencing hearing and report on the following:
   a. What crime(s) was the defendant convicted for?
   b. Was a pre-sentence investigation report prepared? If so, summarize its content if it was discussed in court.
   c. Was a private pre-sentence investigation report prepared? If so, summarize its content.
   d. Were witnesses called? If so, summarize the testimony of each one.
   e. Were victim impact statements presented? If so, summarize each one.
   f. Did the defendant exercise the right of allocution? If so, summarize what he/she said.
   g. Summarize the arguments of the prosecutor and the defense attorney.
   h. What sentence was imposed? Summarize the judge's rationale for giving this sentence.

True or False Questions

1. Indeterminate sentences are unconstitutional.
2. Enhancements must relate to facts about the current crime.
3. Two defendants who commit the same crime must receive identical sentences.
4. A person who is on probation can be prohibited from doing acts that are legal.
5. A person who is given an intermittent sentence serves part of the term in prison and part in county jail.
6. A person who has been convicted of a crime can be required to pay restitution to the victim of the crime.
7. If an inmate is serving concurrent sentences, both sentences start on the same day.
8. The judge decides whether sentences will be served concurrently or consecutively.
9. A pre-sentence investigation report must be prepared prior to sentencing the defendant.
10. The defendant has the right of allocution in felony cases but not misdemeanor cases.

Chapter 14

Appeals

Outline

Key Terms

advance sheets
amicus curiae
appellant
appellant's opening brief
appellant's reply brief
automatic appeal
clerk's transcript
collateral attack

direct appeal
discretionary appeals
motion to proceed
  in forma pauperis
petition for writ of *certiorari*
petition for writ
  of *habeas corpus*
prayer

reporter's transcript
respondent
respondent's opening brief
slip opinions
writ of *certiorari*
writ of *habeas corpus*

Learning Objectives

Learning Objectives

After reading this chapter, the student will be able to

- Describe the court procedures used when an appeal is taken.
- Explain the defendant's right to counsel and other necessary services when appealing a conviction.
- Identify when the defense and prosecution are permitted to appeal before trial begins.
- Explain when a defendant is permitted to appeal after pleading guilty.
- Describe the process for a direct appeal after a conviction.
- Describe the appellate process after a judge has imposed the death penalty.
- Identify the process used when a person convicted in state court appeals his/her case to the United States Supreme Court.
- Explain the procedures used to obtain a writ of *habeas corpus*.

All 50 states provide for appeals after convictions. This involves an elaborate process of written briefs and oral arguments. The defendant automatically has the right to one appeal; subsequent appeals are at the discretion of the courts. *Habeas corpus* relief may be available for the defendant after the normal appellate avenues have been exhausted.

14-1 The Appellate Process

The American justice system assigns the task of assessing the credibility of witnesses to the jury, or to the judge if the case is heard without a jury. For this reason, it is very rare for an appellate court to become involved in the issue of whether the jury correctly weighed the evidence in a case, except when the court finds that there was no credible evidence to support an element of the crime. If there are witnesses giving different versions of the facts, the appellate court defers to the judgment of the jury (or trial judge) who observed the behavior of the witness as well as heard what was said. Occasionally an appellate court will rule that the testimony of a witness was so inherently improbable that it was not worthy of belief. This usually occurs when the timing of the events testified to, or the physical layout of the scene, makes it impossible for the events to have occurred or for the witness to have observed them.

The appellate process is designed to review the legal issues of a case. This usually relates to legal documents filed and arguments made at the pretrial hearings and trial. The judge's rulings during trial on objections made by the attorneys are also potential issues on appeal. Extensive documentation is needed because the judges who will hear the appeal were not present during the trial. Two documents are used for this purpose: the clerk's transcript and the reporter's transcript. The federal rules of appellate procedure require these transcripts to be combined in one appendix, with consistent page numbering to make referencing them easier. The **clerk's transcript** contains all the documents used in the case: warrant applications and warrants (if any) with proof of service and inventory of items seized; criminal complaint; indictment (if any); motions to suppress evidence; discovery motions; clerk's minutes (also called docket entries) regarding what occurred on each court day; information on jury selection; jury instructions (if preprinted instructions are used); verdicts; and notice of appeal. The **reporter's transcript** contains a verbatim account of what was said in court. What the attorneys say, the judge's comments, and the testimony of the witnesses are recorded. In lower courts, such as those handling misdemeanors, the reporter's transcript may be replaced by a statement, agreed to by both attorneys, which summarizes the facts.

Reporter's transcripts may also be available for grand jury proceedings, preliminary hearings, and suppression hearings. Figure 14-1 shows a sample page from a reporter's transcript.

These transcripts are necessary to challenge rulings the judge made on oral objections. They will show whether the objection was made in a timely fashion and if the attorney stated the correct grounds for the objec-

Figure 14-1
Sample of Reporter's Transcript

```
        A  68                                            375

   1    A L B E R T    S T E I N E R, called as a witness having
10 2            been first duly sworn by the Clerk of the Court,
   3            testified as follows:
   4    DIRECT  EXAMINATION
   5    BY MR.  LEVIN-EPSTEIN:
   6            Q    Good morning, ladies and gentlemen.    Good
   7    morning, Mr. Steiner?
   8            A    Good morning.
   9            Q    For the record and so the jurors at this end
  10    can hear you clearly, will you once again state your full
  11    name?
  12            A    Albert Steiner.
  13            Q    Mr. Steiner, at this time, are you employed?
  14            A    No, sir, I'm retired.
  15            Q    How long have you been retired?
  16            A    Approximately three years.
  17            Q    Prior to the time that you entered retirement,
  18    were you employed?
  19            A    I was.
  20            Q    What was your occupation, sir?
  21            A    I was in the fuel oil and oil burner business.
  22            Q    In the fuel oil and oil burner business, did you
  23    have your own company or were you employed by someone else?
  24            A    No, I had my own company.
  25            Q    What was the name of that company?
```

tion. Where legal rulings depend on the facts of the case, such as a question of whether an item was legally seized without a warrant, the reporter's transcript is needed to determine what the officers testified that they did. The clerk's transcript is also needed because the appellate court will review the points and authorities submitted to the judge at the suppression hearing to determine whether the argument for suppression was correctly made. To facilitate review of the record, the appellate court usually requires the attorney appealing an issue to cite the page numbers for any relevant information in the clerk's and reporter's transcripts.

The first document filed in an appeal is the notice of appeal. This may be a preprinted form. Strict rules govern when the notice of appeal may be filed; for example, many states require it to be filed within 30 days of the sentencing hearing but prohibit filing appeals before the final judgment is entered. Failure to file on time waives the right to appeal. The primary function of the notice of appeal is to alert court personnel to prepare the necessary documents and to transfer the files to the appellate court. Figure 14-2 shows a typical format for a notice of appeal.

A copy of the notice of appeal is normally served on the opposing party; court rules may also make it the duty of the person appealing to notify the court reporter that transcripts will be needed. The notice of appeal may include a request for the court to appoint an attorney to handle the appeal because the defendant does not have the financial resources to do so. Figure 14-3 shows the Michigan form used by the judge to grant the appeal, appoint an attorney, and notify the court reporter to prepare the transcript. A defendant who files the notice may abandon the appeal later.

Frequently the attorneys that handle the trial do not process the appeal. Many attorneys specialize in either trial or appellate work because the skills involved are quite different. The trial attorney focuses his/her efforts on preparing the case for trial, presenting evidence, examining witnesses, and making appropriate objections. Public speaking skills are important. The appellate attorney reviews the transcripts and focuses on researching the legal issues and writing persuasive briefs. Some states have the attorney general's office handle appeals in criminal cases instead of the local prosecutor's office; this is more common for felony appeals than for misdemeanors. There may be a statewide public defender's office to handle the appeals for cases in which the defendant cannot afford to hire a lawyer.

The side filing the appeal, called the **appellant,** prepares a brief, stating all the legal issues involved in the appeal. This is called the **appellant's opening brief.** It starts with a summary of the case. The legal maneuvers

Figure 14-2
Notice of Appeal

Notice of Appeal
STATE OF MINNESOTA COUNTY COURT

COUNTY OF _____

	) NOTICE OF APPEAL, BY
	) DEFENDANT, ON THE
_____,)	RECORD TO DISTRICT
Plaintiff,)	COURT FROM COUNTY
)	COURT
vs.)	
)	
_____,)	
Defendant.)	County Court File No. _____

TO: the Clerk of the above-named County Court, and the Prosecuting
     Attorney

PLEASE TAKE NOTICE that the above-named Defendant hereby appeals on the record to the District court for the above-named County from the following Judgement or Orders of the above-named County Court:

_____ Final Judgement of Conviction, entered on the ____ day of
_____, 20 ___.

_____ Order refusing or imposing conditions of release, entered on
the _____ day of _____, 20 ___.

Dated: _____

_____
(Attorney for Defendant)

                              Name:
                              Title:
                              Address:
                              Telephone No.:

Figure 14-3
Claim of Appeal and Order Appointing Counsel

Criminal Procedure		Rule 6.425

Approved, SCAO

Copies to: Trial Court, Court Reporter(s)/ Recorder(s), Appointed Counsel, Defendant, Prosecutor, Court of Appeals, and MAACS

STATE OF MICHIGAN JUDICIAL CIRCUIT COUNTY	CLAIM OF APPEAL AND ORDER APPOINTING COUNSEL	CASE NO.

Court address

Court telephone no.

THE PEOPLE OF THE STATE OF MICHIGAN
v
Defendant name, address, date of birth, and inmate no (if known)

OFFENSE NAME   MCL CITATION   SENTENCE(S)

1. The defendant claims an appeal from a final judgment or order entered on _____ in the _____ Circuit Court, _____ County, Michigan by Judge _____

Copies of the final judgment or order being appealed are attached for the Court of Appeals and appointed counsel.

2. On _____ Date the defendant filed a request for appointment of counsel and a declaration of indigency.

IT IS ORDERED:

3. ☐ The State Appellate Defender Office, 1200 Sixth Avenue, Third Floor North tower, Detroit, MI 48226 (313) 256-2814
OR

☐
Name of Appellate Counsel   Address

City, state, and zip   Telephone no.   Bar no.

is appointed counsel for the defendant in post-conviction proceedings. If appointed counsel cannot or will not accept this appointment, counsel shall notify the court immediately.

4. The court reporter(s)/recorder(s) shall file with the trial court clerk the transcripts checked below and any other transcripts requested by counsel in this case not previously transcribed. Transcripts shall be filed within 28 days for pleas or 56 days for trials from the date ordered or requested. [MCR 7 210 (B)] Reporter(s)/recorder(s) shall be paid as provided by law.

TRANSCRIPT ORDERED	REPORTER/RECORDER NAME, DESIGNATION, AND NUMBER	DATE(S) OF PROCEEDING
☐ a. Jury trial		
☐ b. Bench trial		
☐ c. Plea		
Probation Violation ☐ d. Plea ☐ e. Hearing		
☐ f. Sentence ☐ g. Resentence		
☐ h. Other (specify)		

5. The clerk shall immediately send to counsel a copy of the docket entries and the transcripts ordered above or requested by counsel as they become available. The clerk shall also forward documents upon request by counsel. [MCR 6 433]

Date _____   Judge _____   Bar no.

PROOF OF SERVICE

On this date I served a copy of this claim of appeal on appointed counsel, defendant, court reporter(s)/recorder(s), prosecutor, Court of Appeals, and the Michigan Appellate Assigned Counsel System. I also served a copy of the final judgment or order being appealed on appointed counsel and the Court of Appeals and a copy of the defendant's request for appointment of counsel on appointed counsel, the prosecutor, and the Michigan Appellate Counsel System.

Date _____   Signature _____

cc 403 (12/89) CLAIM OF APPEAL AND ORDER APPOINTING COUNSEL   MCR 6 425 (F), MCR 6 433, MCR 7 210 (B)(3) in the case are summarized: the charges the defendant was arraigned on; the charges the defendant was held to answer on after the preliminary hearing; any charges dismissed before trial; and the charges on which the defendant was convicted. Relevant dates for these actions are usually included, along with references to the page of the clerk's transcript for each. The second part of the summary is a statement of the facts (e.g., at 6:35 P.M. on September 4, 2001, John Jones returned home after work and discovered that his home had been broken into and his stereo was missing, etc.). These facts must be supported by references to testimony in the reporter's transcript.

The legal arguments are the heart of the appellate brief. Figure 14-4 shows a page from an appellant's opening brief. Each issue is usually set out under a separate heading.

Each issue is fully developed, citing the facts, U.S. Constitution and Bill of Rights, state constitution and statutes, and relevant case law. Citations for all statutes and cases are required. Failure to raise an issue in the opening brief waives the right to appeal on that point of law. The brief ends with a **prayer,** which is a request for appellate court action, usually the reversal of the conviction. State law usually sets a time limit, such as 60 days, for the appellant to file an opening brief. This time runs from the time the notice of appeal was filed or the date the transcripts are ready. Continuances may be sought if there is good cause for the delay. The appellant's opening brief is filed with the clerk of the appellate court. Copies are usually served on the opposing party and the trial judge.

The **respondent,** which is the side opposite the appellant, must respond to the appellant's opening brief. If the criminal defendant appeals, the prosecutor or attorney general's staff handles the appeal on behalf of the government. This is true even when the appeal is from a court ruling rather than for something that the prosecutor did. The **respondent's opening brief** is filed to refute the legal claims made in the appellant's opening brief. It normally begins with a summary of the case, but the respondent can accept the one prepared by the appellant. The respondent must counter each issue raised by the appellant; it does not, however, need to raise any additional issues. Figure 14-5 shows the first page of the reply to the issue raised in the case shown in Figure 14-4.

The respondent's opening brief usually takes one of four approaches: it argues that the facts do not support the appellant's argument; it may introduce cases the appellant did not mention; it may argue that cases cited by the appellant are not applicable to the facts of the case; or it may acknowledge that errors occurred but argue that the harmless error rule applies. A combination of these approaches is frequently used. Citations

Figure 14-4
Appellant's Opening Brief

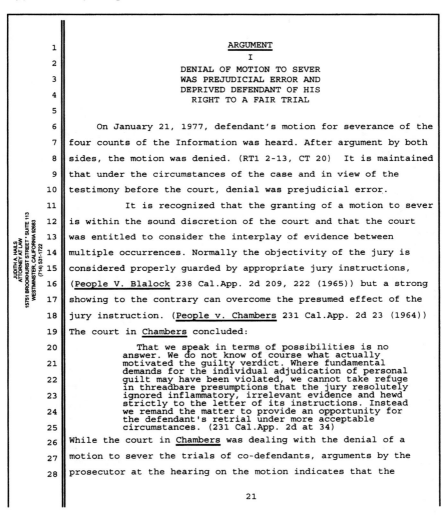

ARGUMENT
I

DENIAL OF MOTION TO SEVER
WAS PREJUDICIAL ERROR AND
DEPRIVED DEFENDANT OF HIS
RIGHT TO A FAIR TRIAL

On January 21, 1977, defendant's motion for severance of the four counts of the Information was heard. After argument by both sides, the motion was denied. (RT1 2-13, CT 20) It is maintained that under the circumstances of the case and in view of the testimony before the court, denial was prejudicial error.

It is recognized that the granting of a motion to sever is within the sound discretion of the court and that the court was entitled to consider the interplay of evidence between multiple occurrences. Normally the objectivity of the jury is considered properly guarded by appropriate jury instructions, (People V. Blalock 238 Cal.App. 2d 209, 222 (1965)) but a strong showing to the contrary can overcome the presumed effect of the jury instruction. (People v. Chambers 231 Cal.App. 2d 23 (1964)) The court in Chambers concluded:

> That we speak in terms of possibilities is no answer. We do not know of course what actually motivated the guilty verdict. Where fundamental demands for the individual adjudication of personal guilt may have been violated, we cannot take refuge in threadbare presumptions that the jury resolutely ignored inflammatory, irrelevant evidence and hewd strictly to the letter of its instructions. Instead we remand the matter to provide an opportunity for the defendant's retrial under more acceptable circumstances. (231 Cal.App. 2d at 34)

While the court in Chambers was dealing with the denial of a motion to sever the trials of co-defendants, arguments by the prosecutor at the hearing on the motion indicates that the

21

JUDITH A. HALS
ATTORNEY AT LAW
15751 BROOKHURST STREET · SUITE 113
WESTMINSTER, CALIFORNIA 92683
(714) 531-1722

for all cases and statutes are required. State law usually establishes a deadline for filing a respondent's opening brief; for example, the respondent's opening brief may be due 30 days from receipt of the appellant's opening brief. The appellate court has the authority to grant continuances. The brief is filed with the appellate court clerk, and copies are served on the opposing side and the trial judge. Upon receipt of the respondent's opening brief, the clerk of the appellate court usually schedules the case for oral arguments.

Figure 14-5
Respondent's Opening Brief

ARGUMENT

I

THE TRIAL COURT DID NOT ABUSE
ITS DISCRETION IN DENYING
APPELLANT'S MOTION TO SEVER

Appellant argues the trial court prejudicially abused its discretion when it refused to sever the four counts of the information. (AOB 21.) Appellant contends had the four counts been served and tried separately, not guilty verdicts would have been returned on each. Appellant notes the deputy district attorney himself argued that if the jury was unaware of appellant's repeated attacks on women, it would be difficult to convict him of any one of those assaults. (RT LF 1-13.)$\underline{4/}$ Appellant argues joinder for that purpose is improper and the trial court abused its discretion in refusing to sever.

Penal Code section 954 allows the joinder of two or more offenses connected in their commission or offenses that are of the same class of crime. The section likewise authorizes severance if good cause is shown and if done in the interest of justice. The denial of the motion to sever is within the sound discretion of the trial court. Denial of the motion will be disturbed only for abuse of

---

4. RT LF refers to the Reporter's Transcript prepared by Court Reporter Louis Frank.

Most states permit the appellant to respond in writing to arguments made by the respondent. The brief prepared for this purpose is called the **appellant's reply brief.** It is usually optional. Figure 14-6 shows a page from the appellant's reply brief in the same case shown in Figures 14-4 and 14-5. New arguments are not usually permitted at this point. State law establishes the time limit for filing this document; it is usually shorter than the time allotted for the opening brief. Local rules may permit the respondent to file a reply brief.

Oral arguments are usually optional at the appellate level. Local custom usually indicates whether an attorney should prepare for them or submit a waiver. The length of oral arguments also varies, with some courts allocating only five minutes per attorney, while others are more generous.

When oral arguments are scheduled, the appellate judges normally review the briefs before the case is heard. In some courts, staff attorneys assist with this process and may even prepare a draft opinion before the

Figure 14-6
Appellant's Reply Brief

```
 1          IN THE COURT OF APPEAL OF THE STATE OF CALIFORNIA
 2                      FOURTH APPELLATE DISTRICT
 3                            DIVISION TWO
 4
 5    THE PEOPLE OF THE STATE OF CALIFORNIA,          4 Crim. No. 9747
 6              Plaintiff and Respondent,          (Sup.Ct.No. C-36468)
 7         v.
 8    TY GLEN CLAYTON,
 9              Defendant and Appellant.
10
11        APPEAL FROM THE SUPERIOR COURT OF ORANGE COUNTY
12            Honorable Mason L. Fenton, Judge Presiding
13                   APPELLANT'S REPLY BRIEF
14
15                           ARGUMENT
16                              I
17                   DENIAL OF MOTION TO SEVER
                     WAS PREJUDICIAL ERROR AND
18                   DEPRIVED DEFENDANT OF HIS
                     RIGHT TO A FAIR TRIAL
19
20
21        Respondent argues that severance would cloak defendant
22   in an aura of credibility to which he is not entitled. This
23   ignores the fact that the prosecution admitted, on the record,
     that in all probability the defense would be successful if
24   severance was granted. Appellant does not seek unfair advantage
25   but merely the protection of the rights to which each person
26   charged with a crime is entitled, namely, that prosecution bear
27   its burden of proving each essential element of each crime
28   (People v. Francisco 228 Cal.App. 2d 355, 358 (1964)) and that
```

case is heard. Some judges listen passively to what the attorney wants to present, while others aggressively ask questions. The judges usually meet after the day's oral arguments have been heard. A vote is taken on each case. One judge from the majority is assigned to write the court's opinion; other judges may write their own opinions, either concurring with the outcome but stating different reasons for doing so or dissenting and stating reasons the case should have been decided differently. Many states have laws that require appellate judges to issue the opinion within a fixed time, such as 90 days, after oral arguments. The opinion is filed with the clerk of the appellate court, and copies are sent to the attorneys for each side and to the trial judge. A copy also goes to the official publisher of the state's appellate opinions.

Only published opinions become precedent. Some states allow the judges to vote on whether an opinion will be published. This is done to reduce the volume of cases in the official reports. An unpublished opinion is still filed in the court record and served on the attorneys and trial judge. It is binding on the parties to the case but cannot be cited by attorneys arguing other cases. The most common reason for not publishing an opinion is that it contains no new issues and the fact pattern has been adjudicated in the past. Many states vacate an opinion if the case is accepted for hearing by a higher court; this leaves only the final decision in the officially published reports.

14-2 The Defendant's Constitutional Rights on Appeal

There is no mention in the Constitution or Bill of Rights of a right to appeal. The Supreme Court has noted, however, that all 50 states and the federal system provide for appeals after convictions. In recognition of the universality of the right to appeal in the American judicial system, the Supreme Court has extended the right to counsel through the first post-conviction appeal. This means that an indigent defendant is entitled to have an attorney appointed to handle the first appeal. The standard for determining if a defendant is indigent is the same as it is at trial: can the person afford to hire an attorney in light of the cost of legal representation for this type of case and the number of dependents that the defendant is supporting? This test is applied at the time appellate counsel is requested. Defendants who paid lawyers to represent them at trial may have exhausted their financial resources and be indigent as far as the appeal is concerned. For this reason, it is more common to find court-appointed counsel handling cases on appeal than it is at trial.

The Supreme Court has held that a defendant's appeal cannot be blocked due to his/her inability to pay fees or purchase documents necessary for the appeal. Some unique features of the appellate process make this decision necessary if the defendant is to be able to pursue an appeal. Many courts have filing fees ranging from $100 to $500 for an appeal. Being required to pay this fee would mean many indigent defendants would forego an appeal; therefore, the filing fee must be waived for them. The transcripts are necessary in many cases because an attorney who did not represent the defendant at trial is appointed to handle the appeal. The documents are frequently lengthy and expensive: the clerk's transcript may cost $1 per page and the reporter's transcript as much as $5 per page. If the rules mandate references to these documents, it is necessary for the government to provide copies to the attorney representing the defendant on appeal. A fourth expense on appeal involves the printing of the briefs. Some courts have rules that require the briefs to be printed—not photocopied. Again, it becomes necessary to pay for the printing of briefs for the indigent or, as an alternative, the appellate rules may permit indigent briefs to be photocopied or prepared by some other, less expensive process.

Not every conviction merits an appeal. Sometimes there are no errors committed at trial serious enough to be grounds for reversal. On the other hand, the Supreme Court has been reluctant to let appointed attorneys be the sole arbitrator of whether the defendant's case will be heard at the appellate level. This has been reinforced by several cases that have been reversed after an attorney wrote a letter stating that the case had no merit. The Supreme Court ruled that an attorney must file a brief discussing all arguable issues prior to requesting to be removed from the case. The appellate court is required to review the brief and appoint another attorney if there are arguable claims of error. Failure to follow this procedure is a prejudicial error which warrants a new appeal. Figure 14-7 shows the form used by the United States Court of Appeals for the Seventh Circuit when an attorney has asked to withdraw from the case because he/she does not believe there are appealable issues involved. Note the procedures the defendant can follow to obtain another attorney.

In some cases a defendant whose case is on appeal may be allowed to remain free on bail or OR. This rarely occurs if the defendant was in custody while awaiting trial. Most states leave the decision to release the defendant to the trial judge. The convicted defendant is usually seen as a flight risk and must show a strong justification for being allowed out of jail at this point. If the defendant was given a sentence that did not include incarceration, the judge is not likely to require him/her to return to jail pending appeal.

Figure 14-7
Motion to Withdraw

FORM OF NOTICE FOR DEFENDANT COUNSEL'S

MOTION FOR LEAVE TO WITHDRAW UNDER

CIRCUIT RULE 51(a)

To:_____
(Name)

_____
(Street Address or Prison Box)

_____
(City, State, Zip Code)
You are the appellant in a case now pending in this court: Case No.

_____

_____
v.
_____

Your attorney filed a brief on _____, 20 _____, stating a
belief that your appeal is frivolous and requesting permission to withdraw
from the case. Please be advised as follows:

1) You have 30 days from the date this notice was mailed in which to
   raise any points that you choose which show why your conviction
   should be set aside.

2) If you do not respond within 30 days, the court may affirm or
   dismiss your appeal. An affirmance or dismissal would mean that
   your case would be finally decided against you.

3) If you want to make a showing why the court should not affirm or
   dismiss your appeal and believe that there is a very good reason
   why you will not be able to file your objections with the court
   within the 30-day limit, you should *immediately* write to the court
   and ask for additional time up to 30 days. If additional time is
   granted, you must file your reasons why the court should not
   affirm or dismiss your appeal before your additional times expires.

4) You do not have a right to another attorney unless this court finds
   that your showing requires that your case be further briefed or
   argued. If the court finds that your case should be further briefed
   or argued, an attorney will be appointed for you who will argue
   your appeal.

If you want to write to this court, you should address your letter to:

> Clerk of the Court
> United States Court of Appeals
> 219 South Dearborn Street
> Chicago, Illinois 60604

Be sure, when writing, to show clearly the name and number of your case.

Notice mailed _____, 20 ___

_____

Deputy Clerk, U.S. Court of Appeals
Attorney for appellant

_____
(Name)

_____
(Street Address)

_____
(City, State, Zip Code)

_____
(Area Code and Telephone Number)

14-3 Pretrial Appeals

State laws vary, but some legal issues can be raised on appeal before trial. The advantage of the appeal at this stage is that the issue can be settled before trial, thus avoiding problems with double jeopardy. Even if double jeopardy would not be a problem, early resolution of the issue saves the cost of a second trial if the conviction is reversed due to the erroneous ruling of the lower-court judge. Delays caused by good faith appeals cannot be used as a grounds for dismissal for lack of a speedy trial.

All of the actions discussed in this section are appealable, but some states require the appeal to be made before trial, others want the issue raised in the direct appeal that follows conviction, while a few permit an appeal at either time. Attorneys handling the case must check the local rules and determine when to file the appeal. Failure to file the appeal in a timely manner may result in the court's refusal to consider the issue later.

Pretrial appeals challenge the rulings of judges presiding over arraignments, preliminary hearings, and pretrial proceedings. Sometimes they also challenge the actions or composition of the grand jury. Either the defense or the prosecution can appeal these actions because double jeopardy has not attached at this stage of the proceeding. Although the case may list the court as a party, such as *Jones v. Superior Court,* the arguments made on appeal are handled by the prosecution and defense. If the prosecution appeals, the defense must file a brief in support of the action taken by the judge. The opposite is true if the defense appeals: the prosecution files a brief, arguing that the judge's ruling was correct.

The most common issues appealed after the arraignment deal with the wording of the criminal complaint: jurisdictional facts; statute of limitations; and stating a cause of action. Section 9-4, "Challenges to the Pleadings," discusses many of these issues. The defense must raise the issue by filing a motion in the court where the arraignment occurred. If denied, it may be appealed. If the defense motion was granted by the trial judge, the prosecution may appeal. The clerk's transcript, which contains the complaint and other documentation from the arraignment, as well as the dialogue contained in the reporter's transcript, are important for these appeals. No witnesses testify before the appellate court. An appeal normally goes to the next higher court. For example, if arraignments are held in Municipal Court and felony trials in Superior Court, the appeal from a ruling made at the arraignment in Municipal Court would be heard in Superior Court.

Holding the defendant to answer at the end of the preliminary hearing can be challenged before trial in some states. In addition to the issues that can be raised to challenge the complaint, the defense can allege that there were insufficient facts presented to establish a *prima facie* case. The verbatim transcript of the testimony at the preliminary hearing is crucial for this purpose. Occasionally the prosecution files an appeal from a ruling at this stage of the case. Pretrial appeals from the preliminary hearing are usually heard in the same court that hears challenges to the criminal complaint.

Many states permit Fourth and Fifth Amendment challenges to the evidence before the trial begins. Section 9-5, "Challenges to the Evidence," discusses many of these issues. For example, the defense may claim the murder weapon was unconstitutionally seized or that the confession was obtained in violation of the defendant's *Miranda* rights. A motion requesting a hearing on these issues must be filed. Depending on the timing of the motion, it may be filed in the court that handled the arraignment or, in felony cases, the court that will hold the trial. The judge's ruling on the motion can be appealed by either side. Five things are usually important source documents for use during this type of appeal: the verbatim transcript of portions of the preliminary hearing where testimony was taken from people involved in the search or interrogation; the verbatim transcript of portions of the suppression hearing where testimony was taken regarding the search and/or confession; the points and authorities submitted before the suppression hearing by both sides; the transcript of oral arguments made by both sides at the suppression hearing; and the judge's ruling, including any written opinion, giving reasons for his/her resolution of the matter.

14-4 Appeal After a Guilty Plea

A defendant has the right to counsel when entering a guilty plea. The issue of inadequate representation can be raised in a plea bargain case based on the same standard it would be if a trial had occurred: the defendant was entitled to a competent counsel; reversal is required only if having competent counsel would have altered the outcome. Important constitutional rights must be waived on the record when the judge accepts the plea: trial by jury; confrontation and cross-examination of witnesses; and proof beyond a reasonable doubt. The defendant is entitled to withdraw a plea if he/she did not knowingly waive these rights; it can also be withdrawn if the defendant was coerced into entering the plea.

It is generally agreed that the defendant has the right to the plea bargain that he/she agreed to. If the judge rejects the agreement, the defendant has the right to withdraw the plea. Refusal to permit the defendant to do so is grounds for reversal on appeal. In many courts it is recognized that the judge retains discretion to impose sentence, and the plea bargain can cover only the charges involved. When this is incorporated into the bargain, the defendant cannot appeal because of the sentence imposed.

The dialogue of what occurred in court on the day the plea bargain was entered is crucial to determining whether errors occurred. The verbatim transcript of the hearing becomes the key evidence on appeal. If the issue is incompetence of counsel, the transcript frequently provides insufficient information on why the attorney performed in the manner he/she did. A **writ of *habeas corpus*** is needed to determine this issue. Section 14-8, "*Habeus Corpus*," discusses how *habeas corpus* is handled.

Some states have a seemingly contradictory procedure: a defendant whose motion to suppress evidence is unsuccessful can enter a guilty plea and still appeal the ruling on the suppression motion. This saves trials in many cases: defendants whose only defense rested on the suppression of evidence do not take up court time with trials in order to retain the right to appeal Fourth and Fifth Amendment issues. The transcript of the suppression hearing is usually the key to the appeal in these cases.

14-5 Direct Appeal of a Conviction

The appeal of a conviction that is taken immediately following sentencing is referred to as a **direct appeal.** To obtain further appeals after that time, the defendant must petition the court for its permission to appeal. These are called **discretionary appeals.** The constitutional right to have an attorney appointed if the defendant is indigent applies to direct appeals but not discretionary appeals.

A direct appeal is limited to issues presented in the trial record (clerk's and reporter's transcripts). The most common issues relate to jury instructions which tell the jury how to apply the law to the facts. Search and seizure issues and *Miranda* questions are common. Local laws may state that issues raised on pretrial appeals cannot be relitigated as part of the direct appeal. There are also issues that may be non-appealable unless specific procedures, such as filing an exception to the admission of evidence, were complied with at trial. The contemporaneous objection rule applies to many things that occur at trial and prohibits appeal regarding evidence that was admitted at trial without an objection.

Some issues cannot be raised on direct appeal because there is nothing in the trial record about them. Incompetence of counsel is a good example. The trial record contains verbatim accounts of what was done but usually does not show whether the attorney was following a tactical plan or was unprepared or unaware of the issues involved. *Habeas corpus* is the appropriate procedure to raise these issues. Section 14-8, "*Habeus Corpus,*" explains procedures that are used to obtain a writ of *habeas corpus*.

Nearly all appeals following convictions are taken by defendants. Double jeopardy does not protect a convicted defendant from being retried on the same charges if he/she wins a direct appeal. There is one exception: cases in which the appellate court held that there was insufficient evidence to support a conviction. On the other hand, if the jury finds the defendant not guilty or the judge orders an acquittal, the prosecution cannot refile the charges no matter what happens on appeal. Perjury or subordination of perjury can be filed if the defendant lied under oath or had other witnesses do so during the trial, but the charges the defendant was acquitted on cannot be refiled.

Occasionally the prosecution will appeal to settle a point of law, usually because the trial judge directed a verdict of acquittal based on an unusual interpretation of how the law applied to the facts of the case. These appeals may be important because of the legal precedent that they set, but they have no effect on the defendant because double jeopardy protects him/her from being tried again.

14-6 Appeals When the Death Penalty Has Been Imposed

Many states set up different appellate procedures if the defendant was convicted of a capital crime and sentenced to death. The first step is usually to require the trial judge to review the case more carefully and grant a motion for a new trial if he/she believes that reversible error occurred. The judge may also have the authority to enter the conviction for murder but disregard the jury's verdict recommending the death penalty. These actions are done before the case is transferred to the appellate court.

State law frequently designates one court to hear all death penalty appeals. The state's highest court is commonly used for this purpose, and the intermediate-level appellate courts are bypassed. When this is done there is only one appeal within the state court system, but it is more thorough than what normally occurs. Many states also make review by this appellate court mandatory, sometimes called an **automatic appeal,** if the death penalty has been imposed.

Greater care is usually exercised when appointing an attorney to handle the appeal. In many states a list of appellate attorneys is used for this purpose. Unlike the average case where any licensed attorney may be appointed, the court may require proof that the attorney has sufficient experience to adequately handle the life-and-death issues to be addressed. More time may be authorized for the preparation of the appellant's briefs. Any page limits that apply to appeals are usually waived, so that the attorney may devote as much space to each argument as he/she believes necessary.

Courts that hear death penalty appeals usually take more time considering them than they do other cases. The opinions are usually longer and demonstrate more detailed application of the law to the particular facts of the case. Many states require the court to consider whether the punishment is proportional to the crime, in addition to considering the defendant's guilt. This means the judges compare the current case with other capital punishment cases they have decided: the sentence should be reversed if it seems disproportionately harsh, compared with the facts of other death penalty cases that have been affirmed.

14-7 Discretionary Appeals

All appeals after the direct appeal are discretionary. The normal process is for the side that lost the direct appeal to file a petition asking the higher court to take the case. If a conviction was reversed on direct appeal, the higher court can reverse the first appellate court, thereby reinstating the conviction, without violating double jeopardy. The justices review these petitions and decide which ones will be heard. Usually a positive vote of nearly a majority of the justices is needed before the petition is granted. This process is followed in many states and for most cases heard by the United States Supreme Court.

Most defendants face two problems when seeking a discretionary appeal: they do not have an attorney to handle the case and they cannot afford the fees involved (filing fees, printing costs, etc.). Defendants cannot invoke the Sixth Amendment or equal protection as grounds for the courts to provide the services they seek. The right to counsel ends with the direct appeal. States are free to address these issues as they wish, as long as they do not totally cut off access to the courts. At a minimum they must provide law libraries in the prisons, appropriate writing materials, and postage to mail legal documents. "Jailhouse lawyers," inmates who help other inmates with legal matters, cannot be prohibited unless other forms of assistance are available.

Due to the fact that defendants frequently write their own petitions for discretionary appeals, many courts have accepted petitions that the clerk's office otherwise would refuse to file. Many are handwritten. The legal issues may be poorly worded. If the justices vote to hear the case, an attorney may be appointed by the state, even though the federal constitution does not mandate it.

State defendants can petition the United States Supreme Court to hear their cases on the grounds that there was a constitutional error. The first step usually is a **motion to proceed** *in forma pauperis,* such as the one shown in Figure 14-8. The literal meaning of *in forma pauperis* is "like a poor person." Granting of this motion excuses the defendant from paying

Figure 14-8
Motion for Leave to Proceed *in Forma Pauperis*

No. _____   ฿) **ORIGINAL**

IN THE

SUPREME COURT OF THE UNITED STATES

October Term, 1992

PAUL PALALAUA TUILAEPA,

            Petitioner,

vs.

THE STATE OF CALIFORNIA,

            Respondent.

93 - 5131

Supreme Court U.S.
FILED
7-8-
OFFICE OF THE CLERK

MOTION FOR LEAVE TO PROCEED

IN FORMA PAUPERIS

    The petitioner, PAUL PALALAUA TUILAEPA, requests leave to file the accompanying petition for writ of certiorari, without prepayment of costs and to proceed in forma pauperis. Petitioner has been granted leave to so proceed before the California Supreme Court. Petitioner's affidavit in support of this motion is attached hereto.

Dated: **7/6/93**

            Respectfully submitted,

            Howard W. Gillingham

            Howard W. Gillingham
            4370 Tujunga Avenue
            Suite 105
            North Hollywood, CA 91604

            Counsel for Petitioner

filing fees and complying with some of the court rules, such as the one that mandates that all briefs be printed.

Once the motion has been granted, the defendant can file a **petition for writ of *certiorari*,** such as the one shown in Figure 14-9. The **writ of *certiorari*** is the document the court issues accepting a case on

Figure 14-9
Petition for Writ of *Certiorari*

No. 00-1260

In the Supreme Court of the United States

UNITED STATES OF AMERICA, PETITIONER

v.

MARK JAMES KNIGHTS

ON PETITION FOR A WRIT OF
CERTIORARI TO THE UNITED STATES COURT OF APPEALS
FOR THE NINTH CIRCUIT

PETITION FOR A WRIT OF CERTIORARI

BARBARA D. UNDERWOOD
Acting Solicitor General
Counsel of Record

JOHN C. KEENEY
Acting Assistant Attorney
General

MICHAEL R. DREEBEN
Deputy Solicitor General

MALCOLM L. STEWART
Assistant to the Solicitor
General

KIRBY HELLER
Attorney

Department of Justice
Washington, D.C. 20530-0001
(202) 514-2217

discretionary appeal. The petition must state constitutional grounds for the appeal and convince the justices to hear the case. The petitions are reviewed in conference and votes taken. At least four of the nine United States Supreme Court justices must vote in favor of issuing the writ of *certiorari*. This does not mean that the defendant is assured of winning the case: two justices may have voted to hear the case because they wanted to affirm the conviction, while two others voted for it so they could reverse it. The grant of *certiorari* states what issues will be heard. Occasionally the justices will ask the parties for supplemental briefs on additional issues. Once the Supreme Court grants *certiorari*, it appoints an experienced attorney to prepare the necessary briefs and pays for printing briefs and other expenses.

The Supreme Court works on a yearly term, which begins the first Monday in October and closes the last week in June or first week in July. The parties file briefs similar to those used for direct appeal in state court. Figure 14-10 shows the introduction to a petitioner's brief. The prosecution's brief is usually prepared by the state attorney general's staff.

Figure 14-10
Petitioner's Brief in *United States v Knights*

CONSTITUTIONAL PROVISION INVOLVED

The Fourth Amendment to the United States Constitution provides:

The right of the people to be secure in their persons, houses, papers, and effects, against unreasonable searches and seizures, shall not be violated, and no Warrants shall issue, but upon probable cause, supported by Oath or affirmation, and particularly describing the place to be searched, and the persons or things to be seized.

STATEMENT

1.　On May 29, 1998, respondent Mark James Knights was placed on summary probation for a drug offense under California law.[1] Summary probation in California does not involve direct supervision by a probation officer. App., *infra*, 4a. As a condition of probation, however, respondent signed a form by which he agreed to "[s]ubmit his * * * person, property, place of residence, vehicle, [and] personal effects, to search at anytime, with or without a search warrant, warrant of arrest, or reasonable cause by any probation officer or law enforcement officer." C.A. E.R. 73, App., *infra*, 4a. The consent-to-search term, sometimes known as the "Fourth Waiver," see *United States v. Ooley*, 116 F.3d 370, 371 (9th Cir. 1997), cert. denied, 524 U.S. 963 (1998), is a common term of probation in California. The California Supreme Court has held that the Fourth Waiver constitutes a valid consent to search. See, *e.g.*, *People v. Bravo*, 43 Cal. 3d 600, 605-611 (1987), cert. denied, 485 U.S. 904 (1988).

[1]See C.A. E.R. 58, 73. On that same date, respondent was sentenced to 90 days in jail, to commence on July 3, 1998. *Id.* At 58, 67.
Source: *http://supreme.1p.findlaw.com/supreme_court/briefs/00-1260/2000-1260.pet.aa.pdf.* page 6.

One or more **amicus curiae** may also file briefs. *Amicus curiae* means "friend of the court." An *amicus curiae* brief is filed by someone (a person, an organization, or a government entity) who wishes to present a viewpoint for the justices to consider. The party wishing to participate files a petition, requesting the court's permission to do so. After the request is granted, a brief is filed, which is usually in the same format as the opening brief of the side the *amicus* supports. Examples of *amicus curiae* in criminal cases include the International Association of Chiefs of Police filing a brief supporting what the police did and the American Civil Liberties Union filing a brief in support of the defendant's allegations that police actions were unconstitutional. The justices consider these briefs when deciding the case.

Oral arguments before the Supreme Court are very formal. Specific time limits are set and strictly enforced. Justices frequently interrupt the attorneys to ask questions. The justices meet in a conference once a week and discuss the cases that they have heard. A vote is taken. Someone from the majority is assigned to write the opinion. The draft opinion is circulated to the other justices, and those who agree with it sign it. Justices also have the option of writing their own opinions. A justice may sign more than one opinion; for example, a justice might sign the majority opinion because of agreement with the outcome of the majority opinion (conviction affirmed) but disagree with the legal rationale given by the majority and write a concurring opinion. Dissents are also written, sometimes with justices signing more than one. An opinion may concur and dissent (i.e., it may concur with part of the majority opinion and dissent as to other parts).

Opinions by the Supreme Court are read aloud in court on the day they are released. Copies, called **slip opinions,** are given to the parties and distributed to those who subscribe to this service. Opinions also become available across the country by electronic mail almost immediately. The official version may not appear in *United States Reports* for nearly two years, but other publishers issue **advance sheets** within a few weeks, containing the text of the opinion.

14-8 *Habeus Corpus*

Article I, Section 9, paragraph 2 of the United States Constitution provides

> The privilege of the *Writ of Habeas Corpus* shall not be suspended, unless when in Cases of Rebellion or Invasion the public Safety may require it.

The writ of *habeas corpus,* sometimes called the "great writ," is used to challenge illegal confinement. This writ orders a government agency to bring the petitioner to court and explain the legal basis for the detention. It can be used to challenge confinement in jail or prison due to illegal arrest; denial of reasonable bail for a bailable offense; illegally obtained conviction; conviction due to incompetent representation of counsel (either at trial or on appeal); or failure to release the person after the sentence has been served. *Habeas corpus* has also been used to challenge inhumane prison conditions. It can also be used to challenge involuntary confinement in a mental hospital. One prerequisite is that the person still be in custody when the petition is sought. Some courts consider a person in custody for the purpose of challenging an illegal arrest or conviction if he/she still has charges pending or is on probation or parole. Inmates may be able to use *habeas corpus* to secure reversals of their convictions, even though they have unsuccessfully raised the issue on direct appeal if an appellate court decision in another case involving issues raised in their case was applied retroactively.

Habeas corpus cases are considered civil, not criminal; therefore, the inmate does not have the constitutional right to have an attorney appointed to handle the case. It is referred to as a **collateral attack** on a conviction, meaning that it is not part of the normal appellate process. Both state and federal laws provide for *habeas corpus,* although it is sometimes classified as one of several postconviction remedies and the name *habeas corpus* may not be used. Normally the case must proceed through the state courts before it can be filed in the federal system.

Inmates in state prisons and county jails can file the federal equivalent of *habeas corpus* in the United States District Court if their constitutional rights were violated either pretrial or while in custody. In recent years the U.S. Congress has enacted laws imposing a variety of restrictions to reduce the number of cases heard in this manner. The most common one is that state inmates cannot proceed in federal court if they had a "full and fair hearing" on the same Fourth Amendment issues in state courts. This is a procedural approach to blocking access to federal courts: the opportunity to be heard on the issues is controlling; whether the judge made the correct decision on the constitutionality of the police action is not considered.

The first document filed with the court in a *habeas corpus* proceeding is the **petition for writ of *habeas corpus.*** This is frequently a preprinted form, such as the one in Figure 14-11. Many jails and prisons keep copies of the form on hand for inmate use.

The person filing this petition must allege facts that indicate that he/she is being illegally confined. The court assigns a judge to review the petition. The writ of *habeas corpus* will be issued if the judge determines that the facts, if true, indicate illegal confinement. This document, as

Figure 14-11
Petition for Writ of *Habeus Corpus*

ATTORNEY OR PETITIONER WITHOUT ATTORNEY (*Name and Address*)	TELEPHONE NO.	FOR COURT USE ONLY

PETITIONER'S BIRTH DATE:

SUPERIOR COURT OF CALIFORNIA, COUNTY OF

IN THE MATTER OF *(NAME)*: Petitioner	CASE NUMBER:

PETITION FOR WRIT OF HABEAS CORPUS–Penal Commitment

1. Petitioner is being unlawfully restrained of liberty at *(specify name of treatment facility)*:
   by *(specify name of persons having custody if known)*:

2. Petitioner was admitted to the treatment facility on *(date)*: and is currently detained pursuant to:
   - [ ] Penal Code § 1026 (not guilty by reason of insanity)   [ ] Penal Code § 1026.5(b) (extended commitment)
   - [ ] Penal Code § 1370 (incompetent to stand trial)   [ ] Penal Code § 2684 (prisoners transferred to state hospital)
   - [ ] Penal Code § 2962 (mentally disordered offender)   [ ] Former W & I § 6300 (MDSO)
   - [ ] Other (specify):

3. **Check at least one box:**
   a. [ ] Petitioner is illegally confined for the following reason:

   b. [ ] Petitioner has been denied the following rights without good cause (Penal Code section 2600):

4. Petitioner has no adequate and speedy remedy at law.

5. Have you made any previous requests for relief from this confinement? _____ *If your answer is yes,* state the nature and grounds for your request, the date it was made, and the result:

6. Petitioner requests that this court *(check all that apply)*:
   a. [ ] Issue a Writ of Habeas Corpus to the director of the facility named in item 1, commanding that the petitioner be brought before this court at a specified time and place.
   b. [ ] Order the facility personnel to release petitioner from said restraint.
   c. [ ] Order that all rights to which petitioner is entitled as a patient be observed.
   d. [ ] Grant such other relief as this court deems appropriate.

I declare under penalty of perjury under the laws of the State of California that the foregoing is true and correct.
Date:

▶

....
(TYPE OR PRINT NAME)

_____
(SIGNATURE OF PETITIONER OR PERSON REQUESTING WRIT ON PETITIONER'S BEHALF)

Form Approved by the Judicial Council of California MC-270 (New January 1, 1994)

PETITION FOR WRIT OF HABEAS CORPUS–Penal Commitment
(Mental Health)

Calif. Rules of Court, rule 260

shown in Figure 14-12, orders the person holding the inmate in custody to bring the petitioner to court for a hearing.

The writ of *habeas corpus* is directed at the sheriff if the inmate is being held in county jail; for inmates in state prison, the writ usually names either the warden of the prison or a high-ranking official in the state's Department of Corrections. The court clerk serves the writ on the appropriate person.

A return is usually filed to the writ of *habeas corpus*. The return is the written reply by the person who is holding the petitioner in custody. It states the legal grounds for the confinement and includes appropriate documentation, such as a copy of the conviction. The return is filed with the court and a copy served on the petitioner.

A hearing is held on the writ of *habeas corpus*. Witnesses testify under oath and are subject to cross-examination. If the issues raised center on releasing the petitioner on bail or failure to release the defendant at the end of a sentence, the testimony of jail or prison officials may be required at the hearing. If the allegation is incompetency of counsel, the hearing centers around the testimony of the allegedly incompetent attorney. Challenges to police conduct may require the testimony of the law enforcement officers involved.

If the petitioner establishes his/her case at the *habeas corpus* hearing, the judge has the authority to discharge the inmate. In most cases this means to release the person from jail/prison; in cases challenging prison conditions, it may be an order to improve the deficient conditions or transfer the inmate to an appropriate facility. The inmate may be arrested before leaving the custodial facility if the prosecution intends to refile the charges.

Figure 14-12
Writ of *Habeus Corpus*

Special Proceedings		Rule 3.303

Approved, 9CAO

ORIGINAL - COURT
1ST COPY - CUSTODIAL OFFICER
2ND COPY - TRANSPORT OFFICER

3RD COPY - PROSECUTION
4TH COPY - RETURN

STATE OF MICHIGAN
JUDICIAL DISTRICT
JUDICIAL CIRCUIT

WRIT OF HABEAS CORPUS

CASE NO.

Court address

Court telephone no.

IN THE NAME OF THE PEOPLE OF THE STATE OF MICHIGAN:

TO _____ THE AGENCY OR PERSON HAVING
CUSTODY OF _____
NAME   I.D. no.   Date of birth

☐ To bring prisoner to court in the case of:
People of
V

☐ To inquire into detention/custody of:

YOU ARE ORDERED to:

1. ☐ Answer this writ, stating the authority under which you ☐ restrain the named prisoner. ☐ exercise custody over the minor child.
File your answer with the ☐ court ☐ judge by _____. Date

2. ☐ Deliver the person named in this writ into custody of _____
Name/Title/Agency
for the following purpose: _____
(To testify, for preliminary examination, trial, to be held pending court appearance, etc.)
Immediately after the prisoner completes his/her appearance, the prisoner shall be returned to your custody.

3. ☐ Bring the person named in this writ before the Honorable _____
at _____, on _____ at ____ m.
Location of court   Date   Time
Bring this writ with you.

Clerk of the Court

By: _____

Date

CERTIFICATE OF ALLOWANCE OF WRIT

I, _____ ,P _____ , certify that the above writ of habeas corpus
Name of Judge   Bar no.
was allowed by me on _____ , ☐ Fees are allowed in the amount of $ _____.
Date

_____
Judge

MC 203 (11/85)   **WRIT OF HABEAS CORPUS**   MC LA 600.4301 et seq.; MSA 27A.4301 et seq., MCR 3.303, 3.304

Chapter Summary

The appellate process provides an opportunity to correct mistakes made in the trial courts. Rulings on the admissibility of evidence may be reversed if they were raised in a timely fashion at trial. It is rare for an appellate court to reverse a conviction due to insufficient evidence unless no testimony was presented about at least one element of the crime: decisions on the credibility of the witnesses are left to the jury.

Direct appeals are based on the record of what occurred at pretrial hearings and the trial. A notice of appeal is filed with the trial court. The attorney for the appellant reads the clerk's and reporter's transcripts to find issues, researches relevant law, and prepares the appellant's opening brief. The opposing party's attorney prepares the respondent's opening brief, which addresses each issue raised by the appellant. The appellant may file a reply brief to respond to statements in the respondent's brief. Oral arguments are heard and the judges write an opinion in the case. Opinions that appear in the officially published reports become precedent for future cases.

A defendant who cannot afford to hire an attorney has a constitutional right to have one appointed to represent him/her through the end of the direct appeal. This includes obtaining copies of necessary documents, such as the clerk's and reporter's transcripts, and waiving filing fees for the appeal. An appointed attorney who wishes to withdraw must file a brief, discussing all possible issues, before being dismissed from the case. Another attorney must be appointed to complete the appeal if the court believes there are any non-frivolous issues.

In some states appeals may be taken before the trial starts. This usually occurs when there are serious legal questions regarding dismissal of the charges (or failure to do so), constitutionality of a search, or appropriate use of *Miranda* warnings. Some states allow the defendant to enter a guilty plea but retain the right to appeal search and seizure issues. Failure of the judge to honor a plea bargain agreed to by the defense and prosecution may also be appealed.

The appeal that normally follows immediately after the conviction is called a direct appeal. It is limited to items that can be determined by reading the transcripts of the case. *Habeas corpus* must be used if it is necessary to call witnesses. Time limits are usually set for direct appeals, and if no action is taken the defendant is deemed to have waived this right. Most appeals to higher courts, such as the state's highest court or the United

States Supreme Court, are considered discretionary appeals because the judges have the discretion to grant or deny requests for an appeal to be heard.

Death penalty cases are frequently an exception to the normal appellate rules: many state statutes designate the state's highest court as the court to hear the direct appeal if the death penalty was given by the trial judge. The court may be required to consider whether the death penalty was imposed in what appears to be an arbitrary manner. Proportionality may be considered—that is, whether the current case represents as serious an offense as other cases in which the death penalty has been affirmed.

A defendant who appeals waives double jeopardy and submits to a second trial unless the conviction is reversed for insufficient evidence. Prosecution appeals cannot reverse acquittals, but they can prevent the rulings of a lower-court judge from becoming established precedent. The prosecution can seek discretionary review when the direct appeal results in the reversal of a conviction, and if successful the original conviction will again become effective. Pretrial appeals by either side do not affect double jeopardy: charges that have been dismissed can be refiled and evidence that was ruled inadmissible can be admitted if the appellate court rules the lower court acted incorrectly.

The United States Supreme Court hears most of its criminal cases via writs of *certiorari*. The party seeking review presents a petition, trying to persuade the justices to hear constitutional issues in the case. At least four justices must vote in favor of considering the case. Once the writ is granted, briefs are filed by both sides and other parties, called *amicus curiae*, who are interested in the case. Formal oral arguments are heard. The opinion normally is issued during the term in which the oral arguments were heard.

Habeas corpus is used to challenge illegal confinement ranging from pretrial detention due to false arrest to inhumane prison conditions, which violate the Eighth Amendment. The initial petition must state sufficient facts to show that a legal issue is involved. If so, a writ of *habeas corpus* is issued, directing the custodial authorities to bring the petitioner to court for a full hearing. In recent years rules enacted by the United States Congress have become more restrictive in order to prevent state inmates from using *habeas corpus* to relitigate Fourth Amendment issues that were previously decided in state courts.

Study Questions

Study Questions

1. Check the laws of your state and explain
   a. the time limit after a conviction for filing a direct appeal.
   b. how the defendant's appellate attorney is selected.
   c. how much time the appellant is given to file an opening brief.
   d. how much time the respondent is given to file an opening brief.
   e. what time limits are imposed on reply briefs.
   f. when oral arguments are held.
   g. what, if any, time limits apply to issuing an opinion in the case.

2. Check the rules for your local court and explain
   a. what court hears pretrial appeals:
      1. felony cases
      2. misdemeanor cases
      3. other grounds for determining the appropriate court
   b. what documents are required for pretrial appeals.
   c. what court hears appeals from misdemeanor convictions.
   d. what documents are required for a misdemeanor appeal.
   e. what court hears appeals from felony convictions.
   f. what documents are required for a felony appeal.

3. If possible, go to oral arguments before your local appellate court. Prepare a report on one case you heard argued. The report should describe
   a. the charges.
   b. the facts of the case.
   c. the legal issues raised.
   d. the oral arguments by the attorneys.
   e. the interaction between the justices and appellate attorneys.

4. Check the laws in your state and describe how an appeal is taken to the state's highest court.
   a. How does a defendant petition the high court for a hearing?
   b. How many justices must vote to accept the case?
   c. If the case is accepted, is an attorney appointed to present the case to the high court?
   d. What time limits apply to preparing briefs by each side?
   e. Where are oral arguments held?
   f. Are there time restrictions on oral arguments? If so, what are they?
   g. Are there time restrictions on how soon the opinion must be issued after oral arguments? If so, what are they?

5. Check the laws in your state regarding *habeas corpus.*
   a. What forms or other paperwork requirements apply to filing a petition for writ of *habeas corpus?*
   b. Which court reviews these petitions?
   c. Are there restrictions on the types of cases that can be heard via *habeas corpus?* If so, explain.
   d. How long does the respondent have to reply to the petition?
   e. How soon after filing the reply is a hearing held on the petition?
   f. How does a state inmate file a *habeas corpus* petition in your local federal court?

True or False Questions

1. A defendant who does not take a direct appeal after being convicted waives the right to take it at a later time.
2. The prosecution files the first brief in a direct appeal.
3. The Sixth Amendment right to appointed counsel does not apply during appeals.
4. Appeals are not allowed while the case is pending in the trial court.
5. Appeals are not allowed when the defendant enters a guilty plea.
6. A direct appeal is restricted to issues previously raised in the case.
7. States are free to design separate appellate procedures for defendants who have been sentenced to death.
8. A defendant, who wishes to have his/her case heard by the U.S. Supreme Court, must file a petition for writ of *certiorari.*
9. For a case to be heard by the U.S. Supreme Court, the justices must vote unanimously to hear the case.
10. Evidence not introduced at trial can be considered at the hearing on a writ of *habeas corpus.*

Chapter 15

Corrections

Outline

Key Terms

boot camp
conditional discharges
conditions of probation
day fine
death warrant
general deterrence
halfway houses
ignition interlock devices
incapacitation
informal probation

intensive probation
Interstate Agreement
  on Supervision of
  Probationers and Parolees
Interstate Corrections
  Compact
preliminary revocation
  hearing
probation
rehabilitation

retribution
return on death warrant
revocation hearing
sexually violent
  predator laws
specific deterrence
suspended sentences
technical violation

Learning Objectives

Learning Objectives

After reading this chapter, the student will be able to

- Explain four rationales for punishing convicted criminals.
- Explain the factors a judge considers when placing a person on probation.
- Describe at least five common conditions placed on probationers.
- Describe the procedures that must be complied with to revoke probation.
- Explain how parole dates are established and changed.
- Explain how inmates accumulate good time and how it can be lost.
- Describe the inmate's due process rights at jail or prison disciplinary hearings.
- Explain how parole functions.
- Describe what occurs at a parole revocation hearing.
- Describe three recent innovations in corrections.

There are many legal procedures that must be followed after the defendant begins serving his/her sentence. Due process must be satisfied if probation or parole is revoked. In some circumstances a hearing must be held prior to imposition of punishment for violation of prison rules. The procedures followed prior to an execution must follow rigid legal guidelines. Special procedures have been instituted in many states to keep convicted violent sexual predators from being returned to the community.

15-1 Rationales for Corrections

The criminal justice system revolves around the concept that a person can control his/her behavior and those that do not conform to the criminal law should be punished. The type of punishment imposed varies with the severity of the offense and the level of the defendant's blame-worthiness, but it also depends on the reasons for punishment. Four main rationales are used—retribution, deterrence, rehabilitation, and incapacitation—sometimes more than one of these is in use at the same time. Other considerations, such as the high cost of incarceration and prison overcrowding, also play important roles in these decisions. Historical trends can be discerned; no one rationale stays in fashion. Which ones are currently used is normally determined by the local legislature.

15-1a Retribution

Criminal punishments in primitive societies were usually a family matter: the family of the victim took revenge on the offender. It frequently took a symbolic form, such as the proverbial "eye for an eye, and a tooth for a tooth." For more serious offenses **retribution** was carried out at the tribal level. As societies became more civilized, the government assumed the function of retribution: it imposed punishment for the injuries inflicted on innocent people. In doing so it prohibited individual members of society from extracting their own vengeance. The victims' rights movement, which has emerged in recent years, is a modified version of retribution: the victim is entitled to have the criminal punished.

15-1b Deterrence

Deterrence is based on the concept that punishment will deter criminal activity. It has two interrelated concepts: specific deterrence and general deterrence. **Specific deterrence** punishes a person in order to deter that individual. In other words, if John Jones is sent to jail for petty theft, he is unlikely to steal again. If it is determined that the individual will respond to less severe punishment—for example, probation—then it is not necessary to incarcerate the defendant.

General deterrence punishes a person as an example to society. There needs to be some reason to believe that others would be deterred by the punishment imposed. Publicizing the punishment may serve this purpose. For example, John Jones is sent to jail for petty theft as an example to all thieves, in hopes that it will deter them from stealing. This approach would find it necessary to punish John Jones for being a thief, even if it could be determined that he would never steal again, if others would interpret a lenient sentence as an indication that they could get away with stealing.

15-1c Rehabilitation

Rehabilitation is based on the idea that the defendant's behavior can be changed. It usually emphasizes counseling and job training, so that the person will not want to commit additional crimes and will be able to be gainfully employed. It places heavy reliance on psychologists and other counselors. Rehabilitation is frequently linked to indeterminate sentencing, so that the inmate can be kept in custody until he/she displays appropriate behavior and attitudes. It is more likely to be used in prisons than jails because of the length of time needed to effect these changes. A diagnostic study is usually done shortly after the defendant enters prison to determine psychological problems the defendant may have, as well as job skills that are needed. Inmates who want to become productive members of society can benefit from this. On the other hand, many inmates become savvy to what is expected and quickly learn to say and do what their counselors want in order to gain early release. Inmates who do not want to be rehabilitated and refuse to cooperate serve the longest sentences.

15-1d Incapacitation

Incapacitation is based on the idea that keeping criminals off the streets makes society safer. It does not pretend to change long-term behavior; nor does it consider whether the sentence will deter crime. Studies of individuals who support themselves by robbery, burglary, and theft show that hundreds of crimes can be prevented by keeping these offenders in prison for long terms. The logic of incapacitation does not fit cases in which the defendant was convicted for an isolated offense and is not likely to commit other crimes.

15-2 Probation

Probation, suspended sentences, and **conditional discharges** involve releasing the convicted offender into the community, frequently without serving time in jail. For convenience in this chapter, all three will be referred to as "probation." Some defendants are released with little or no supervision, sometimes called **informal probation;** others report regularly to probation officers. A condition of all of these releases is that the person commit no new crimes. A new offense, or a violation of other conditions placed on the release, will result in incarceration without a new trial.

Most state sentencing laws are written so that the judge has the option to place the defendant on probation unless the code section contains specific language restricting this discretion. This allows the judge to consider both the defendant's background and the current offense when deciding whether probation should be imposed. Figure 15-1 lists the factors that are typically considered. Some code sections prohibit the use of probation. An intermediate approach appears in some codes: the statute states that probation is prohibited except in unusual circumstances where the interest of justice would be served by not incarcerating the defendant. Prior to granting probation under one of these laws, the judge usually must state on the record what the unusual circumstances are that justify placing the defendant on probation.

Figure 15-1
Factors Considered When Deciding to Place Defendant on Probation

Based on Rule 4.414 of California Rules of Court

Facts relating to the crime, including:

1. The nature, seriousness, and circumstances of the crime as compared to other instances of the same crime.
2. Whether the defendant was armed with or used a weapon.
3. The vulnerability of the victim.
4. Whether the defendant inflicted physical or emotional injury.
5. The degree of monetary loss to the victim.
6. Whether the defendant was an active or passive participant.
7. Whether the crime was committed because of an unusual circumstance, such as great provocation, which is unlikely to recur.
8. Whether the manner in which the crime was carried out demonstrated criminal sophistication or professionalism on the part of the defendant.
9. Whether the defendant took advantage of a position of trust or confidence to commit the crime.

Facts relating to the defendant, including:

1. Prior record of criminal conduct, whether as an adult or a juvenile, including the recency and frequency of prior crimes; and whether the prior record indicates a pattern of regular or increasingly serious criminal conduct.
2. Prior performance on probation or parole and present probation or parole status.
3. Willingness to comply with the terms of probation.
4. Ability to comply with reasonable terms of probation as indicated by the defendant's age, education, health, mental faculties, history of alcohol or other substance abuse, family background and ties, employment and military service history, and other relevant factors.
5. The likely effect of imprisonment on the defendant and his or her dependents.
6. The adverse collateral consequences on the defendant's life resulting from the felony conviction.
7. Whether the defendant is remorseful.
8. The likelihood that if not imprisoned the defendant will be a danger to others.

State law usually specifies the length of probation that a judge may impose. Some states standardize the length of probation, such as one year for misdemeanors and three years for felonies. Others allow the judge to impose probation for any length of time up to the maximum length of incarceration that could have been imposed.

15-2a Conditions of Probation

Probation serves two purposes: it gives the probationer the opportunity to demonstrate that he/she can be rehabilitated while giving the court the authority to impose sanctions without a new trial if the defendant fails to abide by the conditions of probation. In addition to probation's forbidding the commission of new crimes, most probationers are required to comply with a list of rules imposed to assist in rehabilitation. Two legal restrictions apply to imposing the conditions of probation: the condition must be related to rehabilitation and/or supervision of the probationers, and it must be authorized by state law. Figure 15-2 shows a sample list taken from Arkansas statutes. The restrictions, called **conditions of probation,** fall into several general categories: commit no crimes; earn an income and support a family or go to school to learn job skills; participate in a counseling program; avoid persons and places associated with the commission of crimes; and make restitution.

Two more conditions are added in many states: (1) submit to searches and seizures and (2) undergo drug testing. The search and seizure restriction is considered important for detecting criminal activity by the probationer. When these conditions are included, accepting probation is tantamount to waiving Fourth Amendment rights. The main questions regarding this condition are: "Who is authorized to conduct the search?" and "Under what circumstances?" Some states allow only probation officers to conduct these searches. Others permit police officers who encounter probationers in the field to search them. Sometimes a computerized database must be checked prior to the search to verify that the person has the search and seizure condition. Some states require that a police officer have at least a suspicion that the probationer is involved in criminal activity before a search is permitted, unless the probation officer is present. The search and seizure condition usually applies to search of the probationer's residence; some states permit unannounced entry to conduct residential searches, while others do not waive knock notice. It is important for police officers to know the law of the state they work in, so that evidence they find when searching probationers will be admissible in court.

Drug testing usually is made a condition of probation if the conviction was for drug-related charges, the defendant was under the influence of drugs at the time of arrest, or the defendant has a history of drug abuse. Some programs require routine testing at every visit to the probation officer. Others use random testing; some use both. Precautions must be instituted that protect privacy while the urine sample is given, but, at the same time, ensure that the probationer does not submit "clean" urine obtained from a person who does not use drugs. Careful labeling of urine specimens and accurate testing are also necessary.

Probationers can be required to pay the cost of supervision and counseling programs that they attend. Repayment of court costs as well as the

Figure 15-2
Conditions of Probation

Based on Arkansas Code 5-4-303

(a) If the court suspends imposition of sentence on a defendant or places him on probation, it shall attach such conditions as are reasonably necessary to assist the defendant in leading a law-abiding life.

(b) The court shall provide as an express condition of every suspension or probation that the defendant not commit an offense punishable by imprisonment during the period of suspension or probation.

(c) If the court suspends imposition of sentence on a defendant or places him on probation, as a condition of its order, it may require that the defendant:

(1) Support his dependents and meet his family responsibilities;

(2) Work faithfully at suitable employment;

(3) Pursue a prescribed secular course of study or vocational training designed to equip him for suitable employment;

(4) Undergo available medical or psychiatric treatment and enter and remain in a specified institution when required for that purpose;

(5) Participate in a community-based rehabilitative program or work-release program which meets the minimum state standards for certification and for which the court may impose reasonable fees or assessments on the defendant to be used in support of said programs;

(6) Refrain from frequenting unlawful or designated places or consorting with designated persons;

(7) Have no firearms in his possession;

(8) Make restitution or reparation to aggrieved parties, in an amount he can afford to pay, for the actual loss or damage caused by his offense;

(9) Post a bond, with or without surety, conditioned on the performance of prescribed conditions; and

(10) Satisfy any other conditions reasonably related to the rehabilitation of the defendant and not unduly restrictive of his liberty or incompatible with his freedom of conscience.

* * * * *

(e) If the court places a defendant on probation, as a condition of its order, it may require that the defendant:

(1) Report as directed to the court or the probation officer and permit the probation officer to visit him at his place of employment or elsewhere;

(2) Remain within the jurisdiction of the court unless granted permission to leave by the court or the probation officer; and

(3) Answer all reasonable inquiries by the court or the probation officer and promptly notify the court or probation officer of any change in address or employment.

---

expenses incurred for a public defender can be added. Installment payments are frequently established to facilitate collection of these fees. Equal protection prohibits incarceration for failure to pay these expenses if the person is legitimately unable to pay. Prior to revoking probation because complete payment has not been made on time, the court must inquire into the facts to establish whether the probationer has made good faith efforts to do so.

Jail can be made a condition of probation. For example, the sentence might be one year probation with the condition that the defendant serve 30 days in jail. When this is done, the defendant usually serves the jail term first and then is placed on probation. In most states, judges retain the discretion to permit the jail time to be served as weekends or in some other manner. Mandatory jail as a condition of probation, meaning that the judge is required to impose the jail term, has become a popular approach to sentencing in driving under the influence and spousal battery cases, particularly if the defendant has already been placed on probation for a prior conviction for the same crime.

The probation department is usually organized at the same level as the court of general jurisdiction (i.e., the county or similar political boundaries). When a defendant is convicted for a crime committed in the county, the case is normally supervised by a probation officer employed by that county. The conditions of probation frequently require the probationer to obtain permission before leaving the jurisdiction. Juveniles may need a transfer to another county because their parents are moving there. Employment opportunities, family responsibilities, and other situations may make it desirable for adult probationers to move to another part of the state. State laws or administrative regulations usually specify a procedure to permit probation officers in another part of the state to supervise the case. For example, New York Criminal Procedure Law §410.80 allows the judge to designate any other probation department in the state to handle the case. Under this law the sentencing court has the option to retain jurisdiction over the case for revocation proceedings or to delegate it to the court where the case is transferred. The laws usually specify which county is responsible for the expenses incurred in supervising the probationer.

Some states permit early termination of probation. For example, Arizona Rule 27.3 permits the judge to terminate probation at any time upon motion of the probation officer or the judge's own motion. A hearing is held after such a motion is made, and the prosecutor has the opportunity to make arguments in favor of continuing probation. If the motion is granted, the probationer is unconditionally discharged in the same manner as if the entire sentence had been served.

A number of states now have specialized courts, such as drug court, that handle only one type of case. Judges in many of these courts take an active role in the case after the sentence is imposed. The defendant frequently must report directly to the judge with progress reports about rehabilitation programs. These judges may appear to assume the role of the probation officer while retaining the authority to revoke probation when violations are proven.

15-2b Supervision of Probationers Who Move Out-of-State

In some cases it may be desirable for the probationer to move out-of-state before the end of his/her sentence. The **Interstate Agreement on Supervision of Probationers and Parolees** is an agreement signed by all 50 states, the District of Columbia, Puerto Rico, the Virgin Islands, and the United States Congress (for federal probationers). For ease of discussing this interstate agreement in this chapter, the jurisdiction in which the original conviction occurred will be called the "sending state" and the one where the person wishes to be transferred will be called the "receiving state"; "probation" will be used, although the interstate agreement applies to both probation and parole; and "probationer" will be used to refer to both persons on probation and parole.

The interstate agreement permits transfer if the probationer is a resident of, or has family residing in, the receiving state and can obtain employment there or if the receiving state accepts supervision of the person asking for the transfer. The receiving state has the right to investigate the probationer's proposed home and prospective employment before accepting a transfer. Once a person has been accepted, supervision will be done under the same standards as those that apply to probationers who were convicted in the receiving state.

Officers of the sending state have the right to arrest their probation violators in the receiving state. The decision of the sending state to revoke probation is not reviewable by the receiving state. The right to challenge extradition is waived, but the probationer still has the right to a full revocation hearing. The receiving state has the right to block the return of the probationer to the sending state if there are any criminal charges pending against the probationer or if he/she is suspected of having committed a crime within the receiving state. The probationer must be returned after prosecution is complete and/or the probationer has served his/her sentence in the receiving state.

15-2c Revocation Hearings for Probationers

Probation can be revoked for a violation of any condition placed on the defendant. These fall in two categories: an arrest for another crime or an arrest for a violation of a condition that is not itself criminal (sometimes called a **technical violation**). The probation officer usually has authority to arrest for any violation of the conditions of probation. He/she may also obtain a warrant for the arrest of the violator; such warrants can usually be served by both probation officers and police. A typical law authorizing arrest for violation of probation is shown in Figure 15-3.

Figure 15-3
Arrest for Violation of Probation

Based on Connecticut Penal Code Section 531-32(a)

1. *Arrest based on warrant issued by judge:*
   - At any time during the period of probation or conditional discharge, the court or any judge thereof may issue a warrant for the arrest of a defendant for violation of any of the conditions of probation or conditional discharge, or may issue a notice to appear to answer to a charge of such violation, which notice shall be personally served upon the defendant.
   - Any such warrant shall authorize all officers named therein to return the defendant to the custody of the court or to any suitable detention facility designated by the court.
   - Whenever a defendant has, in the judgment of such defendant's probation officer, violated the conditions of such defendant's probation, the probation officer may, in lieu of having such defendant returned to court for proceedings in accordance with this section, place such defendant in the zero-tolerance drug supervision program established pursuant to section 53a-39d.
   - Whenever a sexual offender, as defined in section 54-260, has violated the conditions of such person's probation by failing to notify such person's probation officer of any change of such person's residence address, as required by said section, such probation officer may notify any police officer that such person has, in such officer's judgment, violated the conditions of such person's probation and such notice shall be sufficient warrant for the police officer to arrest such person and return such person to the custody of the court or to any suitable detention facility designated by the court.

2. *Warrantless arrest by probation officer or upon request of probation officer:*
   - Any probation officer may arrest any defendant on probation without a warrant or may deputize any other officer with power to arrest to do so by giving such other officer a written statement setting forth that the defendant has, in the judgment of the probation officer, violated the conditions of the defendant's probation.
     - Such written statement, delivered with the defendant by the arresting officer to the official in charge of any correctional center or other place of detention, shall be sufficient warrant for the detention of the defendant.
     - After making such an arrest, such probation officer shall present to the detaining authorities a similar statement of the circumstances of violation.
   - Provisions regarding release on bail of persons charged with a crime shall be applicable to any defendant arrested under the provisions of this section.
   - Upon such arrest and detention, the probation officer shall immediately so notify the court or any judge thereof.

To revoke probation, the violation must be established at a hearing, which is usually held before a judicial officer. In *Gagnon v. Scarpelli* (411 U.S. 778, 36 L.Ed. 2d 656, 93 S.Ct. 1756 [1973]), the Supreme Court held that due process rights apply to the revocation of probation. In this context, due process does not encompass all of the rights afforded the accused at a criminal trial. The Court viewed a two-phase system as adequately protecting the defendant's rights. A **preliminary revocation hearing** must be held soon after the person is arrested for violating a condition of probation, unless he/she is legally in custody on other grounds, such as being charged with a new crime. The Court did not set specific deadlines, such as within 48 hours, but state law may provide limits. The probationer must be given notice of the time and place of the hearing, as well as what conditions of probation allegedly have been violated. The defendant has the right to be present at the hearing, to confront witnesses, and to present evidence on his/her own behalf. Normal rules of evidence do not apply to these hearings, and both sides can introduce testimony and documents that normally would not be allowed at trial. Unlike a trial, the right to confront and cross-examine may be restricted in some situations; the Court used the example of a hearing officer determining that the informant would be subjected to risk of harm if his/her identity were disclosed as a reason to deny confrontation and cross-examination. At the end of the preliminary hearing, the fact finder must make a written report on the evidence presented and decisions made. The basic standard for detaining a person in custody is that there was probable cause that a probation violation occurred. In *Pennsylvania Board of Probation & Parole v. Scott* (524 U.S. 357, 141 L.Ed. 2d 344, 118 S.Ct. 2014 [1998]), the United States Supreme Court ruled that the exclusionary rule does not apply to parole revocation hearings (and by inference probation revocation hearings). This means that evidence obtained in violation of the Fourth Amendment is admissible at these hearings.

The preliminary revocation hearing focuses on the facts showing a violation; the probation **revocation hearing** has a wider purpose: it must review the facts and determine whether probation should be revoked. The same basic procedural safeguards apply: notice of charge, notice of time and place of hearing, right to present evidence, and confrontation and cross-examination unless the judge determines there is a valid reason to limit it. The key difference is that the judge may conclude that a violation occurred but the defendant's rehabilitation would be best served by permitting him/her to remain on probation. It is common for a judge to require the defendant to serve a short time in jail before reinstating probation. Figure 15-4 shows a state law providing for revocation hearings that comply with current Supreme Court decisions.

Figure 15-4
Probation Revocation Hearing

Based on Arkansas Statutes 5-4-310

Preliminary hearing shall be held to determine whether there is reasonable cause to believe that there has been a violation of a condition of probation except when probationer has been found guilty in an independent criminal proceeding or the revocation hearing is held promptly after arrest:

1. Hearing is conducted by court having original jurisdiction to try criminal matters as soon as practicable after arrest and reasonably near the place of the alleged violation or arrest.
2. Defendant must be given prior notice of time and place of preliminary hearing, the purpose of the hearing, and the conditions of probation he/she is alleged to have violated.
3. Defendant shall have right to hear and controvert evidence against him/her and to offer evidence in his/her own behalf but court, for good cause, may refuse to allow confrontation. Court may permit introduction of any relevant evidence of the alleged violation, including letters, affidavits, and other documentary evidence, regardless of its admissibility under the rules governing the admission of evidence in a criminal trial.
4. If judge presiding over hearing finds that there is reasonable cause to believe that the defendant has violated a condition of probation, it shall order the defendant held for further revocation proceedings before the court that originally placed defendant on probation: If court does not find reasonable cause, it shall order the defendant released from custody but such release does not bar the court that imposed probation from holding a hearing on the alleged violation.
5. Court holding preliminary revocation hearing shall prepare and furnish to the court that placed defendant on probation a summary of the hearing, including the responses of the defendant and the substance of the documents and evidence given in support of revocation.

Revocation hearing must be held prior to revoking probation:

1. Revocation hearing shall be conducted by court that placed defendant on probation within a reasonable time, not exceeding 60 days, after the defendant's arrest.
2. Defendant shall be given prior written notice of the time and place of the revocation hearing, the purpose of the hearing, and the condition of probation allegedly violated.
3. Defendant has same right to hear and controvert evidence as at preliminary revocation hearing (Item 3 above).
4. If probation is revoked, the court shall prepare and furnish to the defendant a written statement of the evidence relied on and the reasons for revoking probation.

Some states have a procedure whereby the judge places the defendant on probation without sentencing him/her. The defendant is sentenced only if probation is violated. When this type of procedure is used, the hearing at which the sentence is imposed has all the procedural safeguards of a sentencing hearing held after the verdict comes in; the defendant has a Sixth Amendment right to be represented by counsel, and the government must provide one at no charge for indigent defendants. The Supreme

Court concluded that appointing an attorney is ordinarily not necessary at the preliminary and final revocation hearings in cases where the defendant has already been sentenced. The judge should review each case involving indigents and appoint an attorney if the following factors indicate legal counsel is needed: cases in which the probationer denies committing the alleged violation or asserts that there were substantial reasons justifying what was done or mitigating guilt; complex cases whose facts are difficult to develop or present; and cases involving probationers who are not capable of speaking effectively. Many states now appoint counsel automatically for the poor in revocation proceedings, even though the Supreme Court has not required it.

A probationer may leave the state without permission and be arrested for committing a crime or violating probation while in another state. If so, it may be necessary to institute extradition proceedings unless the case was transferred to the state where he/she was arrested under the Interstate Agreement on Supervision of Probationers and Parolees. In these cases the probationer may be tried on the crime committed in the state where he/she was arrested before being returned to face revocation proceedings. Authorities from both states usually discuss the potential consequences of a trial on the new charges versus revocation of probation and decide which best suits the case. If revocation is instituted, the preliminary revocation hearing is held in the state where the new offense occurred to facilitate the presentation of evidence on the violation.

15-3 Jail and Prison Sentences

In many states the judge sentences the defendant to serve time in prison but leaves decisions on which facility will be used to the correctional authorities (referred to in this section as the state's department of corrections). The department of corrections normally transfers all new inmates to a diagnostic unit, where interviews are conducted and necessary tests performed to determine any special needs of the inmates. Classification is done according to security risks and other criteria and assignments to appropriate prison facilities are made, unless state law or regulations provide otherwise. Inmates may normally be reclassified based on their behavior while in custody. Transfers to another facility may be made for disciplinary reasons or to avoid overcrowding.

15-3a Good Time

Good time credit is frequently given to inmates who abide by prison rules. The formula used to compute good time is set by either the state legislature or the Department of Corrections. Some states offer one day of good time credit for every two days in custody. How good time is used is established by law: it usually reduces the amount of time spent in custody by either shortening the sentence or making the inmate eligible for parole sooner. Other incentives, such as credits for inmates who work, go to school, or participate in medical research while in custody, are used in some states.

15-3b Disciplinary Hearings

Hearings are not required prior to disciplining an inmate if the relevant statute gives correctional administrators discretion to make a choice, such as assigning an inmate to a specific prison or cell block. A hearing is required to satisfy due process if the disciplinary action will inevitably affect the duration of the inmate's sentence. Regulations must be posted for inmates to read that specify what conduct will trigger disciplinary action and what punishment will be given. For example, a rule might prohibit assaults on fellow inmates and state that up to 90 days of good time can be lost for a single incident if the misbehavior could be prosecuted as a misdemeanor. Loss of good time is an administrative procedure and provides no double jeopardy protection against criminal charges for offenses committed in custody.

Emergency measures, such as the transfer of inmates immediately after a riot, may be done without a hearing, but punishment can be imposed only after a hearing. The Supreme Court in *Wolff v. McDonnell* (418 U.S. 539, 41 L.Ed. 2d 935, 94 S.Ct. 2963 [1974]), established minimum procedural safeguards for prison disciplinary hearings. Written notice of the alleged violation must be given at least 24 hours before the disciplinary hearing. In an effort to accommodate the security needs of jails and prisons, the Court held that the inmate should be allowed to call witnesses and present documentary evidence in his/her defense as long as doing so is not unduly hazardous to institutional safety or correctional goals. Prison authorities have the right to refuse to call witnesses who may create a risk of reprisal or undermine authority, as well as to limit access to other inmates for the purpose of collecting statements or compiling documentary evidence. Correctional officers who submit the charges do not have to testify in the presence of the inmate. Inmates have no constitutional right to cross-examine witnesses.

Hearing officers at the disciplinary proceeding need to be impartial. The Court permits the use of correctional officers for this purpose as long as they are not involved in the incident the inmate is being disciplined for. Their decisions must not be arbitrary. The fact finder is required to make a written statement regarding evidence relied upon and the reasons for the disciplinary action taken. Inmates have no right to have an attorney present at disciplinary hearings, even if they can afford to hire one. Assistance in the form of a fellow inmate or staff person should be provided for illiterate inmates or where the complexity of the issues makes it unlikely that the inmate will be able to adequately collect and present evidence.

15-3c Interstate Corrections Compacts

Sometimes it is desirable to transfer an inmate to a facility in another state. Two common reasons for this are overcrowding of one state's prisons and the need to send an inmate to a specialized rehabilitation or treatment facility, including mental health institutions, not available in the state. The **Interstate Corrections Compact**—and some regional compacts, such as the Western Interstate Corrections Compact—were designed to make it easier for states to transfer prisoners. Inmates sent to another state remain within the jurisdiction of the court where the conviction was entered, and that state has the right to demand their return. The sending state is financially responsible for the expenses of the inmate. The receiving state must provide regular written reports on the inmates in its care. When it is time to release the inmate, he/she must be returned to the sending state, unless the inmate agrees to be released at another location.

The Interstate Corrections Compact makes no mention of inmate consent to the transfer. The Supreme Court reviewed the case of an inmate who was convicted in Hawaii and was transferred to another state. It determined that the language of the Hawaii statute left sufficient discretion with the administrators so that a hearing was not constitutionally required. Some states have made consent a prerequisite to an out-of-state transfer. For example, California Penal Code §11191 requires that the inmate be informed of his/her rights and be given the opportunity for a private consultation with his/her attorney or a public defender before giving consent; it also gives the inmate the right to revoke consent at any time after five years has elapsed.

15-3d Interstate Agreement on Detainers

An inmate may be wanted by authorities in another state due to an outstanding warrant, violation of probation or parole, or escape from jail or prison. The Interstate Agreement on Detainers permits a hold to be placed on the inmate, so that the other state may take the inmate into custody before he/she is released from custody. These holds are usually grounds to deny parole. The interstate agreement allows the inmate to request that the out-of-state charges be adjudicated prior to his/her scheduled release from custody. Section 2-1, "Peace Officers," discusses these procedures in detail.

15-3e Pardons and Commuted Sentences

Most state governors have authority to grant pardons to convicted persons and to commute sentences. These acts are usually based on two distinctly different grounds: the defendant was wrongly convicted or the defendant has led an exemplary life since conviction. The parole board is frequently directed to forward case files to the governor if it deems a pardon appropriate. Individual inmates may submit their own cases. State law usually establishes procedures that must be followed. Pardons based on living an exemplary life usually require the person to wait at least 10 years after release from custody before applying.

15-4 Parole

Parole in many ways resembles probation. It releases an offender into the community under supervision, but the freedom can be rescinded without a conviction for committing a new crime. Unlike probation, parole comes at the end of a prison sentence. The inmate normally has to earn the right to be released on parole. Failure to satisfactorily complete parole usually results in a return to prison to complete the time remaining on the term. The process of parole, from the determination of release dates through the revocation of parole, is usually administered by the department of corrections or another state agency, rather than the courts.

15-4a Eligibility

State law establishes when an inmate will be released and whether or not the inmate will be on parole. A variety of approaches is used. Determinate sentencing states may impose a fixed length of parole, such as one year, at the end of every sentence. Parole is more likely to be used in conjunction with indeterminate sentencing, with behavior in prison being considered when setting a release date; when released, the inmate may be on parole for the entire time remaining on the original sentence. Some states have abolished parole.

State law establishes minimum eligibility for parole, such as first offenders must serve one third of the maximum sentence, and one half of the maximum sentence must be served by second offenders. State law indicates whether good time credits are applied when determining the earliest date an inmate is eligible for parole.

Occasionally parole is granted for humanitarian reasons. State law may provide detailed guidance for the parole board, or it may be left to the board's discretion. Some states give the governor the power to grant parole in special situations. The most common reason to grant this type of parole is terminal illness.

15-4b Hearings to Set Release Dates

Setting a parole date is an administrative function. In states with indeterminate sentencing, release dates are usually set by an agency, referred to in this chapter as the parole board, which is separate from the staff of the prison. The inmate is normally given an opportunity to appear before the parole board and make a statement; disciplinary records and other staff input are also considered. Some states permit victims, or families of victims who died as a result of the crime, to submit material for consideration and/or to appear and make a statement. The trial judge and prosecutor may also be given an opportunity to input information for consideration by the parole board. Predictions of the inmate's behavior after release are also considered. For example, laws of Connecticut (§54-125), Massachusetts (127 §130), and other states require the parole board to consider two factors: (1) if there is a reasonable probability that the inmate will live and remain at liberty without violating the law and (2) whether release is compatible with the welfare of society. If parole is denied, the inmate is usually entitled to a new hearing; for example, state law may require a hearing every two years.

Once the parole date has been set, it can still be revoked if the inmate does not maintain a good disciplinary record or if the parole board discovers additional evidence indicating that parole is not appropriate. The Supreme Court has viewed the setting of parole dates as a discretionary function. As a result of this distinction, there is no right to have a hearing and to present witnesses if a parole date is revoked or changed. Decisions to revoke the parole date cannot be arbitrary. A few states allow the governor to intervene to block the release of an inmate from custody. This type of intervention may be restricted to a few specified offenses, such as murder and forcible rape.

15-4c Conditions of Parole

When a person is released on parole, he/she remains under the jurisdiction of the state agency that operates the prisons. This gives the state the right to dictate the conditions of release and to require the parolee to return to prison if the conditions are violated. One of the most common restrictions relates to residence. The parolee may be required to live in one county;

changes can be made, but only with the consent of the parole officer. The right to control where the parolee lives is also used to place the inmate in a halfway house immediately after release from prison. **Halfway houses** are residential facilities in the community which provide a higher level of supervision for parolees than a parole officer can give. Parolees usually stay for one to six months, during which time they look for employment and begin jobs. Drug testing, curfews, and other conditions may be attached to living at the facility. Inmates usually pay a fee to help cover the cost of operating the halfway house.

Other conditions of parole are usually imposed to assist the inmate's return to society. The universal one is that the parolee commit no new crimes. Many conditions are similar to the conditions of probation discussed in section 15-2a, "Conditions of Probation." The parolee is required to meet regularly with a parole officer to discuss progress. Gainful employment or satisfactory progress in vocational training is normally required. Associating with known criminals and habituating places where undesirable people congregate are usually forbidden. Drug tests may be required; excessive alcohol consumption is prohibited.

Some states now refuse to permit rapists, child molesters, and some other criminals to be paroled in the area where the crime victim resides. Some communities have successfully petitioned the parole board to deny permission for a parolee to move to their area, even though the offense did not occur there. Requiring the department of corrections to notify the victim when the inmate is released is also becoming common.

15-4d Supervision of Parolees Who Move Out-of-State

Parolees may have a legitimate need to move to another state. The Interstate Agreement on Supervision of Probationers and Parolees establishes the legal framework for this to occur. When the interstate agreement is used, parole supervision is assumed by authorities in the state where the person relocates. See section 15-2b, "Supervision of Probationers Who Move Out-of-State," for a detailed discussion of this interstate agreement.

15-4e Revocation of Parole

A violation of a condition imposed on a parolee can result in revocation of parole. Not all violations are handled in this manner because some violations are minor and do not warrant return to prison. The Supreme Court, in *Morrissey v. Brewer* (408 U.S. 471, 33 L.Ed. 2d 484, 92 S.Ct. 2593 [1972]), established the requirements for parole revocation hearings. In most respects they are the same as those for the preliminary and final revocation hearings discussed in section 15-2c, "Revocation Hearings for

Probationers," for probation violators: notice of charges; notice of date and place of hearing; confront and cross-examine witnesses in most instances; present evidence on own behalf; and written statement by fact finder. A subsequent case clarified that the right to appointed counsel does not automatically apply, but parolees who are unable to represent themselves, due to either illiteracy or the complexity of the case, are entitled to some form of help.

One major difference between probation and parole revocation hearings is the agency that presides over the hearings. Since the parolee is still under the jurisdiction of the department of corrections, the case does not return to court; someone within the Department of Corrections or parole agency makes the decision. The Supreme Court noted that this needs to be an impartial fact finder. The parole officer initiating the revocation proceedings and any supervisors who reviewed the decision before it was finalized do not qualify. Other parole officers may judge whether revocation is justified.

The result of revocation is return to prison, usually to serve out the remainder of the original sentence. A variety of circumstances can alter this outcome. State law must provide for each. If a parolee is arrested on new charges, a determination is usually made whether to revoke parole or prosecute the new offense. Revocation has the advantage of being quicker and having a lighter burden of proof. It is frequently used if the parolee would serve a longer term when returned to prison than he/she would receive for the crime committed while on parole or if there are problems with the evidence in the new case. The lower burden of proof for revocation makes it possible to revoke parole even though there was an acquittal on the new charges. Figure 15-5 on page 363 shows a typical statute dealing with these issues.

15-5 Execution of Death Sentences

Death penalty cases are among the most complex and time-consuming matters handled by the courts. Inmates sentenced to die are usually isolated on death row for many years while the direct appeal is taken and numerous collateral attacks on the conviction are attempted. Clemency petitions are presented to the governor after all tactics using the courts have been exhausted. Assuming none of these are successful, a death warrant is issued. The **death warrant** is the official document, signed by the governor, ordering the execution. The date and approximate time for the execution are specified. After it has been signed by the governor, it is delivered to the head of the Department of Corrections, who also signs it and forwards it to the warden of the prison in which the execution will take

Figure 15-5
Computation of Parolee's Sentence after Revocation of Parole

Based on Massachusetts Statutes 127 §149

Arrest and Detention:

If a permit to be at liberty has been revoked, the parole board may order the arrest of the holder of such permit by any officer qualified to serve civil or criminal process in any county, and order the return of such holder to the prison or jail to which he was originally sentenced. A prisoner who has been so returned to prison or jail shall be detained therein according to the terms of his original sentence.

Computation of Period of Confinement:

- In computing the period of his confinement, the time between the day of his release upon a parole permit and the day of issuance of a parole violation warrant shall be considered as part of the term of his original sentence.
- The time between the day after the issuance of the parole violator warrant until the service of said warrant shall not be considered as any part of the term of his original sentence.
- Service of the parole violation warrant shall be made effective forthwith upon arrest and imprisonment of the parole violator unless he is convicted of commission of a crime or found guilty of violating the conditions of federal or another state's parole or probation, then service of said parole violation warrant shall not be effective until the expiration of any additional sentence by parole or otherwise.
- If the parolee is found not guilty of the additional crimes charged or not guilty of violating the conditions of parole or probation then service of the warrant on the parolee shall be made effective on the date of this issuance of said warrant and the time served by him as a result of the parole violation warrant lodged as a detainer shall be considered as part of the original sentence.
- If the disposition of the new criminal charges or charges of violation of probation or parole is without a finding of guilt, the parole board may retroactively serve the parole violation warrant.
- The provisions of this section shall not be deemed to proclude the board from withdrawing a parole violation warrant at any time. In computing the period of the parolee's confinement, the time between the day after the issuance of the parole violation warrant until the withdrawal of said warrant shall not be considered as any part of the term of the parolee's original sentence.

---

place. If the execution is delayed due to legal maneuvers or other technical problems, a new death warrant must be issued. After the execution, a document, known as the **return on death warrant,** must be completed, stating the exact date and time the execution took place and other details. The return is filed with the court and becomes part of the case file.

Last-minute appeals and stays of execution by federal judges have become very common in death penalty cases. It is therefore imperative that prison staff have absolutely up-to-date records on the status of each legal challenge pending as the scheduled time of execution approaches. Two common law rules also must be noted because they have become part of our legal system. One tradition is that pregnant women cannot be executed. This merely requires postponement of the execution until after the baby is born.

A person must be sane at the time of the execution. This rule apparently was based on the idea that the defendant might provide some information at the last minute that would demonstrate innocence and result in a reprieve. Due to this tradition, it is necessary to have a mental health expert evaluate the inmate's sanity shortly before the execution. If the inmate is not sane, the execution must be postponed. Court proceedings to declare mental incompetence are normally instituted and treatment provided. After the court determines the inmate is again sane, a new death warrant can be sought. Incurable insanity permanently blocks the execution.

The extraordinary number of legal maneuvers by most death row inmates has led some to question the sanity of any inmate who refuses to allow appeals on his/her behalf. As long as the person has been determined to be sane, there is no legal basis for forcing an inmate to permit others who oppose capital punishment to petition the courts on his/her behalf.

15-6 Innovative Sentencing

Correctional administrators and legislators frequently initiate new programs aimed at reducing recidivism, alleviating overcrowding, and/or curtailing the cost of incarceration. Penitentiaries were colonial America's attempt to improve corrections; probation was one of the contributions of the late nineteenth century. More recent additions include electronic monitoring, which was discussed in Chapter 9, and a variety of other alternatives reviewed in Chapter 13 ("three strikes and you're out," "use a gun, go to jail," work furlough, intermittent sentencing, community service orders, and restitution for the victim). This section will briefly cover a few more recent techniques.

Driving under the influence of alcohol (DUI) has gained recognition as a serious social problem. A variety of approaches has been taken, including increasing the fines, requiring the suspension of driver's licenses, and making a short jail sentence a mandatory condition of probation. Requiring convicted DUI defendants to install **ignition interlock devices** is one of the newer approaches for keeping drunk drivers off the roads. The driver must breathe into the interlock device before starting the engine. The car will not start if the sensor in the interlock device detects alcohol above a predetermined percentage. The defendant must pay for the equipment and installation and have it calibrated frequently. Periodic reports to probation officers are also required. Figure 15-6 shows the form used by California courts to order the installation of such devices.

Figure 15-6
Order to Install Ignition Interlock Device

NAME AND ADDRESS OF COURT:	FOR COURT USE ONLY
NAME OF DEFENDANT: STREET ADDRESS: MAILING ADDRESS: CITY AND ZIP CODE: HOME TELEPHONE NO.: WORK TELEPHONE NO.: DATE OF BIRTH: SOCIAL SECURITY NO.: DRIVER'S LICENSE NO.:	
DATE OF COURT ORDER:	CASE NUMBER:
ORDER TO INSTALL IGNITION INTERLOCK DEVICE	

THE COURT ORDERS under Vehicle Code Section ☐ 23246 ☐ 23235

1. Defendant *(name)*: _____ **shall not drive motor vehicle** unless it is equipped with a functioning ignition interlock device.

2. Devices shall be installed on the following vehicles owned or operated by defendant:

   Make   Model   Year   Color   License Plate No.   V.I.N.
   a.
   b.
   c.

3. Installation shall be no later than *(specify date no later than 30 days from date of conviction)*:

4. Defendant shall present this form to the installer at the time of installation.

5. Defendant shall return completed Ignition Interlock Installation Verification form to the ☐ court ☐ probation department no later than *(specify date no later than 30 days from date of conviction)*:

6. Defendant shall take vehicles to the installer for calibration ☐ every 60 days ☐ *(other frequency–specify)*: following the date of installation.

7. ☐ Defendant shall make payments directly to the installer and shall adhere to the following payment plan for installation of the ignition interlock device:

8. Without a court order, the device may not be removed before *(specify date one–three years for § 23246, three–five years (period of probation) for § 23235)*:

9. ☐ Defendant's employer requires defendant to drive a vehicle owned by the employer within the course and scope of defendant's employment. Defendant shall provide the employer with the Notice to Employers of Ignition Interlock Restriction form no later than *(date)*: and keep a copy of the notice in defendant's possession or keep the original or a copy in the employer's vehicle.

10. Defendant shall maintain current insurance and registration on all vehicles owned.

11. Defendant shall surrender his or her driver's license to the court (if driving privilege not suspended or revoked) until proof of installation is submitted to and verified by the ☐ court ☐ probation officer.

12. Defendant shall report on the operation of each ignition interlock device installed to the ☐ court ☐ probation officer at least ☐ once every six months (§ 23246) ☐ once each year (§ 23235) or ☐ *(other greater frequency–specify)*:

13. For proceedings under Vehicle Code section 23235, defendant shall pay a fine of *(specify amount–not more than $1,000 for convictions under Vehicle Code § 23152; not more than $5,000 for convictions under Vehicle Code § 23153, punishable under § 23185 or § 23190)*: $

14. Other *(specify)*:

Date: ▶

_____ JUDGE

Defendant: Call installer within 48 hours of this order to arrange for installation of devices. The court will provide you with a list of certified installers.

Distribution: Court, Probation Department, Defendant   *(Continued on reverse)*

Form approved by the   **ORDER TO INSTALL**   Vehicle Code § 23235 et. seq. and
Judicial Council of California   **IGNITION INTERLOCK DEVICE**   § 23246 et. seq.
ID-100 (New July 1, 1993)   **(Ignition Interlock Device)**

Intensive probation gives the probation officer a reduced caseload, so that more time can be spent with each client. It is usually used for juveniles who are not capable of performing well under normal supervision. The time that the probation officer spends with each client, sometimes as much as 10 hours per week, is designed to accomplish several purposes: provide additional guidance, so that the client will not become a habitual criminal; supervise activities in the community, so that the client will develop contacts with law-abiding people and avoid known criminals; and monitor behavior, so that probation can be revoked and the client placed in custody if it appears that criminal activity is occurring. Reducing caseloads so that this type of supervision can occur increases the cost of probation, but the expense is still considerably less than what incarceration would cost. Success in reducing recidivism also greatly reduces the long-range cost to society.

Boot camp is a recent approach to treating first offenders, particularly juveniles. It is a special jail program, sometimes run by the probation department, which is modeled after military boot camp. Strict discipline, exhausting routines, and an emphasis on personal hygiene and maintenance of the housing areas are stressed. The purpose of boot camp is to instill good habits in offenders and to increase their self-esteem. Pride instilled by hard work will, it is hoped, carry over to their lives outside of custody. As with intensive probation, boot camp is more expensive than traditional jails but is designed to have a greater positive impact on the lives of those who complete the course.

Day fines have been used in England and Europe for more than 20 years. A **day fine** makes the fine proportional to the defendant's income. The purpose of day fines is to make the deterrent value of a fine the same for rich and poor defendants. For example, rather than setting a fine at $100 for everyone, the fine is set at one day's wages; a rich person might pay $500 but a poor person only $20.

15-7 Prevention of the Release of Sexually Violent Predators

The correctional system has authority over the offender until his/her sentence has been served. Some offenders, particularly child molesters, still pose a serious threat to the public if released. **Sexually violent predator laws** are designed to provide a mechanism to prevent these dangerous inmates from being returned to the community. The Supreme Court approved this type of procedure (*Kansas v. Hendricks*, 521 U.S. 346, 138 L.Ed. 2d 501, 117 S.Ct. 2017 [1997]). Some state laws apply to both convicted sex offenders and some who escaped the justice system; for example, the original Kansas law applied to violent sex offenders if (1) convicted and a prison sentence was served; (2) never convicted because he/she was found incompetent to stand trial; (3) acquitted based on not guilty by reason of insanity; and (4) found not guilty because of a mental disease or defect (Kan.Stat.Ann. §59-29a03(a), §22-3221).

Sexually violent predator laws are complex because they must protect due process rights. Some states apply them only to crimes against young children. Definitions must clearly state which sex crimes are covered, the level of violence, and any other prerequisites (such as committing two or more offenses within the past 10 years); terms may be defined in ways that are unique to these proceedings. These statutes must be designed to protect the public; in most cases double jeopardy prevents their use for punishment. Criteria must be established that demonstrate that the person currently poses a danger to others. This may be based on a different clinical diagnosis than the mental health system normally uses to commit a patient. For example, the Kansas law reviewed by the Supreme Court used the following definitions:

> A "sexually violent predator" is any person who has been convicted of, or charged with, a sexually violent offense and who suffers from a mental abnormality or personality disorder which makes the person likely to engage in the predatory acts of sexual violence (Kan.Stat.Ann. §59-29a02[a]).

> A "mental abnormality" is a congenital or acquired condition affecting the emotional or volitional capacity which predisposes the person to commit sexually violent offenses in a degree constituting such person a menace to the health and safety of others (Kan.Stat.Ann. §59-29a02[b]).

The goal of sexually violent predator laws is to complete the legal process required to commit the inmate to a mental hospital before his/her scheduled release date from prison. A full court hearing must be held to determine if the defendant qualifies for civil commitment. This implies the standard due process rights of notice and a hearing, including calling witnesses on one's own behalf and cross-examining witnesses who testify for the opposing side. Although civil, many of the laws now in existence mandate proof beyond a reasonable doubt and appoint counsel to represent indigent inmates.

Involuntary confinement in a mental hospital requires frequent reviews, and the patient must be released if he/she is no longer dangerous to him-/herself or others. Sexually violent predator laws must observe the same considerations. Frequently they authorize confinement for a specific period, such as two years, and authorities can renew the petition at the end of that time in order to block release if a person is still dangerous. On the other hand, the patient can request a hearing and be released once there is sufficient evidence that he/she no longer poses a threat to society.

Chapter Summary

Punishing convicted offenders is based on four rationales: retribution, deterrence (both specific and general), rehabilitation, and incapacitation. A combination of these is probably in use in your state today.

Probation was designed to give offenders a second chance. It is now widely used in both misdemeanor and felony cases. A person who is placed on probation must agree to comply with the conditions the court places on his/her release. The Interstate Agreement on Supervision of Probationers and Parolees can be used to transfer a case to another state if a person under supervision has a valid reason to move there.

Violation of the conditions of probation can result in the offenders serving time in jail. Probation cannot be revoked without formal hearings to determine whether the probationer committed the alleged offense and, if so, whether revocation is merited. Minimum due process rights for a hearing to revoke probation require a hearing shortly after the probationer is taken into custody; notice of alleged violation as well as time and place where the hearing will be held; the presentation of evidence of violation and an opportunity to cross-examine witnesses in most cases; the right to present evidence on one's own behalf; and an impartial fact finder who makes a written report on the hearing. The final hearing has similar procedural rights but must also consider what action should be taken against the violator. There is a right to counsel only if the probationer denies the charges or otherwise appears unable to present the case him-/herself. It also is necessary to institute extradition proceedings if the probationer fled the state without permission and is arrested in another state.

Defendants sentenced to incarceration are usually evaluated when they first arrive at a jail or prison in order to determine what special needs they have. Inmates may be transferred to other facilities for a variety of administrative reasons, including reducing overcrowding at specific prisons. Good time and credits for other activities are earned by inmates and applied toward their release dates. A disciplinary hearing is required if the punishment will affect the inmate's release date. Minimum due process requirements for these hearings include notice of the time and place of the hearing; notice of the charges; right to be present and to present evidence, except that prison officials may limit the right to call witnesses if necessary for institutional security; an impartial fact finder and a written report on the disciplinary action taken and the reason for doing so. Cross-examination by the inmate may be denied. There is no right to counsel at these hearings, but illiterate inmates and those with other special needs may have the right to have a person assigned to assist them.

State law specifies when an inmate is eligible for parole. The case is heard by the parole board. A parole date will be set if it is decided that the inmate should be released; this date may be changed without a hearing. When the inmate is paroled, he/she will be subject to conditions similar to those placed on probationers. A violation subjects the parolee to return to prison to serve the time remaining on the original sentence. Revocation cannot occur without hearings similar to those used to revoke probation. These hearings are usually held before fact finders designated by the parole board or parole officers rather than a judge. As with probation, the final decision may be that the parolee should remain in the community, rather than be returned to prison, even though the violation did occur.

After the appeals have been completed in death penalty cases, a death warrant must be issued authorizing the execution. This warrant, signed by the governor, gives the date for the execution. Delays caused by last-minute appeals may make it necessary to issue another death warrant at a later date. After the execution the return on death warrant is completed and sent to the court.

New approaches are frequently tried. Some of the more recent ones include electronic monitoring; work furloughs; intermittent sentencing; community service orders; restitution; "three strikes and you're out"; "use a gun, go to jail"; ignition interlock devices for drunk drivers; intensive probation; boot camp; and day fines. Other innovations will constantly change the operation of corrections.

Sexually violent predator laws are designed to prevent the release of inmates who may prey on the public after their prison sentences have been served. Technically these laws are civil statutes and not part of the criminal justice system. Correctional authorities must carefully plan so that all due process rights are complied with and all procedures are completed prior to the date the inmate is scheduled for release.

Study Questions

Study Questions

1. Check the laws of your state regarding probation.
   a. How long is the probation for a misdemeanor?
   b. How long is the probation for a felony?
   c. What crimes are ineligible for probation?
   d. What crimes have a mandatory jail sentence as a condition of probation?
   e. What standard conditions of probation are imposed.
   f. Are probationers required to submit to searches? If so,
      1. under what circumstances?
      2. what level of suspicion is required?
      3. who is authorized to conduct the searches?
   g. Are probationers required to submit to drug testing?
2. Attend a probation revocation hearing. Prepare a report.
   a. What were the original charges for which the defendant was placed on probation?
   b. What did the defendant do that resulted in the revocation proceeding?
   c. What evidence was presented at the hearing?
   d. Was it determined that the defendant violated probation?
   e. Was probation revoked?
   f. Did the judge reinstate probation? If so, under what conditions?
3. Check the laws of your state to see if inmates are released on parole. If so,
   a. are there any offenses for which parole is not granted?
   b. what agency is responsible for setting parole dates?
   c. when does an inmate become eligible for parole?
   d. is a parole hearing held? If so, when and where?
   e. once parole is granted, how long will the inmate remain on parole?
   f. what agency is responsible for supervising parolees?
   g. what conditions are usually placed on the parolee?

4. If parole is used in your state, determine the procedures used for revoking parole.

   a. Who has the authority to arrest a parolee for a violation?

   b. Where is the preliminary revocation hearing held?

   c. Who acts as fact finder at the preliminary revocation hearing?

   d. Where is the parolee detained between the time the preliminary revocation hearing is held and the revocation decision is made?

   e. What is the maximum time allowed between the preliminary and final revocation hearings?

   f. Where is the final revocation hearing held?

   g. Who acts as fact finder at the final revocation hearing?

5. Check with your local probation department, county jail, parole officer, and state prison and determine which of the following programs are in use in your area.

   a. boot camp

   b. community service orders

   c. day fines

   d. electronic surveillance

   e. halfway houses

   f. ignition interlock devices

   g. intensive supervision

   h. intermittent sentencing

   i. restitution

   j. "three strikes and you're out"

   k. "use a gun, go to jail"

   l. work furlough

   m. any other innovative programs in use

6. Check the laws of your state to determine if your legislature has enacted sexually violent predator laws. If so,

   a. what crimes do they cover?

   b. how many offenses must the person have committed?

   c. do they apply to situations where the suspect was not convicted? If so, explain.

   d. how long prior to the inmate's release date should the Department of Corrections start these proceedings?

   e. what court will determine if the inmate is a sexually violent predator?

   f. what is the burden of proof?

   g. will an attorney be appointed to represent the inmate?

   h. if the judge rules that the inmate is a violent sexual predator, how long can he/she be held in a secure mental health facility?

   i. what are the procedures to renew this commitment?

True or False Questions

1. Punishment is the only constitutional rationale for sentencing defendants who have been convicted.
2. Judges may impose conditions of probation only if the defendant was convicted of a felony.
3. A person on probation must ask his/her probation officer for permission to leave the jurisdiction where the conviction was entered.
4. It is mandatory that the probationer be sent to jail if any of the conditions of probation were violated.
5. A parolee does not have the right to call witnesses at a parole revocation hearing.
6. States are constitutionally required to grant "good time" at the same rate.
7. A prison disciplinary hearing is mandatory for all violations of prison rules.
8. The Interstate Corrections Compact allows a parolee to request a transfer to another state to finish serving parole.
9. States are free to set their own standards for eligibility for parole.
10. The execution in a death penalty case cannot be held if the defendant is not mentally competent at the time of the execution.

Chapter

Chapter 16

Civil Suits

Outline

Key Terms

answer
civil forfeiture proceedings
Civil Rights Act
class action
color of state law
compensatory damages
consent decree
constitutional tort
demurrer
deposition
general damages

in propria persona
injunction
intentional torts
interrogatories
judgment on the pleadings
lis pendens
negligent torts
plaintiff
preponderance
 of the evidence
punitive damages

res judicata
sovereign immunity
strict liability torts
summary judgment
tort
tort claims acts
wrongful death

Learning Objectives

Learning Objectives

After reading this chapter, the student will be able to

- Explain four rationales for punishing convicted criminals.
- Explain how sovereign immunity applies to civil suits against government agencies.
- Differentiate between torts and crimes.
- Describe at least three torts that can be filed against police officers for acts done in the line of duty.
- Explain the purpose of wrongful death lawsuits.
- List the types of monetary damages that can be awarded in civil suits.
- Explain how the federal Civil Rights Act applies to the actions of law enforcement officers.
- Give examples of police activities that can result in Civil Rights Act suits against police officers.
- Explain defenses police officers have against Civil Rights Act suits.
- Explain the types of legal relief available to a plaintiff who successfully pursues a Civil Rights Act suit.
- Describe the purpose of forfeiture proceedings against a criminal defendant.

As our society has become increasingly litigious, the number of civil suits against criminal justice personnel has increased dramatically. These cases are usually based on one of the following legal grounds: violation of rights afforded by the U.S. Constitution and Bill of Rights or violation of state tort law. The procedures for bringing both types of cases are similar but the defenses differ. There is also a civil forfeiture proceeding that can be instituted by the government to seize the profits of criminal activity.

16-1 Civil Suits Under State Law

If one person is injured by another, civil law allows the injured party to recover monetary damages from the person who caused the injuries. Some actions, such as assault and battery, are covered by both civil law and criminal law. The individual who was harmed must institute the civil suit; the state handles the criminal proceedings. This does not violate double jeopardy, even if part of the defendant's sentence includes paying restitution.

16-1a Types of Tort

A **tort** is a civil wrong that does not arise out of a contract. Torts range from incurring damage to a car during an automobile accident to killing someone. The amount of money that a victim can recover due to a tort depends largely on the financial loss involved and the intent of the person who caused the harm. There are three basic classifications of tort: intentional, negligent, and strict liability. **Intentional torts** result from an intentional act: the person intended to do the act but may not have intended to harm anyone. Intentional acts done in bad faith result in the payment of higher damages to the victim.

Negligent torts are based on carelessness: a person did not comply with the standard of care required by law. For this type of tort to arise, there must be a duty to act. Normally a person is not required to do anything, but, if he/she decides to act, due care must be taken not to injure others. There are some situations, such as seeing a neighbor's child playing in the street, that signal danger but do not impose a duty to act. The law may impose a duty to act, such as the parents' responsibility for the safety of their children, which results in liability when nothing is done. The child playing in the street is an example of this: a parent or babysitter who allows the child to play in a hazardous place may be liable for injuries.

Strict liability torts are the result of social policy that imposes an absolute duty. These torts normally involve public health and safety. Restaurants may be strictly liable if they serve contaminated food; manufacturers may have strict liability for distributing hazardous products. The party that brings a strict liability suit does not have to show that the defendant had knowledge that his/her conduct was wrongful or that there was any intent to harm others.

16-1b Tort Claims Acts

The doctrine of **sovereign immunity** protects government agencies from civil suits. Most states have enacted laws, frequently referred to as **tort claims acts,** permitting suits in specified situations. There is also a federal tort claims act that applies to damages caused by federal employees. Normally these laws permit civil suits against the state, city, or other government entity under the same circumstances. People who wish to sue the government must be able to point to specific laws that authorize their suits. Sometimes the state statutes have separate sections for different functions, such as operating motor vehicles or managing jails; if so, the appropriate one must be cited. For convenience, this chapter will refer to all claims as if they were filed against a city police department. Figure 16-1 shows two typical state laws that waive sovereign immunity.

Tort claims acts frequently require that a claim be submitted to the city within a designated period, such as 100 days after the event in question,

Figure 16-1
Two Sample Tort Claims Acts

Based on Alabama Statutes 11-47-190

No city or town shall be liable for damages for injury done to or wrong suffered by any person or corporation, unless said injury or wrong was done or suffered through the neglect, carelessness or unskillfulness of some agent, officer or employee of the municipality engaged in work therefore and while acting in the line of his duty, or unless the said injury or wrong was done or suffered through the neglect, carelessness or failure to remedy some defect in the streets, alleys, public ways or buildings after the same had been called to the attention of the council or other governing body or after the same had existed for such unreasonable length of time as to raise a presumption of knowledge of such defect on the part of the council or other governing body and whenever the city or town shall be made liable to an action for damages by reason of the unauthorized or wrongful acts or the negligence, carelessness or unskillfulness of any person or corporation, then such person or corporation shall be liable to an action on the same account by the party so injured.

Based on Texas C.Pr.&R. 101.0215

(a) A municipality is liable under this chapter for damages arising from its governmental functions, which are those functions that are enjoined on a municipality by law and are given it by the state as part of the state's sovereignty, to be exercised by the municipality in the interest of the general public, including but not limited to:

    (1) police and fire protection;

    (2) health and sanitation services;

    (3) street construction and design;

    (4) bridge construction and maintenance and street maintenance;

    (5) cemeteries and cemetery care;

    (6) garbage and solid waste removal, collection, and disposal;

    (7) establishment and maintenance of jails;

    (8) hospitals . . .

which is much shorter than the statute of limitations (see Figure 16-2). Cities are usually given a specified number of days to take action after the claim is filed. Many cases are settled during this period. A person who accepts the city's offer cannot sue the city based on the same facts. A lawsuit can be filed only after a claim has been made in a timely fashion and the city either rejected it or failed to take any action. These cases must be filed in the appropriate civil court before the expiration of the civil statute of limitations.

16-1c Civil Procedure

The person who files a civil lawsuit, called a **plaintiff,** either hires a private attorney to handle the lawsuit or proceeds *in propria persona* (also

Figure 16-2
Notice Requirement for Filing Claims against the Government

Based on Texas C.Pr.&R 101.101

(a) A governmental unit is entitled to received notice of a claim against it under this chapter not later than six months after the day that the incident giving rise to the claim occurred. The notice must reasonably describe:

   (1) the damage or injury claimed;

   (2) the time and place of the incident; and

   (3) the incident.

(b) A city's charter and ordinance provisions requiring notice within a charter period permitted by law are ratified and approved.

(c) The notice requirements provided or ratified and approved by Subsections (a) and (b) do not apply if the governmental unit has actual notice that death has occurred, that the claimant has received some injury, or that the claimant's property has been damaged.

---

referred to as *in pro per*), which means the plaintiff handles the case without an attorney. The complaint is served on the defendant, who must file a formal written reply, called an **answer,** within the period set by state law, typically 30 days. Each side is entitled to discovery of evidence in the hands of the other side and may take the deposition of anyone with information about the case. At a **deposition,** an attorney from each side is present, along with a court reporter. The witness is given an oath to tell the truth and asked questions by the attorney who requested the deposition. The attorney for the opposing side can object to questions but usually is not allowed to cross-examine. The deposition provides useful information when preparing for trial. The transcript may be admitted at trial under the former testimony exception to the hearsay rule if the witness becomes unavailable; it may be used at trial for impeachment if the person making it testifies. **Interrogatories,** or written questions, can be served on the other side and must be answered under oath. Depositions and interrogatories are the main methods used to discover facts needed to go to trial in the case.

Pretrial motions can be made to dismiss the case. A **demurrer** challenges the complaint's technical merits. It is equivalent to a motion to dismiss the complaint in a criminal case. A **judgment on the pleadings** looks at both the complaint and answer and asks the judge to rule that one side has established its case. To win, the pleadings must establish the case without the need for the testimony of witnesses. For example, if one side alleges that the offense occurred and the answer filed by the opponent does not deny it or raise a defense, judgment on the pleadings in favor of the plaintiff is correct. **Summary judgment** is based on the pleadings, legal points and authorities, and documents containing sworn testimony (depositions and interrogatories). The judge grants a summary judgment only if there is no doubt that the case has been established. If there is a question regarding credibility of the sworn testimony or if witnesses have conflicting versions of the facts, the case will not be decided before trial. Settlement conferences are used extensively in civil court to try to save the time and expense of trials.

Civil trials proceed much as criminal trials do. The burden of proof in civil cases is a **preponderance of the evidence,** which means that it is more likely than not that an event occurred. The burden of proof may be allocated so that the plaintiff must prove some issues and the defendant must carry the burden on others. Either side can call the opponent to testify. The Fifth Amendment privilege against self-incrimination applies to civil proceedings to the extent of allowing a witness to refuse to answer if the testimony would subject him/her to criminal prosecution. Answering questions that are the key to financial liability for a civil judgment is not protected. In tort cases either side has the right to request a jury trial. Most states do not require unanimous verdicts in civil cases; many use smaller juries in civil cases than they do in criminal cases.

Either side can appeal after a civil judgment is entered. The losing side may appeal much the same as a defendant does in a criminal case. The winning side sometimes appeals because the jury instructions resulted in too small of a verdict. Double jeopardy does not apply to civil cases, but there is a similar doctrine, called *res judicata,* which prohibits relitigating issues that have already been settled by a final judgment.

16-1d Torts Found in Police Activity

Officers are civilly liable for their intentional, wrongful acts. Police are required to act with due care. Failure to conform to these standards may result in intentional and negligent torts. Strict liability torts usually do not apply to police conduct. The most common torts resulting from police activity are covered in this section. They can be the subject of civil suits only if sovereign immunity has been waived.

Assault and Battery

The intentional tort of battery closely resembles the crime by the same name; the tort of assault usually requires that the victim was placed in fear or apprehension of immediate battery. Battery involves unconsented touching; any force used beyond what is legally justified is also considered a battery. When a suspect alleges the police used excessive force, the case is usually filed as the torts of assault and battery. These cases depend on the credibility of the witnesses and the officers; therefore, pretrial motions to dismiss are usually to no avail. The crux of the determination of what was excessive force is what a reasonable officer would do under the same circumstances; deadly force is authorized only if someone's life is being threatened. The jury (or judge, if the case is tried without a jury) must examine the facts as they existed moment by moment. The plaintiff's version of the facts usually differs substantially from the officer's. Most courts permit the introduction of prior false claims filed by the plaintiff and past incidents of improper use of force by the officers. The plaintiff's history for assaultive behavior may also be introduced if the officers claim they were trying to subdue the plaintiff. Both the officer's personal history for violence and truthfulness and the department's reputation are extremely important. The verdict usually goes to the side that presents the most credible witnesses.

False Imprisonment

Civil false imprisonment is an intentional tort, which covers confinement against a person's will, whether done by physical or psychological force. This applies to cases of false arrest in addition to kidnapping. Failure to release an inmate when his/her sentence expires is also false imprisonment. Unlawful arrest cases usually include civil battery: since there was no right to make the arrest, any force used was unlawful.

Property Damage

Property damage can come under the intentional tort of trespass to chattels or can be the result of negligence. Probably the most frequent property damage claims against police departments are the result of vehicular accidents, ranging from backing into a mailbox to colliding during a high-speed chase. The state tort claims act may require the police department to pay for the mailbox, but frequently the government is exempt from damages for incidents arising from legal pursuits.

One key question in the pursuit cases is whether the officers followed all regulations regarding emergency vehicles. In many states police cars, fire engines, and ambulances are exempt from the normal rules of the road only when using both red lights and siren; under these laws, the city is not exempt if officers are involved in collisions while driving over the speed limit or violating other traffic laws with only their red lights on.

Negligent Conduct

Even when there is no intent to harm, officers are civilly liable for both physical injuries and property damage caused by conduct that falls below the standard of care required of them under the circumstances. This lack of care, called negligence in legal terms and carelessness in everyday language, applies to everything that an officer does. Negligently firing a gun is an example; so is carelessly administering first aid. Reckless driving in situations not qualifying for the exemptions afforded emergency vehicles can also result in liability.

Sometimes officers help someone when they are not required to do so. When they do this, they can be sued for resulting injuries they carelessly cause, even though they had no duty to give assistance. Another problem arises when officers decide to "be nice" to a drunk driver and allow him/her to drive home instead of booking the driver and impounding the car. A number of courts have held that the officers are liable if the drunk causes an accident and injures someone after being released in this manner. Here the duty is to protect the public, not a particular individual.

Other Kinds of Tort

There are many other torts. Malicious prosecution can be brought if false charges are knowingly filed against an innocent defendant. Public statements that damage a person's reputation can result in a case for defamation; truth is a total defense in these cases. Invasion of privacy applies to both true and false statements that result in publicity about a person's private life, unless there is a valid reason for releasing this information to the public. Theft is classified as the tort of conversion of chattels. Inflicting emotional distress is actionable when done intentionally or, under some circumstances, negligently. Some states allow a person who witnessed unjustified injuries to a close family member to recover based on emotional distress. Sovereign immunity applies to all of these torts unless it has been waived by the legislature.

16-1e Liability of the City

An employer is usually liable for the actions of its employees that it authorizes or condones. This is true for government agencies as well as private companies, except when sovereign immunity applies. This type of liability arises only if it is shown that an employee did something wrong. To do so, it is necessary to include both the employee and the employer as defendants in the suit. The main reason for trying to hold the city liable is that it makes it possible to recover more money. Grounds for the city's liability include inadequate training, failure to supervise, negligent preemployment screening, and policies that tolerate wrongful conduct.

16-1f Class Action Suits

A **class action** is a civil suit brought on behalf of a large number of plaintiffs who allege that they have suffered the same wrong. No minimum size is mentioned in most state statutes, but the judge is given discretion to certify a case as a class action if the number of plaintiffs involved is too large to be handled individually. Once certified, the case proceeds, with one or more attorneys representing all potential plaintiffs. State laws regulate the procedures for class actions. It may be necessary to advertise in newspapers to locate all potential plaintiffs so their rights can be protected and to give them an opportunity to share in the money recovered. Some states allow individuals to opt out of the class action and proceed with separate lawsuits.

A class action must have at least one named plaintiff who suffered the purported wrong. The suit alleges that many others have been mistreated in a similar manner. Racial discrimination by national restaurant chains and price fixing by major clothing manufacturers are examples of class actions filed without knowing who all the potential plaintiffs were. Occasionally a class action is brought against a police department that is alleged to have a policy condoning excessive force. Employment discrimination suits against a law enforcement agency have also been handled as class actions.

16-1g Types of Damages in Civil Suits

One of the basic tenets of torts is that "you pay for what you break." In other words, you must reimburse the victim if you wrongfully cause personal injuries or property damage. Another tenet is that the person who in bad faith causes these damages should be punished; this is accomplished by imposing additional monetary damages.

Compensatory Damages

Compensatory damages merely reimburse the victim for his/her expenses. For this reason, they are sometimes called "out-of-pocket" damages. Expenses that can be included range from medical bills to car repairs; necessary adaptive devices, such as wheelchairs and ramps to allow the wheelchair to enter the house, are included. The victim usually can recover for lost wages. This applies even if the victim received paid sick leave while recovering because the sick leave used in this manner reduces benefits available in the future. Some states permit the victim to recover for medical bills, even though an insurance company paid them; others require reimbursement for these expenses to be paid directly to the insurance company.

Receipts are usually required for compensatory damages. An exception to this is when the victim suffered injuries that will require treatment in the future. Part of the judgment can provide funds to pay these bills. For example, the attorney would ask the jury to award $52,000 for treatments costing $100 each, which are required once a week and are anticipated to be needed for the next 10 years ($100 × 52 × 10 = $52,000). Opposing attorneys would try to convince the jury that the treatments were either not needed, less expensive, or not likely to be required for such a long period of time.

General Damages

General damages, sometimes referred to as "pain and suffering" damages, compensate the victim for inconvenience and pain caused by the tort. Injuries that are more painful or take longer to heal result in higher awards. Those that leave scars, particularly disfiguring ones, also merit higher awards. The highest awards usually go to injuries that result in painful, permanent impairments. For example, if the victim sustained a broken leg that did not heal correctly, the attorney might argue,

> You've seen the plaintiff walk. She limps badly. Walking is slow and painful. It throws her spine out of line and causes constant backaches. She will never be able to participate in sports. She will have trouble playing simple games with her children in the park. She will not be able to keep up with her toddler. I think $100 a day is a fair value to put on this severe handicap.
>
> You heard the doctor say that this condition cannot be corrected. This means it will make every step she takes every day of her life more difficult. The actuary testified that the victim has a life expectancy of 43.7 years. She should be compensated for every day she suffers during those 43 years.

If the jury decides to calculate damages for the broken leg according to this attorney's formula, the general damages will be $1,595,050 ($100 × 365 × 43.7). Juries are free to develop their own formulas, as long as they are logically related to the facts. The judge can reduce a verdict that is excessive. Another procedural device available to the judge is to inform the parties that a new trial will be ordered unless they accept what the judge believes is a more reasonable verdict.

Punitive Damages

Punitive damages are designed to punish a defendant who acted in bad faith or intentionally harmed someone. Without punitive damages some people and businesses would intentionally ignore potential danger to others because many victims would not complain, and settling with those who did sue would likely not be expensive.

The jury answers three questions: (1) Did the defendant do the alleged wrongful act? (2) If so, was it done in bad faith? (3) If so, how large a verdict is necessary to make an impact on his/her future conduct? The amount of punitive damages is only indirectly related to the general damages; it is more closely tied to the defendant's ability to pay. For example, most college students would be deterred by having to pay $100; some large companies would consider awards less than $100,000 a victory. The defendant's financial records are admissible if the case gets to the question of how large the punitive damages should be.

Wrongful Death

If someone is killed by a tortuous act, the person responsible must compensate the family. Two items relating to the victim are considered: income from all sources and life expectancy. Anticipated promotions and adjustments for inflation may be estimated by the jury. A history of unemployment and/or failure to support dependents may also be reviewed and factored negatively into the award. The award resulting from the **wrongful death** of a 30-year-old junior executive with an M.B.A. who is currently making $200,000 annually and is considered likely to become CEO might be nearly $50 million (30 years × $200,000 with a 10 percent raise and inflation adjustment per year plus 10 years of retirement at 50 percent of salary for the last year worked); however, an award of $60,000 (5 years × $12,000 social security) might be justified for the death of a 70-year-old man, even though the actions causing the deaths were the same. The family's emotional distress and loss of companionship are calculated separately.

Limitations on Amount of Recovery

Some states have enacted tort reform laws that place a limit on general damages, such as a maximum recovery of $250,000. Even when this has not been applied to all tort cases, statutes may limit how much can be recovered from a government agency. Figure 16-3 shows a statute that restricts how much can be recovered.

Attorney Fees

Most plaintiff's attorneys handle tort cases on a contingency basis. This means that the attorney agrees to accept a percentage of the verdict as payment for the effort expended on the case. If the jury rules in favor of the defense, the plaintiff's attorney receives nothing; therefore, attorneys refuse to take cases if they believe the chance of winning is too low. This serves as an informal screening device for frivolous allegations. The percentage the

Figure 16-3
Limitation on Recovery in Suits against the Government

Based on Texas C.Pr.&R. 101.023.

(a) Liability of the state government under this chapter is limited to money damages in a maximum amount of $250,000 for each person and $500,000 for each single occurrence for bodily injury or death and $100,000 for each single occurrence for injury to or destruction of property.

(b) Except as provided by Subsection (c), liability of a unit of local government under this chapter is limited to money damages in a maximum amount of $100,000 for each person and $300,000 for each single occurrence for bodily injury or death and $100,000 for each single occurrence for injury to or destruction of property.

(c) Liability of a municipality under this chapter is limited to money damages in a maximum amount of $250,000 for each person and $500,000 for each single occurrence for bodily injury or death and $100,000 for each single occurrence for injury to or destruction of property.

(d) Except as provided by Section 78.001, liability of an emergency service organization under this chapter is limited to money damages in a maximum amount of $100,000 for each person and $300,000 for each single occurrence for bodily injury or death and $100,000 for each single occurrence for injury to or destruction of property.

---

attorney receives is usually set in the contract that the injured party signs when hiring the attorney. This contract may require the plaintiff to pay expenses incurred during the suit, such as filing fees and the cost of having a court reporter at the deposition, separate from the contingency agreement. It is not uncommon to have a contract that allows the attorney to keep 30 percent of the recovery if the case is settled before trial and 40 percent if a trial is required. Some states have enacted laws restricting the amount that the lawyer receives.

The defendant normally pays his/her attorney based on an hourly rate. If the defendant is insured, the attorney is usually hired and paid by the insurance company. In tort cases the losing party is normally not required to pay the opposing side's attorney fees. Some states have modified this rule, particularly if the judge finds the suit to be frivolous.

Representation by the City

It is common for a city to provide an attorney to represent officers who are sued for acts performed in the line of duty. If an officer decides to hire an attorney in addition to the one provided by the city, the officer must pay for it. Many cities also have a policy of paying any judgment entered against its officers for acts done in the line of duty. False arrest insurance may also cover the judgment and attorney fees. Most states have policies that prohibit cities from paying punitive damages assessed against their employees. Punitive damages cannot be assessed against a city or government agency in many states.

16-2 Suits Under the Federal Civil Rights Act

The **Civil Rights Act** of 1871 provides redress for violations of constitutional rights by state, county, and city employees. The act provides both civil and criminal penalties; Section 1983 of Title 42 of the United States Code is the most commonly used civil section. Its full text is shown in Figure 16-4.

Due to the historical context in which it was enacted, the Civil Rights Act was originally intended to protect former slaves against oppressive state action. Federal courts were given jurisdiction in order to avoid the hostility of some state courts toward minorities and abolitionists. Section 1983 specifically applies to the deprivation of constitutional rights under **color of state law.** To qualify as acting under color of state law, a person must be acting within the scope of his/her duties as an employee of a state or local government agency. Since the statute makes no reference to racial discrimination, it can be used to vindicate any constitutional violation. Section 1985 prohibits conspiracies by two or more people to prevent someone from holding office; to interfere with court proceedings by intimidating parties or jurors or otherwise obstructing justice; or to deprive any person of equal protection of the laws or voting rights. This section does not require that the actions be done by government employees. In the 1960s and early 1970s the Supreme Court took an expansive approach to the coverage of the Civil Rights Act. Since that time, the trend has been toward a narrower construction.

Figure 16-4
Civil Rights Act of 1871

United States Code Title 42, Section 1983

Every person who, under color of any statute, ordinance, regulation, custom, or usage, of any State or Territory or the District of Columbia, subjects, or causes to be subjected, any citizen of the United States or other person within the jurisdiction thereof to the deprivation of any rights, privileges, or immunities secured by the Constitution and laws, shall be liable to the party injured in an action at law, suit in equity, or other proper proceeding for redress, except that in any action brought against a judicial officer for an act or omission taken in such officer's judicial capacity, injunctive relief shall not be granted unless a declaratory decree was violated or declaratory relief was unavailable. For the purposes of this section, any Act of Congress applicable exclusively to the District of Columbia shall be considered to be a statute of the District of Columbia.

Congress has never expanded the Civil Rights Act to cover actions by federal officers, but in 1971 the Supreme Court created what is called a **constitutional tort** to provide protection in these circumstances. *Bivens v. Six Unknown Named Agents of Federal Bureau of Narcotics* (403 U.S. 388, 29 L.Ed. 2d 619, 91 S.Ct. 1999 [1971]), established the right to sue federal agents for violating Fourth Amendment rights. A wide variety of constitutional deprivations are now covered. There is no corresponding right to sue a federal agency unless sovereign immunity has been waived by statute. Federal agents have qualified immunity for making arrests if a reasonable officer would have believed that the arrest was lawful in light of the established law and the evidence available at the time of the arrest. This form of immunity applies when the officers have a reasonable but mistaken belief that probable cause exists. The question of immunity is normally determined by the judge.

16-2a Actions Covered by the Civil Rights Act

The Civil Rights Act covers all forms of violations of constitutional rights. Suits against criminal justice personnel most commonly focus on violations of the Fourth, Fifth, Sixth, and Eighth Amendments; due process; and equal protection. The act imparts no rights itself: the plaintiff must show that a specific constitutional right has been violated. Actions taken by the police are covered, whether done during a criminal investigation or while assisting in civil matters, such as evictions.

The first step in the analysis is to determine the constitutional standard involved. For example, if the suit is based on violation of *Miranda* rights, the Fifth Amendment standards for confessions will be reviewed to determine if there was a constitutional violation. The second step is to determine the standard of conduct that is covered by the Civil Rights Act. Generally this will require intentional misconduct or reckless disregard of the plaintiff's rights; negligence is not sufficient for recovery.

Immunity must be considered. In *Saucier v. Katz* (533 U.S. 194, 121 S.Ct. 2151, 150 L.Ed. 2d 272 [2001]), the Supreme Court ruled that the immunity issues should be settled as early as possible before trial so the case could be dismissed. Issues relating to immunity are discussed in section 16-2b, "Defenses to Civil Rights Act Suits."

In cases regarding the destruction of personal property, the Court noted that the due process clause is satisfied if the state provides adequate civil or administrative procedures to recover the value of the item lost. If such remedy exists, there is no violation of due process, even if the property was destroyed intentionally. Federal courts also abstain from intervening if there is a criminal prosecution pending in state courts. The plaintiff must wait until the prosecution is completed and then file the case in federal court. Cases involving only the possibility that someone's rights will be violated in the future cannot be litigated.

A growing array of acts is covered by the Civil Rights Act. For example, excessive force by any state or local government employee falls under the Fourth Amendment. Many of these cases could also be filed in state court, but the plaintiff files under the Civil Rights Act in hopes of more favorable results in federal court. As mentioned in section 16-1, "Civil Suits under State Law," the credibility of the officers involved and their history of respecting the rights of others are frequently key issues. Prior incidents of inappropriate force are particularly damaging.

Acts motivated by race, ethnicity, gender, religion, sexual orientation, and so on violate equal protection. Juries charged with deciding these cases must look both at the objective evidence of what occurred and at the subjective reason for the officers' actions. Both on- and off-duty conduct can be introduced to demonstrate that the officer was racist, sexist, or antagonistic toward gays or in some manner demonstrated animosity toward people based on their membership in a protected group. Officers' memberships in organizations that promote or tolerate these attitudes can be used persuasively by the plaintiff. An officer's use of racial epitaphs in private conversations is another example of conduct that is extremely damaging to the officer's credibility when denying improperly motivated on-duty acts.

16-2b Defenses to Civil Rights Act Suits

The main defense is that no constitutional violation occurred. This analysis is based on an objective review of the evidence. The fact that an officer had subjective bad faith does not alter the conclusion that no violation occurred. The second line of defense is that the defendant is entitled to some form of immunity. A historical approach is used to determine who has immunity: those who had tort immunity in 1871, when the legislation was passed, generally have immunity under Section 1983. The Supreme Court also uses this approach to decide whether the immunity is absolute or qualified.

Most actions of local and state law enforcement officers are covered by qualified immunity, which means they are immune from civil damages if they meet all of the following criteria:

1. The officer acted in good faith.
2. The officer made reasonable efforts to learn current constitutional rights.
3. A reasonable officer would have acted in a similar manner under the same circumstances.

This immunity does not apply if the rights violated were clearly established by law at the time of the incident or the officer acted maliciously. Prison officials, including those who act as hearing officers for disciplinary procedures, also have qualified immunity. While testifying in court, all witnesses including police officers enjoy absolute immunity: they are not subject to suit under the Civil Rights Act even though they commit perjury. This does not mean that they have immunity for criminal prosecution for perjury.

Judges have absolute immunity from monetary damage awards for their judicial actions, even when acting in bad faith. This immunity does not prohibit issuing injunctions against a judge's prospective conduct; nor does it extend to personnel decisions relating to courtroom employees. It also does not prohibit awarding the opposing party attorney's fees if a successful suit is brought against a judge.

Prosecutors have absolute immunity for actions taken within the scope of their court-related duties. Qualified immunity applies when legal advice is given to assist police conducting an investigation. Qualified immunity is also applied if the prosecutor is accused of fabricating evidence during a preliminary investigation of the case or of prejudicing the defendant's case by making false statements at press conferences. Public defenders and appointed attorneys do not have immunity for intentional misconduct.

Municipalities are not exempt from suits under the Civil Rights Act. To establish liability, a policy of disregard for constitutional rights must be shown. Merely the fact that the city employed the offending police officer or a single act of misconduct occurred is not enough. The city is responsible for a failure to train if this results in deliberate indifference to constitutional rights.

A city cannot be held liable for the actions of its officers unless the offending officer was named as a party to the suit and was found to have violated a constitutional right. On the other hand, a city cannot claim qualified immunity for its unconstitutional policies by asserting the good faith of the individual police officer. Municipalities are immune from punitive damages. Release-dismissal agreements, in which a person agrees to forego filing a civil suit if the criminal charges are dismissed, have been upheld.

States are immune from suits in federal court under the Eleventh Amendment. State officials, such as the Director of the Department of Corrections, can be sued in their individual capacities. When an individual capacity suit is brought against a state official, the state cannot be required to pay the attorney's fees of the prevailing party.

16-2c Types of Recovery

The same types of monetary awards are possible in Civil Rights Act suits as in torts: compensatory damages, general damages, and punitive damages. The qualified immunity afforded police officers results in cases ending with defense verdicts unless bad faith is involved. Reckless and intentional misconduct usually results in compensatory and general damages as well as punitive damages. Most cases successfully alleging the denial of constitutional rights due to racist conduct result in punitive damages. This also applies to sexist and homophobic conduct. Officers usually pay punitive damages out of their own salaries and savings because most government agencies will not pay them. Figure 16-5 shows a jury instruction used to help jurors in a Civil Rights Act case determine if punitive damages should be awarded.

Other types of relief can also be granted in these suits. An **injunction** (a court order regulating future conduct) can be issued in civil rights cases only if there is an established pattern of violations that leads to the conclusion that constitutional violations will continue unless the court takes action. It is rare that a court finds that this standard has been met.

Consent decrees are entered in some Civil Rights Act cases, particularly class actions. A **consent decree** is a document, agreed to by both sides,

Figure 16-5
Sample Jury Instruction for Punitive Damages under the Civil Rights Act

The following questions, known as "special interrogatories," lead the jury through a process that could end with a monetary award.*

(a) Did John Jones violate the constitutional rights of Paul Q. Plaintiff?

If yes,

(b) Did John Jones act with malice or in reckless disregard of Paul Q. Plaintiff's rights?

If yes,

(c) In your discretion do you find punitive damages are appropriate?

If yes,

(d) What amount of punitive damages do you award to Paul Q. Plaintiff against John Jones? $ _____ .

*John Jones is a police officer, but the jury instructions would not refer to him as Officer Jones.

which states an agreement for future action. Once it is approved by the judge, it has all the legal effect of a judgment at the end of a trial. If it is not complied with, the opposing side can go to court to enforce it. Consent decrees are common in litigation regarding discriminatory hiring practices. Class actions in several cities alleged a denial of equal protection because police departments did not arrest batterers in domestic violence cases. Some of these cases ended in consent decrees that established new patrol policy.

Section 1988 allows the prevailing party in a civil rights suit to recover attorney's fees. To qualify as a "prevailing party," the plaintiff must have received at least some relief on the merits of the claim. Monetary damages qualify; so do injunctions, consent decrees, and out-of-court settlements. Establishing the violation of a right is not enough if the defendant successfully pleads immunity as a defense.

The Supreme Court has rejected the theory that Section 1988 is a form of contingency-fee agreement which limits attorney fees to a percentage of the amount recovered. Instead, the fee is based on the complexity of the case, the total hours devoted to the litigation, and the value to society. For this reason, sizable attorney's fees have been awarded for the vindication of constitutional rights that had limited financial impact on the individual plaintiff. Class actions, due to their complexity, frequently result in large awards for attorney's fees.

In some cases defendants can recover attorney's fees from the plaintiff. Successfully having the case dismissed is not enough: the case must be shown to be frivolous. The courts have been reluctant to award fees to the defendant unless there is a showing that there is no possible basis for the suit. Judges have been reticent to make such awards when the plaintiff is a *pro per* inmate because the lack of merit may be the result of poor draftsmanship, rather than the facts of the case.

16-3 Forfeiture Proceedings Against the Defendant's Property

Forfeiture laws first became popular during Prohibition but have reemerged in the past decade as a valuable tool in the war against drugs. Civil forfeiture laws permit the seizure of property used to commit crimes. It does not violate double jeopardy to convict a person and to file **civil forfeiture proceedings** for assets involved in the same case. Forfeiture laws cover several key issues: what types of property are subject to forfeiture; under what circumstances property may be seized; what court proceedings are required; and disposition of seized items. It is important that law enforcement officers be knowledgeable about what is authorized in the jurisdiction where they work because there is considerable variation among the states.

Some states, such as Utah, have forfeiture laws which apply only to the manufacture and sale of drugs and related activities. Others, such as Indiana, cover a much wider range of crimes (see Figure 16-6). The laws usually cover items used to commit the crime (equipment, vehicles, etc.); some also apply to cash and items purchased with the profits of criminal activity. In 1993 the Supreme Court held that the seizure of real estate without prior notice and hearing did not comply with the Fifth (federal cases) and Fourteenth (state cases) Amendments' protection against deprivation of property without due process. The Court noted that there was no danger of the land being taken out of the jurisdiction, destroyed, or hidden prior to a court hearing. Other civil remedies, including obtaining a restraining order and/or filing *lis pendens* (a document which makes it nearly impossible to transfer title to real estate until litigation has been completed). The Court approved a 1974 case permitting the seizure of moveable property prior to a court hearing. The potential for removing the property from the jurisdiction creates an emergency, which justifies seizure based on a court order issued at an *ex parte* hearing without the defendant being present or represented by counsel. Final proceedings to determine if the items should be forfeited require notice to the owner and a trial where there is an opportunity to refute charges.

Some states permit forfeiture even though there was no conviction, while others make conviction a prerequisite to these suits. Another variation is the burden of proof: some states require proof beyond a reasonable doubt, while others use the civil standard of a preponderance of the evidence. A few have applied different standards, depending on the value of the items and the alleged crime. Many states try to protect innocent third parties by requiring that there be proof that the owner of the property knew, or should have known, that his/her property was being used in the commission of a crime. This type of provision provides a defense for a person who loans a car to a friend, not knowing that the car will be used to transport drugs. Protection is frequently given to banks and other institutions that hold mortgages on property that is seized for forfeiture.

The ruling on forfeiture is made at the conclusion of a civil trial. Two dispositions are usually available if the government meets its burden of proof: (1) sell the property at auction and divide the proceeds between the governmental agencies involved in the case or (2) keep the items for use by a government agency. Some states, such as Indiana, permit the government to use the property for a limited time but ultimately require it to be sold.

Figure 16-6
Items Subject to Civil Forfeiture

Based on Indiana Statutes 34-24-1-1

(a) The following may be seized:

  (1) All vehicles, if they are used or are intended for use by the person or persons in possession of them to transport or in any manner to facilitate the transportation of the following:

    (A) A controlled substance for the purpose of committing, attempting to commit, or conspiring to commit any of the following:

      (i) Dealing in or manufacturing cocaine, a narcotic drug, or methamphetamine

      (ii) Dealing in a schedule I, II, or III controlled substance

      (iii) Dealing in a schedule IV controlled substance

      (iv) Dealing in a schedule V controlled substance

      (v) Dealing in a counterfeit substance

      (vi) Possession of cocaine, a narcotic drug, or methamphetamine

      (vii) Dealing in paraphernalia

      (viii) Dealing in marijuana, hash oil, or hashish

    (B) Any stolen or converted property if the retail or repurchase value of that property is one hundred dollars ($100) or more.

    (C) Any hazardous waste

  (2) All money, negotiable instruments, securities, weapons, communications devices, or any property commonly used as consideration for a violation of IC 35-48-4:

    (A) furnished or intended to be furnished by any person in exchange for an act that is in violation of a criminal statute;

    (B) used to facilitate any violation of a criminal statute; or

    (C) traceable as proceeds of the violation of a criminal statute.

  (3) Any portion of real or personal property purchased with money that is traceable as a proceed of a violation of a criminal statute.

  (4) A vehicle that is used by a person to:

    (A) commit, attempt to commit, or conspire to commit;

    (B) facilitate the commission of; or

    (C) escape from the commission of;

    murder, kidnapping, criminal confinement, rape, child molesting, or child exploitation.

  (5) Real property owned by a person who uses it to commit any of the following as a Class A felony, a Class B felony, or a Class C felony:

    (A) Dealing in or manufacturing cocaine, a narcotic drug, or methamphetamine

    (B) Dealing in a schedule I, II, or III controlled substance

    (C) Dealing in a schedule IV controlled substance

    (D) Dealing in marijuana, hash oil, or hashish

  (6) Equipment and recordings used by a person to commit fraud under IC 35-43-5-4(11).

  (7) Recordings sold, rented, transported, or possessed by a person in violation of IC 24-4-10.

  (8) Property or an enterprise that is the object of a corrupt business influence violation.

  (9) Unlawful telecommunications devices and plans, instructions, or publications used to commit an offense under IC 35-45-13.

For years it was assumed that civil forfeiture laws do not raise double jeopardy issues. The Federal Court of Appeals for the Ninth Circuit and a few other courts have recently held that a criminal defendant can plead a forfeiture judgment as double jeopardy. The Supreme Court will have to settle this issue.

Chapter Summary

Civil tort suits are filed by the aggrieved party to collect monetary damages and other relief from the person who inflicted the injury. A tort is a wrong that did not arise out of a contract. Torts can be intentional, negligent, or based on strict liability. The most common tort suits filed against law enforcement officers are assault and battery, trespass to chattels (property damage), and false imprisonment (false arrest). At common law, government entities had sovereign immunity, which protected them from civil suits; most states have statutes which abolish this immunity and permit suits for damages occurring during specified types of activities. A city is liable for the actions of its employees if it hires unsuitable personnel or if it fails to adequately train or supervise them.

Compensatory damages can be awarded in tort suits; these damages pay the plaintiff's expenses for injuries and property damage caused by the tort. General damages are awarded to pay for pain and suffering. Punitive damages are imposed for intentional bad conduct; these damages are based on the defendant's financial resources in order to punish him/her and deter future tortious conduct. Wrongful death actions enable the family of someone killed due to a tort to recover the income the deceased would have earned if he/she had lived. Some states impose limits on how much can be recovered in tort actions.

The Civil Rights Act of 1871 permits civil suits in federal court for the deprivation of constitutional rights. The most commonly used section (42 U.S.C. §1983) applies to the actions of state and local government employees which deprive people of their constitutional rights under color of state law. The conspiracy section (42 U.S.C. §1985) applies to the actions of two or more people, whether or not government employees, who act together to deprive someone of specified civil rights.

Most law enforcement officers have qualified immunity for their actions, as long as they act in good faith in a way a reasonable police officer would react and they have taken the steps necessary to learn the current rules protecting constitutional rights. Testimony on the witness stand is covered by absolute immunity, as are acts of the judge and prosecutor in presenting the case in court. The plaintiff can recover compensatory, general, and punitive damages in Civil Rights Act cases for actions not covered by immunity.

Injunctions are also available. These are given only if there is an established pattern of conduct; the injunction orders the plaintiff to stop unconstitutional conduct. Failure to comply can be treated as contempt of court. Consent decrees, which are out-of-court settlements reached by the parties, also serve the function of judicial orders. New policies can be imposed as the result of a consent decree.

Civil forfeiture proceedings are authorized in many states. Items used to conduct criminal activity can be seized under these laws; typical examples are cars, boats, and houses used by drug dealers. Portable items may be seized based on a court order issued at an *ex parte* hearing; both notice to the defendant and a court hearing where both sides can present evidence are required prior to seizing real estate. A civil complaint is filed and a trial held to determine if the items are forfeited. Most state laws provide protections for innocent third parties whose property was used by someone else while committing criminal acts. If the judge orders a forfeiture, the property can be sold or retained for use by the agencies involved in the case.

Study Questions

1. Check your state statutes to determine under what circumstances sovereign immunity has been waived to permit civil suits against a police department.
   a. For what actions can a police department be sued?
   b. Does a claim have to be made to the city prior to filing a civil case in court?
   c. Are there time limits on filing claims? If so, what are they?
   d. Are there limitations on the amount of money that can be awarded to a person making a claim against the city? If so, how much?

2. Look in recent newspapers for information on a tort case against a police department. Identify
   a. the plaintiff(s).
   b. the defendants.
   c. the facts alleged by the plaintiff(s).
   d. the type of torts involved.
   e. the defenses.
   f. if case went to trial,
      1. the verdict
      2. the damages awarded, if any
      3. if the verdict was appealed.
3. Look for a Civil Rights Act suit against a police department. Write a report identifying
   a. the plaintiff(s).
   b. the defendant(s).
   c. the constitutional violation alleged.
   d. the facts showing violation.
   e. the immunity that applies.
   f. if the case went to trial,
      1. the verdict
      2. the damages, if any
      3. the attorney's fees, if any
4. Check the *Federal Reporter* or the *Federal Supplement* or ask a librarian or an attorney to help you find a class action that resulted in a consent decree. Prepare a report on
   a. the plaintiffs.
   b. the defendant(s).
   c. the issue in case.
   d. the facts supporting the plaintiffs' allegations.
   e. the defense(s).
   f. the consent decree.
   g. if plaintiff later went to court to enforce consent decree,
      1. what violation of consent decree was alleged?
      2. what action did the court take?
5. Check your state forfeiture laws. Identify
   a. the property subject to forfeiture.
   b. the types of criminal activity that must be involved.
   c. the procedures used to seize property subject to forfeiture.
   d. the types of court documents that must be filed.
   e. the maximum time limits for starting trial on forfeiture.
   f. the burden of proof.
   g. what will happen to the property that is forfeited.

6. Check court decisions and statutes in your state to determine if a defendant in your state can claim double jeopardy if criminal charges and forfeiture proceedings are both filed.

True or False Questions

1. Trial in civil court after the defendant has been acquitted in criminal court for the same actions violates double jeopardy.
2. Negligent torts are unconstitutional because they do not require intent to cause harm.
3. Police officers in the United States are protected from all civil suits based on sovereign immunity.
4. The first document filed in a civil tort case is a complaint.
5. The burden of proof in civil cases and criminal cases is the same.
6. If the defendant wins a civil case, he/she has immunity from criminal charges for the same actions.
7. General damages are used to pay the plaintiff for pain and suffering.
8. Section 1983 of the Civil Rights Act applies only to individuals who violate constitutional rights under the color of state law.
9. Police officers have qualified immunity under the Civil Rights Act only if they act in good faith.
10. Civil forfeiture laws violate double jeopardy if the defendant has already been convicted and fined for the same actions.

A

Abandoned property   The Fourth Amendment does not apply to abandoned property–it can be seized without probable cause. Since no one possesses it, there is no reasonable expectation of privacy that must be protected.

Abstract of the warrant   An abstract of the warrant summarizes the contents of the warrant. It is frequently sent by computer or FAX to the police station when an arrest is being made based on information from the database on outstanding warrants. The actual warrant is usually kept at the courthouse.

Access of press to preliminary hearing   The Supreme Court held that the preliminary hearing must be open to the news media (radio, TV, etc.). Judges and/or state legislatures are free to decide the issue of whether camera crews, tape recorders, and so on will be allowed in the courtroom.

Administrative hearing   Many state and federal agencies hold administrative hearings. In some states, Department of Motor Vehicles holds an administrative hearing to determine if a driver's license should be revoked. These hearings are not part of the court process. Instead of a judge there is a hearing officer, who is usually employed by the agency holding the hearing. Both sides are allowed to present evidence, but the rules of evidence may be more lax at the administrative hearing.

Advance sheets   Advance sheets contain prerelease portions of future volumes of court decisions. The advance sheets are formatted in the same manner as the final publication and have the same page numbers. This makes it possible for lawyers to cite the cases prior to the bound volumes of court decisions being ready for sale.

Aerial searches   Aerial searches are conducted from a helicopter or airplane. A search warrant is not required because the only items that are seen are ones left in plain view. Aerial searches are not restricted to commercial flight routes; police may charter a plane and fly over a specific area.

Affidavit   An affidavit is a written document made under oath. It is used in both civil and criminal cases. When a warrant is being sought, an affidavit is drafted, containing the facts that support probable cause for the warrant.

Affirmation   An affirmation is a statement, made in the format specified by state or federal law, that a person makes who has religious objections to taking an oath. The Fourth Amendment allows warrants to be based on oath or affirmation.

Aggravating circumstances   The judge is usually allowed to impose a longer sentence if there are aggravating circumstances, gratuitous violence; theft of large amounts of money; victimization of the elderly, such as those who are physically or mentally handicapped, or the very young. In death penalty cases, aggravating circumstances are considered during the penalty phase of the trial.

Alcoholic Beverage Control   Most states have an agency that deals with licensing businesses that sell alcoholic beverages. A common name for such an agency is the Department of Alcoholic Beverage Control. Police officers usually have the authority to arrest for violation of the alcoholic beverage control laws. Violations, such as selling to a minor, may result in loss of the business's license to sell alcoholic beverages.

Alibi   Alibi witnesses testify for the defense and state that the defendant was not at the location claimed by the prosecution.

Allocution   The defendant can make a speech explaining to the judge why he/she committed the crime, apologizing to the victim, and/or asking for mercy. The defendant has the right of allocution at the sentencing hearing. The defendant may waive this right.

Alternate jurors   The purpose of alternate jurors is to have replacements available if one or more of the regular jurors must be excused due to illness or other problems. The number of alternate jurors is set by the judge. Alternate jurors are usually selected after the regular jurors have been seated.

Amicus curiae   When a case reaches the United States Supreme Court, people or organizations that support either side may petition for *amicus curiae* status. If this is granted, the petitioner will be allowed to file a brief in the case. Normally *amicus curiae* do not directly participate in the decisions made by the lawyers who are handling the case; they are not allowed to give oral arguments unless the lawyers for the parties to the case consent.

Anonymous informant   An anonymous informant provides the police with information but does not reveal his/her identity. In *Illinois v. Gates* the U.S. Supreme Court allowed officers to use information from anonymous informants if the facts were sufficiently detailed and, where possible, had been verified.

Answer   The first document filed by the defense in a civil law suit is the answer. It contains denials for the specific allegations in the civil complaint and affirmative defenses.

Apparent authority   When seeking consent for a search, the police may rely on a person with apparent authority over the area to be searched. If it later turns out that the person did not have the authority to consent to the search, the search will still be valid.

Appellant   An appellant is the party to a law suit who files an appeal. The appellant is usually the party who lost in the lower court.

Appellant's opening brief   An appellant's opening brief is the first brief filed in an appeal. It establishes the issues for the case.

Appellant's reply brief   An appellant's reply brief is filed in response to the respondent's opening brief. The appellant's reply brief is usually optional.

Arraignment   An arraignment, sometimes referred to as the first appearance, is usually the first court hearing after a person is arrested. The following are usually done at the arraignment: the defendant is given a copy of the charges; the right to counsel is discussed and a public defender appointed if necessary; bail is set; and the date of the next court appearance is set. The arraignment, whether the defendant is charged with a misdemeanor or a felony, is usually held in front of a judge in the court that processes misdemeanor charges.

Attorney general's office   Each state has an attorney general. The most common duties of this office include helping local agencies investigate cases; providing specialized services; maintaining criminal history files; and operating crime labs for the use of smaller police departments. The attorney general represents the state in criminal appeals and some other legal matters.

Automatic appeal   Most states provide for an automatic appeal in death penalty cases. This means that the appeal will be done whether the defense requests it or not. It is common for this automatic appeal to go directly to the highest court in the state that handles criminal cases.

B

Bail   The bail system allows a defendant to be released from custody pending trial as long as the person deposits something of value with the court. The bail is returned if the defendant appears as scheduled. The judge sets the amount of bail. It is usually determined based on the severity of the defense and the defendant's financial resources. Many defendants use a bail bond agency. The bonding company posts a bond with the court and is required to pay the bail only if the defendant does not appear as scheduled. A typical fee for a bail bond is 10 percent of the amount of the bail.

Bail bond   A bail bond is issued by a bail bond company and deposited with the court. It represents the company's promise to pay the bail if the defendant does not appear when scheduled.

Bench trial   A bench trial is a trial held without a jury. The judge decides if the defendant is guilty or innocent.

Bench warrant   A bench warrant authorizes the arrest of a person and is issued by a judge initiative. The most common reason for a bench warrant is that the person did not appear in court or that the person has been convicted.

Bills of attainder   Bills of attainder are bills passed by the legislature that convict one or more persons for committing a crime. This removes the case from the judicial process.

Booking search   The U.S. Supreme Court has interpreted the Fourth Amendment as allowing a thorough search of the person at the time of booking as well as a thorough search of items in that person's possession. Some states restrict the right to conduct strip searches of people being booked for misdemeanors.

Boot camp   In corrections, a boot camp is a regimented jail program with the type of discipline used in military boot camps. The program is usually aimed at juveniles and young adults and aims at developing self-discipline and reducing the recidivism rate.

Bureau of Alcohol, Tobacco, and Firearms (ATF)   This federal agency has three main components: supervising the alcoholic beverage industry; monitoring the tobacco industry; and regulating the firearms industry. In all three cases, the agents are also concerned with verifying that federal taxes have been paid. ATF also has jurisdiction over thefts of explosives and bombings.

C

Case management system   A case management system is an organized database, whether in a computer or on paper, which makes it possible to locate information about the case. Typically included are the names of all the defendants in the case; the names and addresses of potential witnesses; an inventory of the evidence; laboratory test results; and actions taken in the case.

Case-in-chief   A case-in-chief is the portion of the trial where an attorney calls witnesses and presents evidence in order to meet his/her burden of proof.

Cash bail   A defendant, or his/her family and friends, can post bail in cash. When this happens, the money is returned if the defendant appears as scheduled.

Central Child Abuse Index   This is a database, frequently operated by the state's attorney general, that contains the names of people suspected of abusing children. Many states include the suspect's name, even though charges are not filed if the case was not unsubstantiated. The names of children who have been victimized are also included in many states. Officers investigating child abuse can check this index to see if the suspect has previously been suspected of child abuse.

Chain of custody (chain of possession)   In order to introduce evidence in court, the prosecution must establish what has happened to each piece of evidence from the time it came into the possession of the police until it is introduced in court. This usually involves calling each person who has had possession of it (even briefly) and having him/her explain what was done.

Challenge for cause   During jury selection, either side can use a challenge for cause to remove individuals who have already made up their minds on the issue of the defendant's guilt. There is no limit on the number of challenges for cause, but the judge must have strong evidence indicating the prospective juror will not consider the facts of the case and the law given in the jury instructions.

Challenge to the pleadings   A challenge to the pleadings is an attempt to have one or more of the charges dismissed before trial because of errors in the pleadings. A challenge to the pleadings is made by filing a formal motion with the court.

Chambers v. Maroney   This leading U.S. Supreme Court cases allows officers to search a vehicle based on probable cause without obtaining a warrant. Only the portions of the vehicle where the officers have probable cause to believe evidence is concealed may be searched. The officer's right to search is as extensive as a judge could authorize in a warrant based on the same facts.
    The search may be conducted at the scene, or the vehicle may be towed and searched at a later time.

Change of venue   When a motion for a change of venue is granted, the trial is moved to a different court district. The most common reason for a change of venue is that it would be impossible to find an unbiased jury at the location where the crime occurred.

Character   Character is the sum of a person's personal behavior. The defense is entitled to put the defendant's character in issue and claim that he/she is a "good person" and therefore would not commit a crime. The prosecution is not allowed to make generalized attacks on the defendant's character unless the defense put character in issue. Particular character traits may be in issue due to the nature of the case. If this is the case, the prosecution may introduce evidence of the defendant's reputation on these traits. Character is normally introduced via "character witnesses," who testify about a person's reputation.

Charge bargaining   Charge bargaining is similar to plea bargaining, except that it occurs before the charges are filed. The prosecutor and defense attorneys meet and reach an agreement on what charges will be filed; the defendant then pleads guilty to the charges.

Children's Protective Services   This agency, frequently operated at the county level, is a social work agency dedicated to assisting children who have been abused and/or neglected. If it is deemed appropriate, the social worker will remove the child from the home, arrange for foster care, and handle the necessary paperwork to take the case to court.

Chimel v. California   *Chimel* is the leading U.S. Supreme Court case on the extent of a search that can be done at the time of a custodial arrest. The person being arrested may be searched, as well as the area under his/her immediate control.

Citation   A citation is a form of release where the defendant is released based on a written promise to appear in court at a designated time. Citations are most common in traffic cases, but some states allow officers to use citations in misdemeanor cases.

Citing out   Citing out is the process of releasing a person from custody on a citation.

Civil forfeiture proceedings   Civil forfeiture proceedings involve a civil law suit, technically filed against specific items of property, in which the government seeks to enforce laws that require individuals involved in crime to forfeit items used to commit the crime and/or the profits of the crime.

Civil Rights Act   There have been many acts passed by Congress to protect civil rights. The one most often used to sue criminal justice personnel is the Civil Rights Act of 1871, which is found in Title 42 of the United States Code. Two commonly used sections are 42 U.S.C. 1983, which provides redress for a violation of constitutional rights under the color of state law, and 42 U.S.C. 1985, which provides redress for a conspiracy to violate constitutional rights.

Class action   A class action is a civil law suit by a large group of plaintiffs who were subjected to the same wrong. Once a court certifies a case as a class action, one group of attorneys represents all the victims, both known and unknown. Money recovered will be divided between all of these victims after attorney's fees and expenses have been paid.

Clerk's transcript   A clerk's transcript is prepared by the court clerk's office when a case is appealed. It includes copies of all the court documents in the case. Depending on the complexity of the case, it may include the complaint, the information, pretrial suppression motion and points and authorities, pretrial discovery motions, daily logs kept by the clerk in the courtroom, the list of   potential jurors, jury instructions, and verdict forms.

Closed Container Rule   The original Closed Container Rule stated that officers may seize a closed container based on probable cause, but a search warrant must be obtained in order to open it. In subsequent cases the Court made exceptions for property in a person's possession at the time of booking; the probable cause search of a car; the search of a car based on reasonable suspicion; and the search of a car incident to an arrest.

Closing statements   Closing statements are made by the attorneys after all the witnesses have testified. They summarize the case and try to present the evidence in the light most favorable to the side making the argument.

Code pleading   Code pleading is one of two formats used in writing the accusatory pleadings (complaint, information, or indictment). Code pleading allows the prosecutor to list the name of the crime and the code section but does not require the facts of the case to be listed in the pleading. Either the state legislature or local court rules designate which form of pleading will be used.

Collateral attack   A collateral attack is an attempt to set aside a conviction other than a direct or discretionary appeal.

Color of state law   Suits filed under the Civil Rights Act, 42 U.S.C. 1983, must be based on a violation of constitutional rights under color of state law. This means that the person who violated the plaintiff's rights was acting with authority bestowed by a state statute. For example, a police officer conducting an illegal search is considered to be acting under color of state law.

Common law   Common law is the body of precedent that has accumulated over the years. It is frequently used to refer to the body of law that came to the American colonies from England.

Community service order   A community service order usually states that a defendant is required to perform a specific number of hours of community service. A judge may give the defendant a community service order in addition to other types of sentences. In some cases the judge specifies which agency the defendant should work for.

Compensatory damages   In a civil suit the successful plaintiff can recover compensatory damages. Compensatory damages are based on the rationale that the defendant must reimburse the plaintiff for expenses caused by the defendant's actions—for example, medical bills or damaged property repair.

Competency to stand trial   The legal standard for competency to stand trial is that the defendant must understand the nature of the proceedings and be able to assist with the defense. The defendant must be mentally competent during all phase of the court proceedings. This is a due process right; therefore, the judge and prosecutor have a duty to raise it if the defense does not. The judge will stop the criminal proceedings. In many cases there is a delay to allow time for mental health experts to examine the defendant and submit reports. A hearing will be held on the issue of competency. The defendant will be sent to a mental health facility for treatment if he/she is found to be incompetent. The criminal proceedings may resume if the defendant recovers.

Complaint   A complaint is the first formal document filed with the court in most cases. It must contain the following information: the name of the court, the name and address of the plaintiff (prosecutor's office), the name of the defendant, and the charge(s). For each charge the complaint needs to specify the date the crime was committed (to satisfy the statute of limitations) and the location (to establish the geographical jurisdiction of the court).

Concurrent sentences   If the defendant is convicted of committing more than one crime, the judge must decide if the sentences will be served concurrently. Concurrent sentences are served at the same time: the time served for all of the crimes combined is equal to the time served for the crime with the longest sentence.

Conditional discharges   Conditional discharges resemble probation. At the sentencing hearing the judge places the defendant on conditional discharge. The defendant is required to comply with a set of rules (similar to the conditions of probation). If the defendant violates the rules, the judge has the authority to cancel the conditional discharge and order the defendant to serve his/her sentence in jail or prison.

Conditions of probation   When a person is placed on probation, the judge imposes a number of rules, which the probationer must follow. These rules are called the conditions of probation. Typical conditions of probation include commit no crimes, report to the probation officer at specified intervals; maintain gainful employment or attend school; do not associate with known criminals; and so on.

Confidential informants   Confidential informants provide information for the police with the understanding that the informant's identity will not be revealed. This type of information can be used when seeking a warrant because the police have the ability to verify the reliability of the informant.

Consecutive sentences If the defendant is convicted of committing more than one crime, the judge must decide if the sentences will be served consecutively. Consecutive sentences are served in sequential order. The total time served is the sum of all of the sentences (minus good time, etc.).

Consent decree In a civil case, the parties can settle out-of-court. If the settlement involves more than the payment of money, a consent decree will be entered, stating what each side agrees to do. A judge reviews the consent decree; if the judge accepts it, the consent decree has the same legal status as other court orders. Failure to comply with the consent decree is contempt of court.

Constitutional tort The Civil Rights Act, found in 42 U.S.C. 1983, does not apply to federal employees. In *Bivens v. Six Unknown Agents* (1968), the Supreme Court ruled that victims of unconstitutional acts by federal employees have a right to sue that is similar to that found in the Civil Rights Act. This right to sue is a constitutional tort.

Contemporaneous Objection Rule The Contemporaneous Objection Rule applies in court proceedings. If one attorney wishes to object to what the opposing side is doing, he/she must immediately state the objection and the reason behind it. For example, if the attorney asked the witness, "What did he say?" the opposing attorney would say, "Objection, calls for hearsay." The judge would allow both sides to argue the point and then the judge would make a ruling on whether the questions should be answered. The objection is rarely allowed if the attorney waits until after the question has been answered.

Continuance A continuance is a delay in a case. In most circumstances one of the attorneys must ask the judge for a continuance. Opposing counsel has the opportunity to respond to the request. The next court date is usually set when a judge grants the continuance, so that both sides know the length of the delay.

Contract cities Contract cities do not have their own police departments. They contract with another agency, such as the county sheriff, to provide all necessary police services.

Controlled delivery A controlled delivery occurs when police seize an item and then have it delivered to the intended recipient. Surveillance is maintained during this delivery. The court has ruled that the fact that either the police or the person who originally opened the package resealed the package prior to the controlled delivery does not give the addressee a reasonable expectation of privacy in the contents.

Coroner The coroner, usually a county-level official, is responsible for determining the cause of death. The coroner may hold a formal hearing, called an inquest, on this issue. If the coroner rules that the death was at the hands of another, the case is given to the prosecutor who must decide what charges, if any, to file.

Coroner's jury   In some states the coroner has the right to hold a hearing, called an inquest, and empanel a jury to hear evidence and decide if the death was at the hands of another. If the jury votes for "at the hands of another," the case is forwarded to the prosecutor, who will determine what charges, if any, to file.

Count   A count in an accusatory pleading charges one person with committing one crime. More than one count can be listed in the pleadings as long as the counts are related and meet the statute of limitations and geographical jurisdiction requirements set by the state.

Criminal history   A criminal history (sometimes called a "rap sheet") lists all previous cases filed against an individual and their dispositions. Some states include arrests even though charges were not filed.

Cross-examination   The side calling the witness conducts direct examination. Following this, the witness is subject to cross-examination by opposing counsel. The purpose of cross-examination is to bring out information that was not covered on direct and to impeach the witness. Leading questions are allowed during cross-examination.

Cruel and unusual punishment   The Eighth Amendment prohibits cruel and unusual punishment. Most of the cases on this issue that have been considered by the U.S. Supreme Court are about the death penalty.

Cumulative evidence   Cumulative evidence merely repeats evidence that has already been introduced. If there were several eye witnesses, and each gave to police statements that are very similar, their testimony is cumulative evidence. The judge may restrict the number of witnesses who testify if they present cumulative evidence.

Custody   *Miranda* warnings are required only if a person is in custody and being interrogated. For this purpose, custody means that a person has been arrested and is not free to leave. A person who is released at the scene is not in custody; neither is a person stopped under *Terry v. Ohio* but not arrested. A person remains in custody until released; this could include the time spent serving a sentence after conviction. During the entire period a person is in custody, *Miranda* warnings must be given even though the officers who wish to question the suspect have no connection with those who made the arrest.

D

Day fine   A day fine makes the amount of the fine proportional to the income of the individual. For example, the statute might state that the fine is equal to five days' wages. Day fines are used more commonly in Europe than in the United States.

Deadly force   The U.S. Supreme Court applied the Fourth Amendment to the use of force. Deadly force may be used only if a life is in immediate danger. The reasonable appearances test is used to determine if the force was justified.

Death warrant   A death warrant sets the execution date for a person who has been sentenced to death. The death warrant may be executed only on the date specified; if this is not possible, a new one may be issued.

Defendant   A defendant is a person who must defend him/herself against a law suit. In a criminal case the defendant is the person charged with the crime.

Demurrer   In a civil case the defense may file a demurrer to challenge the plaintiff's right to bring the law suit. It argues the legal issues of the case without calling witnesses to establish the factual basis for the suit. When used, the demurrer is the first document the defense files.

Department of Justice   The attorney general (state or federal) usually heads the Department of Justice. The legislative branch usually decides what agencies will be housed in the Department of Justice.

Department of Motor Vehicles   This state-level department issues driver's licenses and revokes them. Vehicle registration is usually processed by this agency. It may also have authority over car dealers, due to their frequent involvement in vehicle registration.

Dependency court   Dependency court handles cases involving children who have been abused, neglected, or abandoned. The judge makes rulings on whether the children should be removed from the home and, in extreme cases, whether the children should be put up for adoption. In a large court system there is usually a court that specializes in these cases. It may be housed in family court or juvenile court if there is not sufficient workload for a specialized court.

Dependent children   Dependent children are in the court system because of abuse, neglect, or abandonment by their caregivers, not due to their own misconduct.

Deposition   In a civil case either side can take the deposition of anyone having firsthand knowledge of the facts in the case. The deposition is taken during a hearing, where the witness is sworn in, the side requesting the deposition asks questions, and a stenographic reporter makes a verbatim record of what is said. Opposing counsel is usually present and has the right to object to questions but is not allowed to cross-examine.

Detention hearing   In juvenile court a detention hearing is held shortly after the juvenile is taken into custody. Its purpose is to determine if the child should remain in custody pending trial. The juvenile and his/her attorney are given a copy of the charges during this hearing.

Determinate sentencing   In states with determinate sentencing, the judge is usually given options, but the sentence that is imposed is a specific number. For example, the defendant may be sent to state prison for 7 1/2 years.

Direct appeal   A direct appeal is taken immediately after a conviction. The state usually sets time limits, such as 60 days after entry of conviction, for filing notice that the direct appeal will be taken. The defendant usually has a right to one direct appeal of the conviction; subsequent appeals are at the discretion of the higher court.

Direct examination   The attorney that calls a witness conducts direct examination of that witness. Leading questions are usually not allowed during direct examination.

Discovery   Discovery is conducted pretrial so that both sides know what evidence will be presented at trial. Both sides are usually expected to exchange lists of intended witnesses. Many states allow discovery regarding the physical evidence and statements made by intended witnesses. The defense does not have to provide information protected by the privilege against self-incrimination.

Discretionary appeals   Discretionary appeals are appeals that are granted only if the higher court wishes to hear the cases. For example, criminal cases are heard by the United States Supreme Court only if four justices vote to accept the cases.

Dismissed with prejudice   When a judge dismisses a case with prejudice, the charges cannot be filed again.

Disposition hearing   In juvenile court, a disposition hearing is held after a trial if the juvenile was "convicted." The purpose of the disposition hearing is to decide what will happen to the juvenile. The alternatives available to the judge include releasing the child to his/her parents and placing the child on probation, placing the child in juvenile hall or a camp, or sending the child to the state's juvenile equivalent of prison.

Diversion   Diversion is the process of sending defendants to counseling and other services in lieu of proceeding with the criminal charges. A formal hearing is held before a judge after the charges are filed and the defense must accept diversion. Diversion programs usually last from six months to two years. If the defendant fails to comply with the conditions of the diversion program, the criminal charges can be reinstated.

Double jeopardy   A person who has been convicted or acquitted cannot be charged with the same crime(s) a second time. The Fifth Amendment prohibits double jeopardy. Double jeopardy does not apply to a pretrial dismissal of the case; dismissal of the case during trial (mistrial); cases resulting in a hung jury (not able to reach a verdict); and the retrial of a criminal defendant who was convicted but had the case reversed on appeal.

Drug Enforcement Administration (DEA)   This federal agency supervises the pharmaceutical industry to make sure its drugs are not diverted into the illegal market. It also has jurisdiction (both inside the United States and abroad) to try to prevent the smuggling of drugs into the United States.

Due process   Both the Fifth and Fourteenth Amendments guarantee due process of law. In a criminal case the defendant has the procedural rights guaranteed by the Sixth Amendment. At subsequent proceedings, such as a parole revocation hearing, the person is entitled to a fair hearing but does not have as many rights as a person who has not been convicted.

E

Electronic monitoring   A defendant released on bail, as well as one on probation or parole, may be required to wear an electronic device, which can be used to determine where the defendant is.

Electronic surveillance warrants   Electronic surveillance warrants authorize the installation of a wiretap or listening device. Federal officers use Title III of the Omnibus Crime Control and Safe Streets Act of 1968 to obtain electronic surveillance warrants. State and local officers can obtain this type of warrant if their legislature has authorized them.

Enhancements   Enhancements are added onto a sentence—for example, one extra year for being armed while committing a crime or five extra years if the defendant has previously served a prison term for a felony.

Equal protection   A person cannot be discriminated against on the basis of race, place of origin, or ethnicity. Over the years this right has expanded to protect against gender discrimination. The Fourteenth Amendment guarantees equal protection.

Ex post facto   A law is considered *ex post facto* if it is retroactive. Three types of situations are covered: a law that makes an action a crime when that act occurred prior to the date the law became effective; a law that increases a penalty for crimes that were committed prior to the date the law went into effect; and a law that changes the rules of evidence, so that it is easier to convict than it would have been on the date the crime was committed.

Exclusionary Rule   The Exclusionary Rule prohibits the use of evidence at trial if the evidence was obtained in a manner that violates constitutional rights.

Exclusive jurisdiction   An agency has exclusive jurisdiction if the legislature has given it the sole right to enforce a specific law. In many instances more than one agency has jurisdiction to handle the case. When this is the case, it is important to have guidelines, so that both agencies know who will make the key decisions.

Executing a warrant (serving a warrant)   An arrest warrant is executed when a person is arrested. A search warrant is executed when the authorized search is performed.

Expert witnesses   Expert witnesses are allowed to testify if the jury needs help in understanding the evidence. Expert witnesses are allowed to give their professional opinions. Either side may call expert witnesses.

F

Fact pleading   Fact pleading is one of two forms of pleadings used in accusatory pleadings (complaint, information, and indictment). In fact pleading, the facts that support the charge must be briefly summarized in the pleadings. Either the state legislature or local court rules designate which form of pleading will be used.

Failure to state a cause of action   The defense can have a charge dismissed if the complaint, information, or indictment fails to state a cause of action. This means that the charge, even if everything in it is true, does not allege all the elements necessary of a crime. If the pleadings contain more than one charge, each charge must be considered separately; only those that fail to state a cause of action should be dismissed. The entire case will be dismissed only if every charge is defective.

Federal Bureau of Investigation (FBI)   This multipurpose federal agency investigates many types of crimes. It has jurisdiction over espionage, threats to kill the president, and many other crimes. If Congress passes a new crime and does not assign jurisdiction to a specific agency, the FBI has jurisdiction to investigate violations of the law.

Felony arrest   The traditional rule is that a police officer is allowed to make a felony arrest based on probable cause that the crime was committed. The crime does not need to occur in the officer's presence.

Filing the complaint   The process of filing the complaint involves taking a complaint to the court clerk's office, where it is stamped "Filed" and date stamped.

Fine   A fine is a specific amount of money a judge orders a defendant to pay to the court. In most states a judge has the authority to impose a fine on anyone convicted of a crime. The code may specify the amount of the fine—for example, the fine for petty theft is $500—or it may give the judge the authority to set a fine within a range—for example, the fine for a misdemeanor is up to $1,000.

First Amendment   The First Amendment provides for freedom of speech and assembly, for freedom to petition the government, for freedom of the press, for the free exercise of religion, and that the government shall not establish religion.

Fitness hearing   A fitness hearing is a court hearing where the judge decides if a case should be transferred from juvenile court to adult criminal court. A fitness hearing is held in juvenile court if the prosecutor filed papers asking to transfer the case to adult court.

Free counsel for the poor–under *Miranda*   During custodial interrogation a suspect has the right to have an attorney present. If an indigent person requests an attorney, he/she must be provided with an attorney if the questioning continues.

Free counsel for the poor–under the Sixth Amendment   The Sixth Amendment right to counsel applies during court proceedings. The U.S. Supreme Court, in a series of cases, established that an indigent person has the right to have government-appointed counsel represent him/her from arraignment through trial and the sentencing hearing; the first postconviction appeal is also covered.

Freedom of speech   The First Amendment guarantees freedom of speech. This is one of the most highly guarded rights, but it does not apply in all situations. Obscenity and "fighting words" are not protected; neither is shouting "Fire!" in a crowded theater. Any laws the government makes to restrict the freedom of speech must be content-neutral.

Frisk   *Terry v. Ohio* allows officers to stop a person based on reasonable suspicion. If there is reasonable suspicion that the person is armed, the officer may do a pat-down of the person's outer clothing and retrieve any weapons that are detected. This pat-down is called a frisk.

Fruit of the Poison Tree Doctrine   The Fruit of the Poison Tree Doctrine is an extension of the Exclusionary Rule. Under the Exclusionary Rule, any evidence obtained in violation of the suspect's constitutional rights is not admissible by the prosecution at trial. The Fruit of the Poison Tree Doctrine operates to make items inadmissible if they were found due to items discovered during an unconstitutional search or confession. For example, a person was detained illegally and searched, a key was found in the person's pocket. The police used the key to open a storage locker and found a cache of illegal drugs. The key is inadmissible under the Exclusionary Rule; the drugs are excluded under the Fruit of the Poison Tree Doctrine.

G

General damages   The purpose of general damages is to compensate the plaintiff for physical and emotional pain and suffering. In a civil suit a defendant who causes injury to the plaintiff must pay general damages.

General deterrence   General deterrence is one rationale for punishment. When general deterrence is used, the sentence is an attempt to deter the general population from committing a crime, rather than just deterring the defendant.

Geographical jurisdiction   A court has geographical jurisdiction if the crime occurred within its boundaries. The legislature establishes the boundaries for court districts.

Good faith exception   The Supreme Court has established a good faith exception to the exclusionary rule. It applies to searches conducted by officers who, in good faith, acted on warrants that appeared to be valid; arrest warrants that had been recalled but court personnel had failed to remove the warrant from the database of active warrants; and statutes that appeared to be valid but were declared unconstitutional after the arrest was made.

Grand jury   A grand jury is a panel of citizens who review criminal cases; if the grand jury finds there are sufficient facts to warrant prosecution, it issues an indictment. The size of the grand jury is set by the legislature. Many states establish a one-year term for the grand jury.

Guilt phase   In cases involving the death penalty, and those in which the defense entered dual pleas of not guilty and not guilty by reason of insanity, the trial is divided into two parts: the guilty phase, where the issue is whether the defendant committed the crime, and a second phase, where the other issues are considered.

H

Halfway houses   Halfway houses are residential facilities for people who have been released from jail or prison. They provide supervision while the staff helps direct job search efforts and other relevant activities. People living in a halfway house are usually allowed to leave the building at will but may have curfews, be subjected to drug and/or alcohol testing, and so on. Spending time in a halfway house is usually mandated by the judge or parole board. Most halfway houses accept people for one to six months.

Held to answer   If sufficient evidence is presented at the preliminary hearing, the defendant will be held to answer. In such a case, the judge will make a ruling after the evidence has been presented and will state which felony charges the prosecutor can take to trial.

Hostile witnesses   Hostile witnesses are people who are called by one side but are biased in favor of the opposing side. If the judge agrees to designate a person as a hostile witness, the side calling the witness may use leading questions and may ask questions designed to show the jury how biased the person is.

House arrest   A person is said to be under house arrest when he/she is released pending trial or on probation and one of the conditions is that he/she must not leave the residence.

Hung jury   A jury that deliberates but cannot reach a verdict is referred to as a hung jury. The prosecutor is usually allowed to refile the charges.

I

Ignition interlock devices   Ignition interlock devices prevent cars from being started. In some states, people who have multiple convictions for driving under the influence are required to have ignition interlock devices placed on their vehicles. In these situations, the device is set up to take a breath sample; the ignition switch will work only if the person passes the legal standard for breath alcohol level.

Illinois v. Gates   This landmark case on obtaining search warrants permitted officers to rely on anonymous informants. Whether probable cause exists is determined based on the totality of the circumstances test.

Impeachment   Impeachment is the process of attempting to discredit a witness. It is usually done during cross-examination. Every witness who takes the witness stand is subject to impeachment by the opposing side.

Implied consent   In many states a person who applies for a driver's license consents to taking blood, breath, or urine tests if stopped on suspicion of driving while under the influence of alcohol or drugs. This is called implied consent. If the person is stopped for suspicion of drunk driving, he/she can be taken to the emergency room or other appropriate facility for tests.

In propria persona (pro per)   This Latin phrase means that a person is representing him-/herself and does not have an attorney.

Inability to perceive events   A witness may be impeached based on his/her inability to perceive the events which he/she has testified about. Two types of impairment result in an inability to perceive: lack of physical ability by witness (poor eyesight, impaired hearing, etc.) and physical barriers that made it impossible to observe the event (poor lighting, a wall blocking the view, etc.).

Incapacitation   Incapacitation is a rationale for punishment. When incapacitation is used, the convicted defendant is sent to jail or prison to keep him/her out of society, thus making the defendant incapable of preying on the public.

Inconsistent statements   After a witness has testified on direct, opposing counsel may ask about specific statements that the witness made prior to taking the stand that are in conflict with the testimony in court. The witness may be impeached if he/she makes inconsistent statements while on the witness stand.

Independent source   The independent source exception to the exclusionary rule allows evidence to be used at trial if it was obtained through an independent source, even though the same evidence was obtained by an illegal act.

Indeterminate sentencing   In states with indeterminate sentencing, the judge sentences the defendant to a period of time with the exact release date determined by the parole board or another agency. For example, a person convicted of second-degree murder might be sentenced to 15 years to life in state prison.

Indictment   An indictment is the official charging document issued by the grand jury if it finds sufficient evidence to merit prosecution.

Inevitable discovery   The inevitable discovery exception to the exclusionary rule allows evidence to be used at trial if the judge is convinced that illegally seized evidence would inevitably have been discovered, regardless of the illegal act.

Informal probation   When someone is placed on informal probation, that person is not required to keep in regular contact with a probation officer. An arrest for another crime, however, may result in the revocation of probation and the person's being sent to jail or prison.

Information   An information is the official charging document that the prosecution files after a preliminary hearing. It contains the felonies for which the defendant was held to answer plus any misdemeanors the prosecution selects.

Injunction   An injunction is a court order that requires a party to the case to do (or to refrain from doing) something. Injunctions are issued in civil rights cases only if the plaintiff can show that there is a pervasive pattern of misconduct; an isolated incident in not sufficient.

Inquest   An inquest is a hearing held by a coroner to determine whether a death was due to natural causes or "at the hands of another."

Insufficient evidence   The level of proof increases as a criminal case moves from the first court appearance to the trial. The judge may dismiss the case if he/she believes there is insufficient evidence to support the prosecution's burden of proof at any point in the case.

Intake   Intake is the process of completing the paperwork necessary for admission to a juvenile facility. It is the equivalent of booking an inmate into a jail.

Intensive probation   When a person is placed on intensive probation, that person is required to report to the probation officer much more frequently than are other probationers. The probation officer handles fewer cases than his/her colleagues and is able to provide a much higher level of supervision for the probationers.

Intentional torts   Intentional torts are civil wrongs, perpetrated by a person who intentionally did an act that the law has declared to be wrong. A person who is found liable for an intentional tort can be required to pay punitive damages in addition to compensatory and general damages. Intentional torts are considered more serious than negligent torts.

Intermittent sentencing   If a defendant receives an intermittent sentence, the sentence can be served in segments. For example, a person sentenced to 30 days in jail may serve 15 consecutive weekends but be allowed to remain free during the workweek.

Interrogation   Interrogation is the process of questioning a person. The Supreme Court has ruled that interrogation includes both direct and indirect questioning. *Miranda* warnings are required prior to custodial interrogation.

Interrogatories   Interrogatories are written questions that must be answered in writing under oath. In civil cases each side may serve interrogatories on the other side. Interrogatories can ask the opposing party to search his/her records for the answers to questions.

Interstate Agreement on Detainers   The Interstate Agreement on Detainers allows a law enforcement agency to place a "hold" on an inmate who is being held in another state. When the inmate is due to be released, he/she is turned over to the agency that placed the hold and then can be prosecuted on the pending charges. If the inmate desires, he/she can demand an immediate trial when the hold is placed, rather than waiting for the end of his/her sentence.

Interstate Agreement on Supervision of Probationers and Parolees   This interstate agreement allows states to transfer probationers and/or parolees to another state. The receiving state will supervise them under the local rules. The most common reason for using this interstate agreement is that the probationer/parolee has family or employment in another state.

Interstate Corrections Compact   The Interstate Corrections Compact allows states to transfer inmates to another state to continue serving their sentences. These transfers most commonly are used to reduce prison overcrowding and to provide necessary treatment facilities (medical, psychiatric, etc.) not available in the home state.

Involuntary civil commitment   An involuntary civil commitment is the confinement of a person to a mental institution for treatment when the person is not willing to sign the admission papers. The legal standard for involuntary civil commitments is that the person is a danger to him-/herself, is a danger to others, or is so gravely impaired that he/she is unable to care for him/herself.

J

"John Doe" warrant   A "John Doe" warrant is a warrant that is issued even though the name of the person to be arrested is not known. At a later date, when the person's name is known, the prosecution can go to court and have the true name inserted. In lieu of a name, the warrant must contain a detailed description of the person to be arrested, so that the arresting officer will know whether or not the correct person is being taken into custody.

Joinder   A joinder is the joining of two or more cases. This consolidation may occur because two defendants were involved in the same crime and it is more efficient to have only one trial. Another reason is because one defendant committed multiple crimes, which were filed separately, but it is more efficient to have only one trial.

Joint jurisdiction   Agencies have joint jurisdiction if each is not the sole agency with jurisdiction over a case. For example, in a bank robbery case the FBI has jurisdiction over the robbery of a federally insured bank; at the same time, the local police department has jurisdiction to investigate a robbery under state law.

Judgment on the pleadings   In a civil suit the judge has the power to enter a judgment on the pleadings if there are no facts in dispute. This judge considers only the complaint and the answer. The most common reason for granting a judgment on the pleadings is that the defense failed to deny key allegations in the complaint. A judgment on the pleadings has the same legal consequences as a verdict at the end of a trial.

Jurisdiction   Two types of jurisdiction must be considered in criminal cases. Geographical jurisdiction means that a court may hear only a case if the crime was committed within the geographical boundaries of the court district. Subject matter jurisdiction is the authority of the court to hear a particular type of case. In criminal cases the issue of subject matter jurisdiction arises if the legislature has given one level of court—for example, the municipal court—authority for misdemeanor trials but not felony trials. In such a situation, the municipal court lacks subject matter jurisdiction to hold a felony trial.

Jurisdiction hearing (adjudication hearing)   In juvenile court the hearing that is equivalent to the trial in adult criminal court is frequently referred to as the jurisdiction hearing.

Jurisdiction of peace officers   The jurisdiction of peace officers is set by the state legislature. Typically the officer has jurisdiction while working in the city that employs him/her, while going anywhere in the state to investigate a crime that occurred in the city that employs the officer, and if he/she observes a crime that threatens public safety anywhere in the state.

Jury commissioner   A jury commissioner is the person in charge of sending out jury summons and making sure that there are enough prospective jurors at the courthouse.

Jury instructions   The judge gives the jury instructions before the jury leaves the courtroom to begin deliberations. Most jury instructions are quotes from the relevant codes and appellate court opinions. Some states have standardized jury instructions and allow the jury to take copies of the jury instructions into the jury room to use during deliberations. Other states allow judges to compose their own jury instructions.

Jury nullification   A jury has the right to vote its conscience and ignore the law. An acquittal obtained in this manner is covered by double jeopardy and the charges cannot be filed again. If the jury ignores the law and returns a conviction, the conviction will be set aside or reversed on appeal.

Jury pool   A jury pool is a group of people whose names are in the database used to send out summons for jury duty. Voter registration records are used. Some states add names from driver's licenses, state identifications cards, and other sources.

K

Knock notice   Officers must comply with knock notice (also called knock and announce) prior to entry into a dwelling, except in emergencies. The standard process is (1) knock or otherwise indicate that you are at the door; (2) announce who you are; (3) announce why you are there; and (4) wait long enough for a cooperative person to open the door. Exceptions apply if the officer is in danger; if there is a serious threat of destruction of evidence; if there is a strong indication that the suspect will flee; or if someone inside is in danger.

Knowing, intelligent, and voluntary waiver   A suspect's answers given during custodial interrogation are admissible by the prosecution only if the suspect has made a knowing, intelligent, and voluntary waiver of his/her *Miranda* rights. "Knowing" means the person has been informed of his/her rights and understands them; "intelligent" means the person possesses at least the minimum level of intelligence required to understand his/her rights; and "voluntary" means the waiver was made without coercion.

L

Lack of jurisdiction   A criminal case must be dismissed if it is established that the court lacks jurisdiction over it. The most common reason for this action is that the crime did not occur inside the court district. Cases dismissed for lack of jurisdiction may be filed in another jurisdiction if the statute of limitations has not expired. If there are multiple charges, the court must consider each charge separately and dismiss only the ones where jurisdiction is lacking.

Lay witness   Lay witnesses are called to testify about what they observed with the five senses (sight, hearing, smell, taste, and feel). Lay witnesses are not allowed to give opinions.

Leading questions   Leading questions are ones that imply the answer. On cross-examination an attorney is allowed to ask leading questions. They are also used for hostile witnesses during direct examination.

Limited admissibility   A fact can be used by a jury for one purpose but not another. For example, when a witness is impeached for a prior inconsistent statement, the statement can be used to challenge the credibility of the witness but should not be used to establish the defendant's guilt.

Line-up   A line-up is an identification procedure where an eye witness is shown a group of people (one of which is the suspect) and asked if the person who committed the crime is present. After indictment or arraignment the suspect has the right to have an attorney present at the line-up. Unduly suggestive line-ups violate due process.

Lis pendens   *Lis pendens* is a document that is filed, usually with the county recorder of deeds, which puts anyone interested in real estate on notice that a law suit is pending regarding ownership of the land. It is rare that anyone purchases land on which *lis pendens* has been filed. While a civil forfeiture proceeding is in progress, *lis pendens* can be filed to prevent the defendant from selling the property.

M

Miranda **warnings**   In the landmark case of *Miranda v. Arizona* (1966), the U.S. Supreme Court mandated that, prior to custodial interrogation, the suspect be advised of the following rights: you have the right to remain silent; anything you say will be used against you in court; you have the right to have an attorney present during questioning; and if you cannot afford an attorney one will be provided for you at no charge.

Misdemeanor arrest   The traditional rule was that a police officer could make an arrest for a misdemeanor based probable cause *only if* the officer observed the crime being committed. When the crime did not occur in the officer's presence, the officer could ask a person who witnessed it to make a "citizen's arrest" or seek an arrest warrant.

Misplaced Reliance Doctrine   The Misplaced Reliance Doctrine states that a person has the right to select who can overhear his/her conversations. If someone hears what is said, and later informs authorities, the speaker cannot claim an invasion of his/her privacy. This rule also applies when someone wearing a microphone or tape recorder is sent to participate in or eavesdrop on conversations. Listening devices surreptitiously installed so that no party to the conversation knows that anyone can overhear require an electronic surveillance warrant.

Mistrial   A mistrial is declared by a trial judge due to errors at trial. It provides no double jeopardy protections for the defendant. Reasons for a mistrial include prejudicial conduct by one of the attorneys; less than the required number of jurors and no remaining alternates; testimony by a witness about topics that have previously been ruled inadmissible; and a hung jury.

Mitigating circumstances   Mitigating circumstances are facts related to the case that justify imposing a lenient sentence. Mitigating circumstances are considered by the jury in capital murder cases when deciding whether to impose the death penalty or life in prison without the possibility of parole. The judge may consider mitigating circumstances when imposing a sentence for other crimes. Examples of mitigating circumstances are a very low level of violence used in what is normally a violent crime; the theft of very small amounts of money; and attempts to return stolen items before being confronted by the police.

Motion to proceed *in forma pauperis*   A person who wishes to petition the United States Supreme Court but cannot afford the expenses for printing briefs, and so on may petition the court to proceed *in forma pauperis.* When granted, this petition allows the use of less expensive briefs, waives filing fees, and so on.

Motive, bias, or prejudice   A witness may be impeached due to motive, bias, or prejudice. On cross-examination the opposing counsel can ask questions to show that there was a motive, bias, or prejudice, which may have, consciously or unconsciously, resulted in the witness being less than objective while testifying. Examples are close family ties to the defendant; a personal dislike for the defendant; racist opinions about members of the defendant's race; and potential financial gain if the person who called the witness wins the law suit.

Mutual aid agreements   Police departments frequently enter into mutual aid agreements, so that they can borrow officers when emergencies arise. Police officers who are working outside the city that employs them due to a mutual aid agreement usually have all the authority of an officer in the city where they are serving. The mutual aid agreement is a formal contract which specifies all the details, including how many officers may be used, who pays them, and other important issues. Mutual aid agreements usually cover natural disasters (earthquake, flood, etc.), riots and civil disturbances, and special events.

N

Narrative questions   Narrative questions prompt a witness to talk about the event in question. This type of question is not favored because witnesses tend to ramble, bring up irrelevant information, and possibly cover items the judge has ruled are inadmissible. A series of more specific questions is preferred.

Negligent torts   Negligent torts are torts based on the assumption that the defendant acted carelessly and must pay to replace what was damaged. The plaintiff may recover both compensatory and general damages.

Neutral magistrate   A neutral magistrate is a person—authorized by law to grant warrants—who can act in an unbiased manner. A judge is not neutral if he/she has a personal interest in the case.

New York v. Belton   This leading U.S. Supreme Court case held that officers who arrest a person in a vehicle may, contemporaneous with the arrest, conduct a thorough search of the passenger compartment of the car.

No bill   If a prosecutor takes a case to a grand jury, but the grand jury finds there is insufficient evidence to warrant a trial, the indictment is endorsed "no bill" of indictment.

Nolo contendere   In many states a defendant can enter a plea of *nolo contendere*, which means no contest. This plea has all the ramifications of a guilty plea in criminal court. Some states do not allow evidence of a *nolo contendere* plea to be admitted in a civil case.

Non-cash bail   A defendant may deposit anything of value for bail. The most common items used for non-cash bond are deeds to real estate and certificates representing shares of stock.

Non-deadly   The U.S. Supreme Court applied the Fourth Amendment to the use of non-deadly force. Whatever force an officer uses must be reasonable, based on all of the circumstances present. Deadly force is authorized only in life-threatening situations.

Not guilty by reason of insanity   Only the defense can enter a plea of not guilty by reason of insanity. Once the plea is entered there are usually two phases to the trial: one addresses the issue of whether the defendant committed the crime; the other addresses the mental issues and determines if he/she is not guilty by reason of insanity. If the defendant is found not guilty by reason of insanity, double jeopardy prevents the prosecution from filing the charges again after the defendant recovers. Defendants found not guilty by reason of insanity are usually sent to a mental hospital under an involuntary civil commitment but may be released if they recover. The most common test used to determine if the defendant was sane at the time of the crime is the M'Naghten test. Under this test the defendant is not guilty if, due to mental disease or defect, he/she is unable to appreciate the nature and quality of his/her acts, or if he/she does not understand whether the acts were right or wrong.

Number of grand jurors   The number of people on a grand jury is set by the legislature. Traditionally it was 23. Some states establish the size of the grand jury based on the population of the county.

Number of votes to indict   The number of votes required for a grand jury to indict someone is established by the legislature. Unanimity is not required, but most states require more than a simple majority.

O

Oath   An oath is a promise to tell the truth. The traditional oath was to tell the whole truth, "so help me God." Many states now recognize written documents made under the penalty of perjury as meeting the requirement of an oath.

Objection overruled   During trial, if an attorney makes an objection and the judge finds it without merit, the judge states "Objection overruled."

Objection sustained   During trial, if an attorney makes an objection and the judge decides to grant it, the judge states "Objection sustained."

"Off-sale" license   A store that has an "off-sale" liquor license may sell cans and bottles of alcoholic beverages but is not authorized to have open containers on the premises—for example, grocery store or liquor store.

"On call" subpoena   A witness may be given an "on call" subpoena if he/she can be trusted to appear in court when called. A person with an "on call" subpoena does not report to the courtroom until notified that it is time to go. For example, a witness who works two miles from the courthouse may be put "on call" on the condition that, when the attorney phones, the witness will arrive at the courthouse within 30 minutes.

"On-sale" license   A business with an "on-sale" license is allowed to serve alcoholic beverages in open containers, such as glasses or open beer bottles—for example, a bar.

Opening statements   Opening statements are speeches, made by attorneys, that summarize a case and explain what each side will attempt to prove. The prosecutor makes an opening statement immediately after jury selection is complete and the jury has been sworn in. The defense has three options: make the statement immediately after prosecution; give an opening statement at the beginning of the defense case-in-chief; or do not make an opening statement.

Out-of-state warrants   The Uniform Criminal Extradition Act gives officers the right to make an arrest based on a warrant issued in another state. The arrested person is then held until the agency that obtained the warrant arranges transportation back to the location where the case will be prosecuted. Extradition proceedings are required unless waived by the defendant.

Own recognizance release   In many states inmates may be released on their own recognizance pending trial if they demonstrate sufficient ties to the community. No money or bond is required for an OR release. Failure to appear in court as directed after being released OR is a separate crime.

P

Past recollection recorded   The past recollection recorded exception to the hearsay rule is used if a witness no longer has sufficient memory to fully and accurately testify but the witness made a written report of the events near the time that they occurred. The witness must be able to testify that the report was made when the events were fresh in his/her memory and that the report is accurate. Statements in the report that would not have been admissible if the witness were testifying about them are not admissible when the report is read into evidence.

Patdown (frisk)   *Terry v. Ohio* allows officers to stop a person based on reasonable suspicion. If there is reasonable suspicion that the person is armed, the officer may do a patdown of the person's outer clothing and retrieve any weapons that are detected.

Peace officer   State law sets the requirements that allow agencies to designate their employees peace officers. Peace officer status impacts several issues: a need to complete mandated training; powers of arrest; the right to carry weapons; and the need to pass background checks.

Penalty phase   At the penalty phase of a death penalty trial, the jury decides whether the defendant will be executed or sentenced to prison for life.

Peremptory challenges   During jury selection each side has peremptory challenges, which can be used to exclude jurors for any reason except race or gender. State law establishes a quota for peremptory challenges.

Petition   The first document filed in juvenile court is usually called a petition. It is the equivalent of the complaint in adult criminal court.

Petition for writ of *certiorari*   Anyone asking the United States Supreme Court to hear his/her case must file a petition for writ of *certiorari*. If four justices vote to grant *certiorari*, the case will be transferred to the Court for a full hearing.

Petition for writ of *habeas corpus*   Anyone asking a court to hold a *habeas corpus* hearing must file a petition for writ of *habeas corpus*, stating the grounds for the request. A judge will review the petition and documents filed by the opposing side and decide if there is a legal issue involved which justifies holding a hearing in the case.

Petitioner   A petitioner is a person (or an agency) who files a petition.

Photographic line-up   A photographic line-up is an identification procedure in which eye witnesses are shown a number of photographs and asked to pick out the person who committed the crime. Photographic line-ups must not be unduly suggestive. The suspect does not have the right to be present or to have an attorney present during this procedure.

Physical layout of the crime scene   An officer at the scene of a crime should make an accurate, to-scale diagram of the layout of the scene, marking the location where each piece of evidence was discovered. In many cases a large display board with the diagram of the crime scene is used while witnesses are testifying.

Physical limitations of the witness   Attorneys (both prosecution and defense) must consider the physical limitations of a witness when deciding what questions to ask. For example, if the witness is known to have a hearing impairment, the attorney should not rely on this witness to establish what the defendant said.

Plain View Doctrine   Under the Plain View Doctrine, evidence found by an officer who is legally at the location where the observation is made can be seized if there is probable cause to believe that the item is evidence of a crime, is contraband, or has other evidentiary value. The officer is not allowed to pick up or move an item and examine it to determine if there is probable cause.

Plaintiff   A plaintiff is a person who files a law suit. In a criminal case the prosecutor's office is the plaintiff.

Plea bargain In a plea bargain, a guilty plea is entered after negotiations between the prosecution and defense on what charges the defendant will plead guilty to and which ones will be dismissed. In some states the sentence is also part of the plea bargain.

Points and authorities This document contains legal research on the topic to be discussed in court and usually cites code sections and case law. Points and authorities accompany many motions made in court.

Poll the jury After a jury verdict is read in court the attorneys are allowed to ask to have the jury polled. To poll the jury is to ask each juror, in open court, whether he/she agrees with the verdict. If a juror changes his/her mind at the time the jury is polled, the verdict is not valid.

Prayer In court documents a prayer is a formal request for court action. It usually appears at the end. If a defendant appeals a criminal conviction, the prayer is that the court will reverse the conviction.

Precedent Prior court decisions establish precedent and must be followed by courts in the future. Only appellate courts establish precedent; their decisions are binding on all courts within their geographical jurisdiction.

Preliminary hearing A preliminary hearing occurs in felony cases a few days after the arraignment. A judge hears testimony from witnesses and decides if there are sufficient facts to justify taking the case to trial.

Preliminary revocation hearing If a defendant will be held in custody for any substantial time awaiting resolution of a probation or parole revocation request, a preliminary revocation hearing must be held to review the facts and determine if there is sufficient evidence to warrant keeping the person in custody pending the final proceedings. If the violation occurred our-of-state or at a location far from the court that imposed the sentence, a preliminary revocation hearing is held in the jurisdiction where the violation occurred in order to obtain testimony from eye witnesses and the arresting officer.

Preponderance of the evidence In a civil case, the plaintiff must prove his/her case by a preponderance of the evidence. The jurors must be convinced that it is more likely than not that the facts favor the plaintiff.

Present memory refreshed A person who will be a witness at a court hearing is allowed to refresh his/her memory before taking the stand. If a person has notes made at the time in question, they can be used to refresh memory while on the witness stand. Opposing counsel has the right to know what was used to refresh memory; if written materials were used, the attorney has the right to see them.

Pre-sentence investigation report In many cases the judge orders a pre-sentence investigation report in order to have more facts available when deciding on a sentence. A pre-sentence investigation report includes a summary of the facts for the present crime, information on the defendant's criminal history, and a social history of the defendant's life. It may also include interviews with the victim and other people who are relevant to the case.

Presumptive sentence (base sentence)   A presumptive sentence is the sentence the legislature selected for use if there are no aggravating or mitigating circumstances. When the state legislature has established presumptive sentences, the sentencing judge is given discretion to impose a sentence, other than the presumptive sentence, if the facts of the case fall within guidelines established by the legislature. The judge may be required to state the reasons for departing from the presumptive sentence.

Pretrial conference   A pretrial conference is held shortly before trial to review administrative details relating to the trial. Both the prosecutor and defense are present to discuss the case with the trial judge.

Prior convictions   A witness may be impeached based on prior his/her convictions. Some states allow impeachment only on felonies.

Probable cause   Probable cause is defined as sufficient facts to make a reasonable person believe that it is more likely than not that specific facts exist. The probable cause requirement is found in the Fourth Amendment. In order to make an arrest or obtain a warrant, there must be probable cause. In the case of an arrest, there must be probable cause that the crime occurred and probable cause that the person being arrested committed the crime. For a search warrant, the probable cause must indicate that the specific items for which there is a legal justification to seize are currently at the location to be searched.

Probable cause hearing   A probable cause hearing is required, at the request of the defendant, if the arrest was made without a warrant and the defendant remains in custody. The Supreme Court specified that the probable cause hearing must be held within 48 hours after arrest; additional time is not allowed if this time period ends during a weekend. The probable cause hearing can be equivalent to an arrest warrant: a judge must review statements made under oath and determine that there was probable cause for the arrest. It is also possible to combine the probable cause hearing with the arraignment, provided the 48-hour limit is met.

Probation   In many cases the defendant may be sentenced to probation and allowed to remain in the community. Conditions will be placed on the probation that restrict the defendant's conduct—for example, the person must not associate with known criminals, must keep a job and support the family, must report to the probation officer at least once a month, and must submit to random drug testing. If the defendant fails probation, the judge will decide whether to send him/her to jail or prison.

Proof of service   A proof of service verifies that a person receives a document. When a legal document is served, the person serving it completes the proof of service and files the document with the court. A judge cannot impose penalties for not complying with court orders or subpoenas if a proof of service is not in the court's file. A person who was subpoenaed cannot be held in contempt of court for not appearing if there is no proof of service.

Protective sweep   A protective sweep is a quick, visual check of an area for people who may harm officers. The U.S. Supreme Court has authorized officers to conduct a protective sweep when making an arrest. To go beyond the immediate area, officers need reasonable suspicion that someone who poses a danger is hiding there.

Public safety exception   The public safety exception to the exclusionary rule allows evidence seized in an emergency to be used in court, even though the defendant's constitutional rights were violated in order to obtain the evidence. It covers brief questions at the time of arrest, seeking information on rescuing victims and recovering weapons that pose a danger to the public. The exclusionary rule applies to lengthy questioning or searches.

Punitive damages   In civil cases the plaintiff can recover punitive damages if it is established that the defendant intentionally did a wrongful act. The amount recovered is based on the jury's estimation of how much money it would take to punish the defendant. This type of damages focuses more on the defendant's wealth than on the plaintiff's injuries.

Q

Question of fact   A question of fact involves analyzing the evidence presented. For example, based on all the evidence, did the defendant commit the crime charged. A question of fact is decided by the jury; if the trial is heard without a jury the judge decides the issue.

R

Reasonable suspicion   Reasonable suspicion is sufficient articulable facts to make a reasonable officer believe that criminal activity is afoot. The U.S. Supreme Court, in *Terry v. Ohio*, authorized police to stop a person for investigation if there is reasonable suspicion.

Recalled warrant   A recalled warrant is one that has been withdrawn by the court and is no longer valid. This occurs when a warrant expires, new facts indicate the warrant should not have been issued, and so on.

Recidivist   A recidivist is a person who has a prior conviction. Many states have laws that impose longer sentences on recidivists who are convicted of crimes after serving their sentences than on first offenders.

Redacting a confession   When there are multiple defendants, each has the Sixth Amendment right to cross-examine witnesses. If one defendant makes a confession that implicates the other and then refuses to take the witness stand, use of the confession would violate the rights of the defendant who is being implicated. To avoid this, sometimes it is possible to reword the confession, leaving out references to defendant(s) other than the one making the statement, so that it can be introduced in court without violating Sixth Amendment rights. The rewording of a confession for this purpose is called redacting a confession.

Rehabilitation At trial, rehabilitation is the process of attempting to restore the credibility of a witness. It occurs after impeachment and is done by the side that originally called the witness. For example, an eye witness may have admitted that he has poor eyesight but during redirect examination it was established that he wore glasses that made it possible for him to see 20/20. Rehabilitation also is one of the rationales for punishment. When rehabilitation is emphasized, the convicted person may be sent to counseling or assisted in learning job skills. Rehabilitation can be conducted as part of a jail or prison sentence or as part of probation or parole.

Relevant evidence Relevant evidence is evidence that tends to prove (or disprove) a point that is at issue in the case. Only relevant evidence is admissible; however, some relevant evidence is not admissible—for example, privileged communications.

Reporter's transcript A reporter's transcript is a verbatim record of what occurred at trial or other court hearing. It is prepared by the court reporter who took the notes, usually on a stenotype machine, while testimony was being given.

Reputation for dishonesty A witness may be impeached based on his/her reputation in the community for dishonesty. This form of impeachment is usually accomplished by calling a character witness, who testifies about the reputation of the person in question. The character witness is subject to impeachment during cross-examination.

Res judicata The civil doctrine of *res judicata* prevents a defendant from being sued in civil court more than once by the same plaintiff for the same wrongful conduct. It is not affected by criminal cases filed against the defendant.

Respondent In juvenile court the person who is being charged is called the respondent. The respondent is the equivalent of the defendant in adult criminal court. In an appeal the respondent is the side who must answer the appellant's allegations. If a criminal defendant appeals a conviction, the defendant is the appellant and the government is the respondent.

Respondent's opening brief A respondent's opening brief is the first brief filed by the respondent in an appeal. It addresses the issues raised in the appellant's opening brief.

Rest the case At the end of a case-in-chief, an attorney rests the case. This is usually done by telling the judge, "The Prosecution rests" or "The Defense rests."

Restitution Restitution is reimbursing the victim for expenses caused by the defendant while committing the crime. In many states a judge may order restitution as part of the defendant's sentence. The amount of restitution is usually set after reviewing the victim's expenses (medical bills, lost wages, property damage, etc.). Money collected as restitution goes to the victim.

Retribution Retribution is one of the rationales for punishment. As societies evolved, the government took over the role of kin exacting revenge for wrongdoings. This is part of the reason for retribution; the other is that the person deserves to be punished for what was done, whether or not deterrence or rehabilitation will be accomplished.

Return on a search warrant   A return on a search warrant states the date and time the warrant was executed and what items were seized. It is frequently printed on the back of the warrant.

Return on death warrant   A return on death warrant states what was done to comply with a death warrant. If an execution occurred, the date and time of the execution is stated.

Revocation hearing   Due process requires that there be a revocation hearing prior to parole or probation being revoked. Witnesses may be called by either side and subjected to cross-examination. The probationer or parolee does not have an automatic right to have an attorney appointed to assist with the hearing if the person has already been sentenced. A judge presides over a probation revocation hearing; parole revocation hearings are usually handled by a parole board.

Right to a speedy trial   The Sixth Amendment provides the right to a speedy trial for all defendants in criminal cases. This right starts at the time the charges are filed (not at the time the crime was committed). Four factors are considered when courts decide if this constitutional right has been violated: the length of the delay, the reason for the delay, whether the defendant invoked the right to a speedy trial or concurred with the continuance, and any prejudice to the case caused by the delay. Many states also have statutory rights to speedy trial.

Right to have an attorney present during questioning   A suspect has the right to have an attorney present during custodial interrogation; he/she also may have one at a line-up or show-up that is staged after arraignment or indictment. An indigent has the right to have an attorney appointed to handle his/her case from the first court appearance through sentencing and the first postconviction appeal.

Right to remain silent   During all criminal court proceedings the defendant has the right to remain silent: he/she cannot be forced to take the witness stand and answer questions. The right to remain silent comes from the Fifth Amendment right not to incriminate oneself. One of the *Miranda* warnings reminds the suspect of this right. The jury is not allowed to infer guilt from the fact that the defendant remained silent.

Roadblocks   The U.S. Supreme Court has allowed the use of roadblocks to check for drivers who are under the influence of alcohol. No suspicion is required to stop a car for this purpose; stops can be random. The Court refused to give officers the authority to conduct roadblocks to check for narcotics activity.

S

Sanity phase   If the defendant enters a plea of not guilty by reason of insanity, there will be a sanity phase of the trial devoted to the issue. Since most defendants file dual pleas of not guilty and not guilty by reason of insanity, most cases have two phases: the guilt phase, which addresses the issue of whether the defendant committed the crime, and the sanity phase, which determines whether the defendant was criminally insane at the time the crime was committed.

Schneckloth v. Bustamonte   This U.S. Supreme Court cases established the rule that police officers do not have to advise a person of his/her right to refuse to consent to a search. The validity of consent is based on whether the consent is voluntary; the totality of the circumstances is considered.

Search incident to the arrest   At the time of a custodial arrest, an officer may conduct a thorough search of the person being arrested and the area under the arrestee's immediate control. The only requirement for doing this search is that there be a legal arrest and the person is being taken into custody. The officer does not need to fear for his/her own safety or suspect that evidence or contraband is concealed on the person.

Secret Service   The Secret Service has two main functions: protection of the president and other dignitaries and the investigation of counterfeiting of federal currency and other documents specified by Congress.   The Secret Service also has jurisdiction over crimes involving electronic transfer of money, ATM cards, and credit cards.

Self-incrimination   A person does not have to answer questions by law enforcement officers or in court about any acts that could be prosecuted at the time this right is invoked. The Fifth Amendment establishes the privilege against self-incrimination. The *Miranda* warnings were designed to protect this right. The privilege against self-incrimination does not cover cases in which the statute of limitations has expired; immunity has been granted to the person being asked questions; or double jeopardy would bar a new prosecution of the case.

Sentencing guidelines   Many states have sentencing guidelines to help judges determine the length of sentences; they also help keep sentences more uniform. The guidelines are a set of rules the judge should follow; sometimes detailed checklists are provided.

Serve a subpoena   A subpoena is an official notice to appear to testify at a court hearing. It is served when it is handed to the person being subpoenaed, whether or not the person takes it or lets it fall on the ground. Many states allow any adult who is not a party to the case to serve subpoenas; some states require service by law enforcement personnel or registered process servers. Service by mail is allowed in some states.

Severed   A case is severed when it is divided into two (or more) cases. The most common reason for severance is undue prejudice to one defendant (usually a lesser participant) when a jury hears the evidence against all the defendants.

Sexually violent predator laws   Sexually violent predator laws enable states to have a person who was convicted of a specified violent sex crime committed to a mental institution after the termination of his/her prison term. A full court hearing is required prior to such action.

Sheriff's department   This county-level agency, headed by an elected sheriff, operates the county jail. It may also have responsibilities for law enforcement in unincorporated areas.

Show-up   A show-up is an identification procedure in which one suspect is shown to an eye witness. It is most commonly done in the field when a person has been detained a short time after a crime, but it can be done at later times as well. The police do not have to establish that an emergency prevented them from conducting a full line-up. The suspect has the right to have an attorney present if the show-up is done after arraignment or indictment.

Sixth Amendment   This amendment to the U.S. Constitution applies to criminal trials and gives the defendant the following rights: to have speedy and public trial, to receive a notice of charges, to be present when the prosecution questions its witnesses, to cross-examine prosecution witnesses, to subpoena witnesses for the defense, to have an impartial jury, and to have the assistance of counsel.

Sixth Amendment rights–assistance of counsel   The Supreme Court has ruled that indigents have the right to have an attorney appointed to handle their cases from arraignment through trial and the sentencing hearing; it also applies to the first postconviction appeal.

Sixth Amendment rights–compulsory process   A defendant has the right to subpoena witnesses to appear in court.

Sixth Amendment rights–confront witnesses   A defendant has the right to be present when prosecution witnesses testify and to cross-examine them.

Sixth Amendment rights–impartial jury   A defendant has the right to a jury that is not prejudiced against him/her. The Supreme Court ruled that this right applies if the crime has a sentence of more than six months in jail. Many states apply it to all crimes.

Sixth Amendment rights–informed of the nature and cause of the accusation   A defendant has the right to know what the charges are before the trial begins.

Sixth Amendment rights–speedy and public trial   A defendant has the right to have the trial open to the public. The right to a speedy trial can be invoked if delays have been so long that the defense case has been prejudiced.

Slip opinions   Slip opinions are usually the first published form of an appellate opinion. They are distributed by the court on the day the decision is issued. While they contain the full text of the decision, they are not formatted in the same layout as the published opinion will be and the pagination does not match what will be in the book when the opinion is published.   For this reason, slip opinions are cited only until the case is available in the advance sheets.

South Dakota v. Opperman   This U.S. Supreme Court case gave police the authority to inventory the contents of vehicles prior to impounding them. The key rationale for the inventory is to prevent theft, to deter false theft claims, and to stop the vandalism of vehicles in inventory lots.

Sovereign immunity   The doctrine of sovereign immunity protects the government from being sued. In modern times, Congress and most state legislatures have passed tort claims acts, which allow suits against the government. When contemplating a suit against the government, it is important to research the passed tort claims act because it is rare for immunity to be waived for all types of cases.

Special circumstances   The Supreme Court mandated that a defendant can be executed only if he/she committed a murder under special circumstances. The legislature must enact a list of situations that make a murder sufficiently heinous to qualify for the death penalty; the items on this list are the special circumstances. The prosecutor has the discretion to file murder charges with, or without, an allegation of special circumstances. If special circumstances are alleged, the jury must vote on them separately. The death penalty can be imposed only if the jury is unanimous on at least one.

Specific deterrence   Specific deterrence is one of the rationales for punishment. The goal of specific deterrence is to deter the person being punished from committing crimes in the future.

Speedy trial   The Sixth Amendment gives a criminal defendant the right to a speedy trial. If a defendant demands that a case be dismissed for lack of a speedy trial due to violation of the Sixth Amendment, the judge will consider the length of the delay; the reason for the delay; whether the defendant invoked the right to speedy trial in order to prevent the delay; and if the case was prejudiced by the delay. Many states have statutes that establish specific time frames for a statutory right to a speedy trial.

Stale information   Stale information is information that is too old to be reliable, and it cannot be used to obtain a search warrant. If the item in question, such as drugs owned by a drug dealer, is likely to be removed from the location, the information may become stale very quickly. Less portable items rarely result in stale information.

State constitution   Each state has a constitution, which establishes the framework for government in that state. States are entitled to construct their own constitutions, as long as their provisions do not violate the U.S. Constitution and Bill of Rights.

State law   The U.S. Constitution and Bill of Rights establish the basic civil rights for everyone in the United States. States are free to pass legislation that gives their citizens *more* rights than required by the Supreme Court's interpretation of the Constitution and Bill of Rights. States may also establish laws in areas not covered by the Constitution and Bill of Rights. In this latter area, the states act independently, and there is no requirement that states have similar laws or punishments.

Statute of limitations   The statute of limitations sets the maximum time that may elapse between the commission of a crime and the filing of the charges. Some crimes, such as murder, do not have statutes of limitations—they can be filed at any time. Misdemeanors usually have a shorter statute of limitations than felonies. In some states more serious felonies have longer statutes of limitations than lesser felonies.

Stipulation   A stipulation is an agreement between opposing attorneys. If the attorneys stipulate to a fact, jurors will be told they must conclude the fact exists and no evidence will be introduced about the fact.

Strict liability torts   Strict liability torts are torts based on public policy, not on the fault of the individual involved. They are usually stated in the civil code or developed through case law. For example, in many states restaurants are civilly liable for serving contaminated food, even though the food was contaminated when purchased from the wholesaler and there was no hint of contamination.

Sua sponte   A judge must give key jury instructions *sua sponte*, meaning that the judge has the responsibility to give the instructions, even if neither attorney requests it.

Subject matter jurisdiction   Subject matter jurisdiction is a court's authority to handle particular types of cases. Many states have more than one level of trial court. When this occurs the court must have subject matter jurisdiction as well as geographical jurisdiction in order to make valid judgments.

Subpoena   A subpoena is an official court document notifying a person to appear and testify in court or another official proceeding. A person who fails to comply with an appropriately served subpoena can be held in contempt of court.

Subpoena duces tecum   A *subpoena duces tecum* is a court order that requires that a person take a specified document to court at a specific time.

Summary judgment   A judge can issue a summary judgment in a civil case based on the complaint, answer, depositions, and interrogatories. No witnesses are called to testify in court. The summary judgment is given if there are no issues remaining unsettled and no key facts in controversy.

Sunset laws   When a legislature passes a law that has an expiration date, the law is referred to as a sunset law. Laws that do not have expiration dates remain on the books until repealed.

Suppression hearing   A suppression hearing is a court hearing that is held to obtain a judge's ruling on the admissibility of an item of evidence at trial. The defense requests a suppression hearing before trial if it believes that evidence in the case is inadmissible due to a search conducted in violation of the Fourth Amendment and/or violation of the suspect's *Miranda* rights.

Suppression motion   A suppression motion is a formal motion made by an attorney, asking the judge to rule that evidence is inadmissible. Copies of the suppression motion are served on the court and the opposing side. A suppression hearing follows. The judge will announce a ruling on the motion after hearing witnesses and oral arguments and reviewing the points and authorities.

Suspended sentences   Suspended sentences are sentences that the judge imposes at a sentencing hearing but rules that the defendant does not have to serve the sentence at that time. Imposition of a suspended sentence is frequently accompanied by an order that the defendant be placed on probation. If the defendant violates probation, the defendant can be ordered to serve the suspended sentence.

T

Technical violation   A violation of the conditions of probation or parole that does not involve criminal activity is called a technical violation. These include failing to report to the probation/parole officer as required; moving or changing employment without notifying the probation/parole officer; and associating with known criminals. Technical violations can result in the revocation of probation or parole.

Telephonic search warrants   Telephonic search warrants are search warrants obtained by giving information under oath to a judge over the telephone. The judge authorizes a search in the same manner as if the information were in affidavits presented in person.

Terry v. Ohio   *Terry v. Ohio* is a landmark U.S. Supreme Court case on the right of an officer to stop a suspect when there is no probable cause to make an arrest. Such stops are allowed if the officer has reasonable suspicion, based on a reasonable officer standard, that criminal activity is afoot. If there is also reasonable suspicion that the person is armed, the officer may conduct a patdown search for weapons.

Testimonial communication   Testimonial communication includes oral and written communication. The Fifth Amendment's privilege against self-incrimination applies to testimonial communication. The following are not considered testimonial communications: participating in a show-up or line-up; giving samples of body fluids (blood, urine, saliva, semen, etc.) for laboratory testing; and providing handwriting or voice exemplars.

Tolling the statute of limitations   Tolling the statute of limitations is extending it. In most states the statute of limitations is tolled if a suspect leaves the state to avoid prosecution. Some states also toll the statute of limitations if the suspect hides from the police, even if the person does not leave the state.

Tort   A tort is a civil wrong not based on a contract.

Tort claims acts   Tort claims acts waive sovereign immunity and allow law suits to be filed against the government. Most tort claims acts specify the types of situations for which the government can be sued. A person can sue the government only if the injuries occurred in a situation covered by a tort claims act.

Totality of the circumstances test   The totality of the circumstances test assesses the facts and determines if probable cause exists. It is used when seeking warrants and when an officer takes action in the field. Both the information available and the reliability of the source are considered, but it is not mandatory that an informant have a history of providing accurate information.

Transfer a case to adult court   Many states have laws that allow a judge to transfer a juvenile to adult criminal court. Usually the prosecutor must file a request with the juvenile court judge and a fitness hearing is held.

Trial brief   A trial brief is prepared by an attorney and presented to the judge shortly before the trial is to begin. This brief summarizes the case, usually by giving a short synopsis of what each witness is expected to say, and presents relevant legal arguments with appropriate citations to statutes and case law. Trial briefs are optional in most courts.

True bill   If a prosecutor takes a case to the grand jury, and the grand jury concurs that the charges should be filed, the indictment is endorsed as a true bill of indictment.

U

Unduly suggestive   Line-ups and photographic line-ups must not be unduly suggestive. They must contain a large enough sample to provide good choices; participants must be dressed in a manner that does not suggest guilt; the people in the line-up must be of similar height, weight, age, race, hair color, etc.; the officer conducting the procedure must not make statements or gestures suggesting which person is believed to be the one who committed the crime.

Uniform Criminal Extradition Act   This act, which is enforced in all states, establishes the procedures for extraditing a person back to the state where the crime was committed. It also authorizes police officers to make arrests based on warrants that were issued in another state. Once the arrest has been made, extradition proceedings will follow unless the defendant waives extradition. Extraditing a person's return to the United States from a foreign country is covered by any treaty signed by the two countries, not the Uniform Criminal Extradition Act.

Uniform Act on Fresh Pursuit   This act allows officers to continue a pursuit, even though the suspect flees into another state. It applies only to felonies. The officers must be in fresh pursuit at the time they cross the state line.

U.S. Code   The United States Code is enacted by the United States Congress. Violations of the U.S. Code are tried in federal court.

U.S. Congress   The members of Congress are elected by the people of the districts they represent. Congress enacts laws, which apply throughout the United States. These laws can be found in the U.S. Code.

U.S. Constitution   The United States Constitution is the supreme law of the land. Any state laws violate the U.S. Constitution are unconstitutional. The states retain the right to enact laws covering issues not assigned to the federal government in the U.S. Constitution.

U.S. Courts of Appeals   The United States Courts of Appeals are the primary appellate courts in the federal system. They are organized geographically into circuits. Congress assigns states to a particular circuit. For example, all cases tried in federal court from the state of New York go to the United States Court of Appeals for the Second Circuit.

U.S. District Court   The United States District Court is the trial court in the federal system. There is at least one U.S. District Court in each state. Larger states have multiple districts. For example, Los Angeles is in the U.S. District Court for the Central District of California.

U.S. Supreme Court   The United States Supreme Court is established in the U.S. Constitution. It has the authority to hear cases involving federal constitutional issues that arise in either state court or federal court.

Unreasonable searches and seizures   Unreasonable searches and seizures violate the Fourth Amendment. Evidence obtained by an unreasonable search and seizure is not admissible to establish the defendant's guilt.

V

Vehicle searches–closed containers   The closed container rule does not apply to most searches of vehicles. The Court made exceptions for probable cause search of a car; search of a car based on reasonable suspicion; and search of a car incident to an arrest.

Vehicle searches–incident to arrest   Incident to the arrest of a person in a vehicle, the officer may conduct a thorough search of the passenger compartment.

Vehicle searches–inventory   At the time a vehicle is impounded, the police have the right to inventory its contents. No probable cause that there is evidence in the car is needed. The rationale for these searches is to cut down on theft while the car is in the impound lot, to deter false theft reports, and to reduce vandalism.

Vehicle searches–probable cause   A vehicle may be searched based on probable cause that there are items subject to seizure in the vehicle. No search warrant is required. The only portion of the vehicle that may be searched is the portion where the items are believed to be.

Vehicle searches–reasonable suspicion   When an officer stops someone in a vehicle pursuant to *Terry v. Ohio*, the passenger compartment may be searched for weapons if there is reasonable suspicion that there are weapons there.

Vehicle searches–voluntary consent   A vehicle may be searched based on the voluntary consent of the owner or a person with apparent authority to consent. The scope of this search is based on what the person authorized.

Venue   A venue is the location where the case should be heard. Many large court districts are divided into smaller areas, each with its own courthouse. Maps are consulted to determine the venue where a case will be heard.

Victim impact statement   A victim impact statement is a statement usually prepared by the victim, or the victim's family if the victim died due to the crime which provides insight into how the crime has changed the victim's life. In most states the victim may personally make the victim impact statement during the sentencing hearing, provide a written statement that is read at the hearing, or forego making a statement. The judge considers the victim's statement but is not bound by it.

Voir dire   *Voir dire* is the process of questioning a person to determine if he/she has the necessary qualifications to serve on a jury or to testify as an expert witness.

Volunteered statements   As used in *Miranda*, volunteered statements are those suspects voluntarily make without any questioning by officers. Volunteered statements are admissible, even though *Miranda* warnings were not given. Follow-up questions after a volunteered statement require a full set of warnings.

W

Waiver of *Miranda* rights   A suspect's answers given during custodial interrogation are admissible by the prosecution only if the suspect made a knowing, intelligent, and voluntary waiver of his/her *Miranda* rights. "Knowing" means that the person has been informed of his/her rights and understands them; "intelligent" means the person possesses at least a minimum level of intelligence required to understand his/her rights; and "voluntary" means the waiver was made without coercion. The waiver may be oral or written. In a few cases it has been implied that the suspect waived his/her rights if the suspect acknowledged that he/she understood the *Miranda* warnings prior to answering questions.

Wants and warrants   This database includes the names of suspects who have outstanding arrest warrants, as well as the names of individuals that law enforcement agencies want for questioning. The database may be operated at the state level (usually by the department of justice) and/or at the county level (usually by the sheriff's department).

Ward of the court   Juveniles become wards of the court if they are "convicted" of crimes or status offenses. Dependent children also become wards of the court. Once a child is a ward of the court, a judge has the power to determine where the child should live and other issues relating to the child.

Writ of *habeas corpus*   If a court grants a writ of *habeas corpus*, a full hearing will be held on the issue of whether the petitioner is being illegally held in custody.

Work furlough   Work furlough programs house inmates in a jail or prison but allow them to leave the facility go to work at their regular jobs outside the facility. These programs are more common for inmates serving relatively short sentences for misdemeanors.

Writ of *certiorari*   Nearly all cases heard by the U.S. Supreme Court are heard because the justices issued a writ of *certiorari*. The party seeking a hearing files a petition for writ of *certiorari*. The justices then vote on whether they want to hear the case. If four justices vote to hold a hearing, a writ of *certiorari* is granted. The case is then transferred to the U.S. Supreme Court and receives a full hearing.

Wrongful death   A wrongful death action is brought in civil court by the surviving family of a person who was killed due to wrongful acts of the defendant. Wrongful death actions can be the result of criminal activity or other non-criminal acts that violate civil law. The family is allowed to recover living expenses that the victim would have paid if he/she had survived. The size of the monetary award is based on the economic status of the victim.

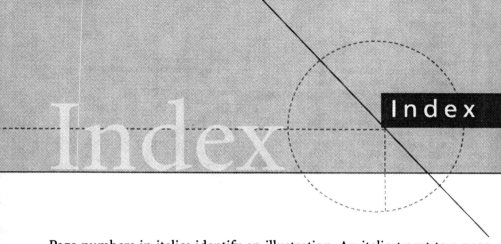

Index

Page numbers in italics identify an illustration. An italic *t* next to a page number (e.g., 176*t*) indicates information that appears in a table.